A VANISHING

NEW YORK

A VANISHING NEW YORK

PHOTOGRAPHS BY JOHN LAZZARO

FOREWORD BY THOMAS MELLINS

Ruins Across the Empire State

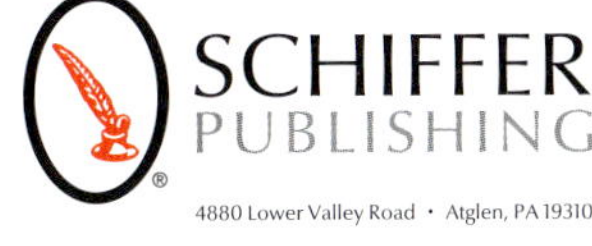

Library of Congress Control Number: 2021942742

Designed by Ashley Millhouse
Type set in Bernina Sans/Garamond
ISBN: 978-0-7643-6358-0
Printed in India

Published by Schiffer Publishing, Ltd.
4880 Lower Valley Road
Atglen, PA 19310
Phone: (610) 593-1777; Fax: (610) 593-2002
Email: Info@schifferbooks.com
Web: www.schifferbooks.com

For our complete selection of fine books on this and related subjects, please visit our website at www.schifferbooks.com. You may also write for a free catalog.

Schiffer Publishing's titles are available at special discounts for bulk purchases for sales promotions or premiums. Special editions, including personalized covers, corporate imprints, and excerpts, can be created in large quantities for special needs. For more information, contact the publisher.

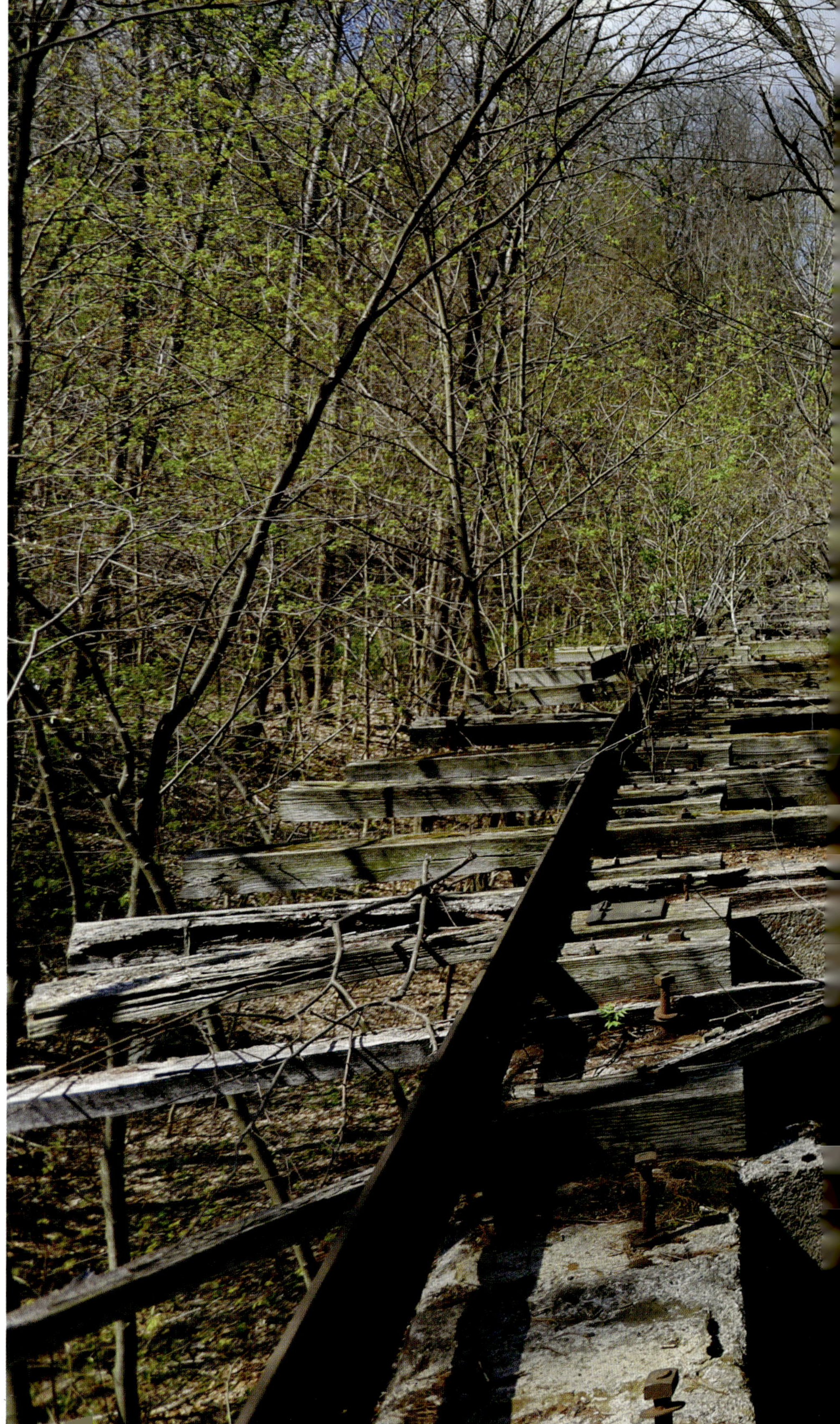

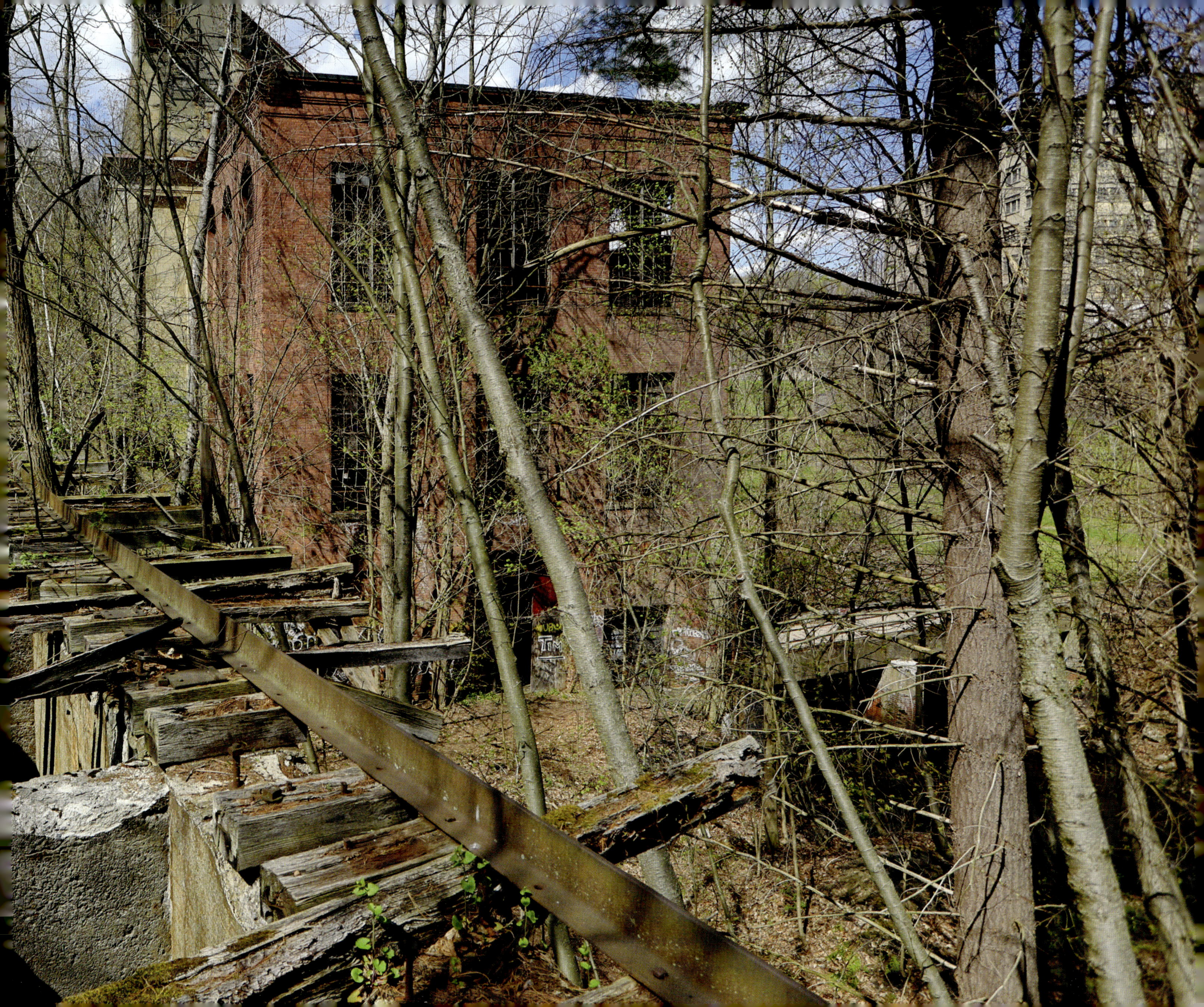

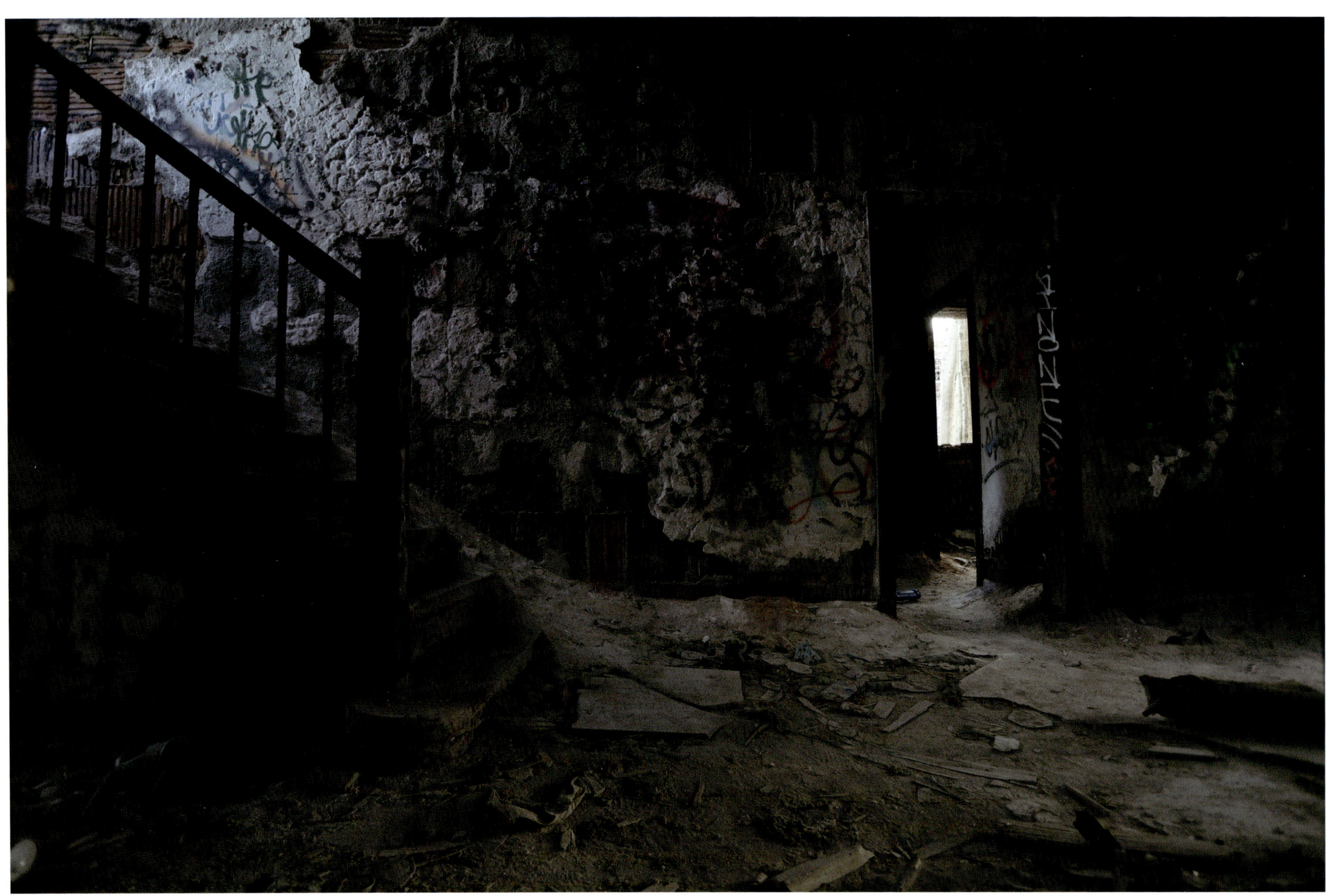

“Insane pavilion” / nurses’ residence, New York City Farm Colony

Is it nothing to you,

all you who pass by?

—Lamentations 1:12

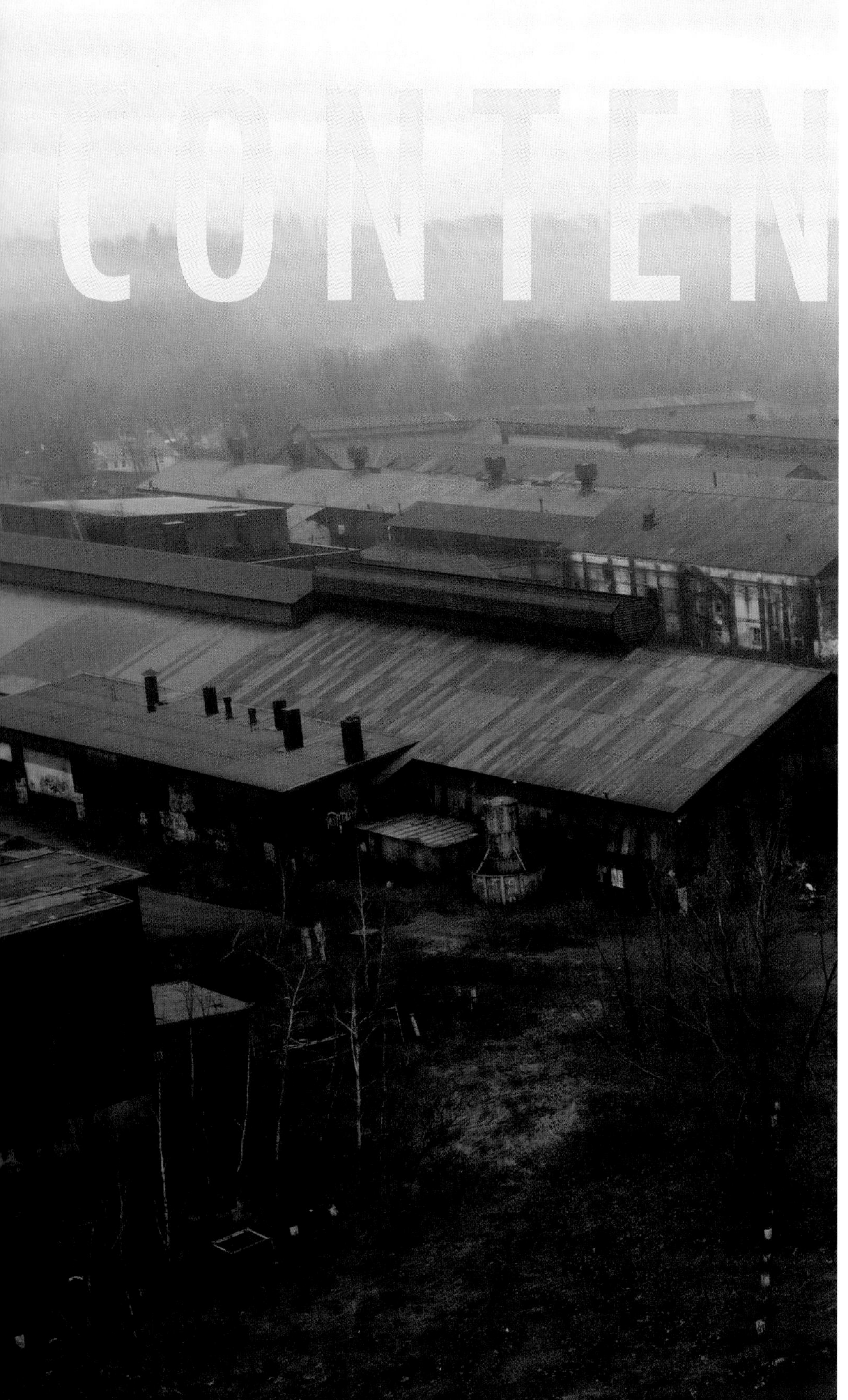

CONTENTS

4. CATSKILLS REGION

5. CENTRAL NEW YORK REGION

6. CAPITAL REGION

7. ADIRONDACK REGION

8. THOUSAND ISLANDS-SEAWAY REGION

9. FINGER LAKES REGION

10. CHAUTAUQUA-ALLEGHENY REGION

11. NIAGARA FRONTIER REGION

FOREWORD

Vital Ruins

Ruins have fascinated us for centuries. In 1810, Lord Byron, writing a letter from Athens, exclaimed, "Hymettus before me, the Acropolis behind, the Temple of Jove to my right, the Stadium in front, the town to my left; eh, Sir, there's a situation, there's your picturesque!"[1] Byron celebrated the associations triggered by his exploration of the monumental ruins of the ancient world in verses that would come to define the modern concept of the Romantic. Perceived to be at once beautiful, familiar, and foreign, ruins inevitably refer to the passage of time and the observer's own mortality, imbuing aesthetics with ache. How else can we explain what the author Rose Macaulay, in her book *The Pleasure of Ruins*, lyrically described as "the romantic and conscious swimming down the hurrying river of time, whose mysterious reaches, stretching limitlessly behind, glimmer suddenly into view with these wracks washed onto the silted shores"?[2]

The photographs in *A Vanishing New York* document a wide range of buildings, from formerly state-of-the-art factories to plush hotels, private estates, public schools, and vast psychiatric facilities and asylums built between the nineteenth century and the 1970s. The featured buildings are located in places scattered throughout New York State, from Buffalo to Staten Island. Most, however, are in "upstate" communities, where agriculture, and later industry, offered great opportunity and produced great wealth.

New York State has historically been overshadowed by New York City, which claims 40 percent of the state's population and has served as the nation's de facto capital in terms of monetary might since at least the end of the Civil War, yet the state's contributions to the nation and the world have been profound. Beginning with the completion of the Erie Canal in 1825, a feat of engineering unsurpassed in the life of the then-young nation, New York State played a crucial role as a connector. The state has long served as a crossroads, bordering or linking to New England, the Midwest, Appalachia, and Canada, as it reaches from the shores of the Atlantic Ocean to those of two Great Lakes. Historically, New York State has served as a critical link between abundant natural resources, and, later, manufactured goods, and seemingly insatiable markets regionally, nationally, and internationally. But in the last four decades, as farms gave way to midwestern agribusinesses and manufacturers closed shop or moved their operations to the South or, more likely, overseas, much the Empire State has suffered as the "empire" decamped.

New York State is strongly associated with ethnic diversity and cultural achievement. Landmark events and larger-than-life personalities, both famous and infamous, define and dominate its history. It has been extensively written about, the subject of countless studies, surveys, accounts, and works of fiction. The state has further entered the public realm through theater, movies, and television. Architecturally, images of Manhattan's skyscrapers, Albany's monumental modernism, and perhaps Frank Lloyd Wright's legacy in Buffalo come to mind. But Lazzaro's eye bypasses landmarks in favor of structures that are often overlooked—or even shunned.

Lazzaro lucidly documents both the totality of a building and its details. Few formal attributes escape his gaze. Yet, it seems that for Lazzaro a building's formal qualities are only part of the story. Architecture is for him a narrative art, not merely the fulfillment of a specific program but a way in which we connect to our environment, our past, our aspirations, ourselves. In this, Lazzaro becomes a colleague of the architects and builders—known and unknown—who designed and constructed the buildings he photographs. Working together across time, this imagined multidisciplinary team weaves together a story of expansion and contraction, achievement and demise. How fitting, since architecture itself can be seen as a type of conversation conducted between generations, present and departed, reflecting who we have been and who we are now.

Lithic evidence of the past is a lens through which we conjure up the secret lives of buildings: the visions realized, the activities enacted, the lives lived there. Ruins tell stories to inquisitive audiences. In this regard, John Lazzaro has not only a gimlet eye, but also keen listening skills, skills that enable him to catalog the realities of the present and, in so doing, reveal the once-vital past.

Lazzaro's photographs are at once trenchant records of buildings marked by decay and elegiac mediations on the nature of decay itself. Ironically, his work also constitutes a visual form of architectural preservation. Lazzaro's haunting images record the past, jog our memories, and, in a sense, keep the past alive, albeit only virtually. And the images are quietly provocative, resonant with questions: What happened there? Why did activity cease? Was the endeavor destined to fail? What will happen to these fragments and remains now?

Though not specifically proscriptive or concerned with advocacy, Lazzaro's work underscores the fragility of the built environments that surround us, as this book's evocative title, *A Vanishing New York*, suggests. To paraphrase T. S. Eliot, buildings do not end with a bang—the power of the wrecker's ball notwithstanding—but with a whimper. Absent significant protest or opposition, the diminishment of the buildings featured in this book unfolded largely without notice. And it is precisely this casualness of loss that Lazzaro's work seizes upon. Be careful, these photographs seem to assert, for the past can slip through our fingers.

At times, New York's ruins recall an economically robust past, defined by efficient production and brisk demand. America's focus on ingenuity, entrepreneurship, and prosperity was embodied by such enterprises as the Newton Falls Paper Company facility, located in the Adirondack Mountains, 50 miles from the Canadian border. The business's evolution, from 1895, when James Newton opened a sawmill, to its closure in 2011, mirrored the area's growth and decline. The business not only provided significant employment for locals, as well as immigrants from as far away as Russia and Latvia, but defined a community. The line between commerce and civics blurred as Newton essentially built a hamlet, complete with prefabricated houses manufactured and distributed by the Sears Company.

The remains of the sprawling, eponymous Kings Park Psychiatric Center, as well as of the related Pilgrim Psychiatric Center and other facilities, bear silent testimony to changing attitudes and practices regarding the treatment of the mentally ill throughout the nineteenth and twentieth centuries. Similarly, the Mid-Orange Correctional Facility in Warwick and Greycourt Women's Prison (later Camp LaGuardia, a work camp for homeless men) in Chester speak volumes about the state's legacy of incarceration.

Though images of the industrial and institutional past dominate here, Lazzaro also turns his camera to New Yorkers' embrace of luxury and glamour. David

Abercrombie's 1925 estate in Ossining still recalls the boom years of the Roaring Twenties, and the Nevele Grande Resort in Wawarsing, parts of which were built as recently as the 1960s, constitutes not merely a single abandoned hotel complex, but also a reflection of the tastes and social mores of the lost world of Catskills resorts.

Winston Churchill famously stated, "We shape our buildings; thereafter they shape us."[3] But what of the buildings we neglect? What of the buildings that due to changes of fortune, as well as economic and demographic shifts—or perhaps mere chance—have become ruins and, in a sense, vanished? Do they too still shape us, albeit in a less obvious way than buildings that remain in use, part of our daily lives? Lazzaro's photographs powerfully suggest that they do.

– Thomas Mellins

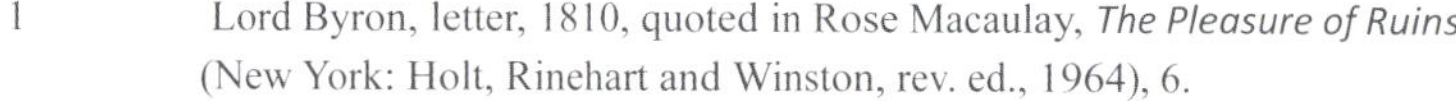

1 Lord Byron, letter, 1810, quoted in Rose Macaulay, *The Pleasure of Ruins* (New York: Holt, Rinehart and Winston, rev. ed., 1964), 6.

2 Macaulay, *The Pleasure of Ruins*, 6.

3 Winston Churchill, speech to the House of Commons, October 28, 1944.

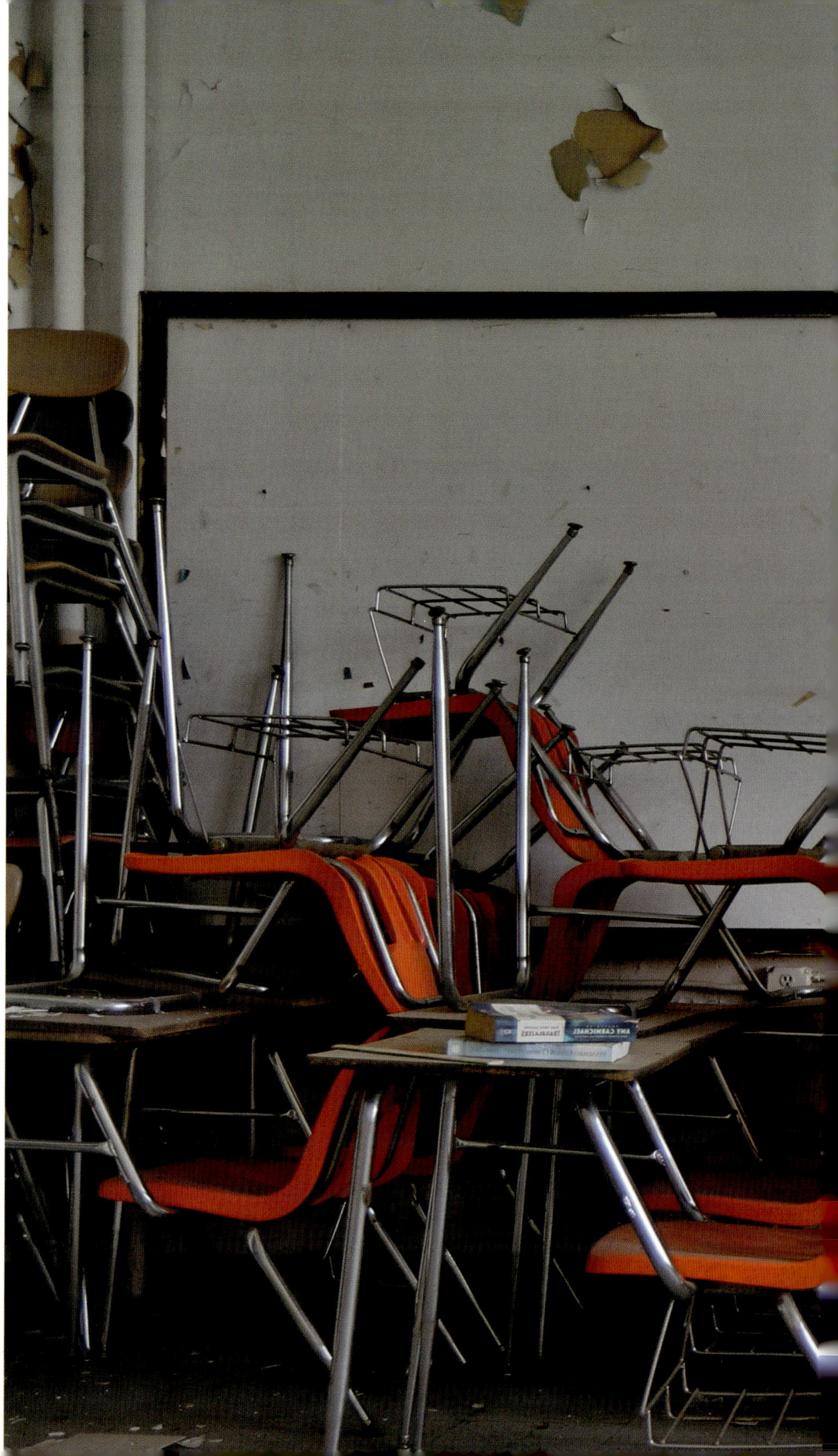

ACKNOWLEDGMENTS

Thank you to the following people for making this book possible:

Pete Schiffer and Cheryl Weber at Schiffer Publishing for their commitment to this project along with their insight and collaboration.

Joan Brookbank, my agent, for her heartfelt and enthusiastic representation, support, and expertise.

Thomas Mellins for his profound knowledge and passion for architecture.

I also appreciate the support and encouragement of my parents Joanne and Tom, my sister Jackie along with family, Melanye, and the many friends that I've made on this incredible journey.

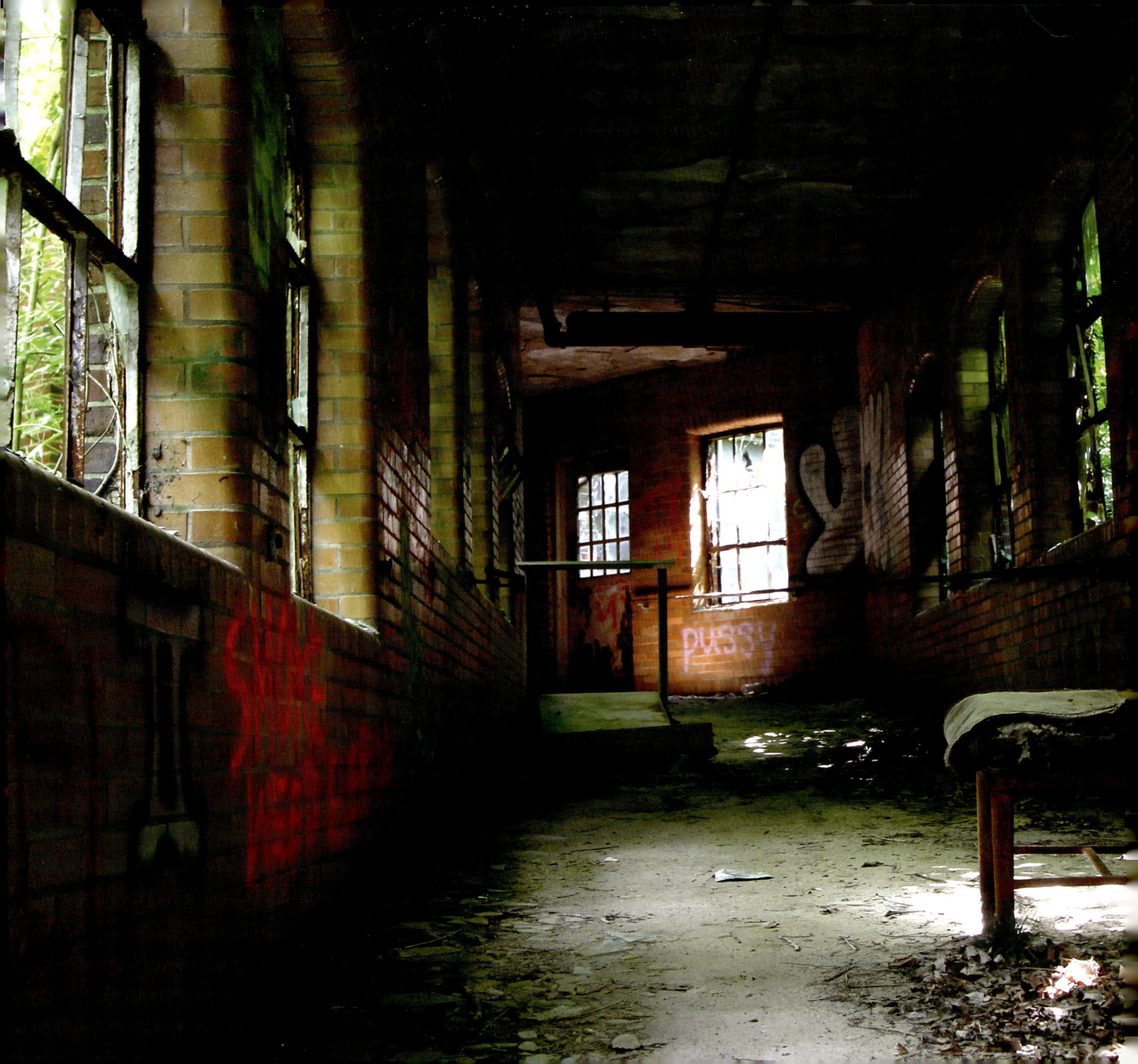
PUSSY

Breezeway corridor connecting Building 136 (medical diagnostic clinic / surgical center) to Building 137 (kitchen / dining hall), Kings Park Psychiatric Center

INTRODUCTION

Like many others, I have been drawn to ruins and abandoned buildings, not just from the perspective of a photographer and documentary filmmaker, but also having an avid appreciation for history and culture. After switching my photography muse from nature to urban exploration some years ago, the idea for *A Vanishing New York* came sometime in 2019 as I was wrapping up my first book, *The Walls Still Talk: A Photographic Journey through Kings Park Psychiatric Center*. After documenting the over century-long history of Kings Park Psychiatric Center, my newfound interest in abandoned hospitals and sanatoriums led me to begin researching and visiting other abandoned locations throughout New York State. From there, I categorized each location by county and then by region in an attempt to show how majestic and diverse New York's ruins are.

New York State is vast. As a Long Islander, it's easy to become overwhelmed and seemingly isolated in the shadow of a metropolis. In fact, a friend and fellow explorer that I met while doing this project told me, "How can you be tied to a city when you have the great outdoors to enjoy?"

The state is divided into eleven regions, over 55,000 square miles; each can be defined by the abandonments left behind. In fact, while undertaking this project, I discovered that the commonalities throughout each region's abandonments show how they each played a role in New York's infrastructure. For instance, the Long Island Region once served as the mental health capital of New York—and arguably the East Coast—as can be seen through the remains of Kings Park Psychiatric Center and Pilgrim Psychiatric Center. The glorious Catskill Region is riddled with the remains of once-vibrant tourist and vacation destinations through the Nevele Grande Resort, Catskill Game Farm, and White Lake Mansion House. The introduction of the Interstate Highway System essentially rendered the railway system in the Finger Lakes Region useless, forcing the Manchester Roundhouse and the Rochester Industrial & Rapid Transit Railway to close as it became far more efficient to transport freight via highways.

The common reason why a location shuts down and ultimately becomes abandoned is due to a financial matter where a business or organization can no longer sustain upkeep costs and is forced to close—the Parksville Pharmacy and Newton Falls Fine Paper Company being perfect examples of this. In some circumstances, there is a darker reason behind an abandonment. A mysterious fire, likely set by the developer of the former Greenpoint Terminal Market in Brooklyn, birthed Skull Silo. The Catskill Game Farm not only faced years of declining attendance but was fined for such things as excess accumulation of manure, poor water drainage, and spoiled food for the animals in captivity. Some hospitals such as Letchworth Village closed because they could no longer provide effective treatment, while others such as Saratoga Homestead closed because treatment for a particular illness was no longer needed. New York State is riddled with abandoned structures holding stories such as these, the most profound and significant being featured in this book.

These ruins of the Empire State are a testament to what happens when New York's remaining vestiges are left to the elements of our own devices. Some will see them as urban eyesores, mere detritus. I, however, see them as sacrosanct, historical keepsakes. And in some cases, these photographs serve as the last remaining evidence of past generations before they ultimately vanish forever.

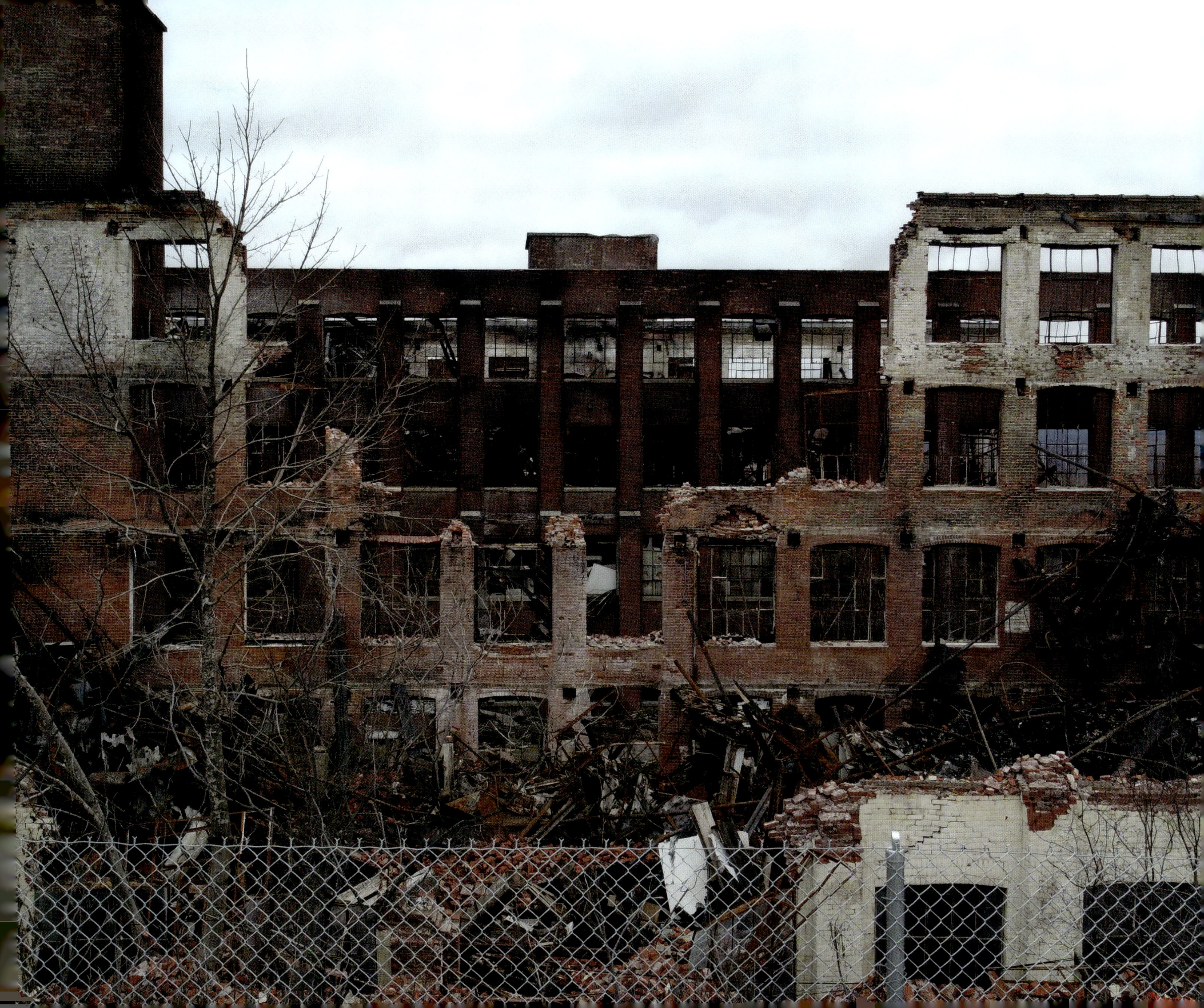

CHAPTER 1.

LONG ISLAND REGION

Kings Park Psychiatric Center

KINGS PARK

In 1885, Kings County purchased 873.8 acres of woods and farmland in St. Johnland—now Kings Park, New York—with the sole purpose of opening a rural branch of the overcrowded Kings County Asylum. Despite local townspeople voting against the idea of a lunatic farm being established in the area, three temporary cottages were constructed, allowing for twenty-three female and thirty-two male patients to occupy them. As a form of therapy, these patients were set to work clearing the land to start the farm that would provide food and future cottages for more patients. By the turn of the century and now under state control, the new hospital officially separated from the Kings County Lunatic Asylum and became the Kings Park State Hospital—a name it would carry until the 1970s. Patients could now be admitted directly into the facility without having to go through its Brooklyn counterpart. The town of St. Johnland became Kings Park likely as a result of the locals wanting a separate identity from the hospital.

The hospital would grow from three wooden cottages to over 150 buildings, which at its max in 1954 would house nearly 10,000 patients. By the end of 1955 and with the advent of Thorazine, 5 percent of the patient population were receiving psychotropic drug therapy. The use of restraints declined by 50 percent. Psychosurgery was declining. New York State completed the Mental Health Study Act, which called for the abolition of state hospitals and the redirecting of federal funds to build community centers for the mentally ill. By this time, the farm buildings were gradually phased out, as it became far cheaper to import food. Another change came in 1965, when Medicare and Medicaid were established. Both contained provisions for mental health treatment, but the care provided by state hospitals was not covered and mentally ill people under the age of sixty-five were ineligible for Medicaid benefits. As a result, large numbers of geriatric patients were transferred from state hospitals to nursing homes. Along the way, the hospital had its name changed to the Kings Park Psychiatric Center (KPPC) as 100 acres of land was sold off since it was no longer needed. The hospital began the slow and steady process of closing its buildings and leaving them abandoned.

The final blow to KPPC came in 1993, when the New York State Community Mental Health Reinvestment Act mandated that all savings realized from the closure of unneeded state psychiatric centers would be funneled into various community mental health programs. This act was propelled partly by the Office of Mental Health's decision to close several facilities. Three years later, KPPC employees gathered in the auditorium of Building 23 to celebrate the closing of the very hospital that had served the mentally ill for 111 years.

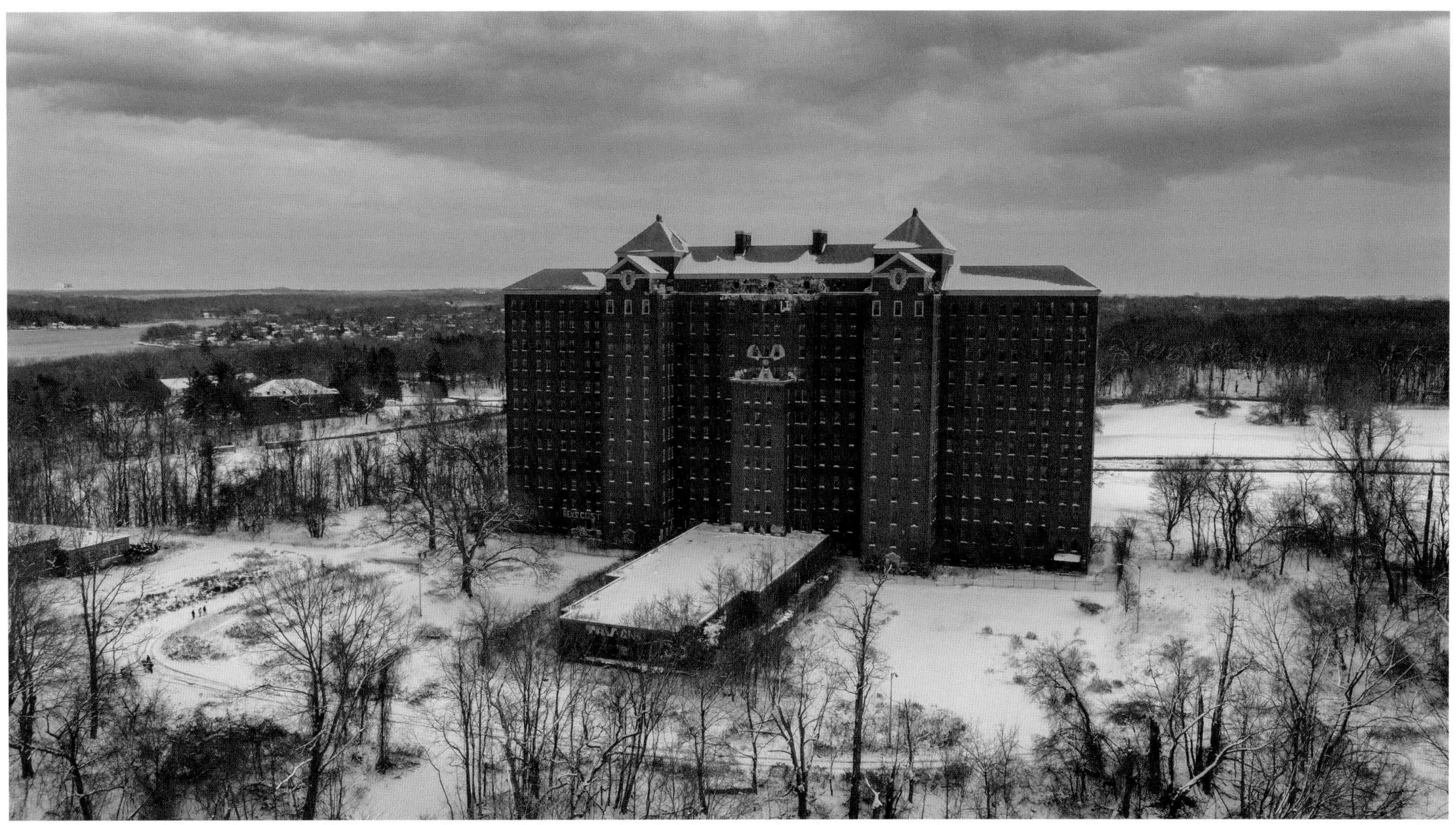

Building 93 (geriatric infirmary / drug treatment), Kings Park Psychiatric Center

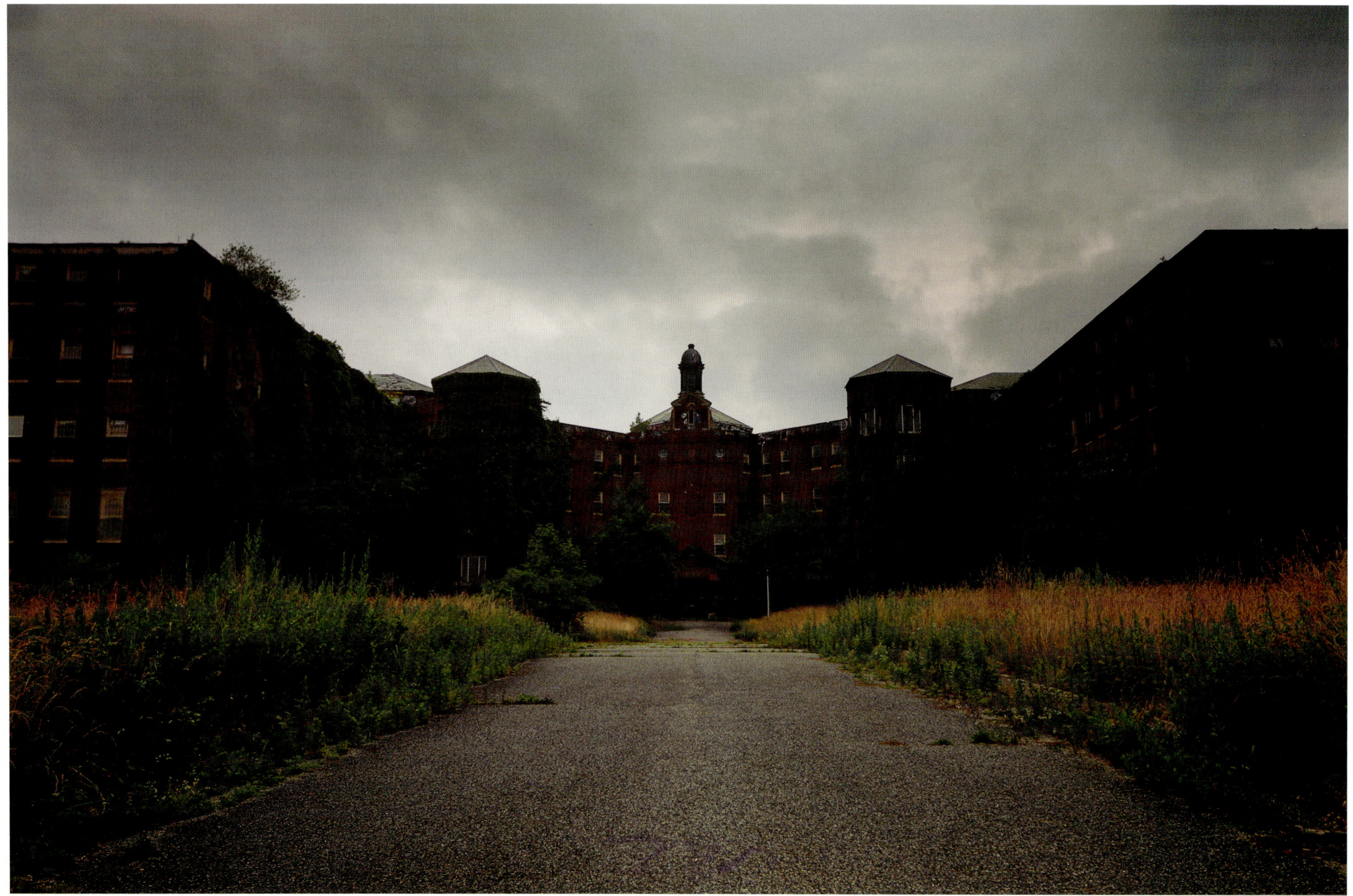

Buildings 41–43 (geriatric/ambulatory care), Kings Park Psychiatric Center

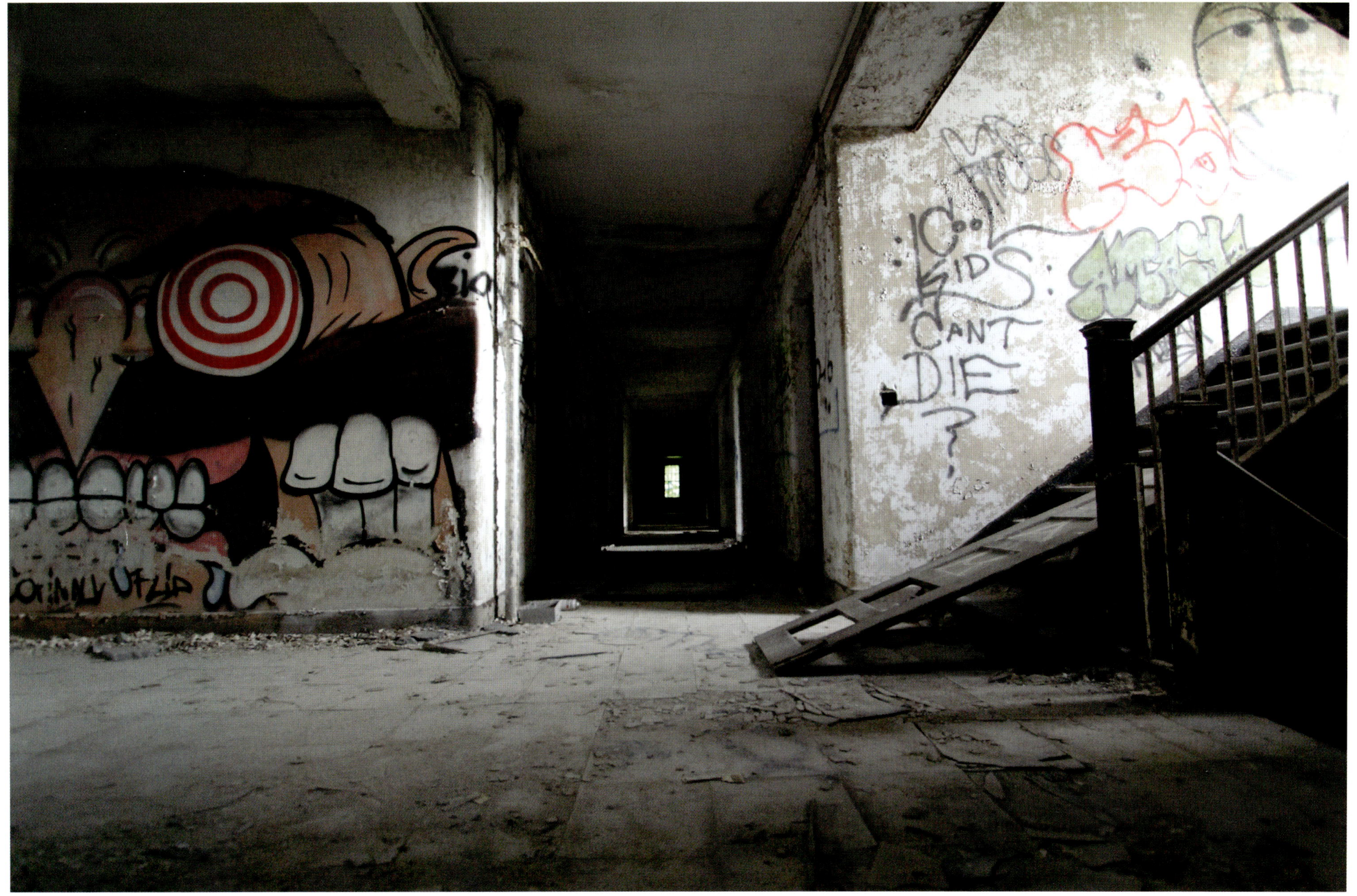

Building 90 (business/clerical offices), Kings Park Psychiatric Center

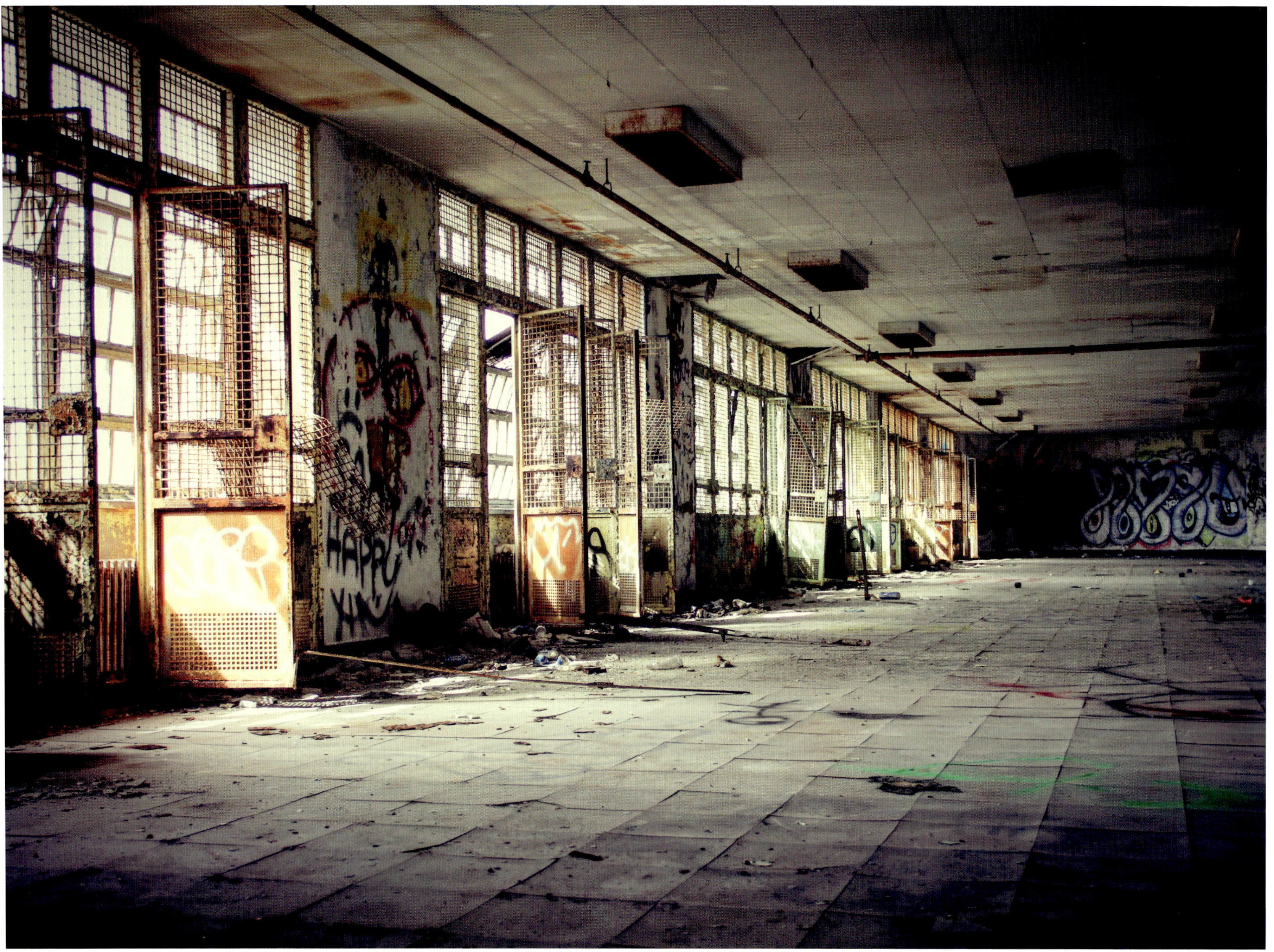

Typical day room in Building 22 (admissions / continued care), Kings Park Psychiatric Center

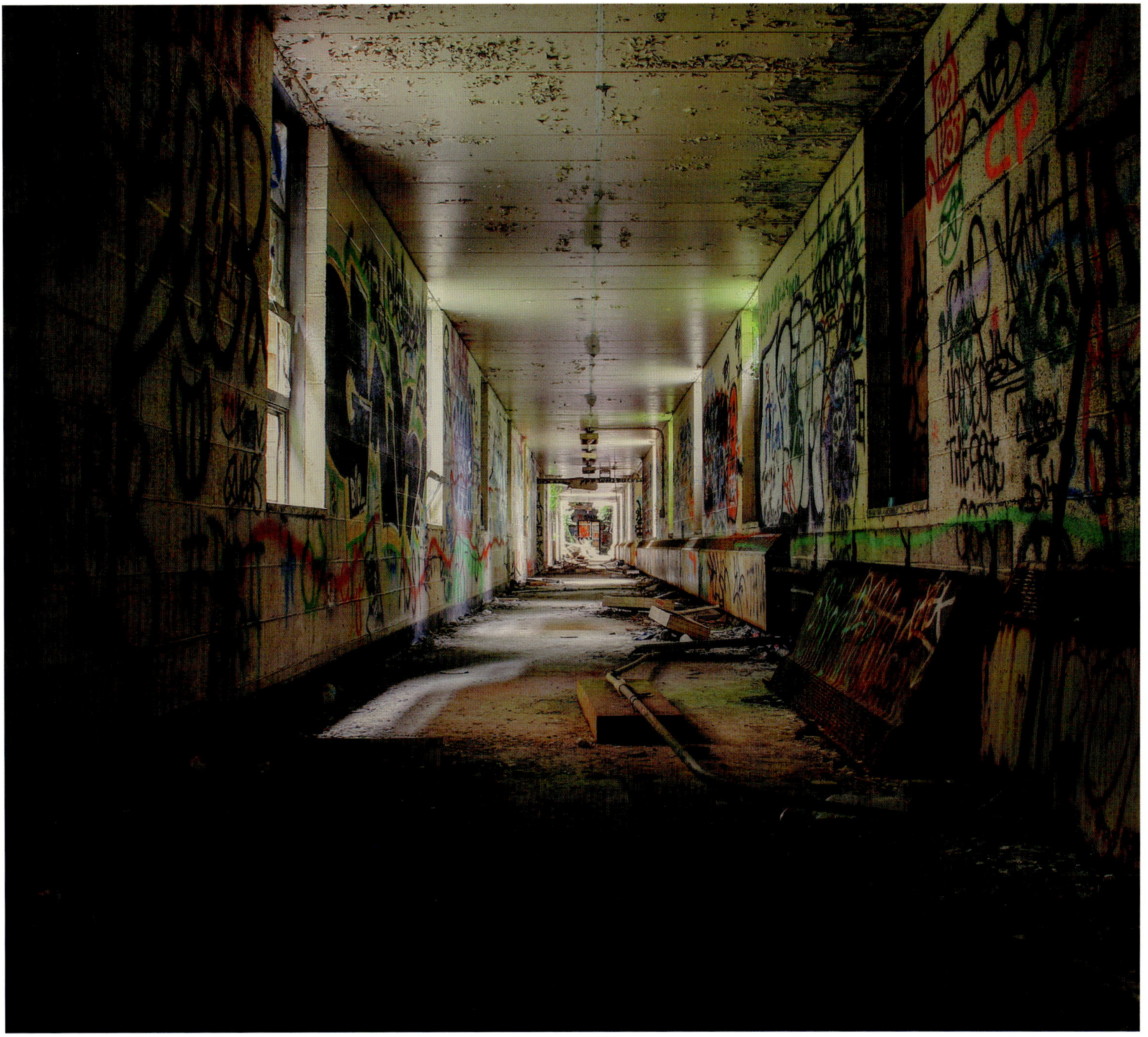

Breezeway corridor connecting Buildings 21/22 (admissions / continued care / drug treatment) to Building 7 (medical/surgical), Kings Park Psychiatric Center

Pilgrim Psychiatric Center

BRENTWOOD

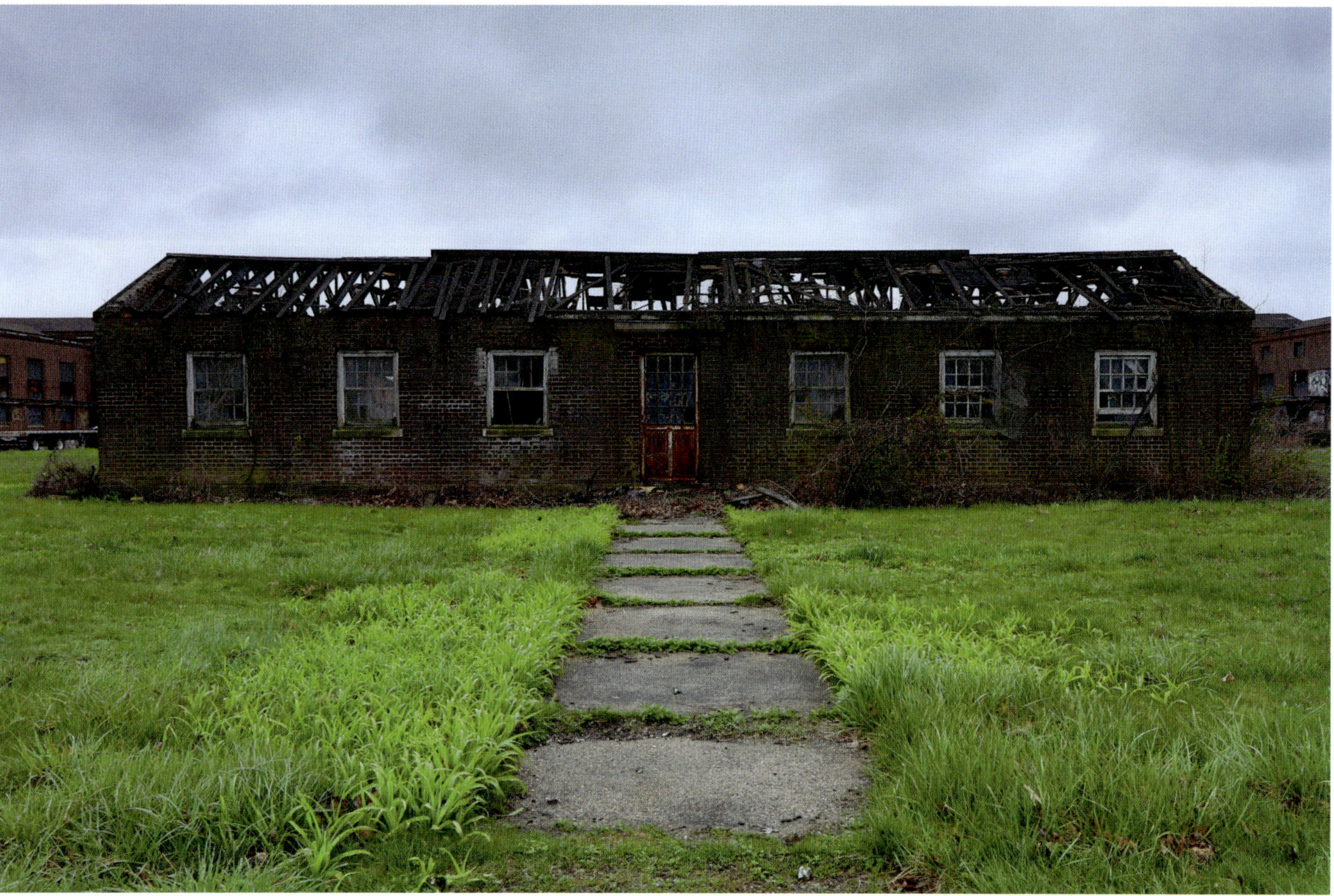

Workshop, Pilgrim Psychiatric Center

By the 1920s, overcrowding at Kings Park Psychiatric Hospital and Central Islip Psychiatric Center had become a serious problem. In order to provide such relief, New York State purchased 1,000 acres of farmland in Brentwood to build Pilgrim State Hospital. It would go on to become the largest state hospital in the world, housing approximately 14,000 patients at its peak. Today, Pilgrim Psychiatric Center still operates, but only at a fraction of its former capacity.

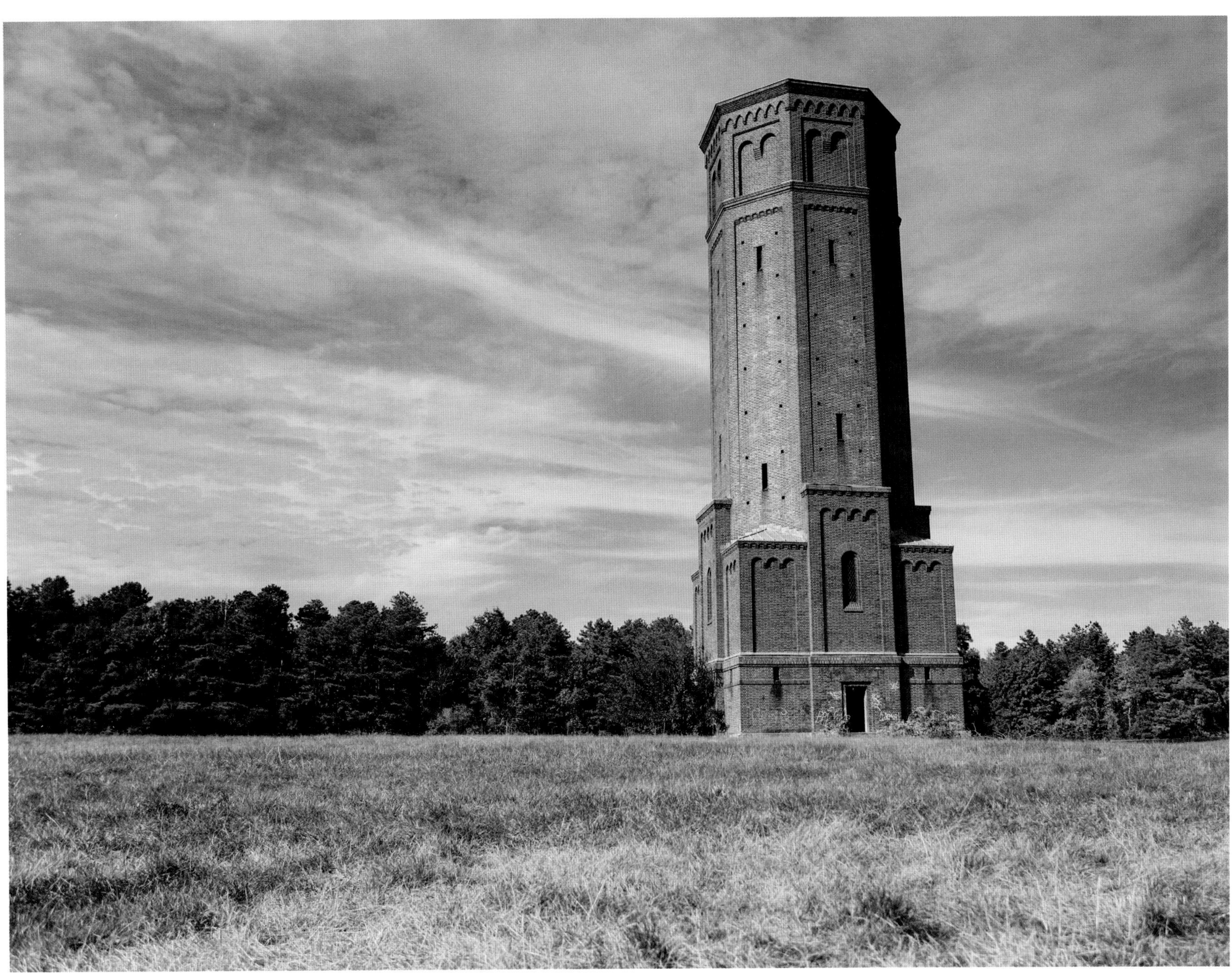

Many buildings sit abandoned on the grounds, including this art deco–styled tower, which supplied water to the entire hospital.

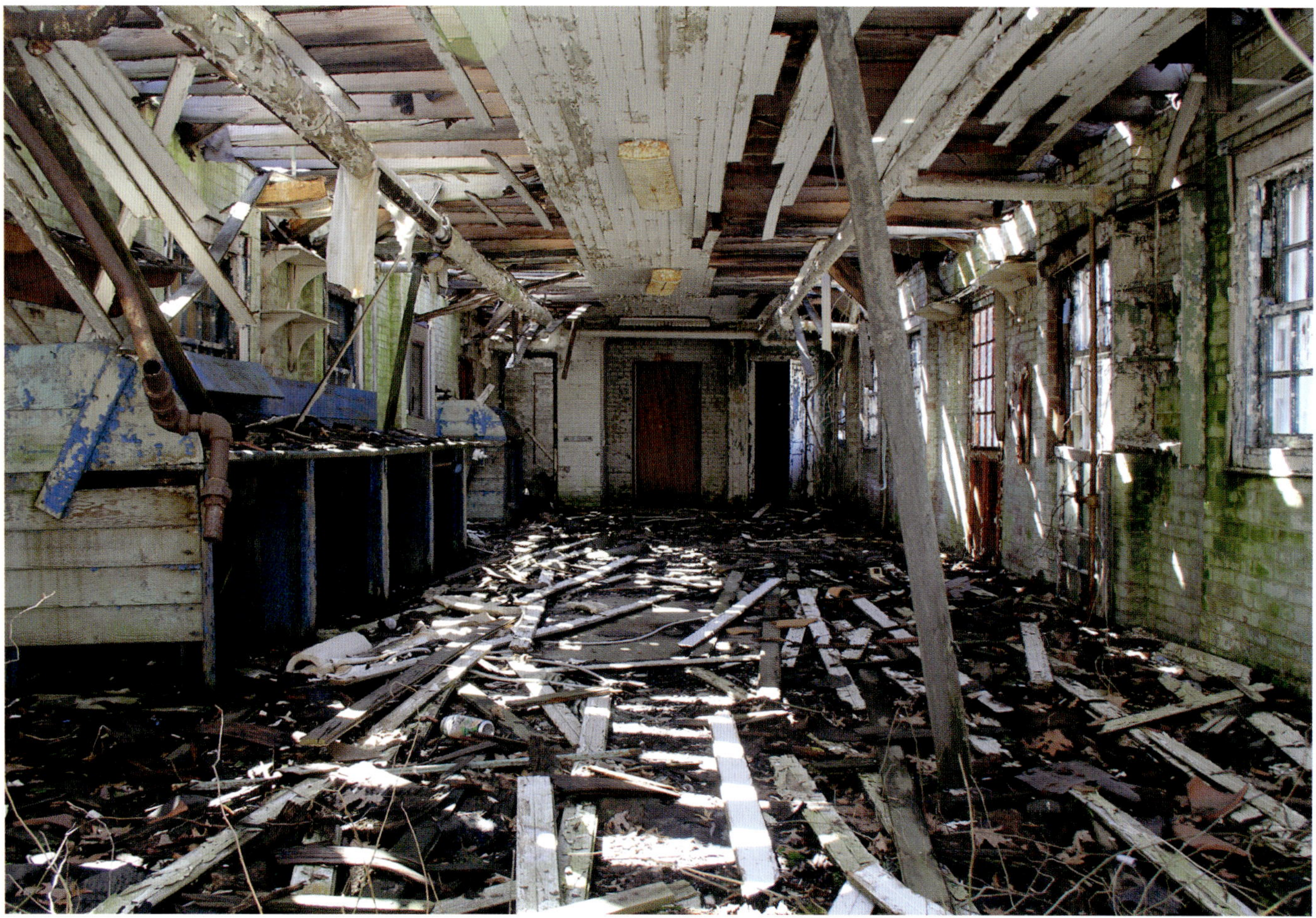

Workshop interior, Pilgrim Psychiatric Center

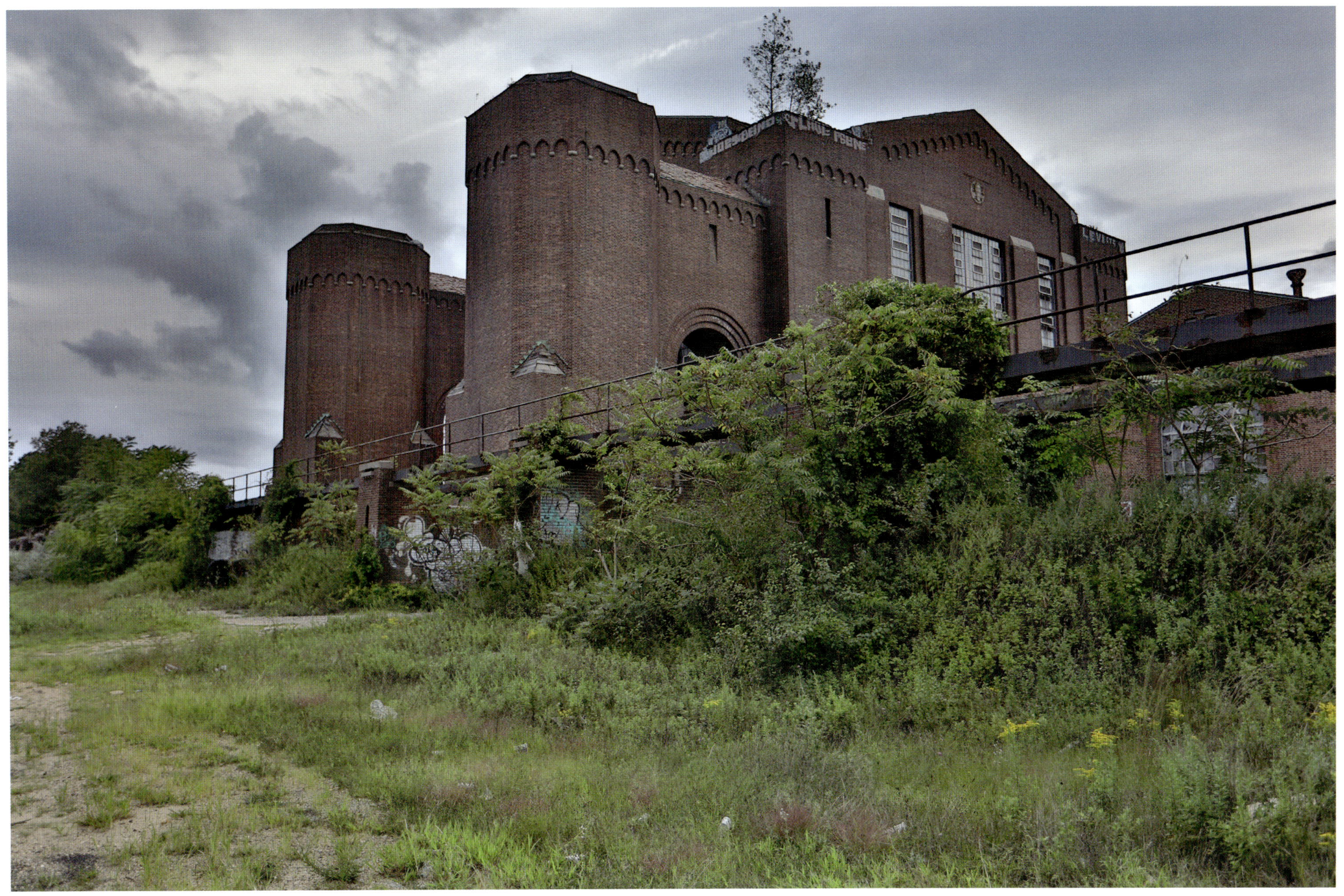

Power plant, Pilgrim Psychiatric Center

Fairchild Republic Factory

FARMINGDALE

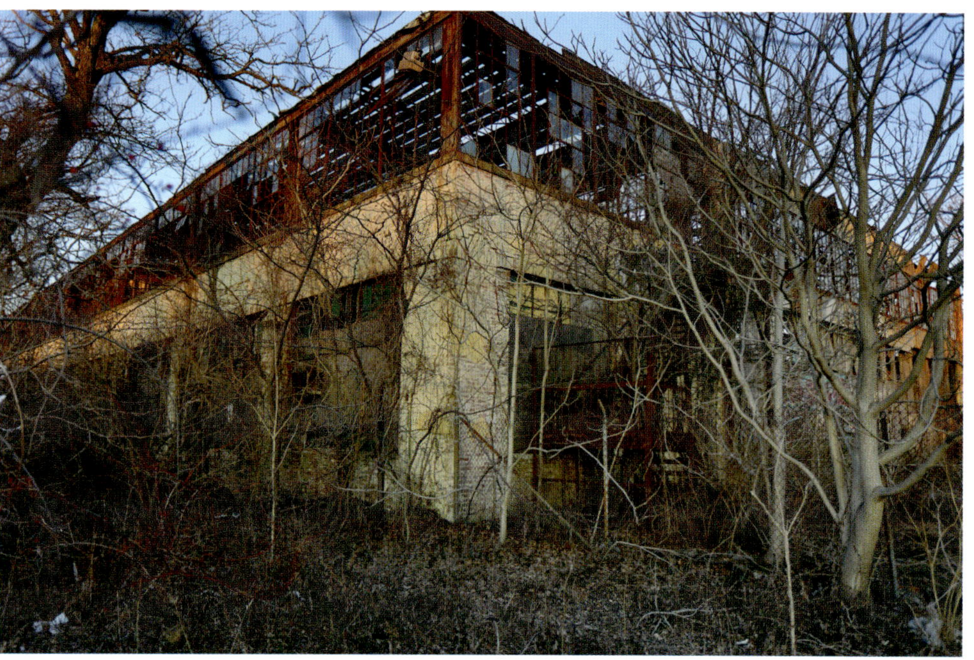

In October 1939, Republic Aviation took over aircraft production in Farmingdale. During World War II, the company produced over nine thousand P-47 Thunderbolt fighters, which were instrumental in the European theater. Later, Republic's F-84 Thunderjets were used during the Korean War, and its F-105 Thunderchiefs in Vietnam. Republic Aviation was renamed the Fairchild Republic Company after its acquisition by the Fairchild Hiller Corporation. Manufacturing ended in 1987, after a decline in building contracts. The factory buildings were abandoned and all archival records were destroyed except for a single document, a purchase order for a block of P-47s, which now sits in the Cradle of Aviation Museum in Garden City, New York.

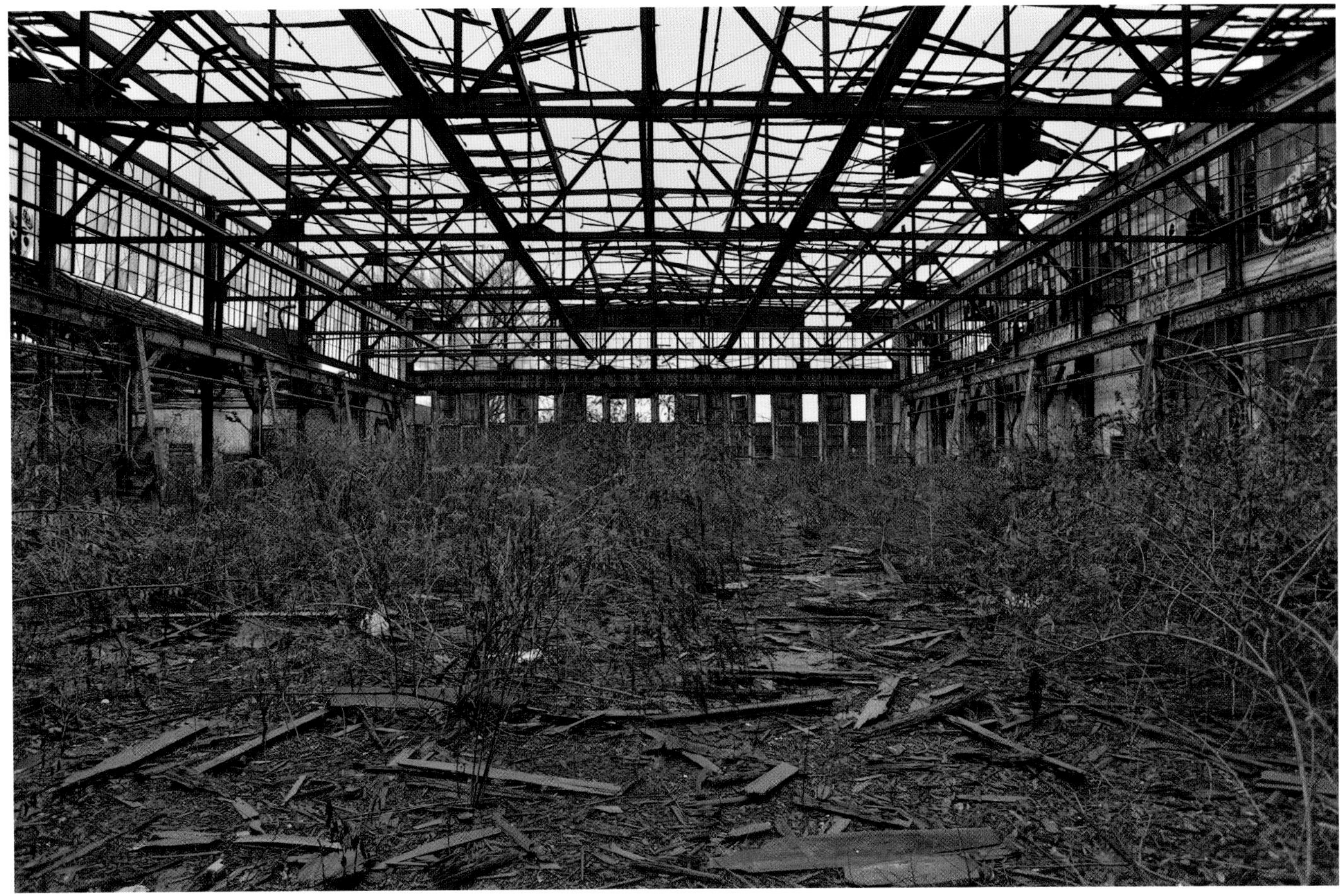

Interior, Fairchild Republic Factory

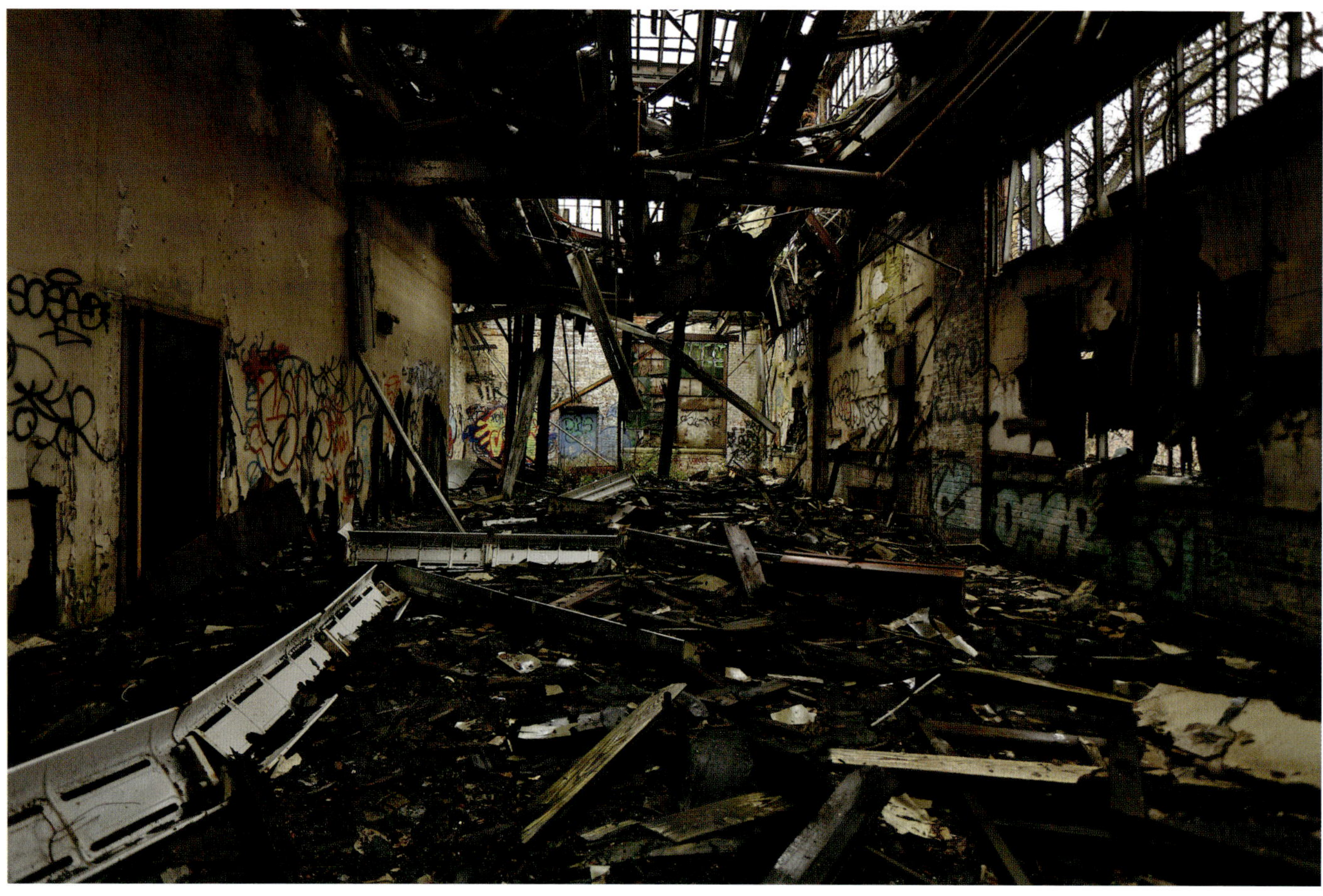

Office, Fairchild Republic Factory

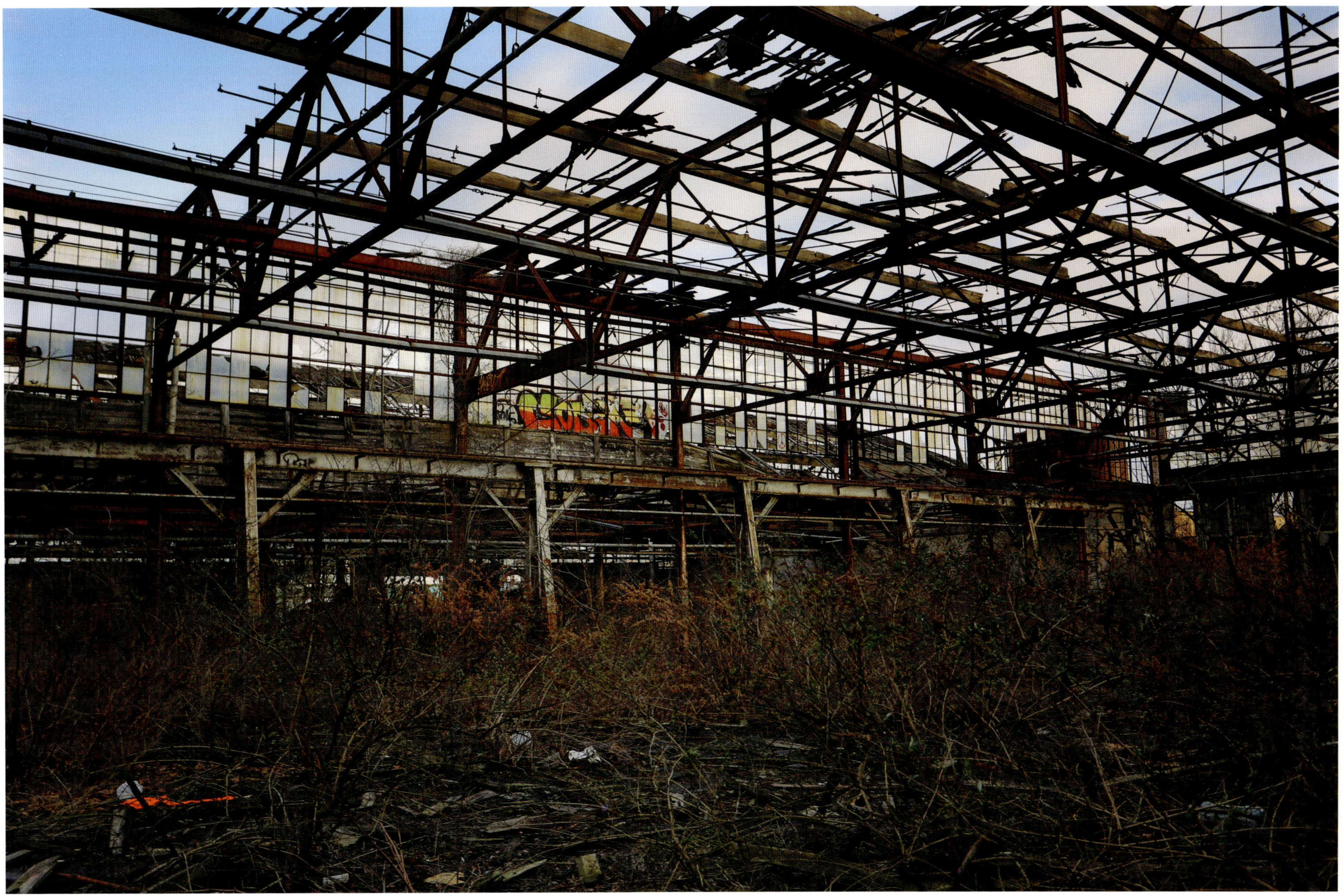

Interior, Fairchild Republic Factory

Camp Hero

MONTAUK

This radar tower at Camp Hero was once a mother station to a network of smaller radio towers situated all along the East Coast. It is said that this collection of radar towers afforded the United States an extra thirty minutes of warning time in the event of a nuclear attack.

What's more interesting is the theory of the Montauk Project, which was the basis of the television show *Stranger Things*. Legend has it that experiments took place beneath the radar tower in secret laboratories connected by an elaborate tunnel system. Children were allegedly taken from the streets and kept below ground, where scientists performed mind control experiments on them.

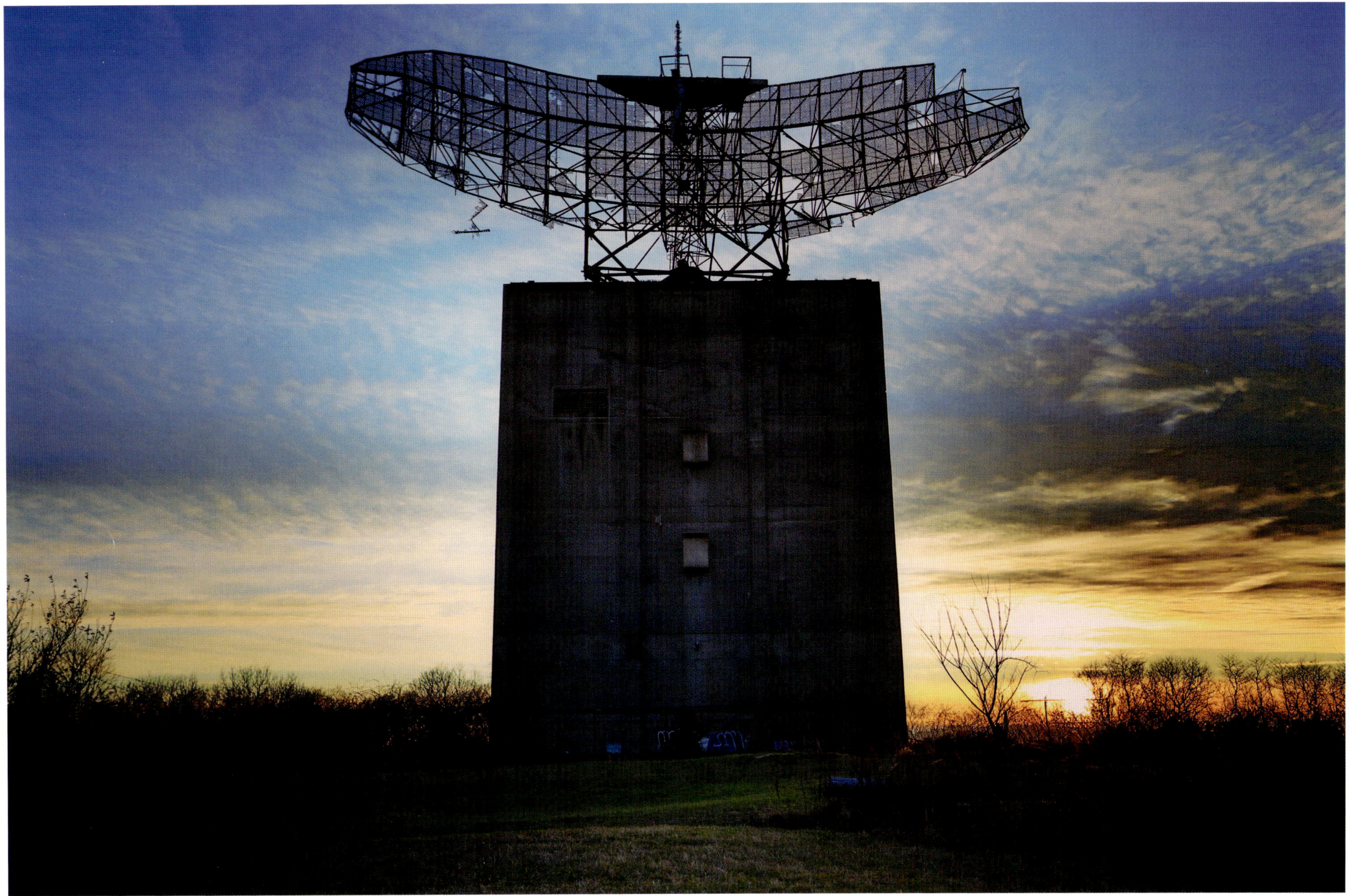

Radar Tower, Camp Hero

Stilt House

NAPEAGUE

This home was abandoned in 1998 as per town order, stating that due to a nonfunctional septic system, the residence could no longer be occupied. Originally, the home sat on a beach 100 feet from the water, as part of a small fishing community in the early 1950s. As of 2020, the house sits 30 feet from shore in Napeague Bay.

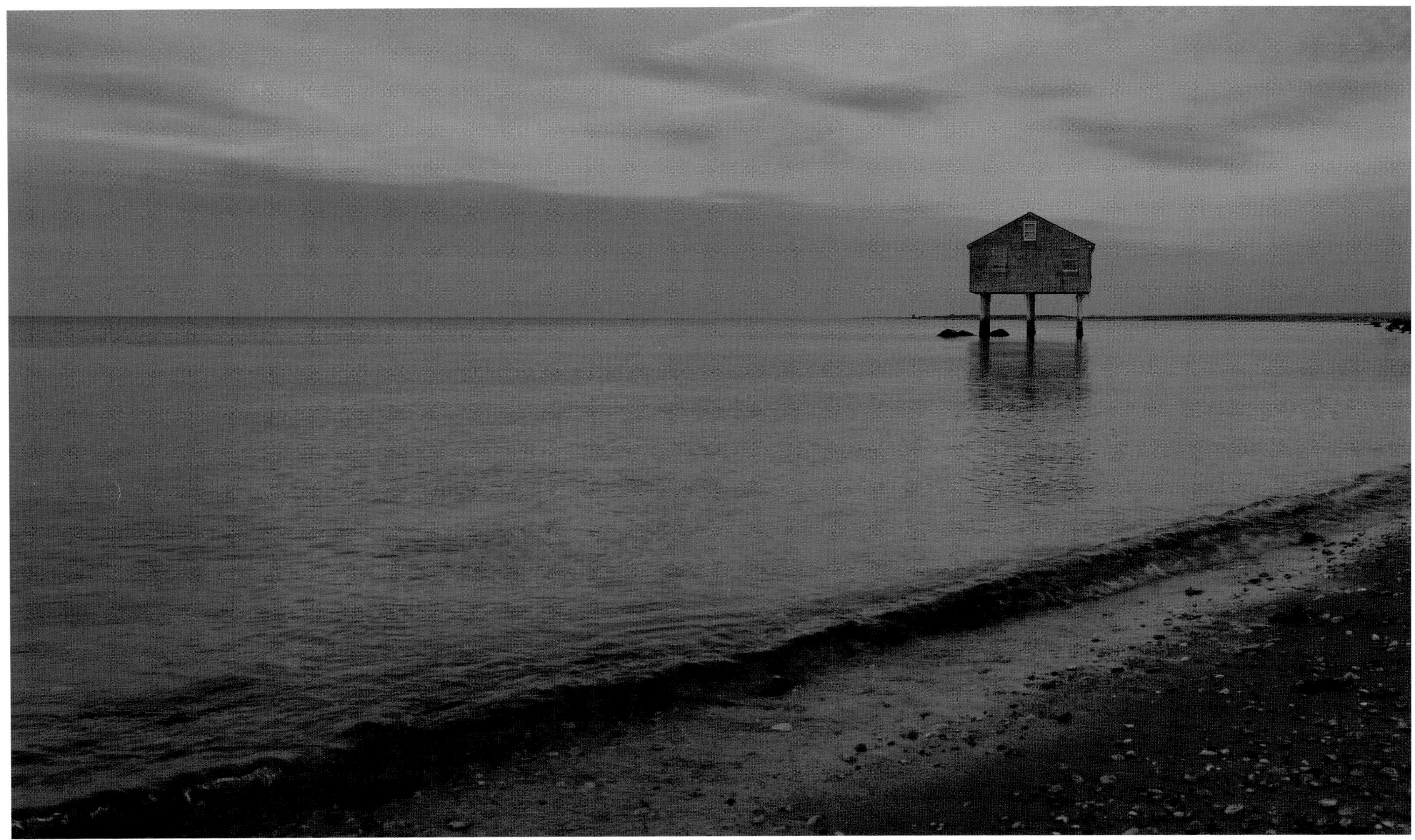

The abandoned house on wooden pilings is known to locals as "Stilt House."

CHAPTER 2.

NEW YORK CITY REGION

New York City Farm Colony

STATEN ISLAND

Seemingly remote and inconspicuous from the rest of the New York metropolis, Staten Island's New York City Farm Colony sits in seclusion among a contiguous wooded parkland known as the Greenbelt. Over a dozen buildings modeled in Dutch Colonial style are hidden in immense vegetation off Brielle Avenue, only to fully emerge in the winter months.

Back in 1829, the New York City Farm Colony was then the Richmond County Poor Farm, where the county's indigent received room and board in exchange for farmwork. After Staten Island merged into New York City in 1898, the Poor Farm was renamed the New York City Farm Colony. Over the coming years, four architectural firms designed additional dormitories and staff buildings following the original design of Renwick, Aspinwall, & Owen: dark, stone walls with red-brick infill and distinct gambrel roofs. City planning and analysis later showed that two hundred residents living on the grounds were able to harvest enough vegetables to feed three thousand people.

By the 1910s, the farm population had grown to 824. Many of the residents, however, were over fifty years of age, with a quarter being over seventy, essentially rendering them unfit for manual farm labor. The Farm Colony evolved into a geriatric hospital and home by the 1950s. But with the advent of social security, the geriatric population decreased, forcing the Farm Colony to close in 1975.

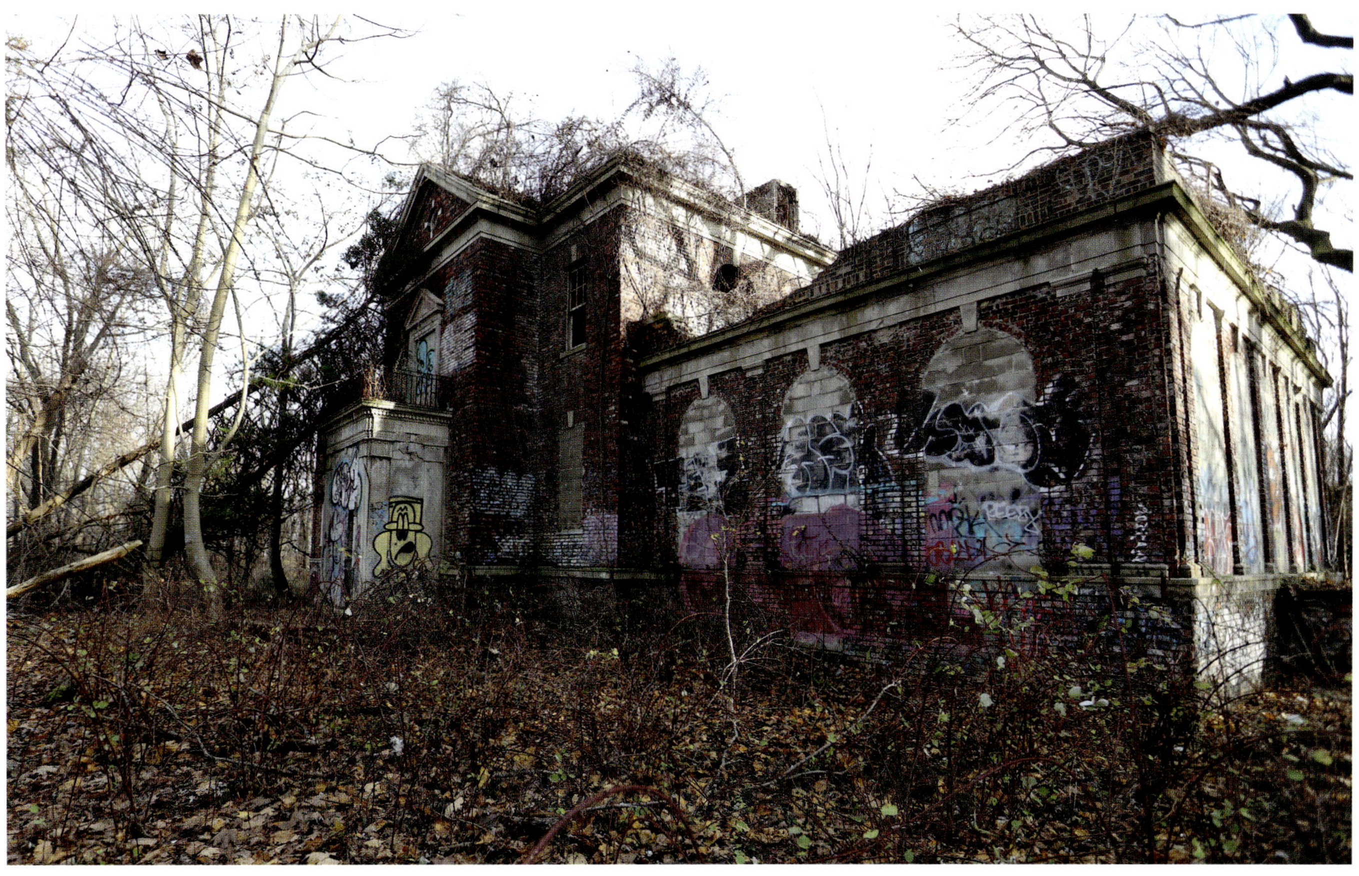

One of the many dormitories remaining on the grounds of the New York City Farm Colony

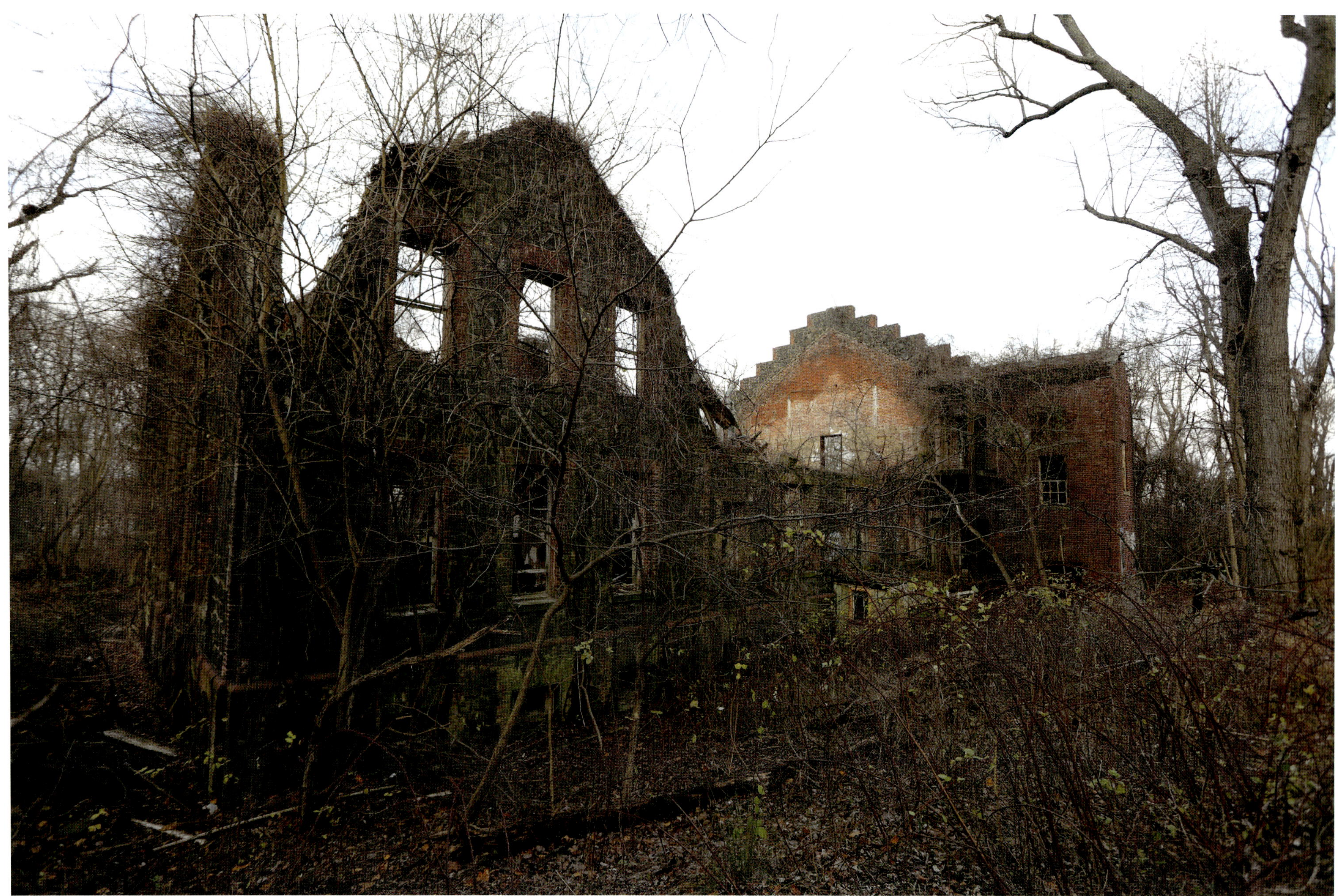

This dormitory is one of the original structures designed by Raymond F. Almirall in 1907.

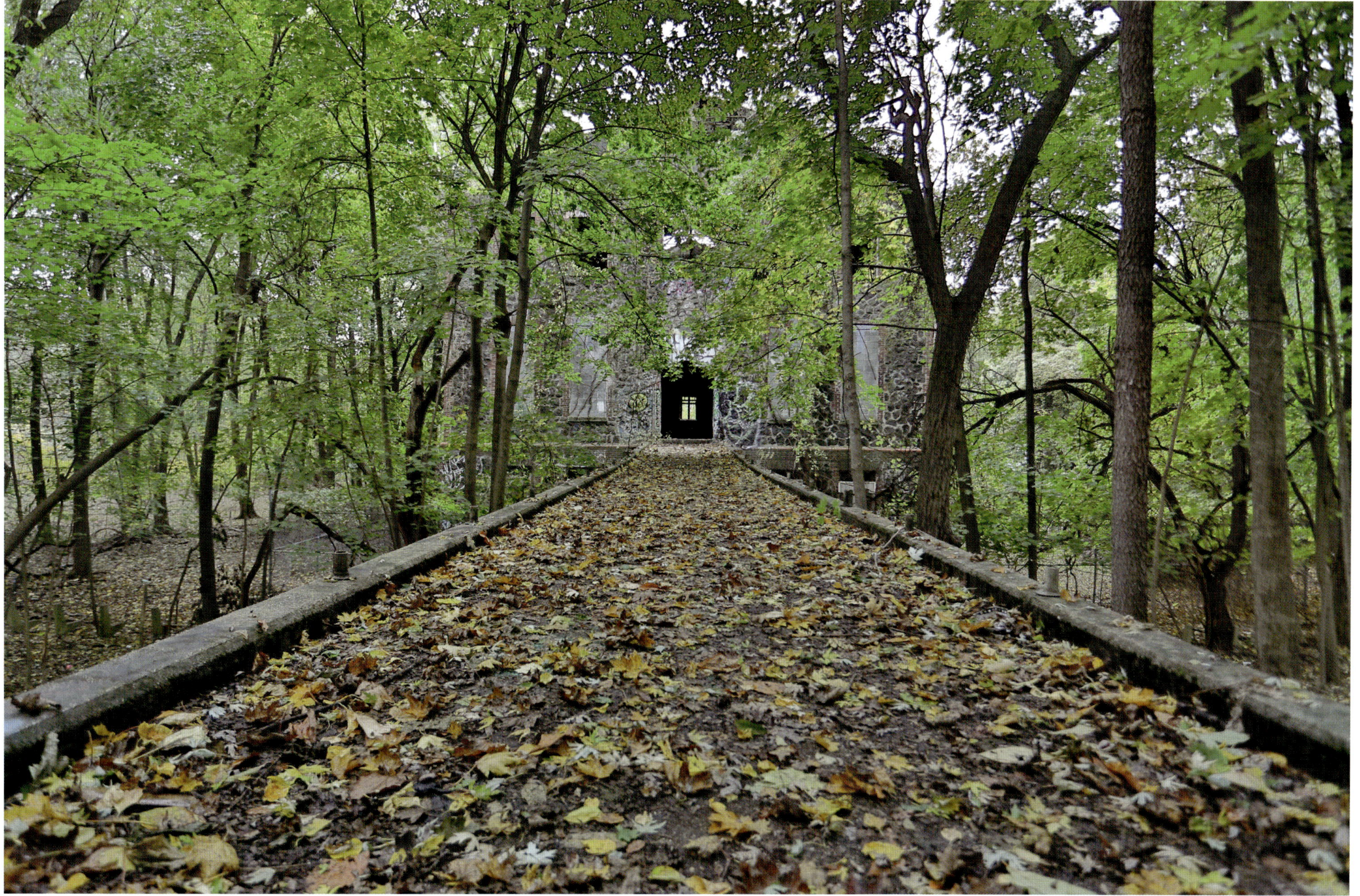

Dining hall and kitchen building (spring), New York City Farm Colony

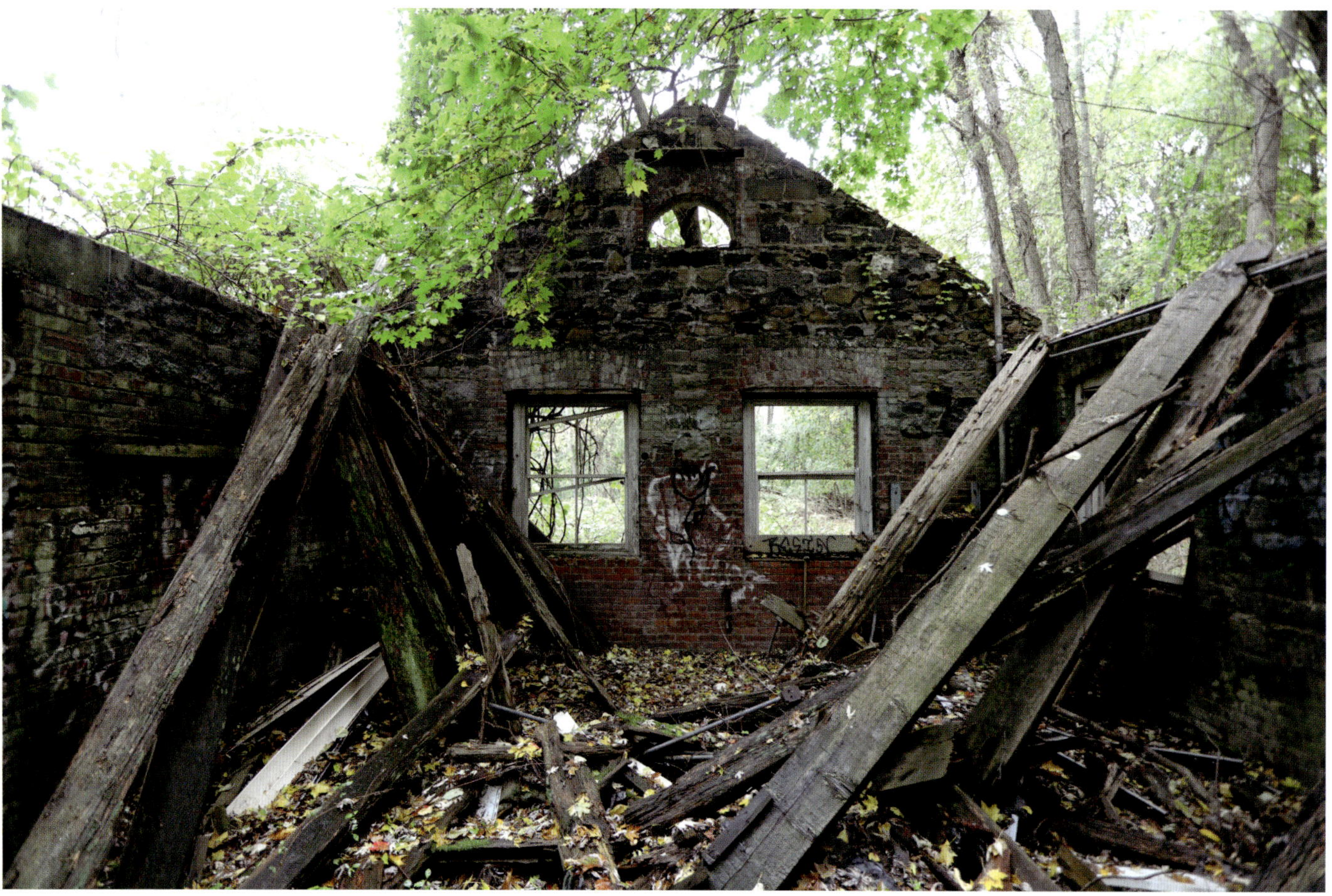

Shop building, New York City Farm Colony

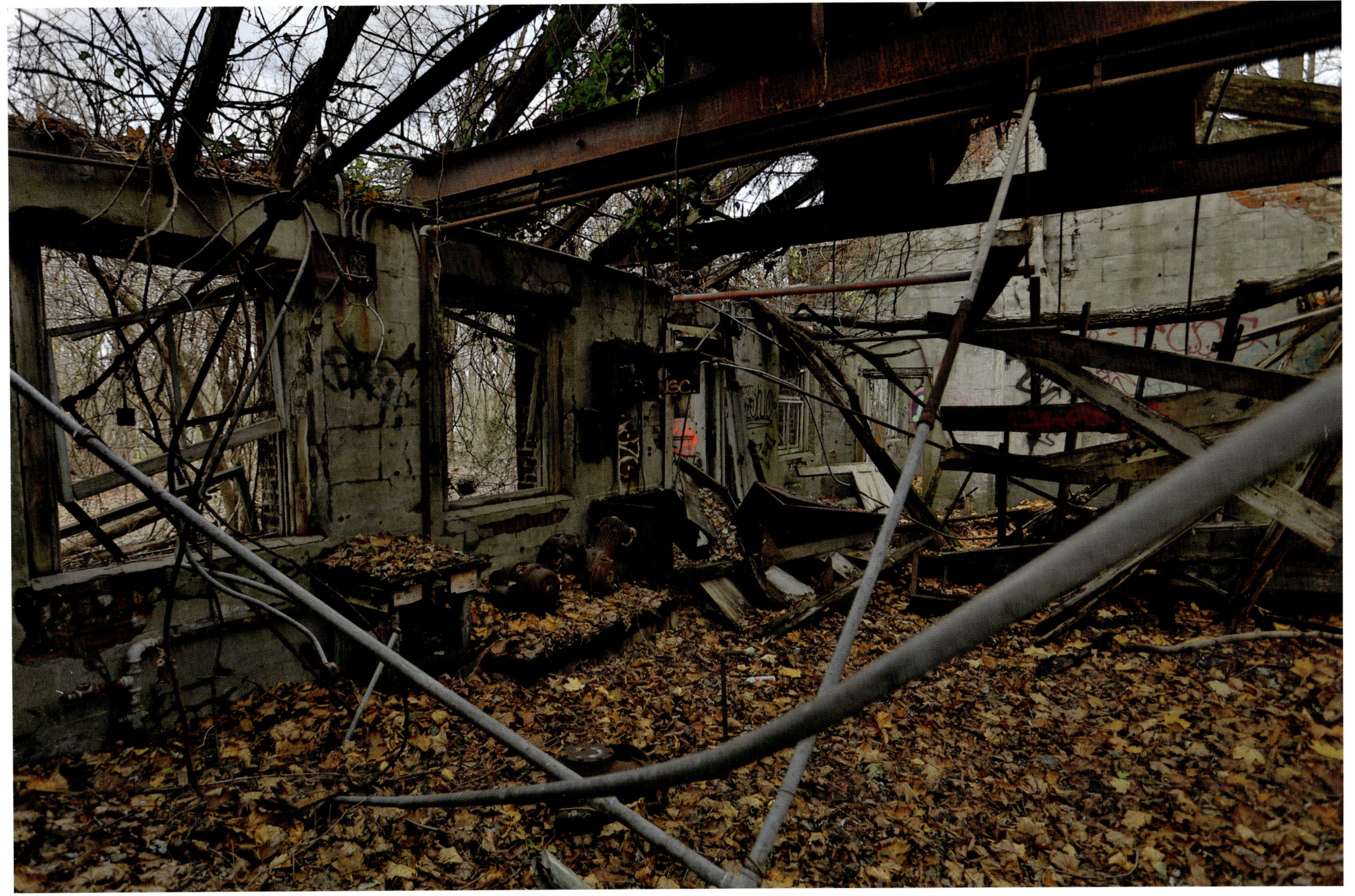

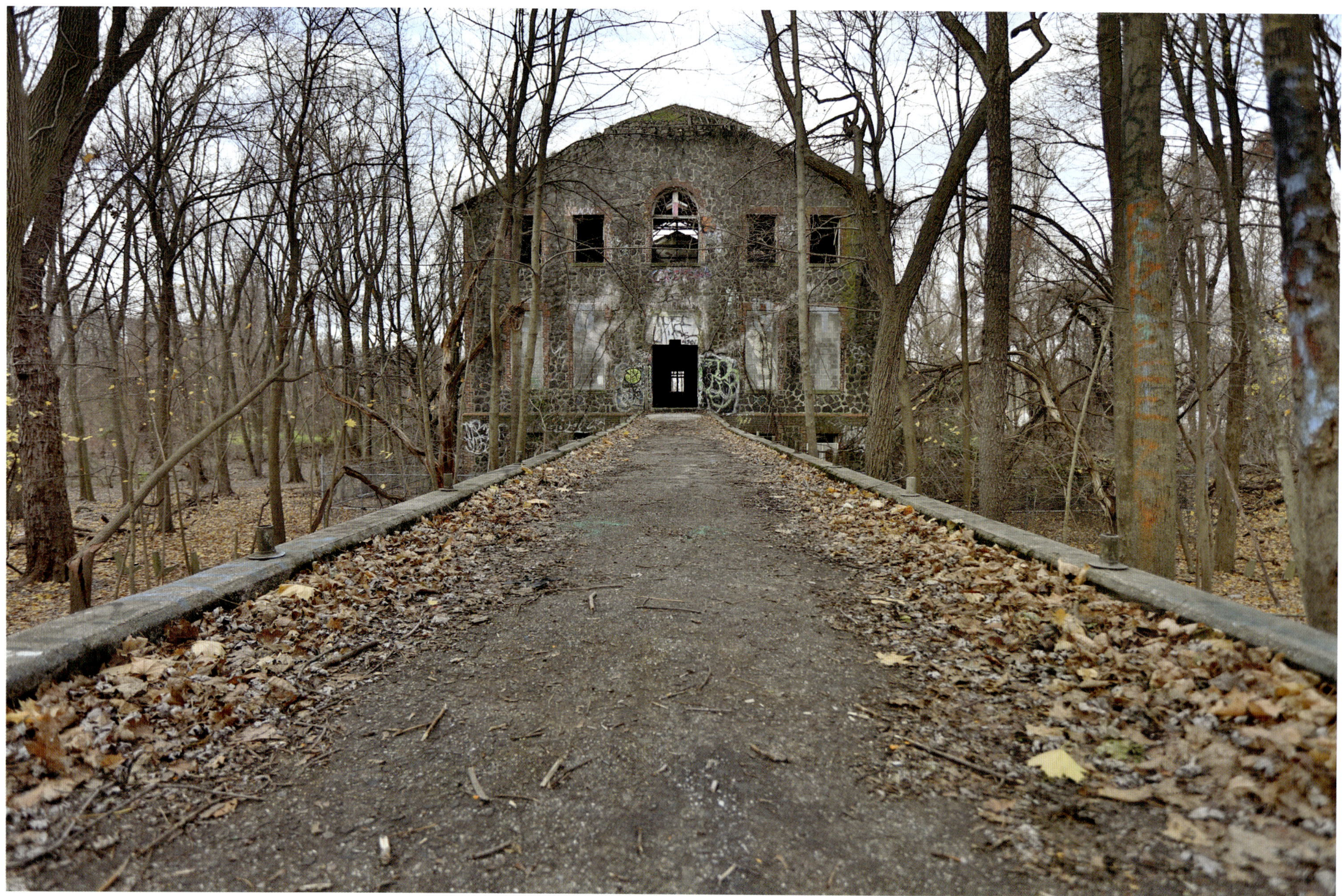

Dining hall and kitchen building (winter), New York City Farm Colony

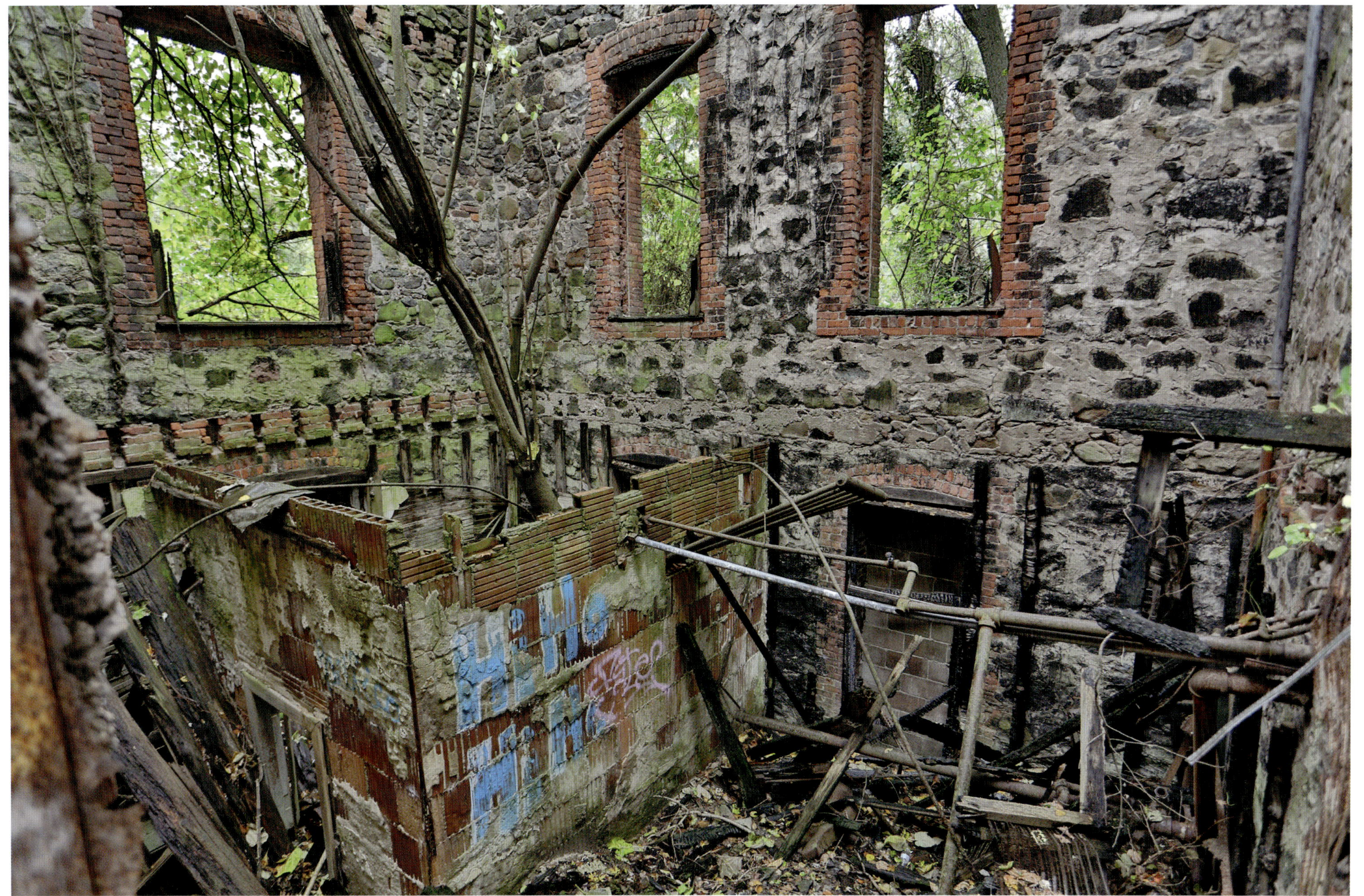

The stone walls with red-brick infill of the dormitory interior were part of Renwick, Aspinwall & Owen's original design.

Skull Silo

BROOKLYN

Around 5:30 a.m. on May 2, 2006, a mysterious ten-alarm fire broke out at the Greenpoint Terminal Market in Brooklyn. Clouds of gray smoke stretched across the East River all the way to the West Side of Manhattan.

The Greenpoint Terminal Market played an important part in American industrial history at the turn of the century. The market buildings dated back to 1890 and were built by the American Manufacturing Company, which happened to be the largest rope manufacturer in the United States. By the 1980s, with the buildings of the American Manufacturing Company long gone, squatters, drifters, and feral dogs and cats had occupied the space.

It took four hundred firefighters thirty-six hours and 9 million gallons of water to fully extinguish the blaze, making it the most extensive operation by the FDNY since 9/11. It is widely speculated that the fire was a result of arson by the developer of the property. This building is one of the few remains of the historic waterfront.

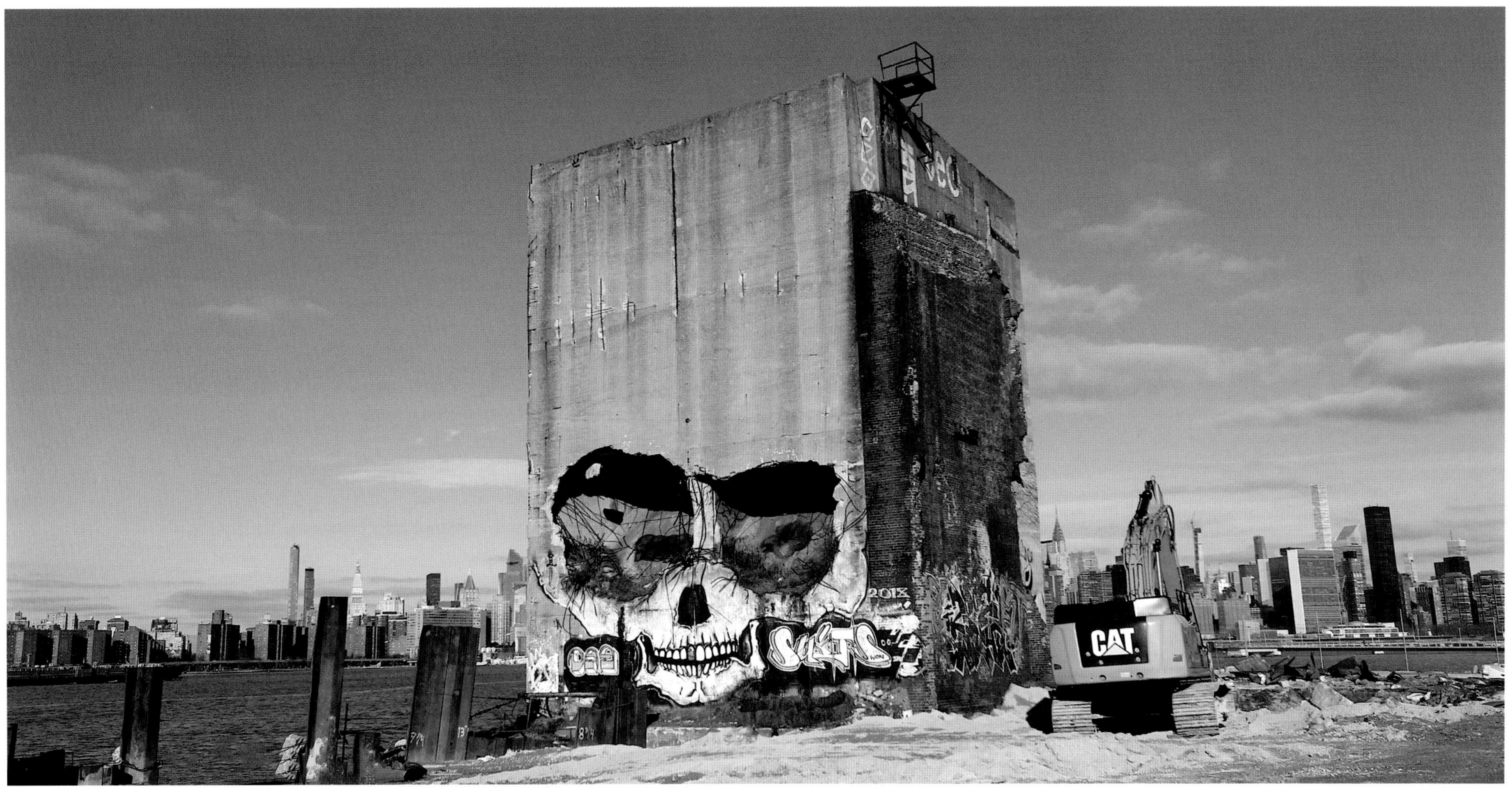

Skull Silo

Old Pier 1

BROOKLYN

In the 1950s, the New York Dock Company sold its shares to the Port Authority of New York, which in turn demolished over 130 warehouses and twenty-five piers along the Brooklyn waterfront in order to accommodate larger ships and cargo. When the Port Authority moved to its New Jersey location, the economic viability of the Brooklyn Marine Terminal took a downturn. By 1970 much of the Brooklyn waterfront developments were barren and decrepit, forcing the Port Authority of New York to end cargo ship operations in 1983. The remains of the old piers are still prominent in Brooklyn Bridge Park.

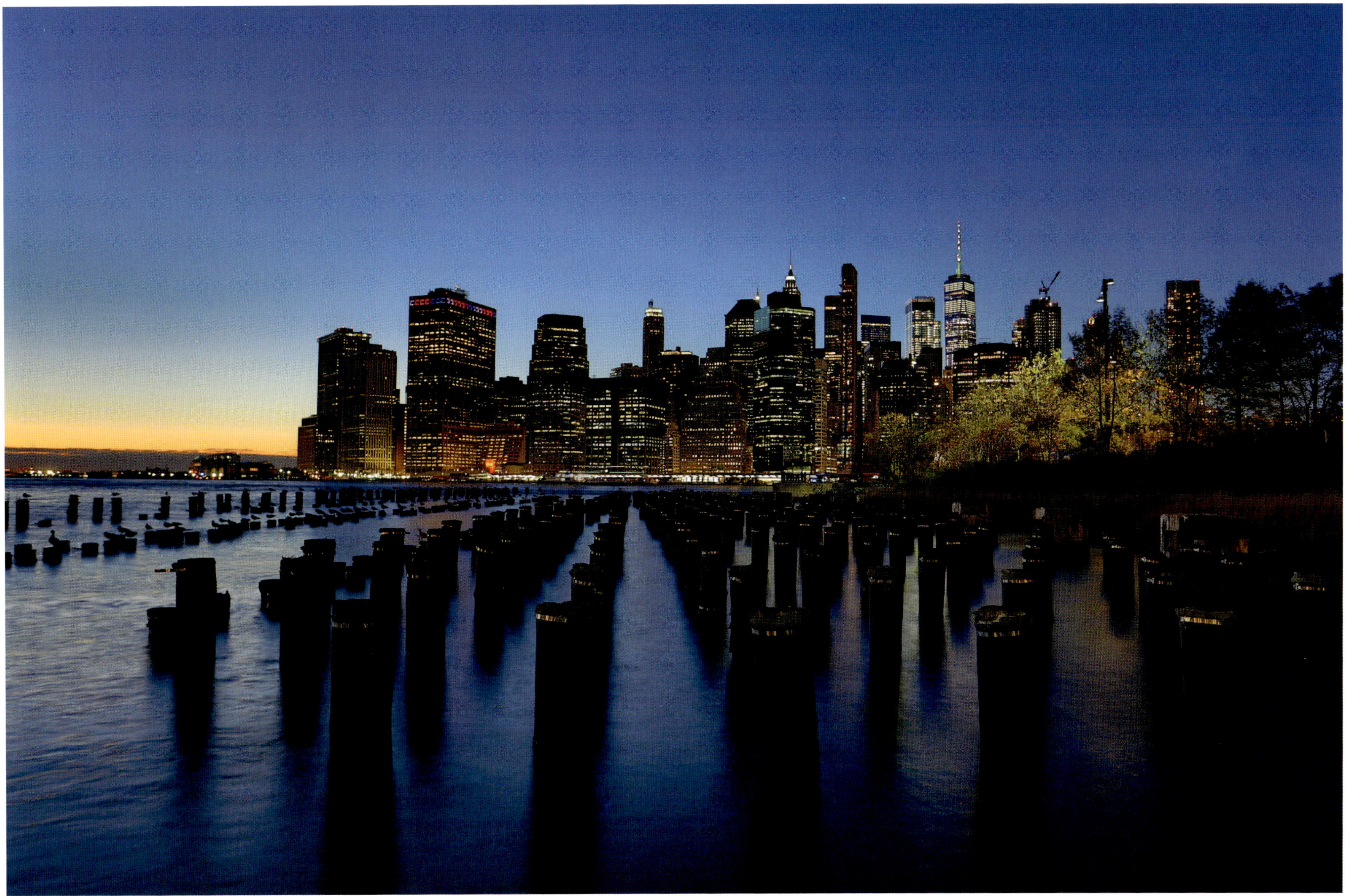

Old Pier 1

Sea View Hospital

STATEN ISLAND

At the turn of the century, pneumonia cases were the leading cause of death in New York City, followed by tuberculosis at a close second. The only prescribed cure for tuberculosis at that time was ample fresh air, rest, and sun, combined with a nutrient-rich diet. Thirty-seven buildings were constructed from 1905 to 1938 adjacent to the New York City Farm Colony on Staten Island to serve as the city's new tuberculosis hospital. While the site for the Sea View complex fell in line with the traditional cure by offering spectacular views of the oceans and Staten Island's Greenbelt, the pioneering research for a cure took place within the hospital.

During the 1940s, Sea View Hospital was running at full capacity and treating bone and glandular tuberculosis, which was not often treated at other hospitals. Many of the doctors serving on the Sea View staff pioneered surgical procedures such as lung collapse, which permitted the self-sealing of tuberculosis lesions and went on to receive national reputations in the field of chest surgery. After streptomycin was developed by Dr. Selman Waksman at Rutgers University in 1943, the antibiotic's culminating step was taken by Sea View's Dr. Edward Robitzek and Dr. Irving J. Selikoff. Together, they conducted the first experiments on humans with a synthetic compound called isoniazid, which aided patients who had failed to respond to the treatments of streptomycin. By 1961, Sea View had phased out all tuberculosis treatment.

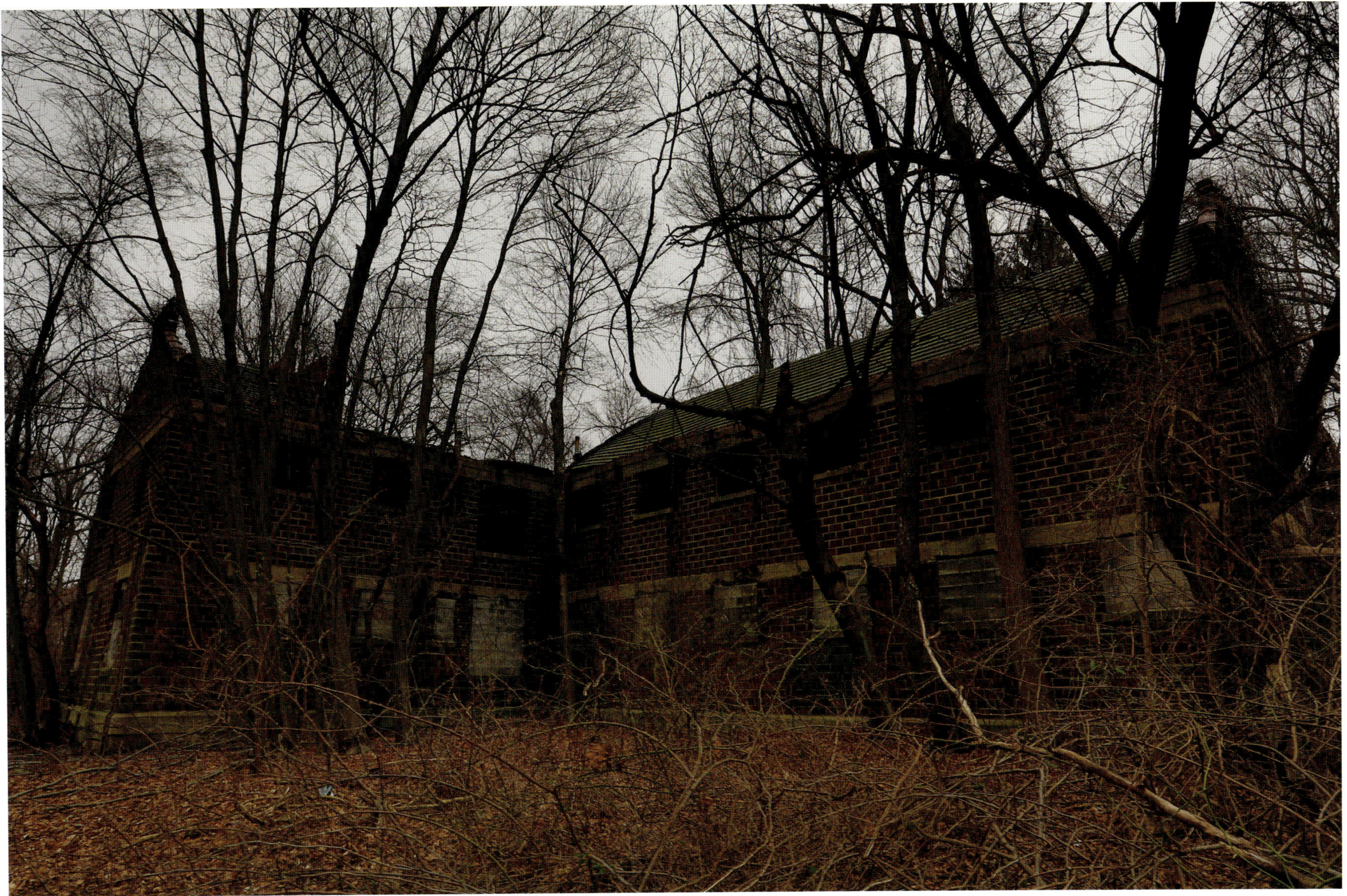

Women's open-air tuberculosis pavilion, Sea View Hospital

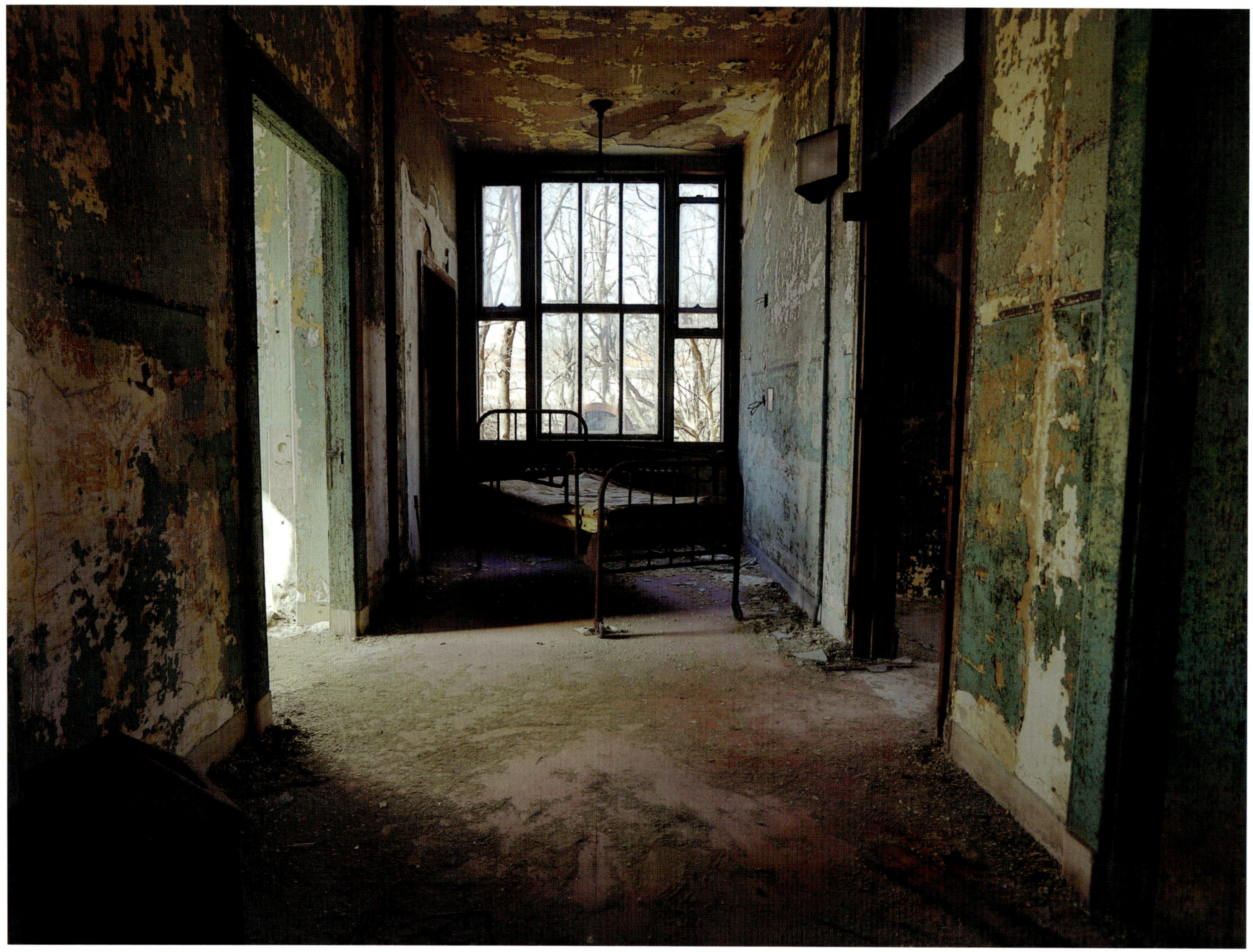

Typical ward in the patient pavilion, Sea View Hospital

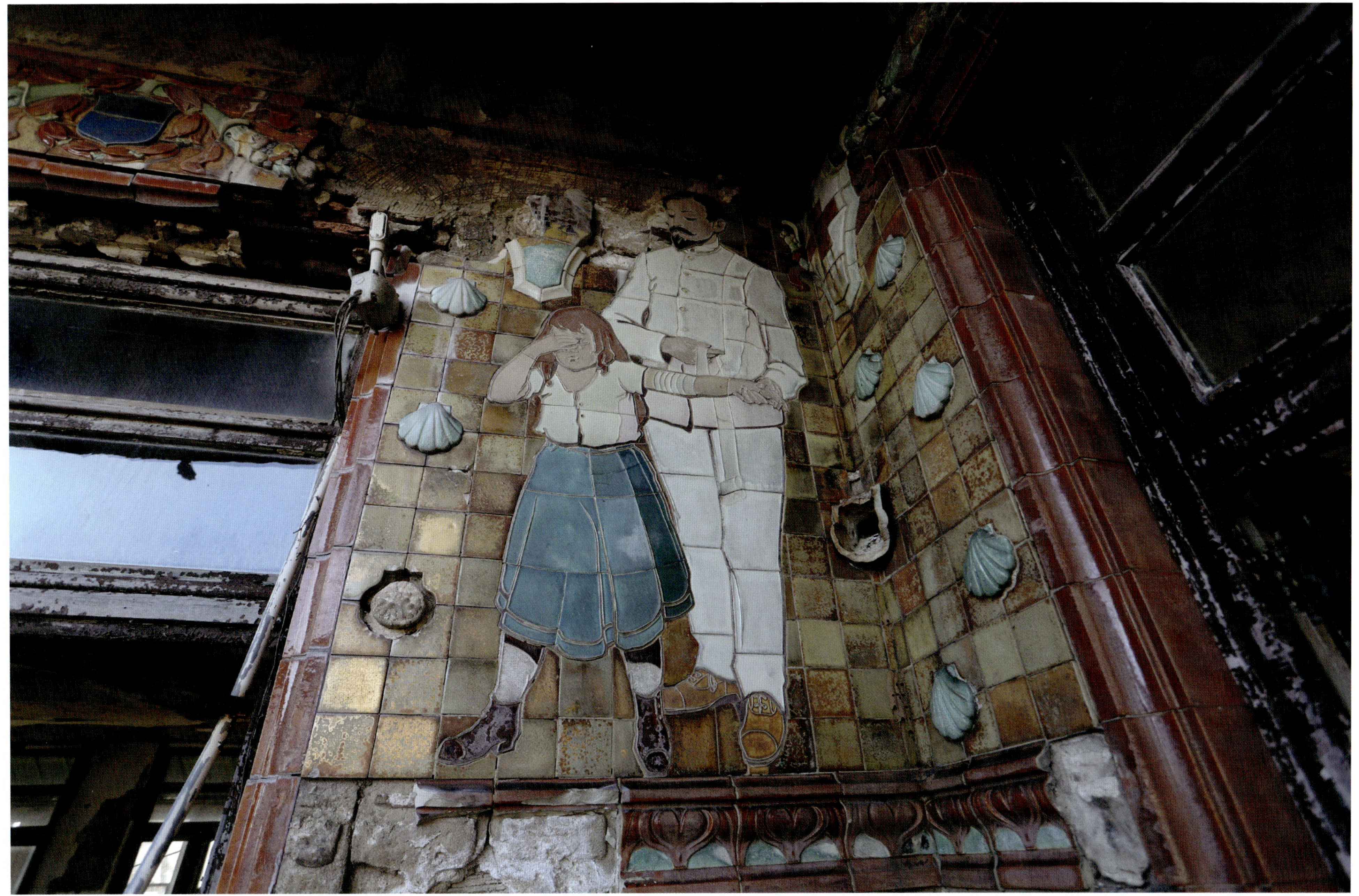

Part of the mosaic frieze just below the roofline that decorates the open-air porches of the patient pavilions

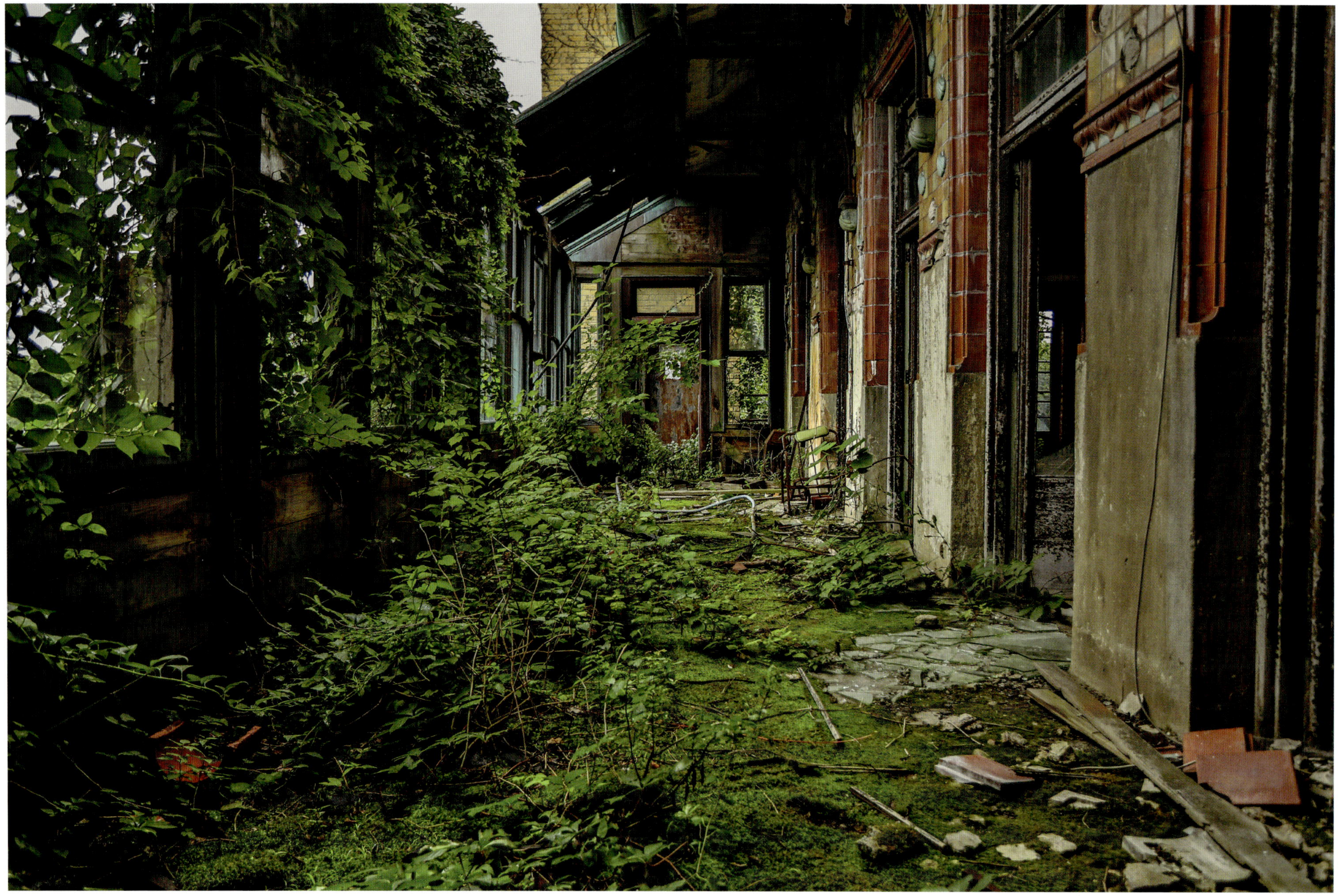

The open-air sleeping porches of the female patient pavilion have a 6-foot-high terra-cotta frieze running beneath its projecting eaves. Sticking out from the wall are the remains of seashells and medallion-like tile decorations, designed to provide a more serene setting in the hospital.

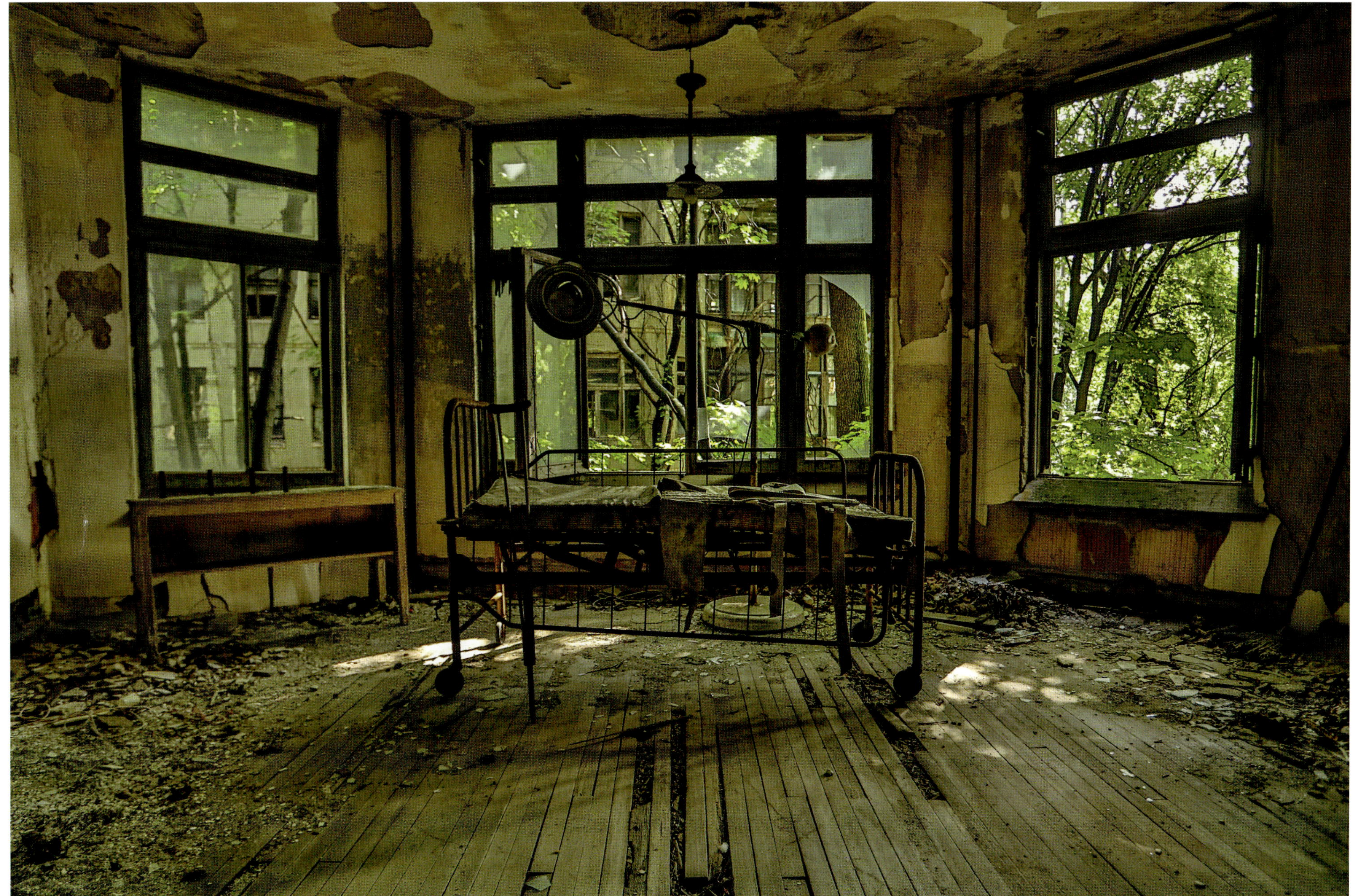

Leftover medical equipment in the patient pavilions

CHAPTER 3.

HUDSON VALLEY REGION

Camp LaGuardia

CHESTER

Originally serving as the Greycourt Women's Prison, which opened in 1924, Camp LaGuardia was a men's work camp that housed and employed the transient male population of New York City. Prior to World War II and through the late 1950s, Camp LaGuardia included a 191-acre farm, which provided food for the residents and to which up to 150 residents were assigned to work. In its heyday, the camp housed more than a thousand homeless men, making it New York City's largest and longest-lasting homeless shelter until its closure.

The history of Camp LaGuardia dates back to 1918, when New York State purchased 300 acres of land in the town of Chester, Orange County, to build a prison for young women, following a sharp spike in female criminal activity in New York City during and after World War I. The construction of Greycourt Women's Prison (also referred to as the Farm Colony at Greycourt) took place over a five-year period as part of a greater Progressive movement in the modernization of New York City's correctional institutions. Greycourt, New York City's version of the State Reformatory at Bedford, became the women's branch of the city's reformatory system and the city's first geographically separate women's prison. It was built in the English Gothic architectural style to avoid the generic appearance of most prison buildings of the time.

By 1930, eighty-one women were incarcerated at Greycourt, well under its maximum capacity of seven hundred inmates. The work component of the rehabilitation program at Greycourt would be transferred to the Department of Public Welfare. With criminality among women on the wane, the depths of the Depression brought about homelessness and alcoholism among men. In 1934, Greycourt Women's Prison was converted into Camp Greycourt, a work camp for homeless men, by New York City mayor Fiorello LaGuardia. Renamed Camp LaGuardia in 1935, the facility was imagined to be self-sustaining by providing a rehabilitative work environment, thus becoming a model for President Franklin Roosevelt's Civilian Conservation Corps. Camp LaGuardia residents would work on the grounds or find employment at the nearby resorts.

By the 1990s, Camp LaGuardia's homeless population had grown to consist more of young males who were drug addicted or mentally ill (or both) and were allowed the leeway to leave the grounds. Incidents such as public urination, lewdness, and the strangulation of a local's pet had put many of the residents of Chester on edge. By the first decade of the 2000s, the New York City homeless population was estimated at 35,000. As part of Mayor Michael Bloomberg's five-year plan to reduce homelessness in New York City, and the reallocation of Camp LaGuardia's $19 million budget to more-long-term solutions such as subsidized housing, city officials announced the closing of the camp in November 2006.

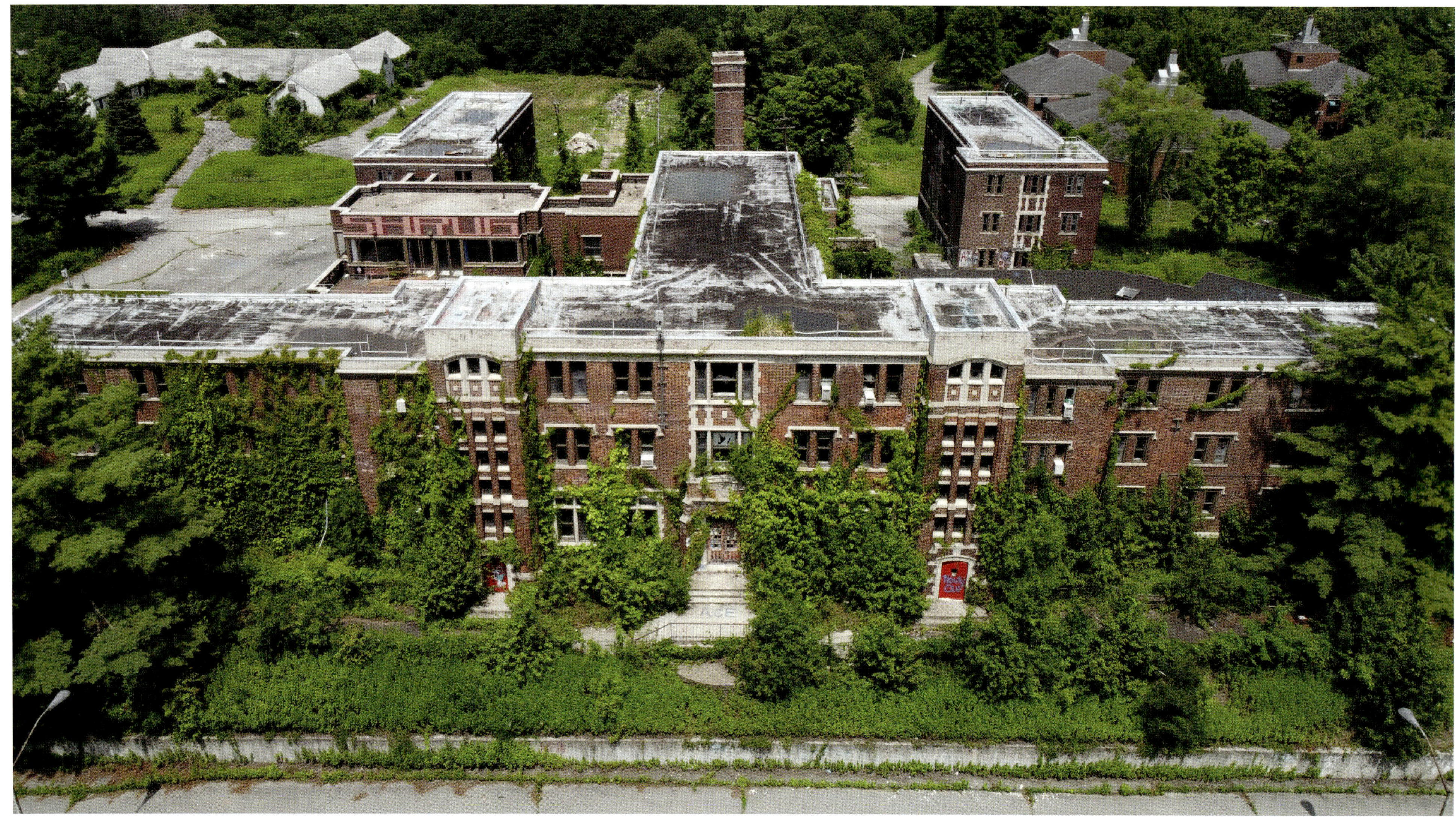

Aerial view of Camp LaGuardia

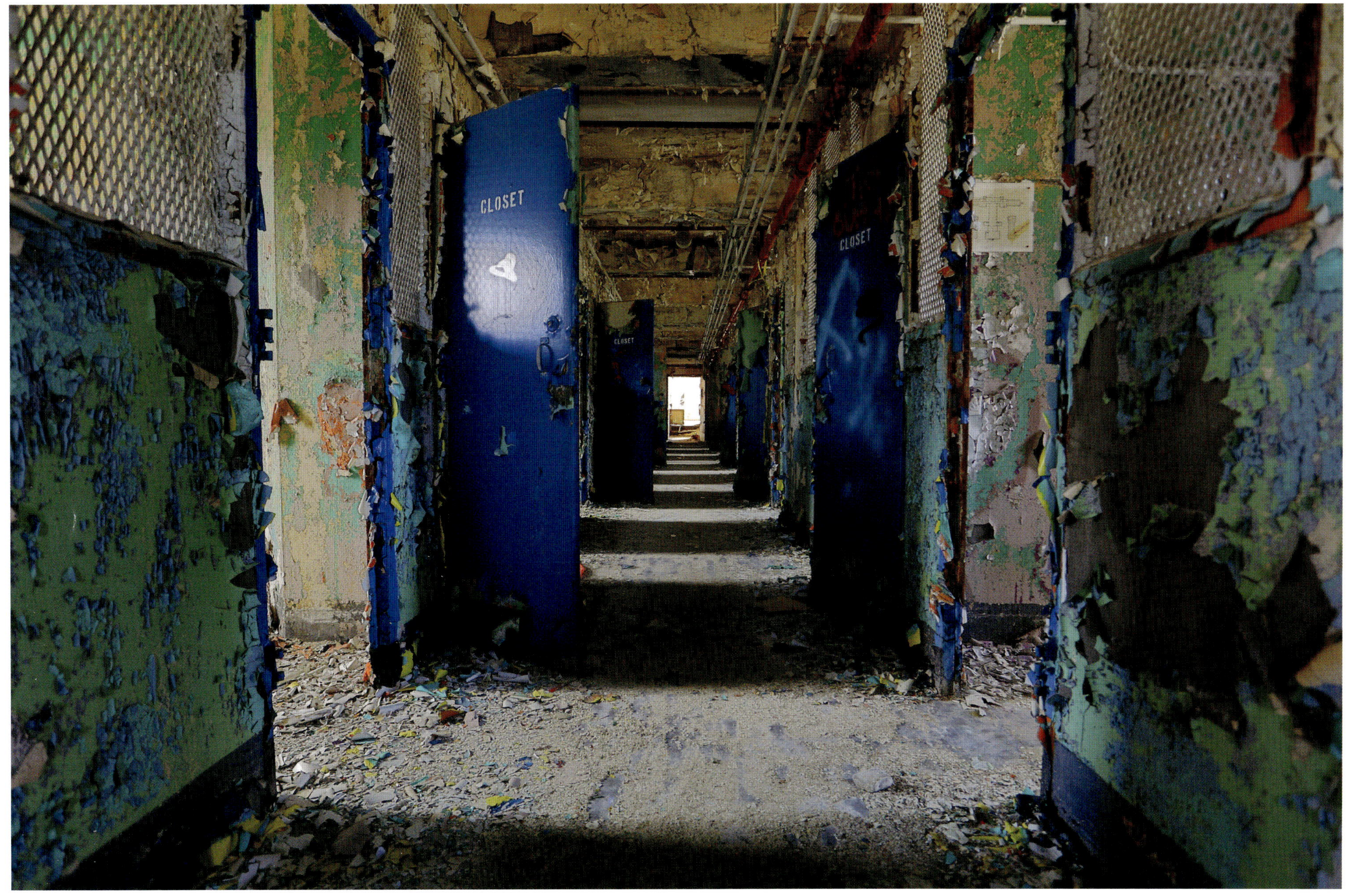

West wing, Camp LaGuardia

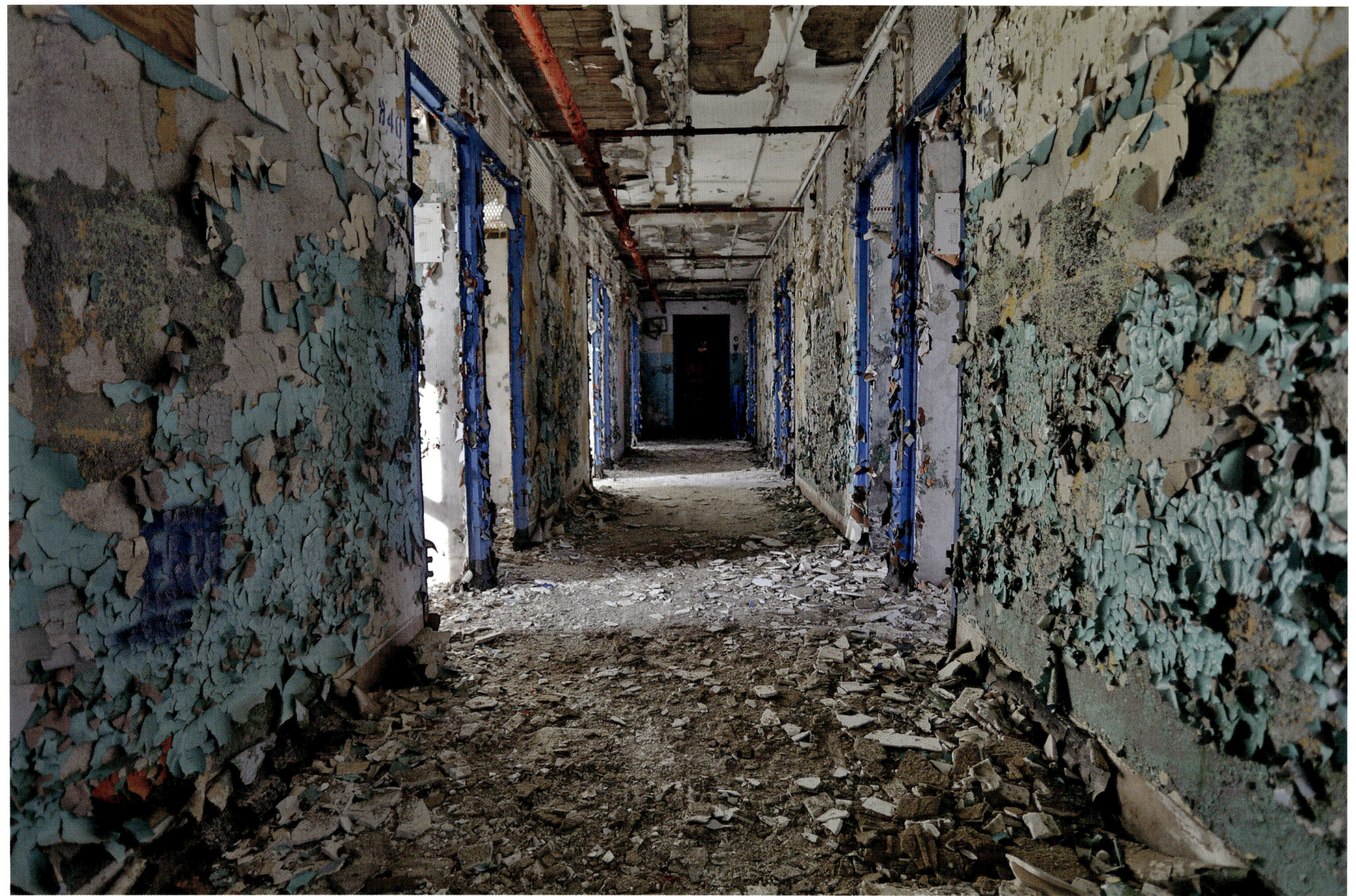

Main building wing, Camp LaGuardia

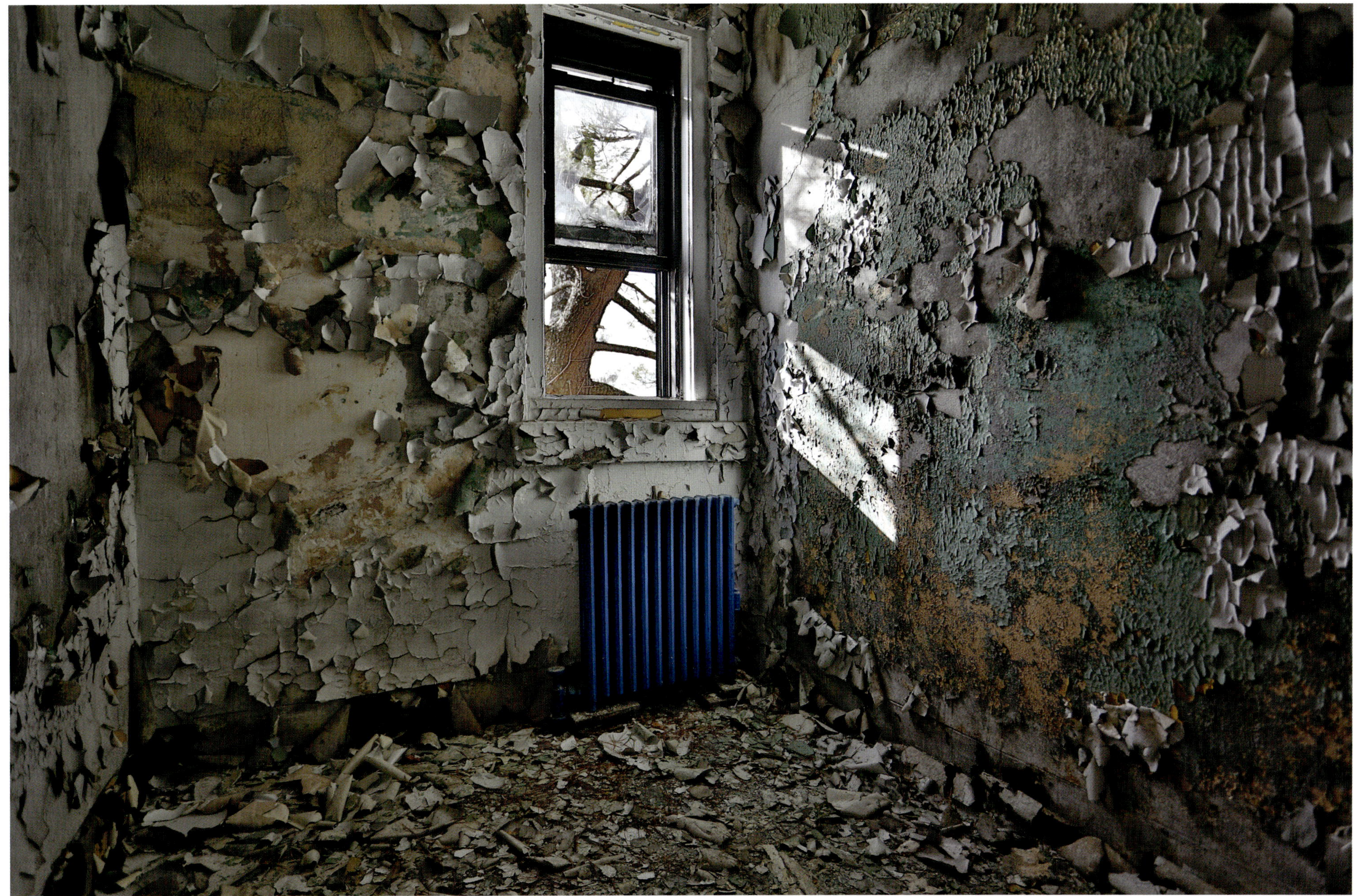

Resident room in the main building, Camp LaGuardia

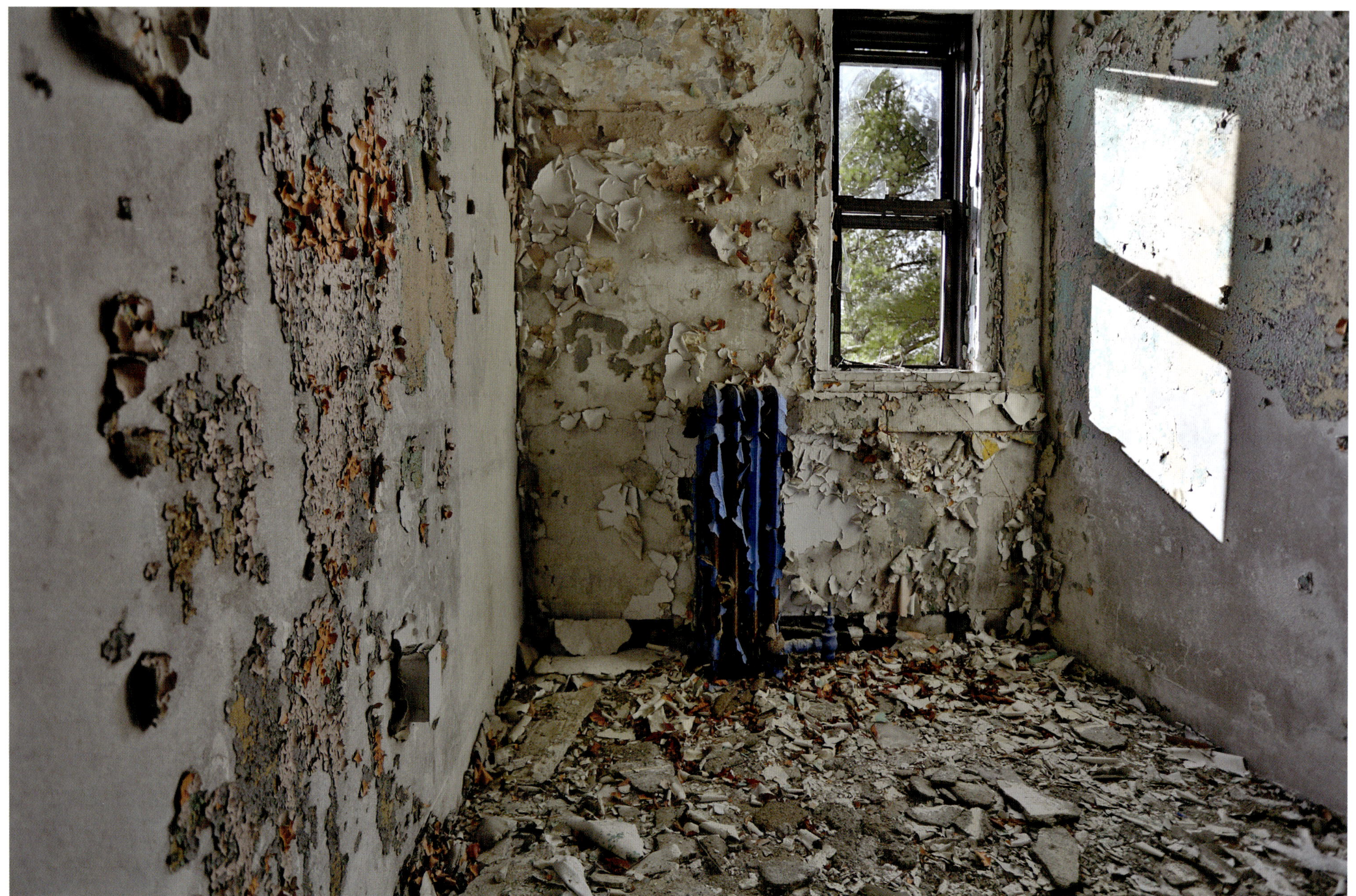

Resident room in the main building, Camp LaGuardia

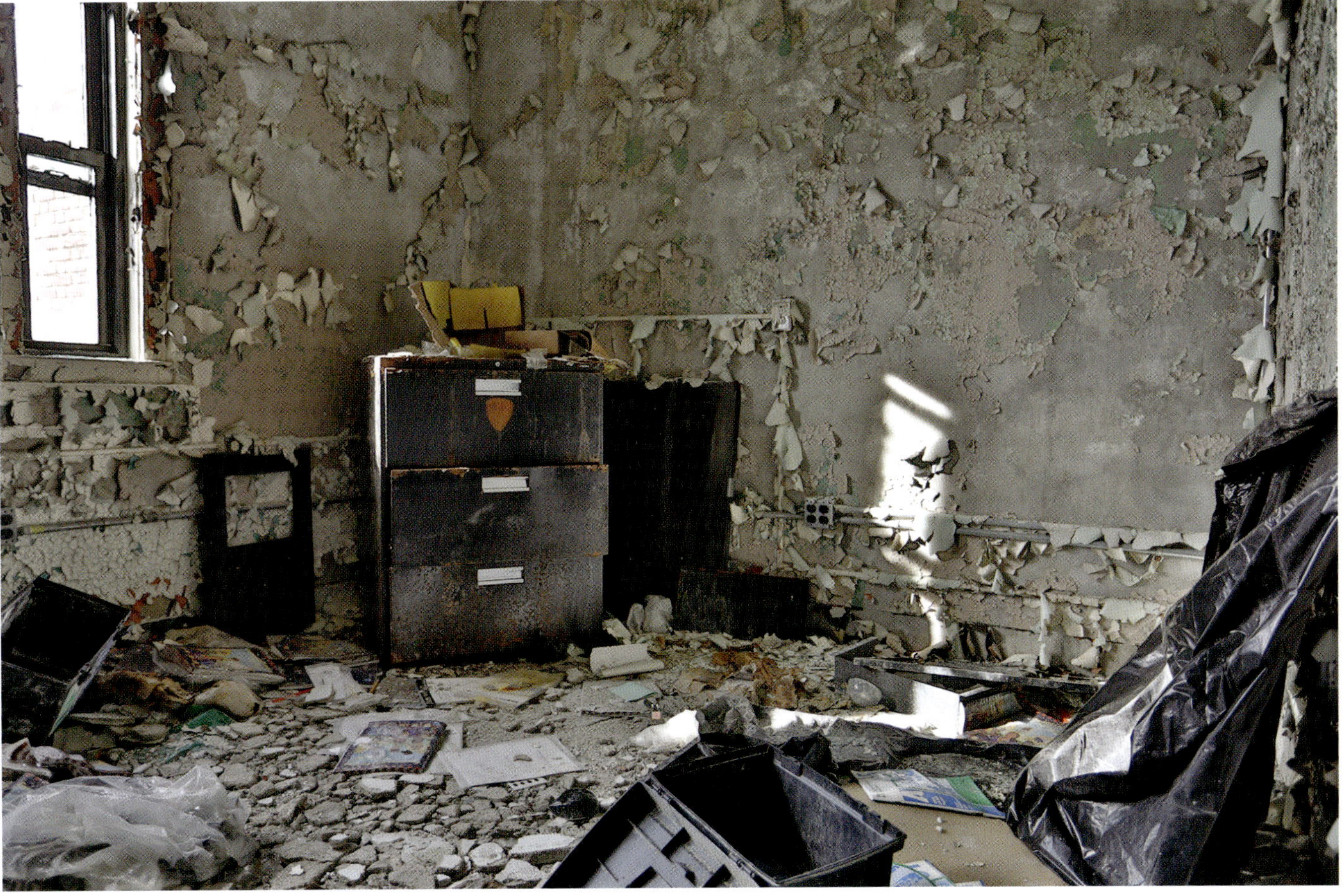

Office room, Camp LaGuardia

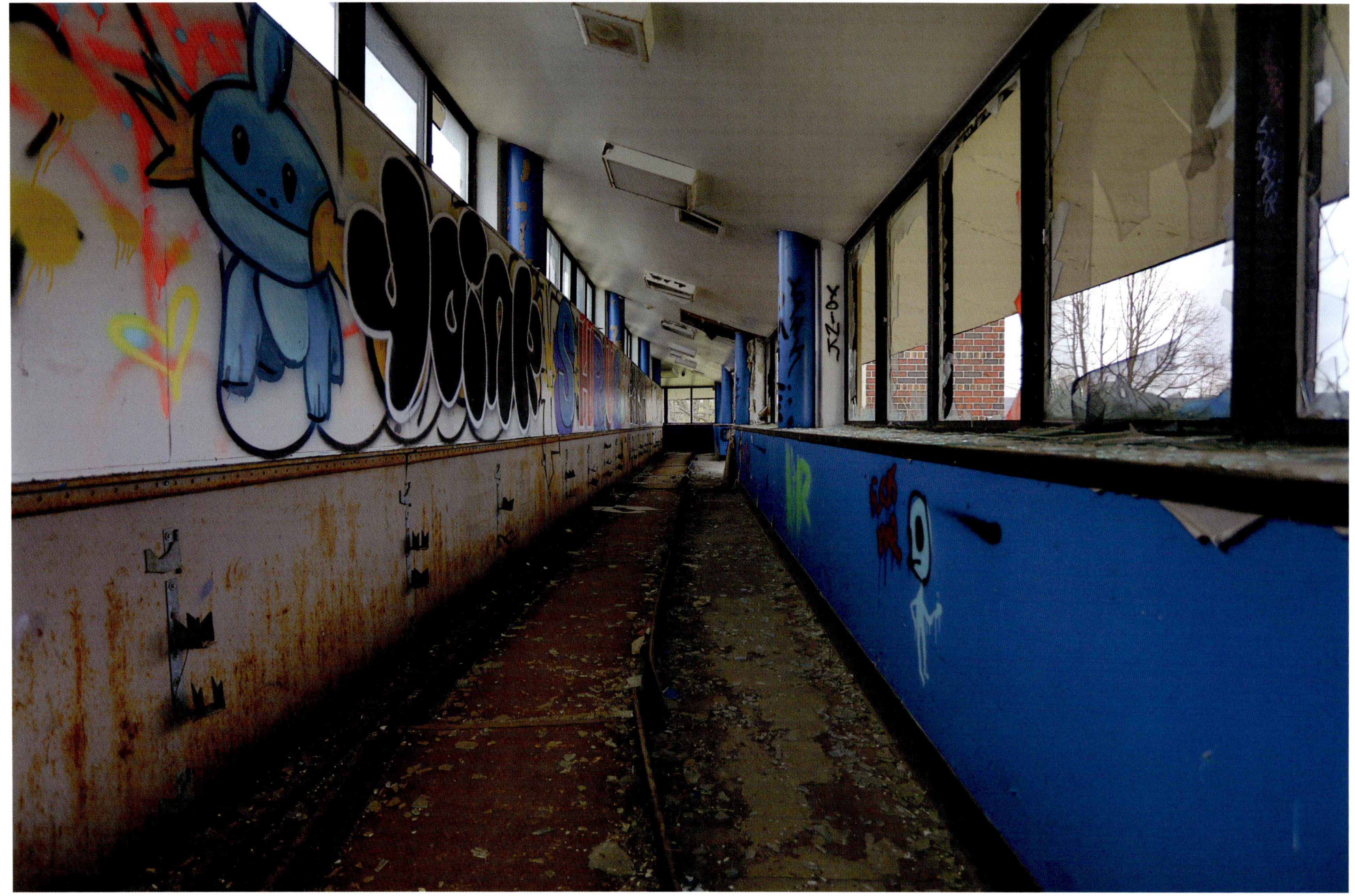

Sky bridge, Camp LaGuardia

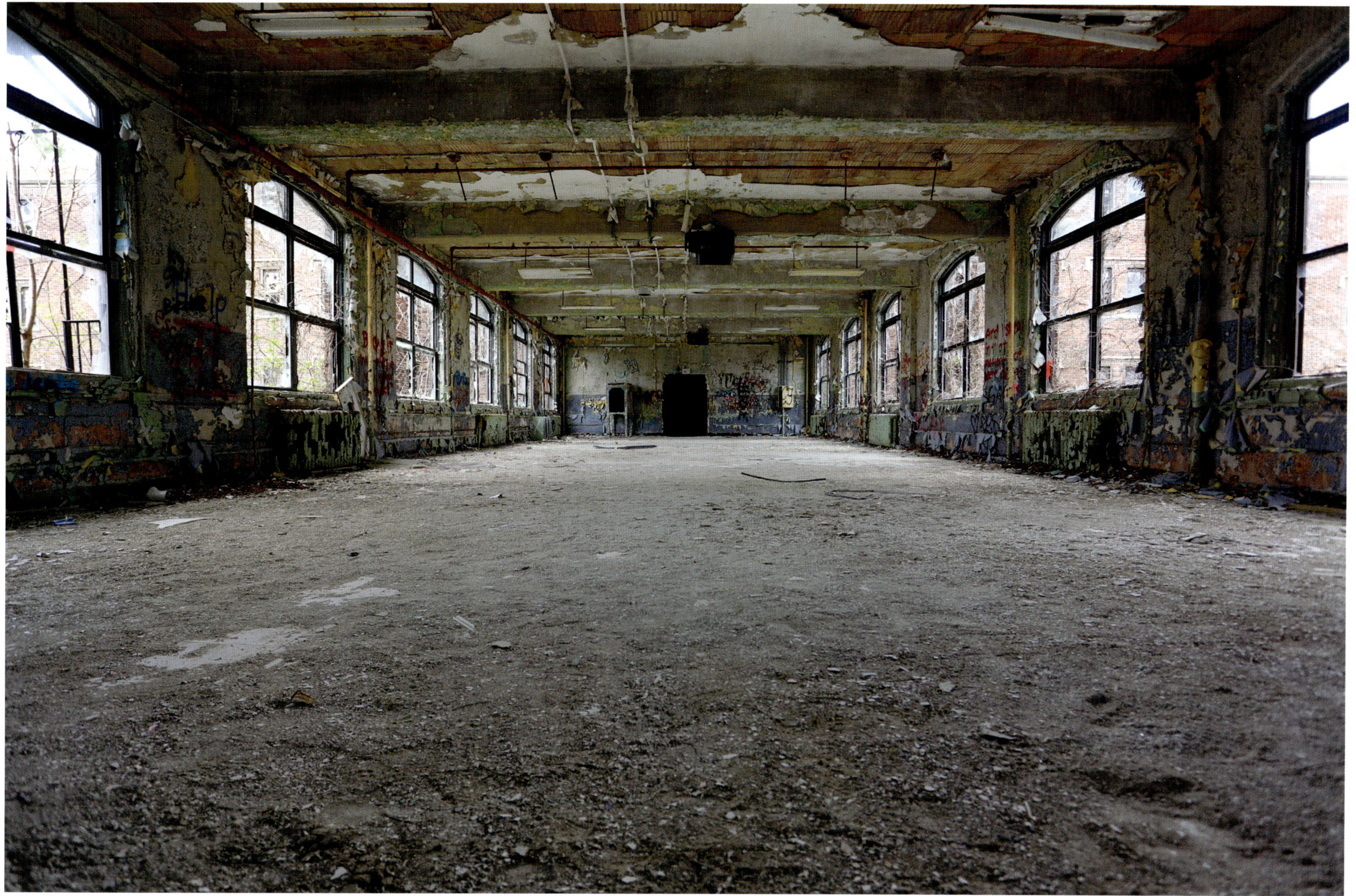

Dining hall, Camp LaGuardia

Letchworth Village

THIELLS

In the midst of New York's Ramapo Mountains, among the rolling hills of Rockland County, lies the bucolic hamlet of Thiells. It was the perfect spot for the president of the New York State Board of Charities, William Pryor Letchworth, to conceive of his new model of progressive care: a self-sufficient village of working farm cottages that would give mentally disabled patients a more humane lifestyle. This "community within a community" was a departure from the high-rise asylums and overcrowded almshouses that had become the standard of care for the mentally ill at the time. In 1907, New York State approved Letchworth's plan and acquired 2,300 acres in Thiells. Modeled after Monticello, Letchworth Village's neoclassical fieldstone buildings afforded abundant sunlight to help aid the treatment of the developmentally disabled. Construction was completed in 1911.

At the time of its opening, patients were categorized into one of three categories of feeblemindedness: idiot, imbecile, and moron. Based on their functionalities, patients helped farm, cook, sew, and care for livestock. Under the direction of superintendent Dr. Charles Sherman Little, research was conducted into the cause of intellectual disability. The village also became the testing site for the first polio vaccine. After trying it on himself, immunologist Hilary Koprowski administered the vaccine to twenty child patients, seventeen of whom developed antibodies to the disease.

By the 1940s, Letchworth Village nearly doubled its three-thousand-patient threshold; yet, new arrivals kept coming in from New York City, overwhelming the staff. It was the same time when a photojournalist named Irving Haberman released photographs of naked patients sleeping on floor mattresses. Many of them appeared to be malnourished. It became clear that the well-intentioned vision of Letchworth Village had taken a dramatic turn. In 1972, Geraldo Rivera's ABC News exposé, *Willowbrook: The Last Great Disgrace*, shined a light on the decrepit conditions due to underfunding at Willowbrook

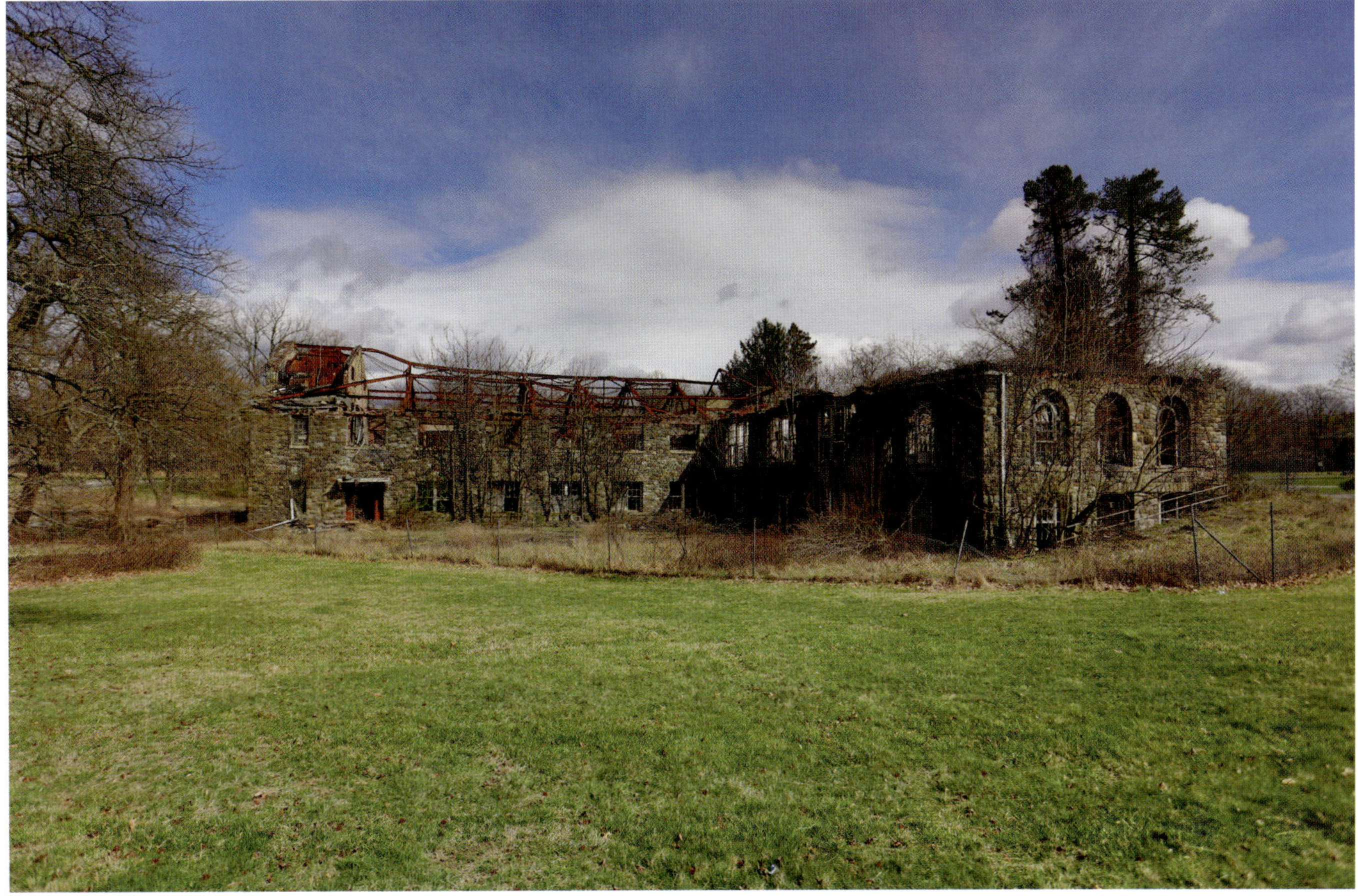

Remains of Stewart Hall (assembly hall), Letchworth Village

State School and Letchworth Village. In the wake of the Rivera report, hospitals all around the country began the long, slow process of deinstitutionalization. Letchworth would move its residents to group homes while cutting down admissions before closing for good in 1996.

Today, many of the buildings still sit abandoned on the hospital grounds. A few miles away, Old Letchworth Village Cemetery serves as a stark reminder of what went wrong. T-shaped markers with only serial numbers mark the resting place of those who lost their lives at the hospital. State agencies funded the installation of a permanent plaque inscribed with the names of the patients, along with a resounding epitaph: “To Those Who Shall Not Be Forgotten.”

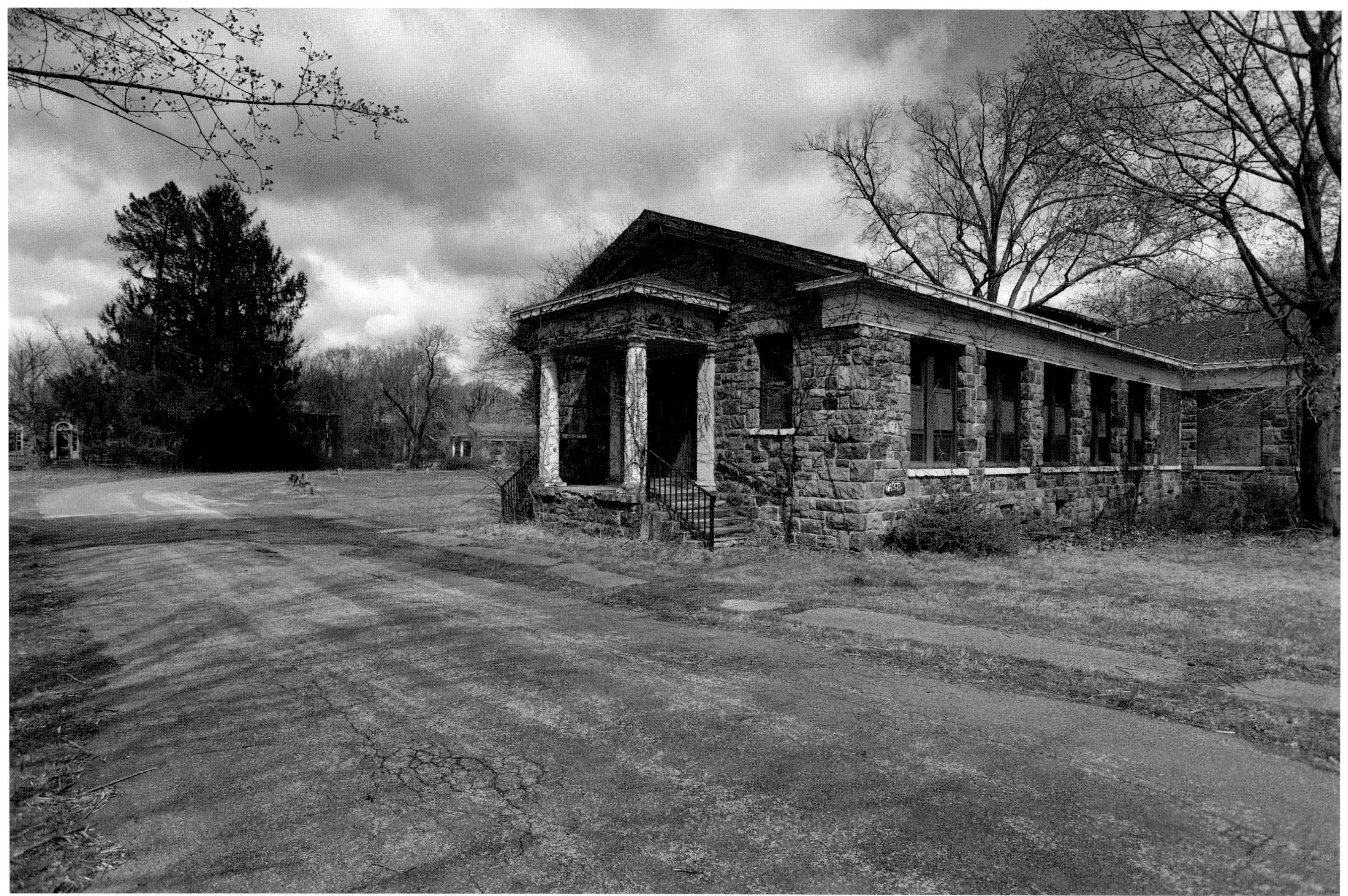

Boys dormitory, Letchworth Village

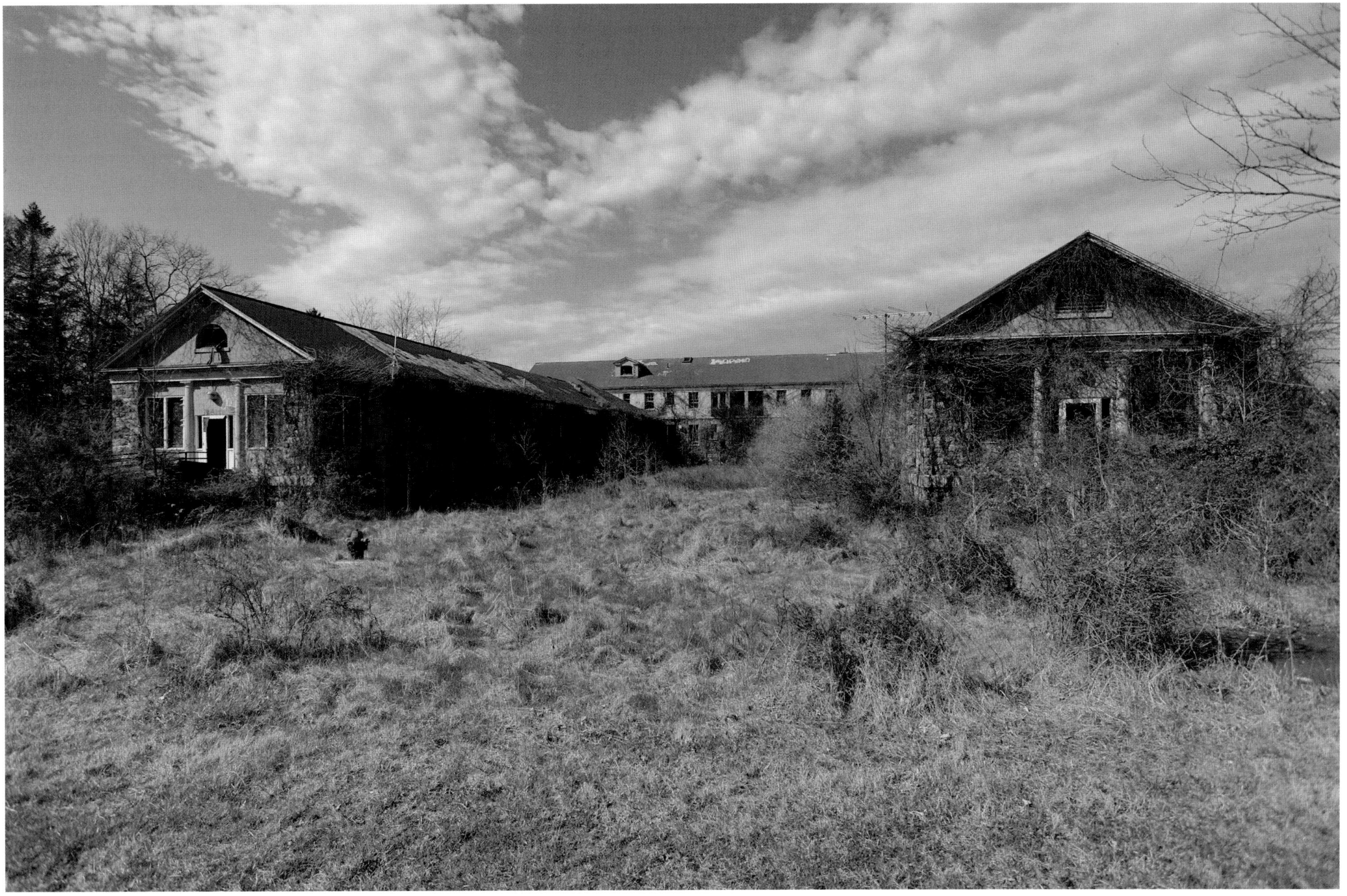

James F. Reville Hospital building, Letchworth Village

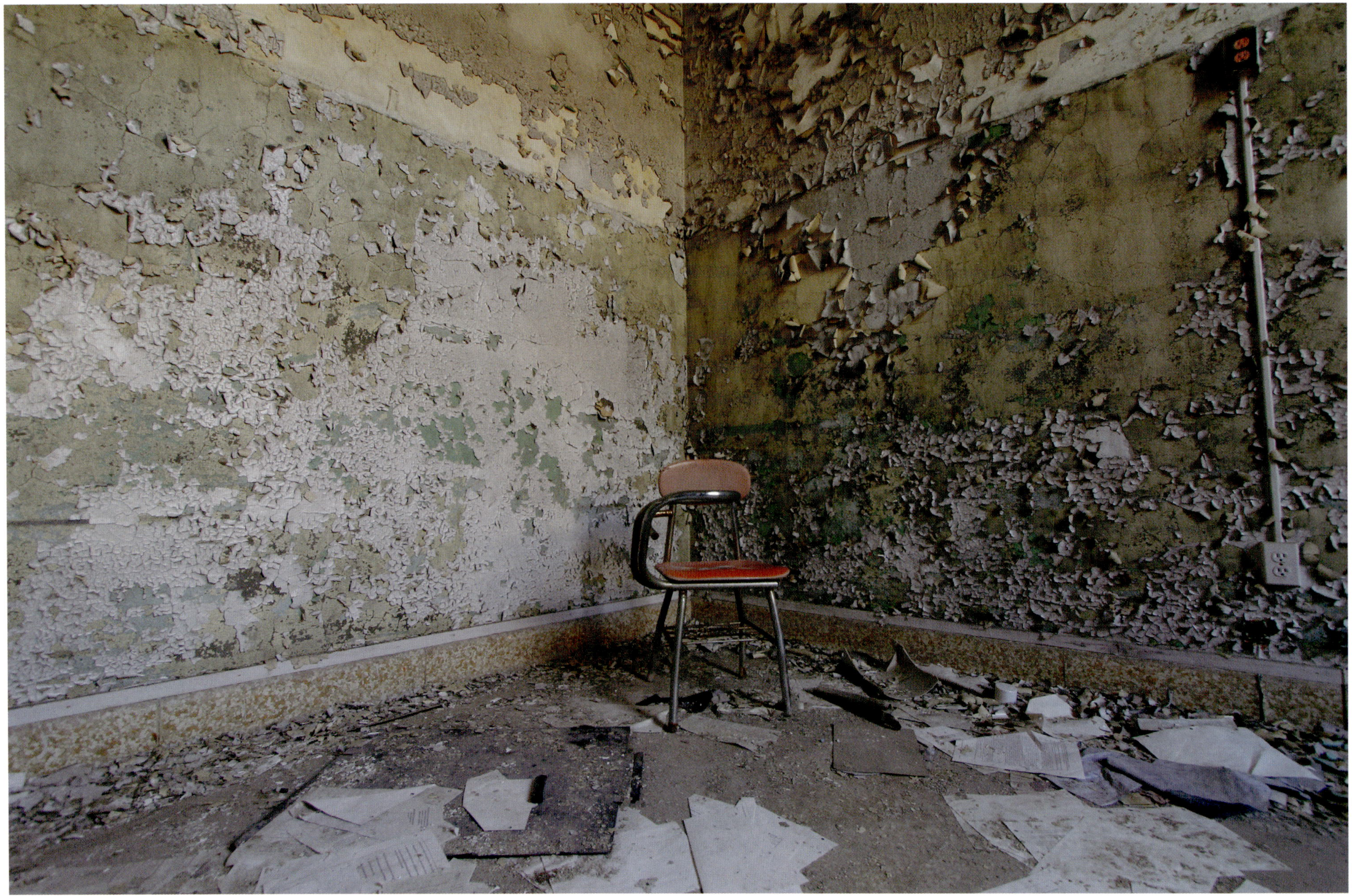

Clerical office, Letchworth Village

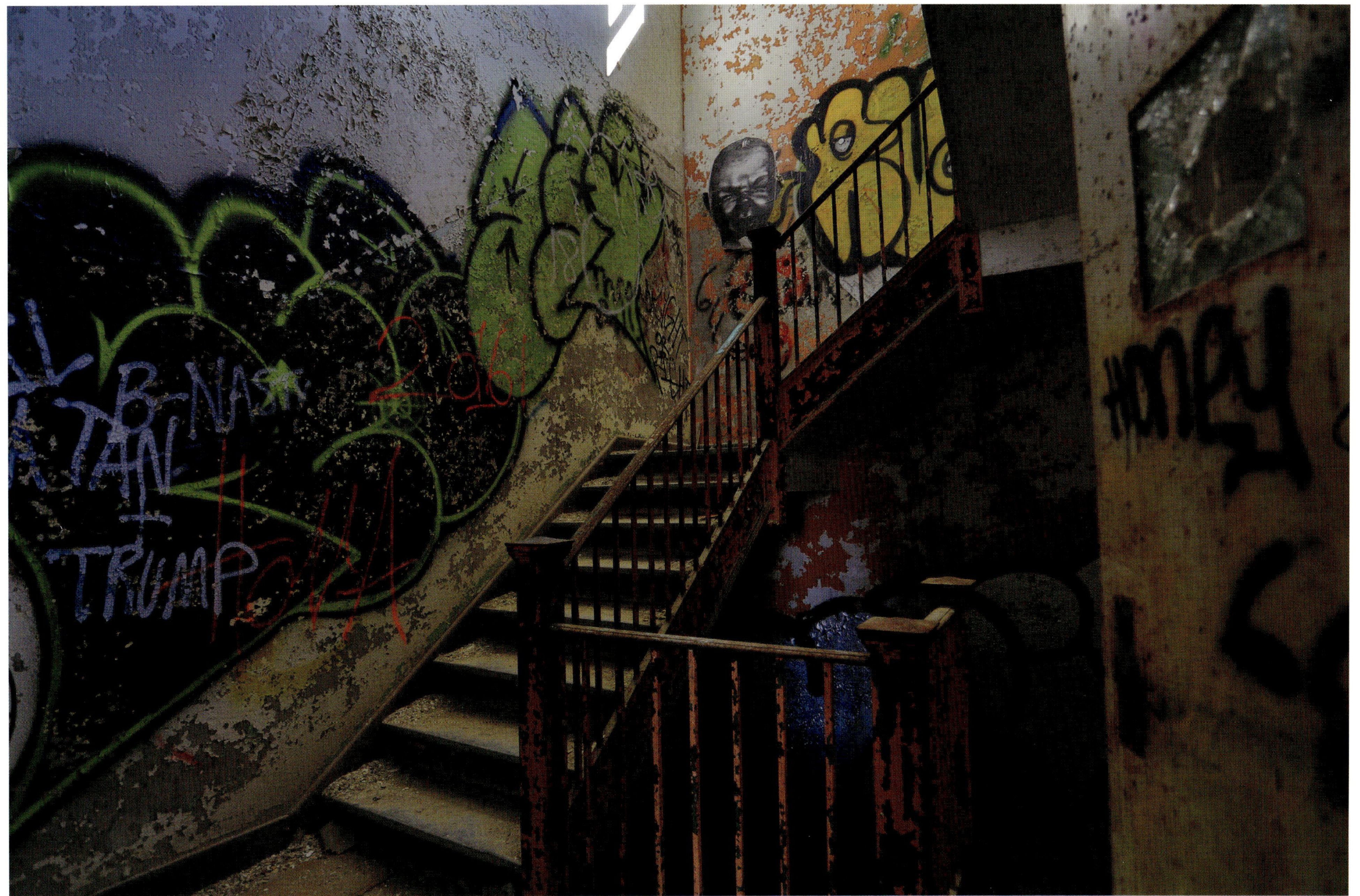

West stairwell, James F. Reville Hospital building, Letchworth Village

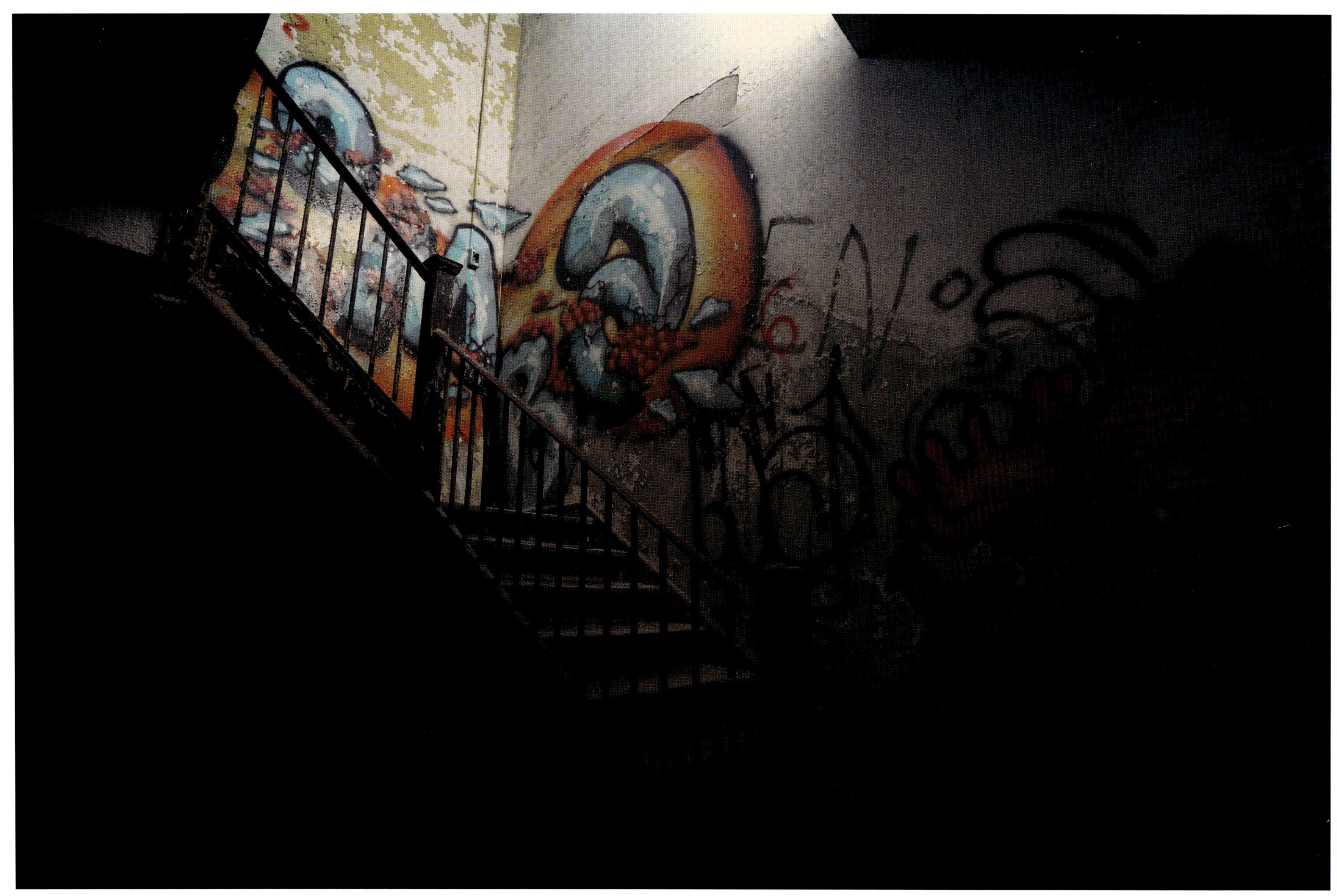

East stairwell, James F. Reville Hospital building, Letchworth Village

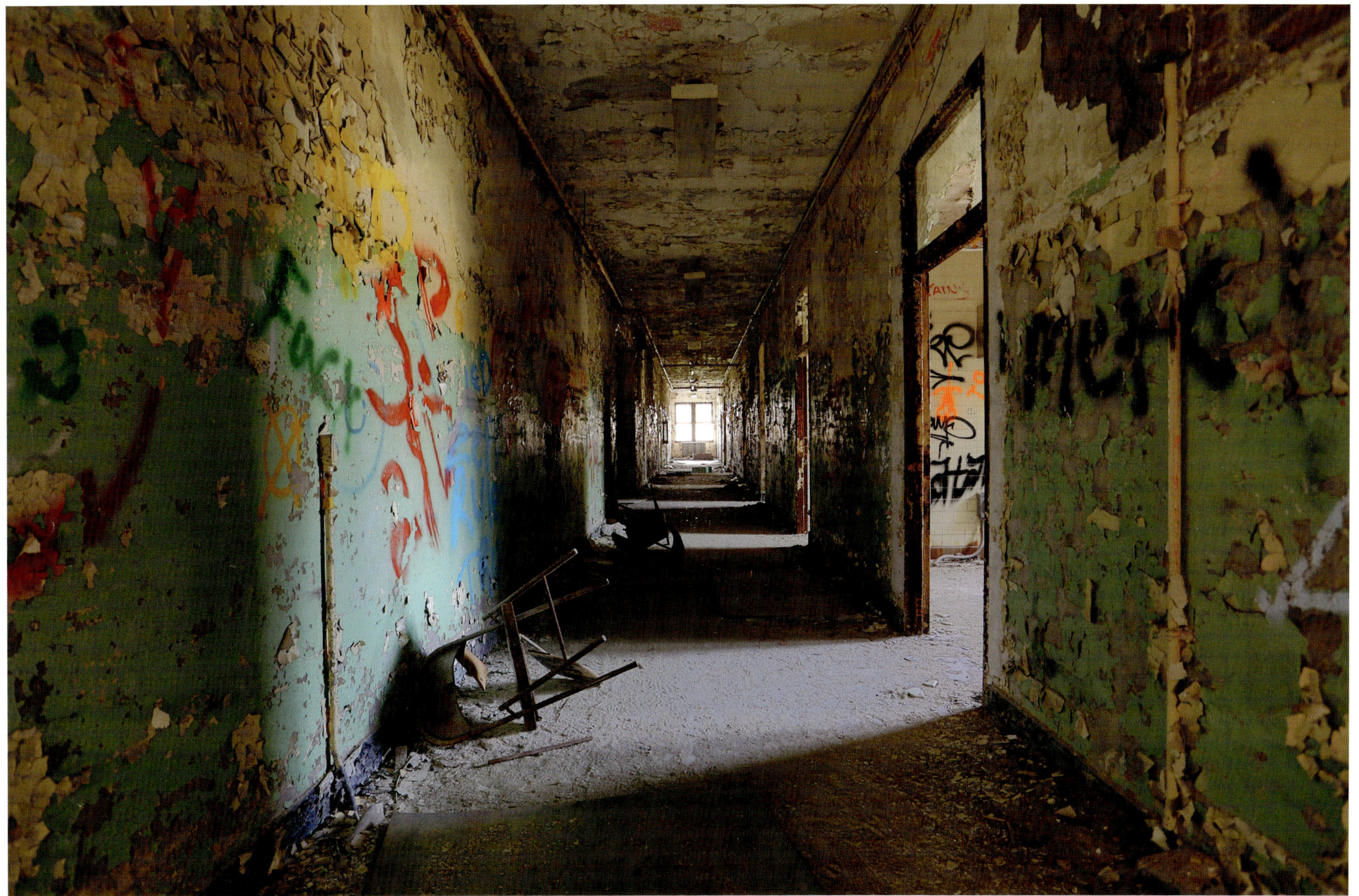

Hospital corridor, Letchworth Village

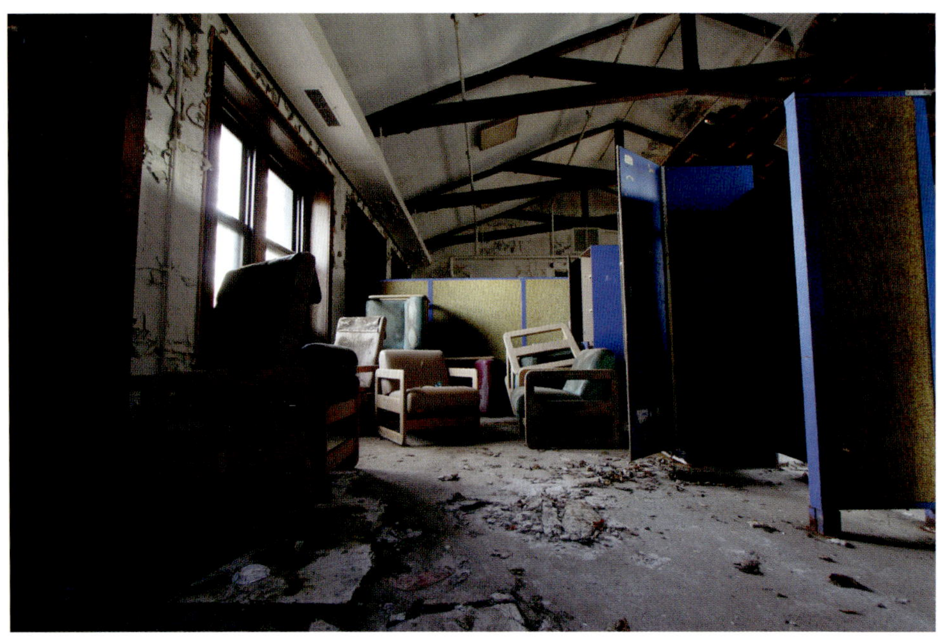

Boys dormitory, Letchworth Village

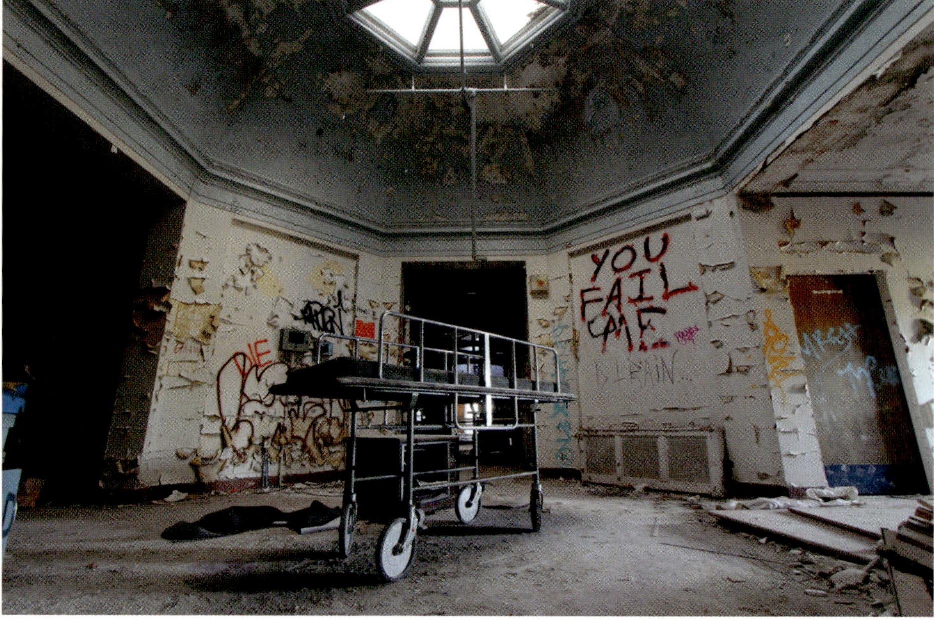

Boys dormitory, Letchworth Village

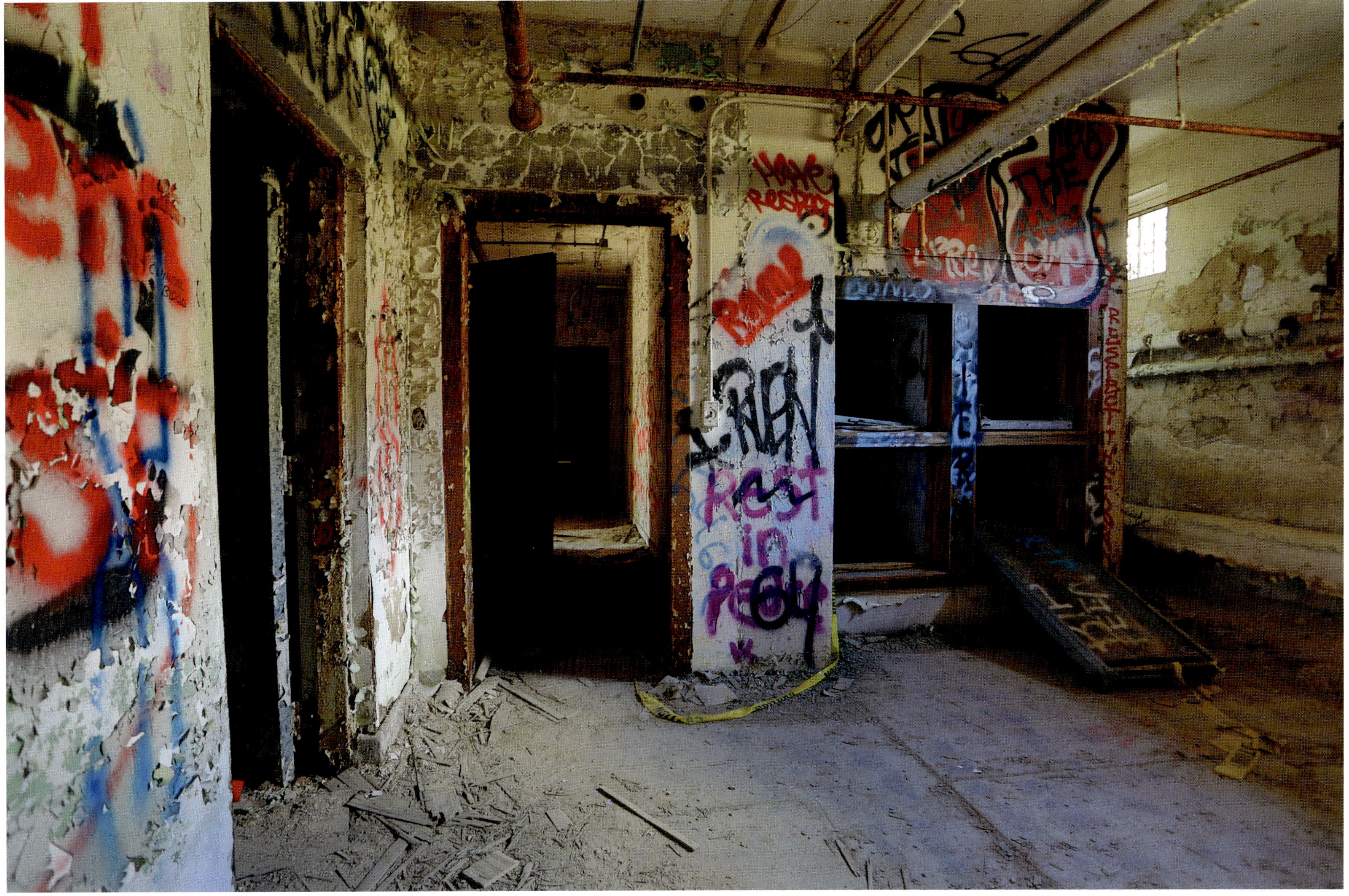

Morgue, Letchworth Village

Mid-Orange Correctional Facility

WARWICK

The practice of housing inmates needing rehabilitation on the grounds of the Mid-Orange Correctional Facility dates back to 1912, when New York City purchased the land encompassing Wickham Lake in Warwick to construct the New York City Farm, an institution to treat men suffering from alcoholism. Its operation was short lived, since the Prohibition Act made the sale of alcoholic beverages illegal in 1920.

And just as the Great Depression was taking hold of the country in 1929, New York State took over the New York City Farm in a prophetic move to turn the grounds into a reform school for boys. Thus, the New York Training School for Boys was born, with the idea that removing youths from their violent, dysfunctional environment and teaching them basic skills such as woodworking, farming, and other vocations would be the path to rehabilitation. But by the 1970s, with the "War on Drugs" well underway, the profile of many of the boys sent to the school had drastically changed. Repeat offenders and escapees were common, so much so that the school had fallen out of favor, which ultimately led to its closure in 1976.

A year later, the school was reopened as the state-operated, medium-security Mid-Orange Correctional Facility. Opening with an inmate population of four hundred, it quickly rose to a thousand, until more facilities were constructed on the grounds. There were several innovative programs for inmates that were implemented at Mid-Orange. In the Puppies Behind Bars program, inmates raised and trained puppies to become guide dogs for the disabled. The Corcraft commercial carpentry shop produced modular housing and components for public projects such as New York's Florida Public Library.

On June 30, 2011, New York governor Andrew Cuomo announced that the Mid-Orange Correctional Facility would close as part of the greater reorganization of New York State prisons.

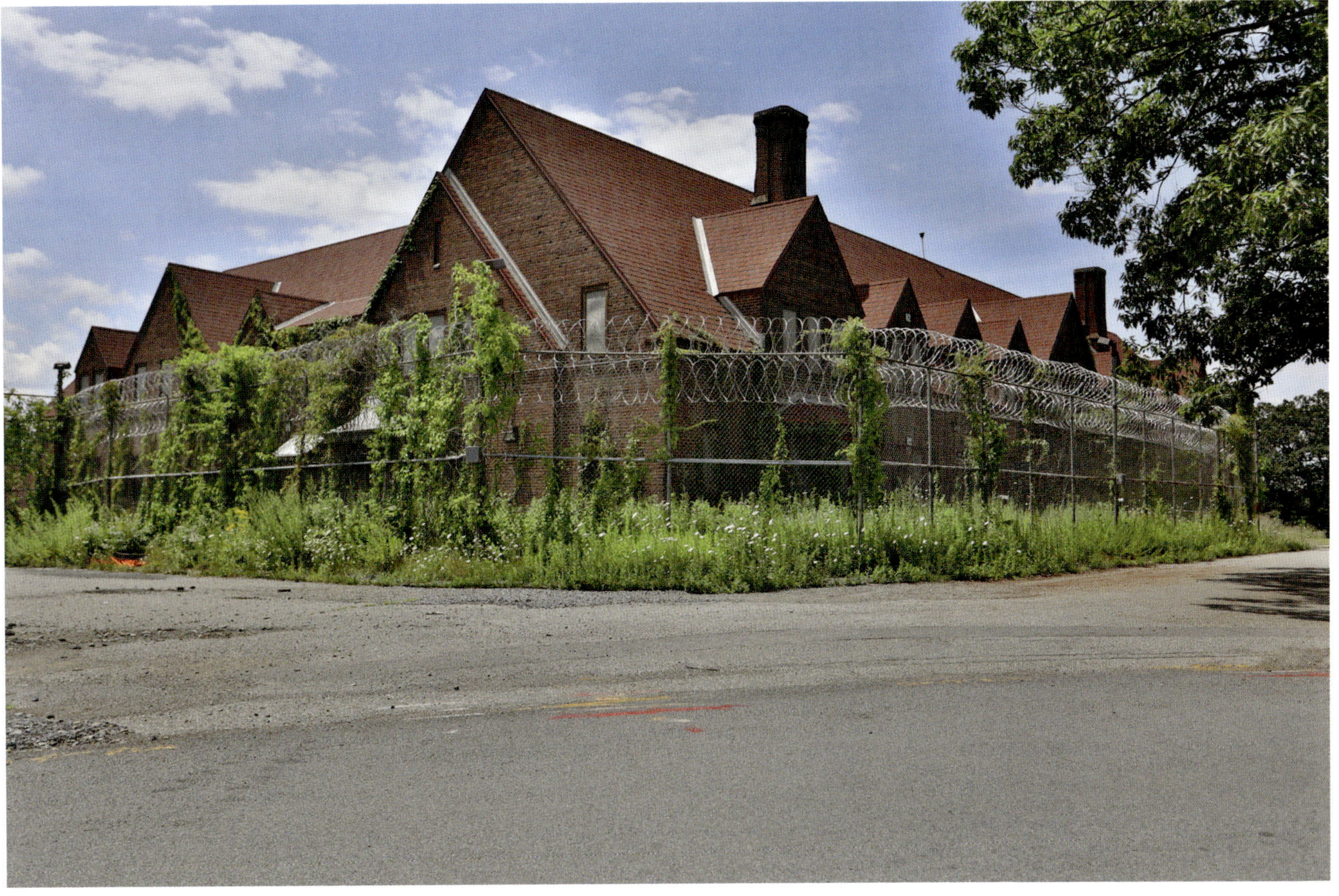

Mid-Orange Correctional Facility

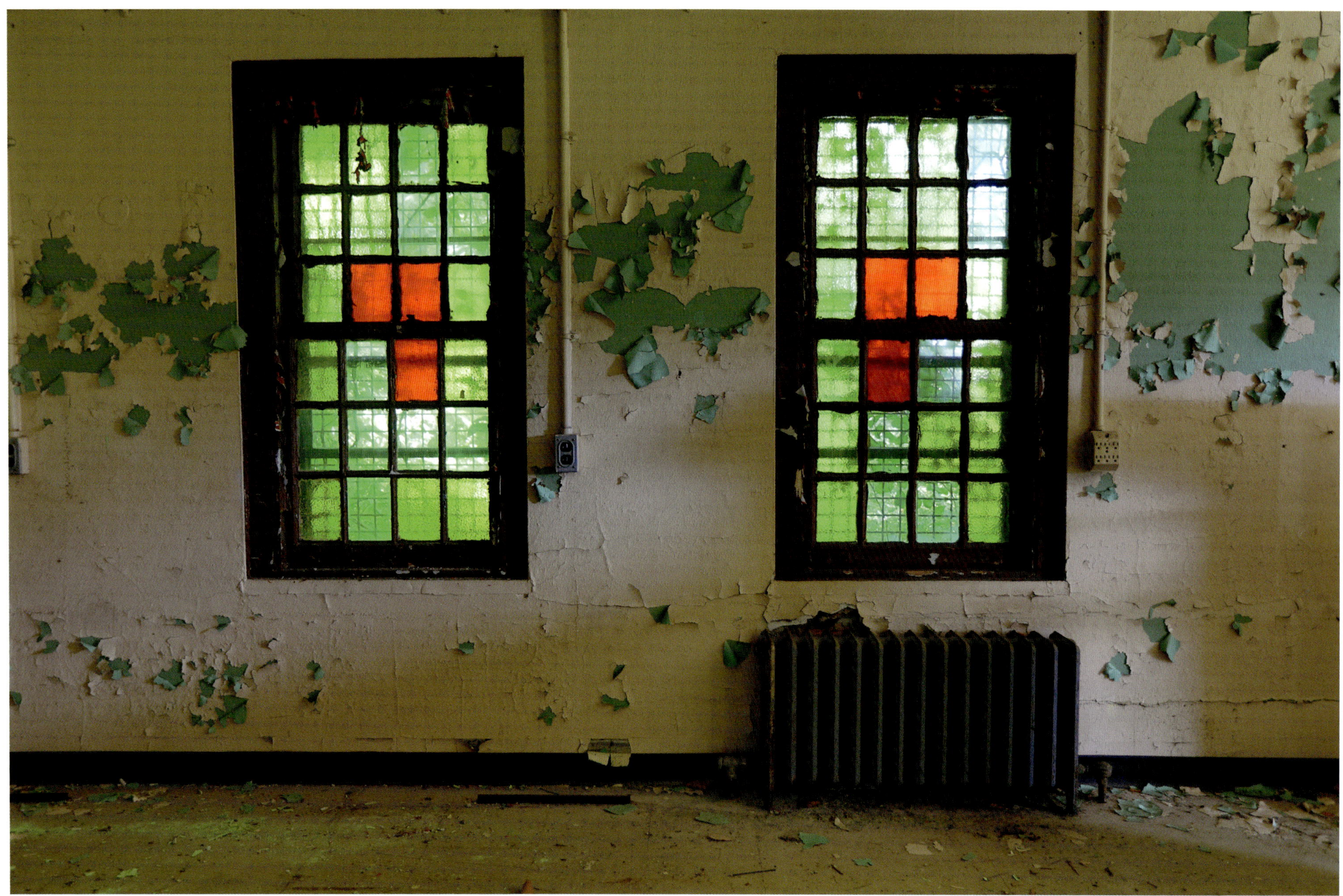

Inmate cottage, Mid-Orange Correctional Facility

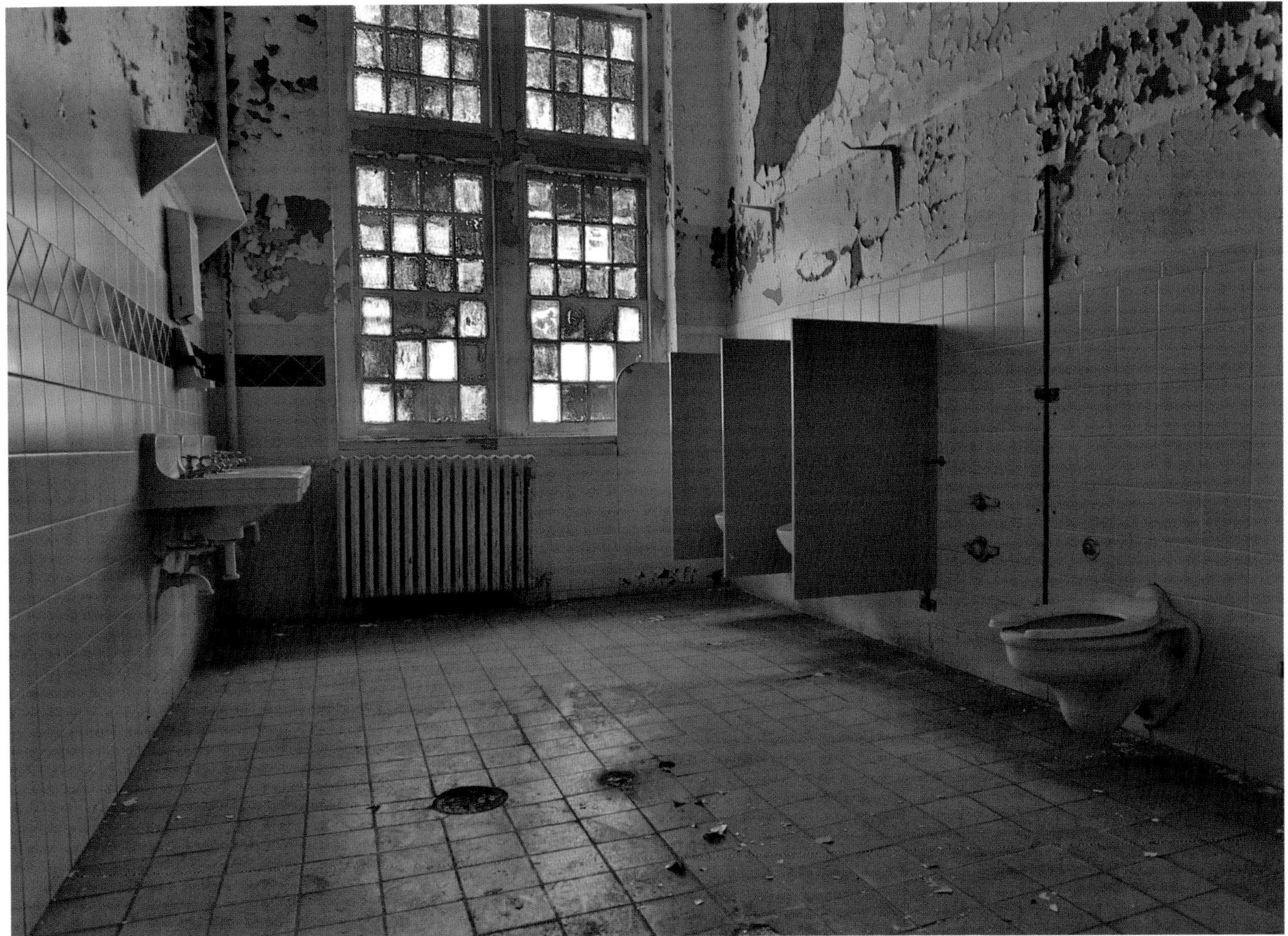

Bathroom, Mid-Orange Correctional Facility

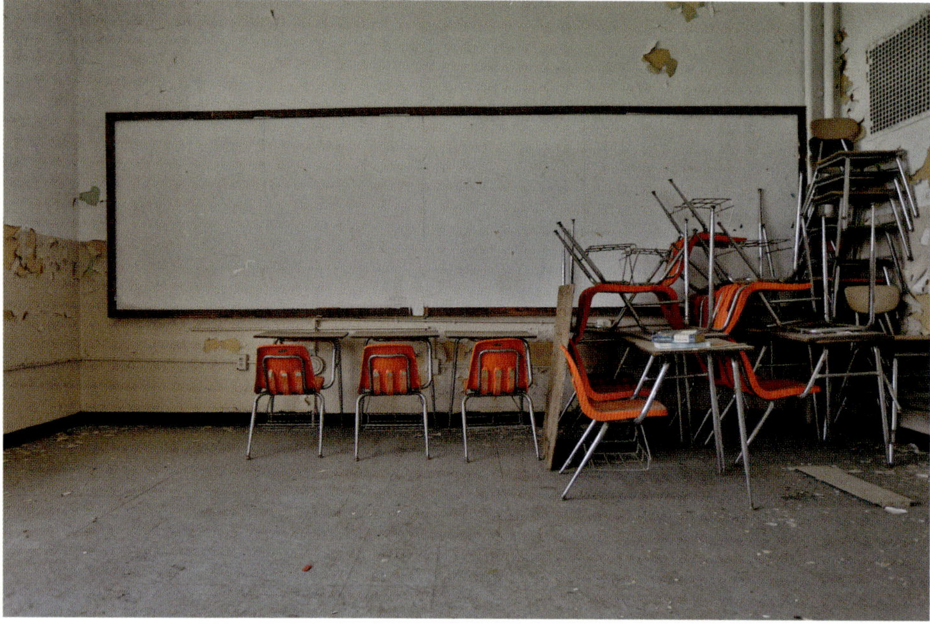

Classroom, Mid-Orange Correctional Facility

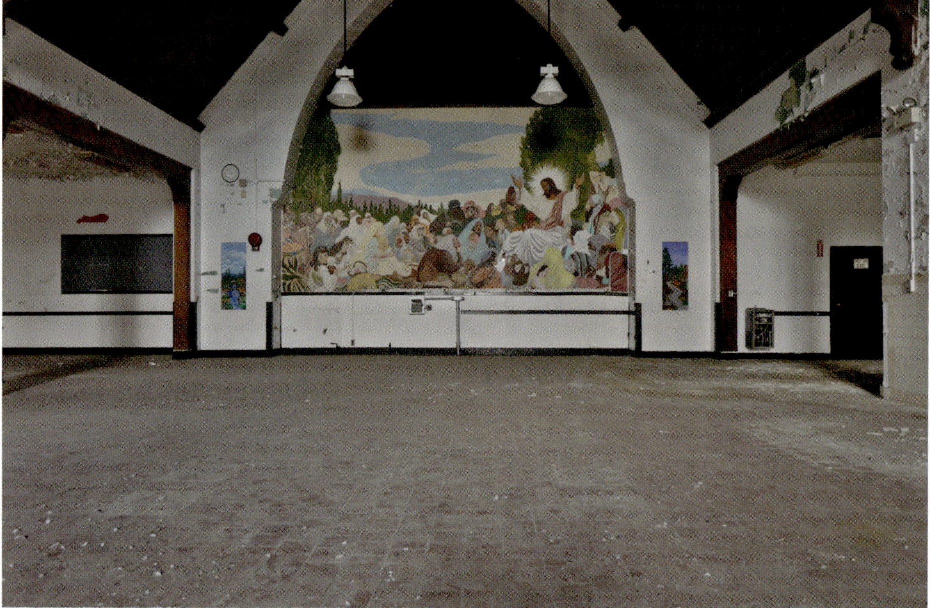

Mural in the dining hall, Mid-Orange Correctional Facility

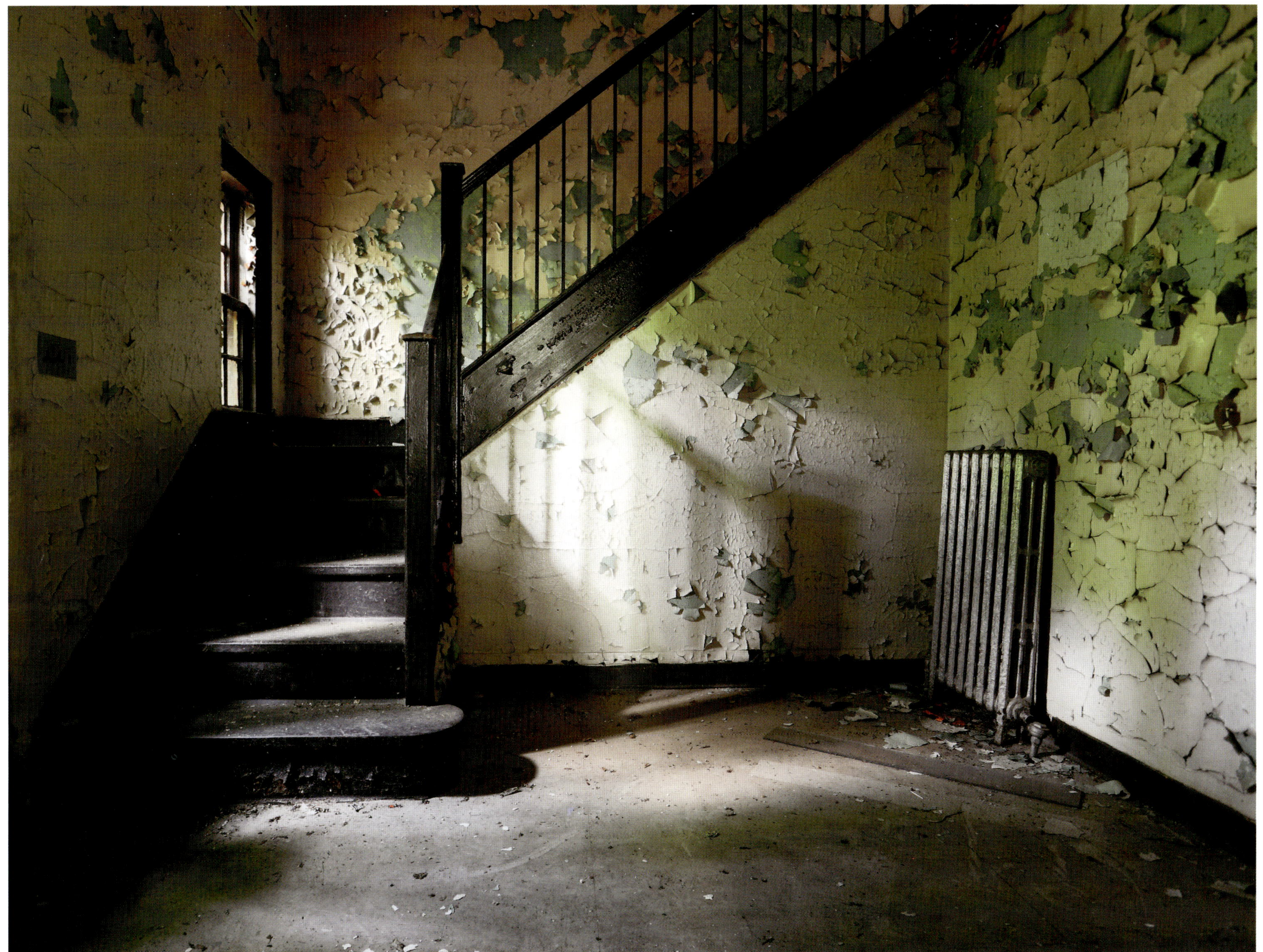

Stairwell in the inmate cottage, Mid-Orange Correctional Facility

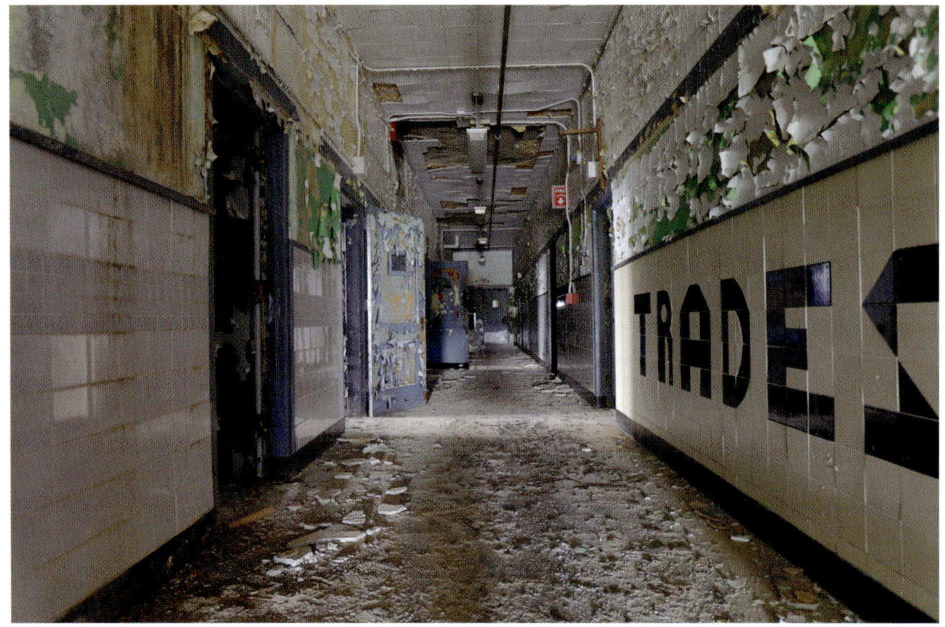

Hallway for trade shops, Mid-Orange Correctional Facility

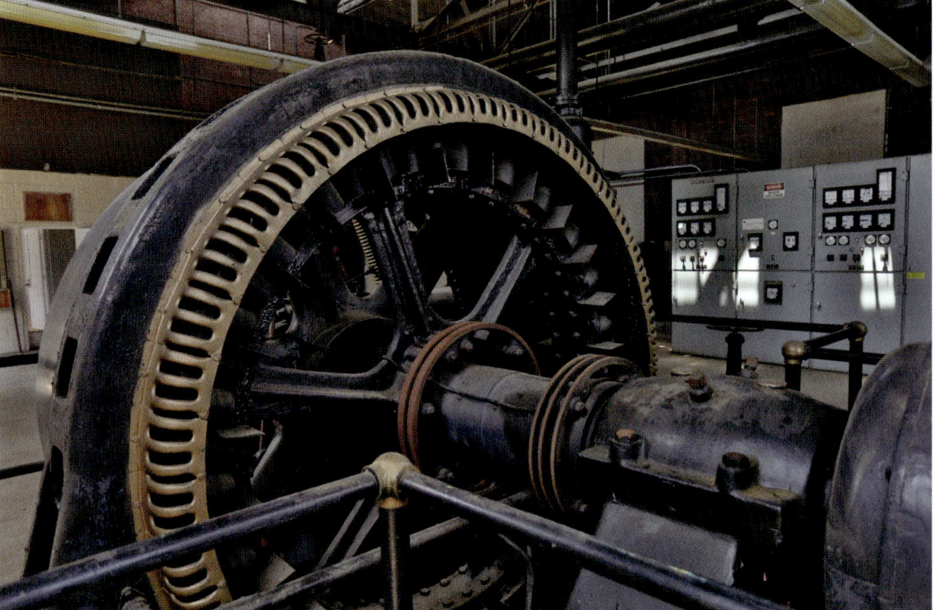

The Ridgway engine, developed by the Elliott Company, dates back to 1926, when steam powered many of America's correctional facilities, including the Mid-Orange Correctional Facility.

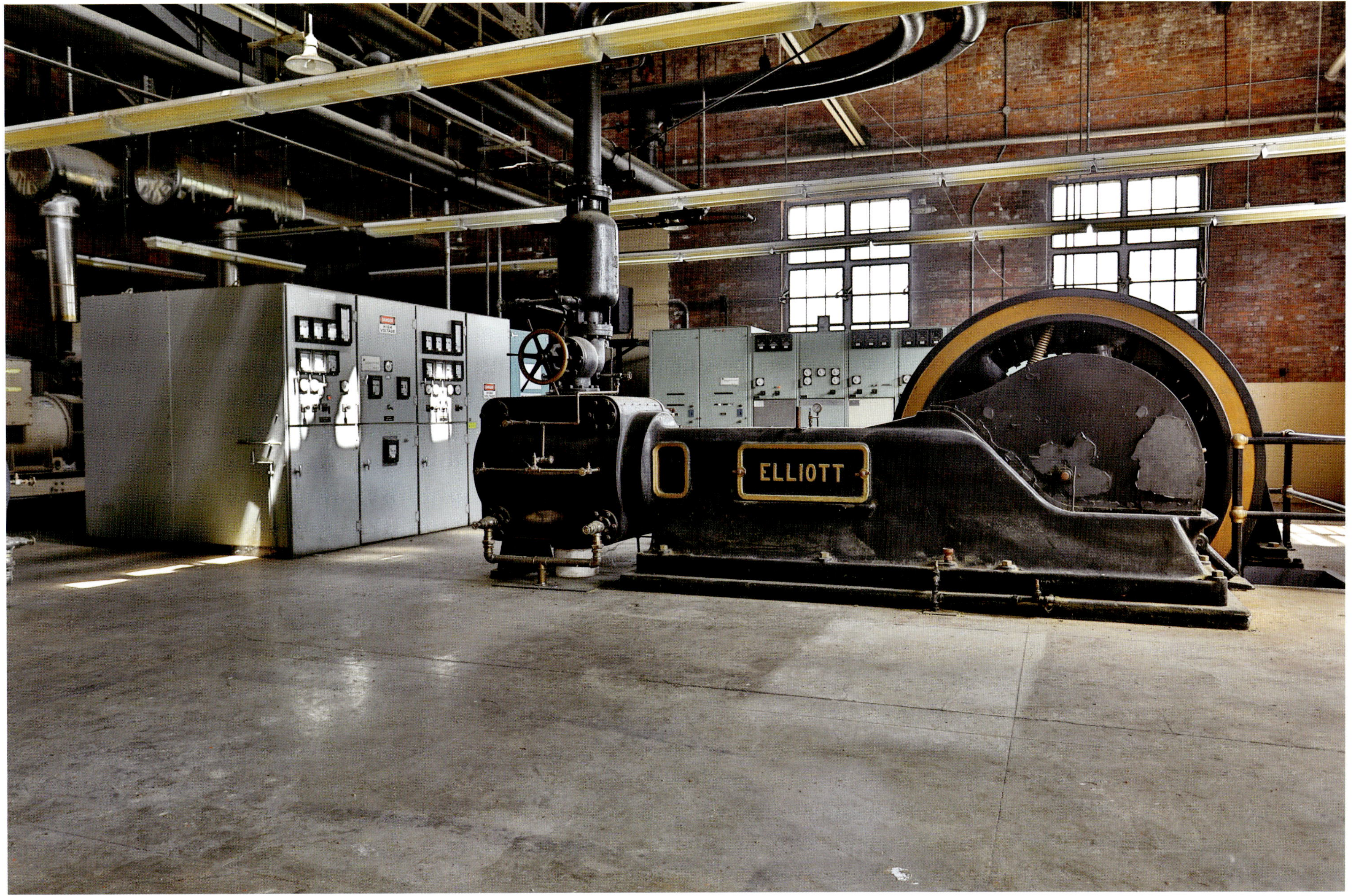
ELLIOTT

David Abercrombie's ELDA

OSSINING

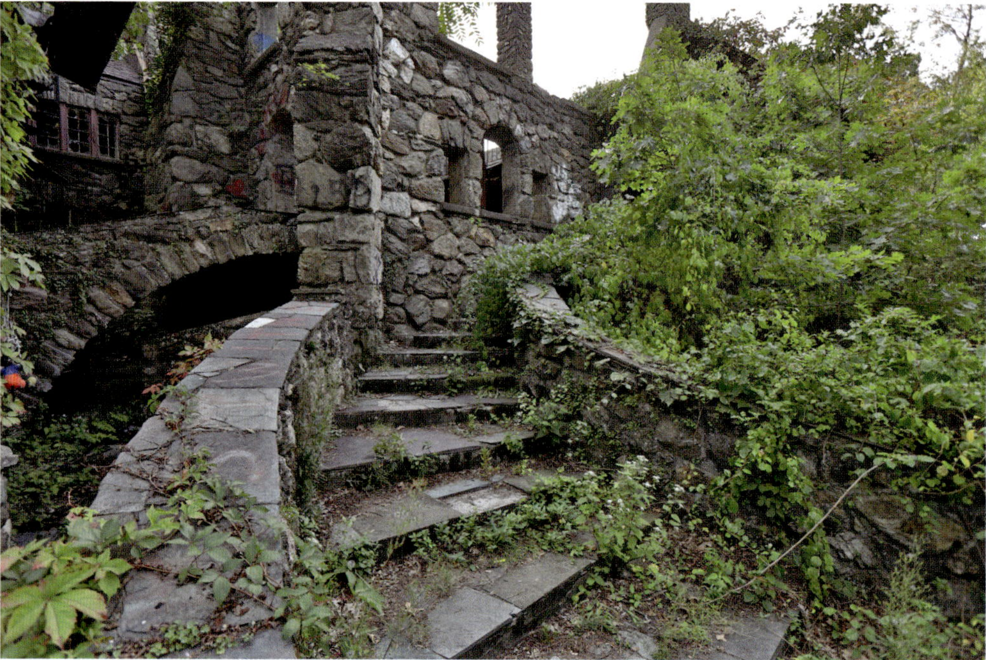

Steps leading to the main entrance of ELDA

Dating back to the days of the Dutch settlers, Ossining, Briarcliff Manor, and the surrounding areas have been the site of elaborate homes and estates that have belonged to prominent New Yorkers. Ossining was a popular real estate venture due to its inexpensive cost of land. While most estates have long been demolished, with the land repurposed, one such remaining site is the ELDA castle. "ELDA" was once home to the founder of the Abercrombie & Fitch Company, David Thomas Abercrombie, and his wife, Lucy Abbott Cate. After marrying in 1896, Abercrombie had four children. ELDA, the name of their estate in Ossining, is actually derived from the first letter of each of their children's names: Elizabeth, Lucy, David, and Abbott.

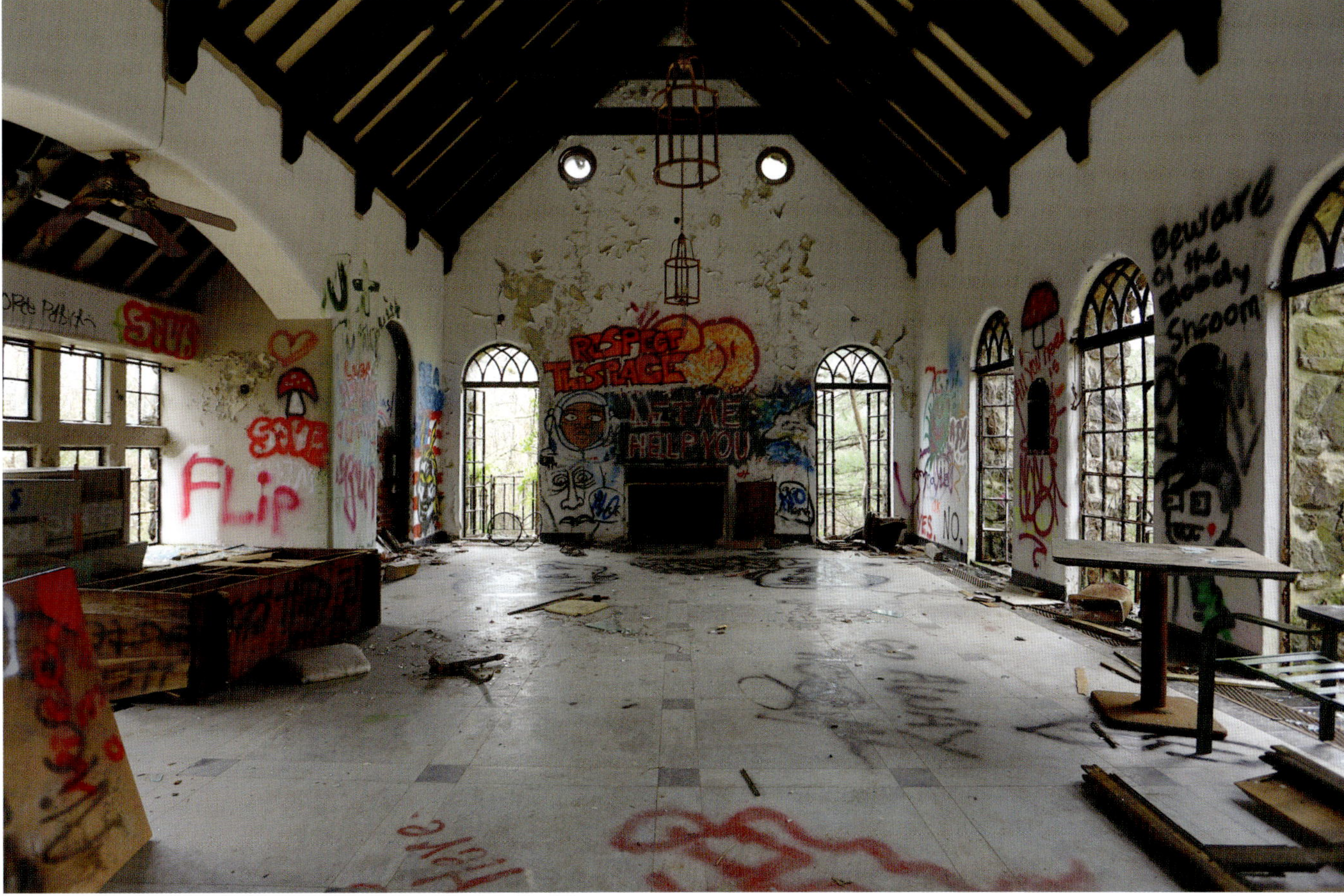

Living room, David Abercrombie's ELDA

Constructed in 1925, ELDA was a 4,337-square-foot steel-girded granite estate consisting of twenty-five rooms, a tower accessed by a winding staircase, and several courtyards and patios. The formal living room consisted of exposed wood beams, green-tiled floor, and a fireplace, alluding to the feel of "great halls" in medieval castles. A flight of curving steps led into the main entrance, which brought visitors into a glass vestibule serving as a conservatory for Lucy's plants. It is likely that Abercrombie's experience as an engineer and land surveyor came into play in the construction of ELDA.

After David Abercrombie died in 1937 and with Lucy Abbott Cate having moved to New Jersey, ELDA was unoccupied for several years. It was rehabilitated in 1964 and would go through several owners before finally being abandoned in 2012.

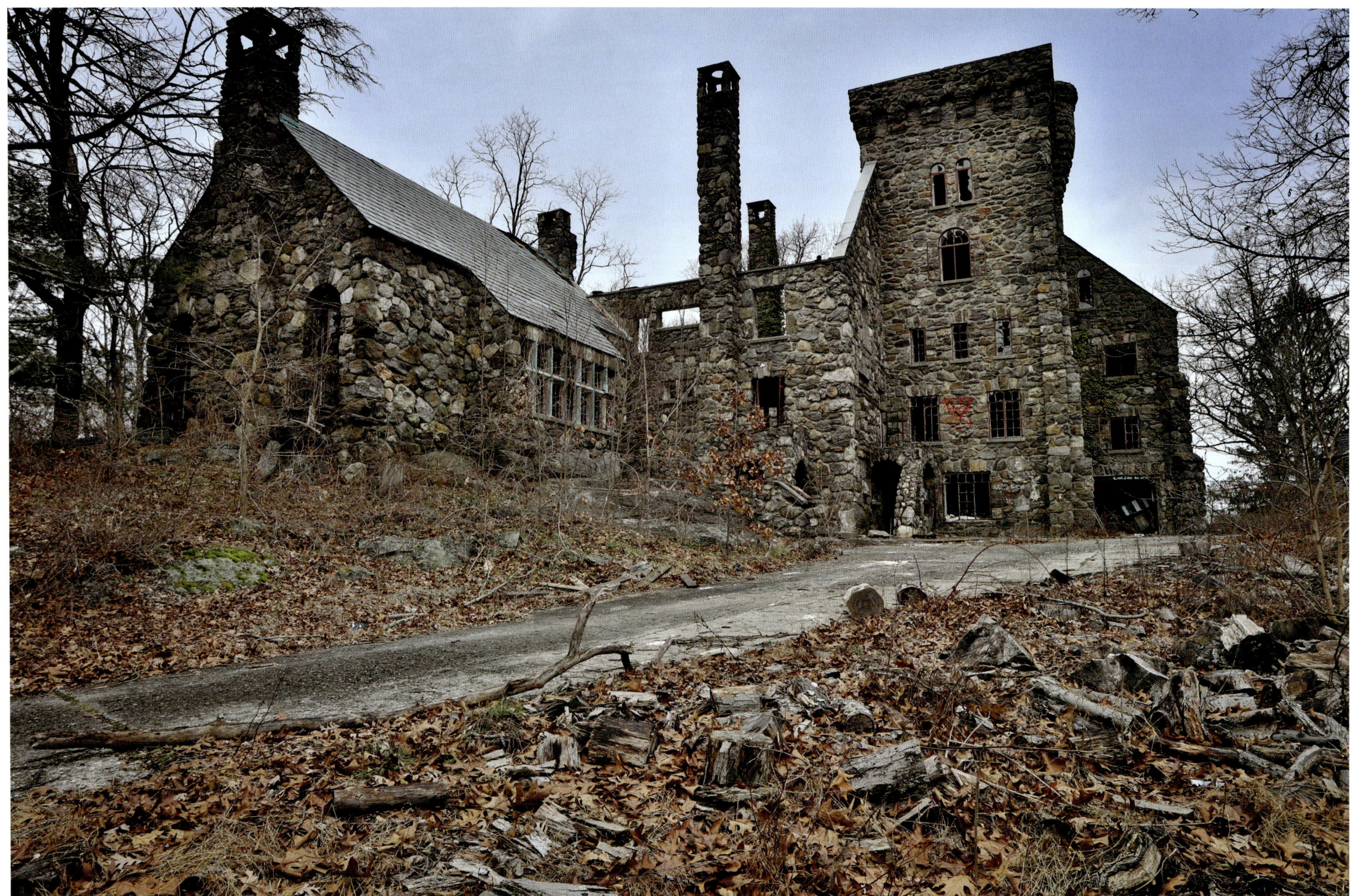

David Abercrombie's ELDA

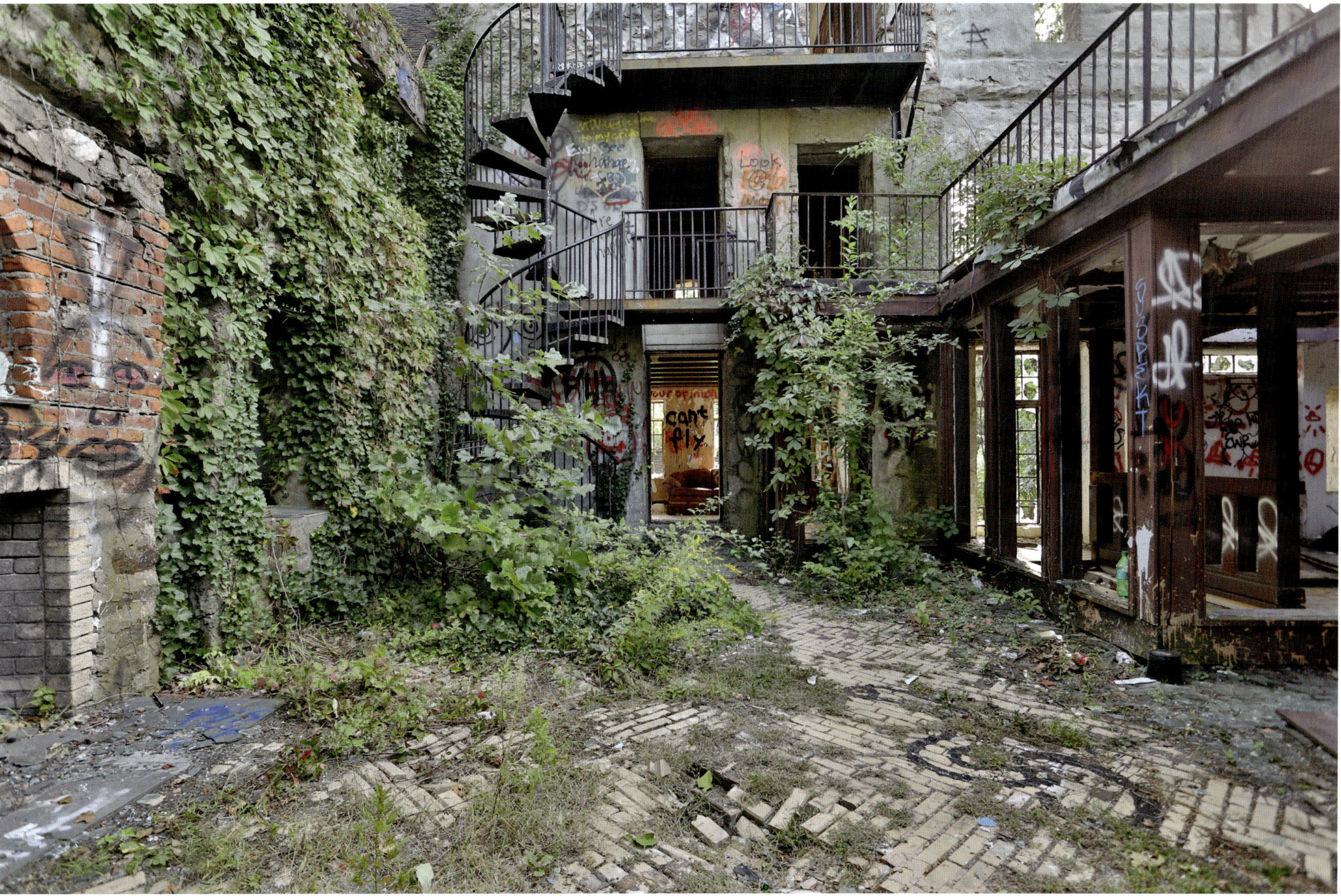

Conservatory, David Abercrombie's ELDA

German Masonic Home

TAPPAN

Sitting on a 20-acre plot of land purchased by German masons in 1872 is the dormant German Masonic Home. The sprawling structure was constructed from 1906 to 1909 and initially served as housing for older members of the freemasonry. At its height, approximately fifty members and their families lived in the home until 1983. The home was then used as a dormitory for Dominican College until 1995 and has been unoccupied ever since. To date, much of the German Masonic Home's more than 110-year-old exterior furnishings remain intact.

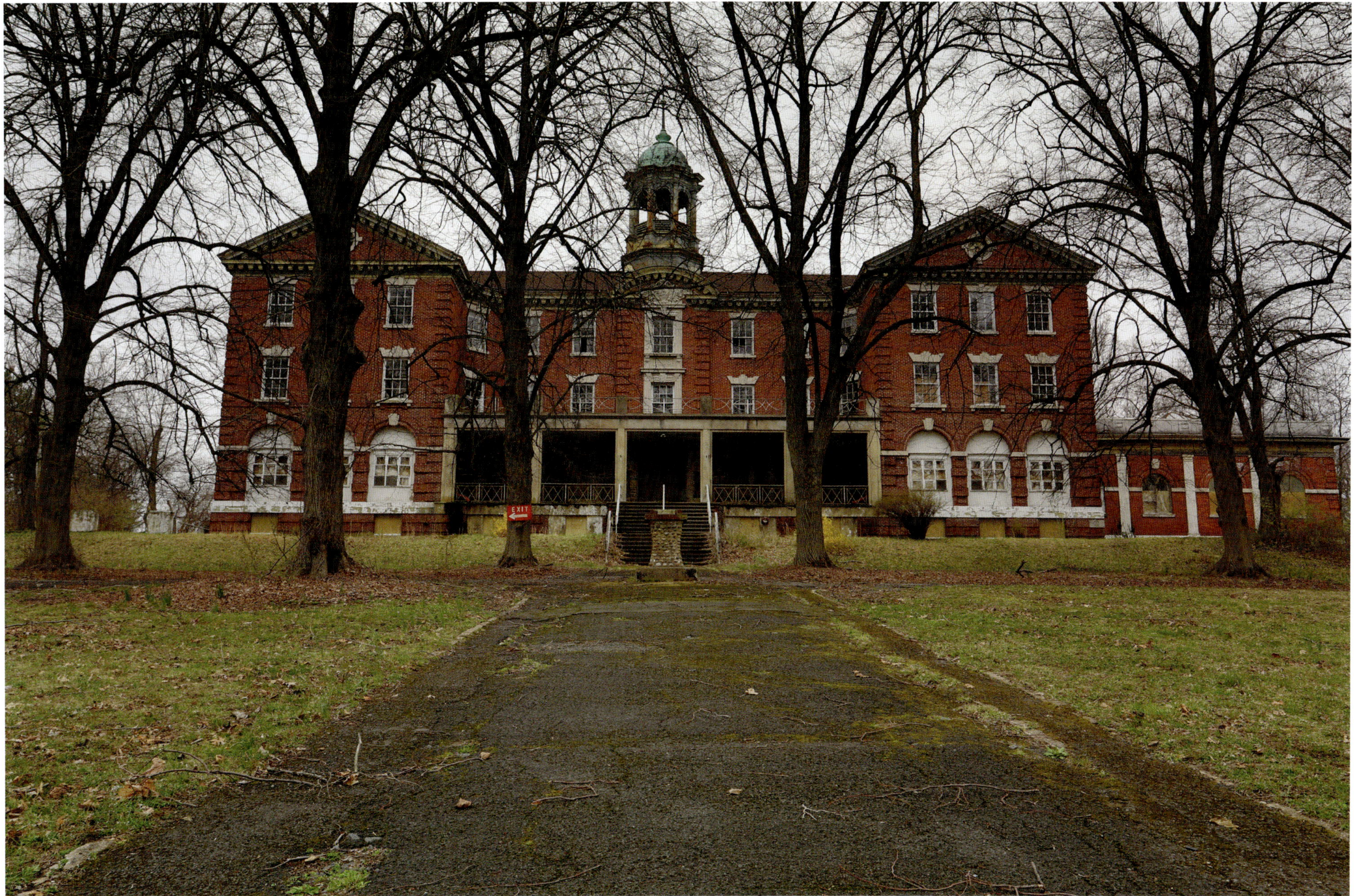

German Masonic Home

Bennett College

MILLBROOK

Millbrook's curio landmark that is Halcyon Hall was once a resort hotel built in 1890 and was designed for guests who cherished reading. In 1907 Miss Bennett's Finishing School for Girls of Irvington, New York, purchased the property. The school would reinvent itself into Bennett College, a two-year college for women offering fashion design, art, music, modern languages, history, dance, and equine studies.

With the rising popularity of coeducation in the 1960s and 1970s, Bennett College faced retention and enrollment issues. Attempts at upgrading the facilities left the college in an even greater financial hole. To make matters worse, Westchester's Briarcliff College had merged with Pace University, eliminating all opportunities for a collaborative merger. Shortly after beginning the 1978 school year, Bennett College was forced to close.

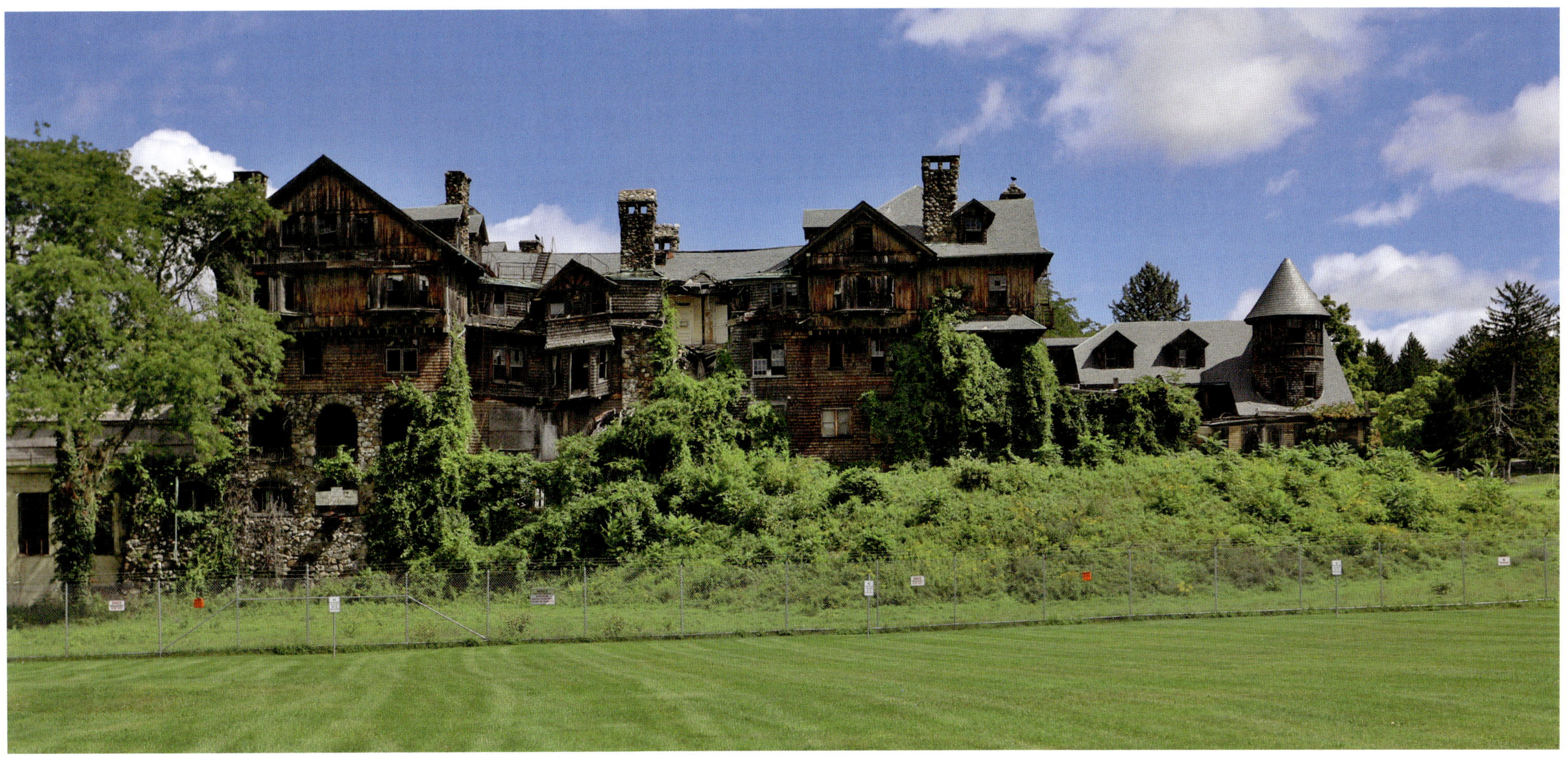

Bennett College

Brandywine Estate

BRIARCLIFF MANOR

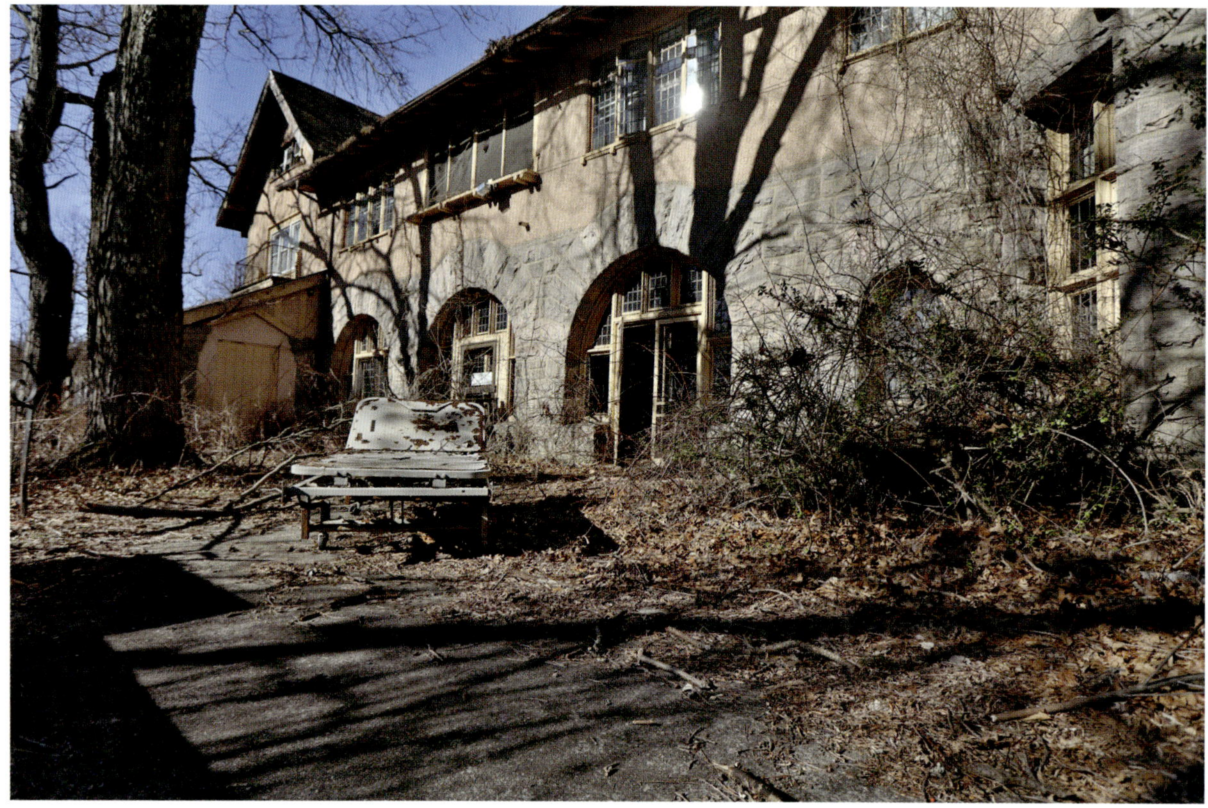

Built in 1909, this forty-nine-room Tudor-style mansion belonged to Isaac Newton Spiegelberg, a prominent railroad businessman. After his death in 1927, the estate went through several owners and a massive renovation before being converted into a nursing home. It was then abandoned after the Briarcliff Manor Center for Rehabilitation and Nursing Care was built nearby.

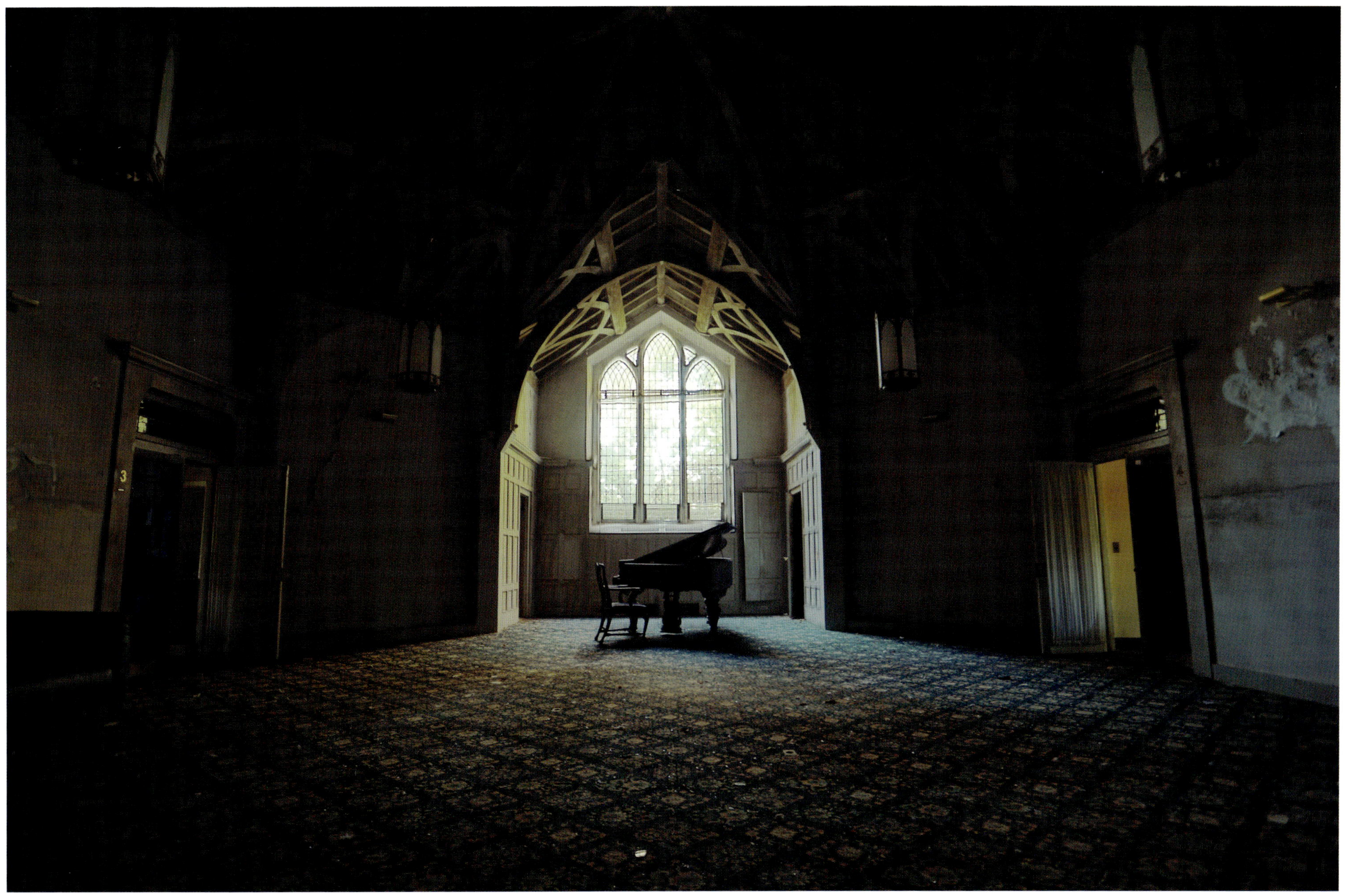

Common room, Brandywine Estate

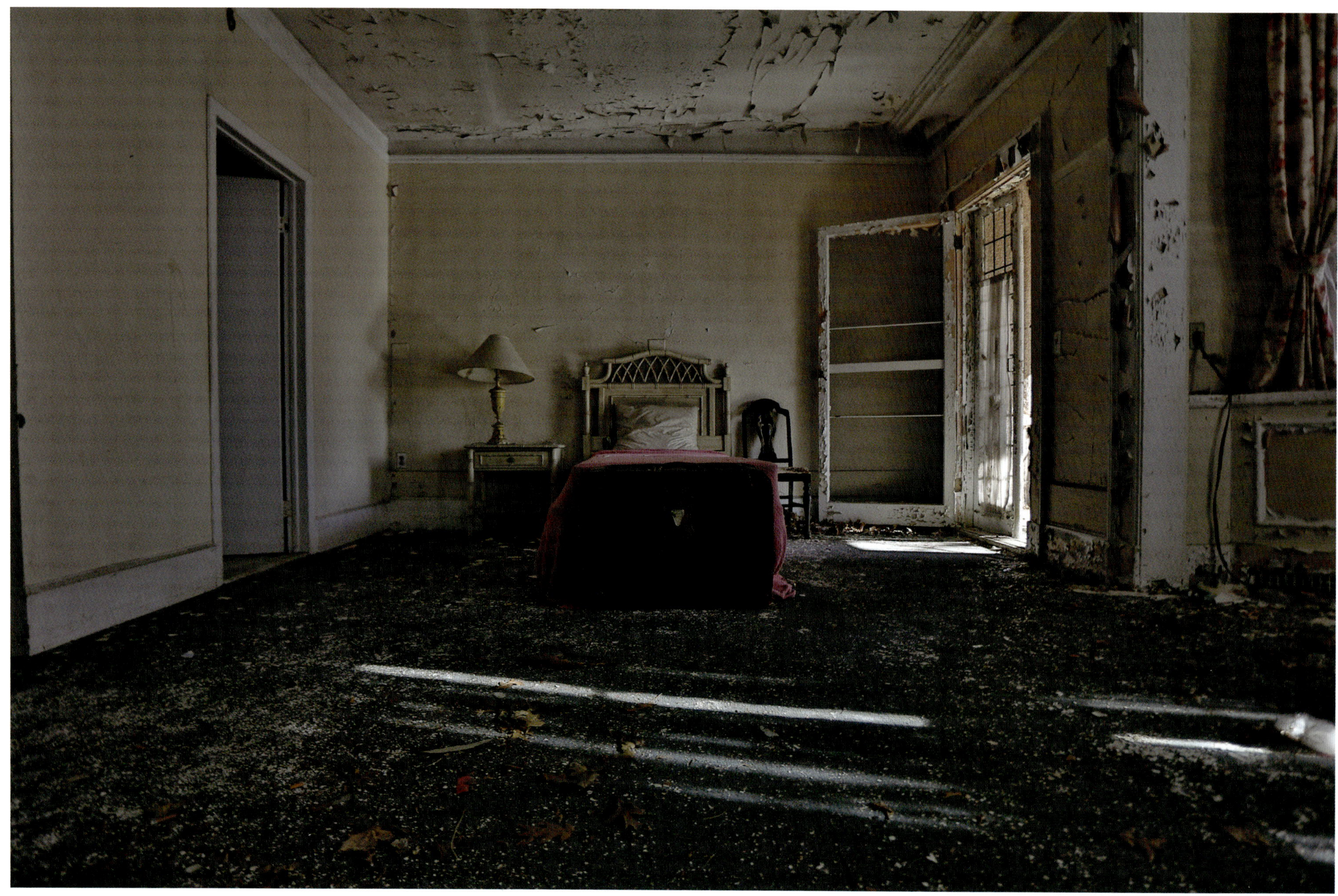

Typical resident room, Brandywine Estate

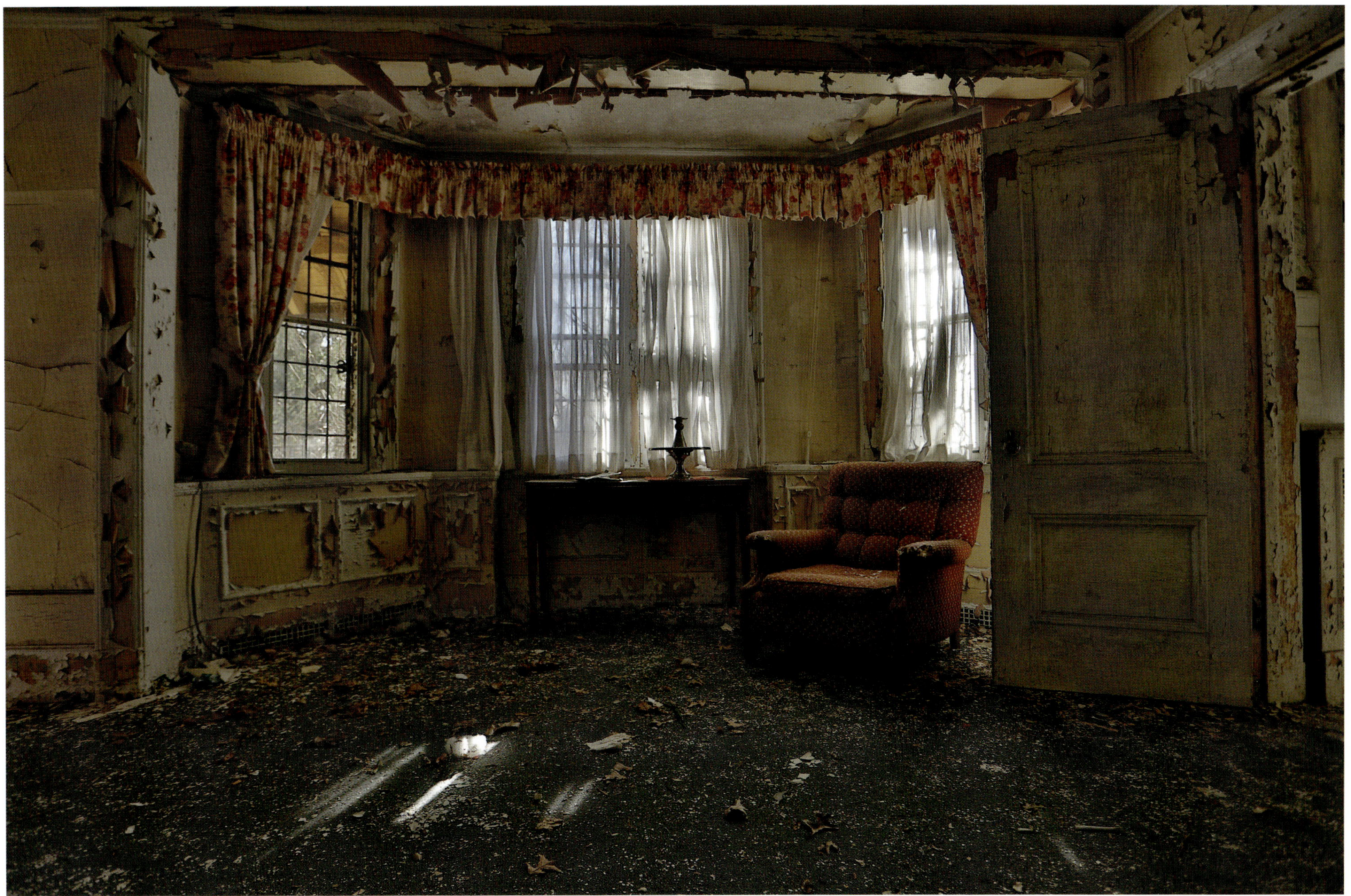

Typical resident room, Brandywine Estate

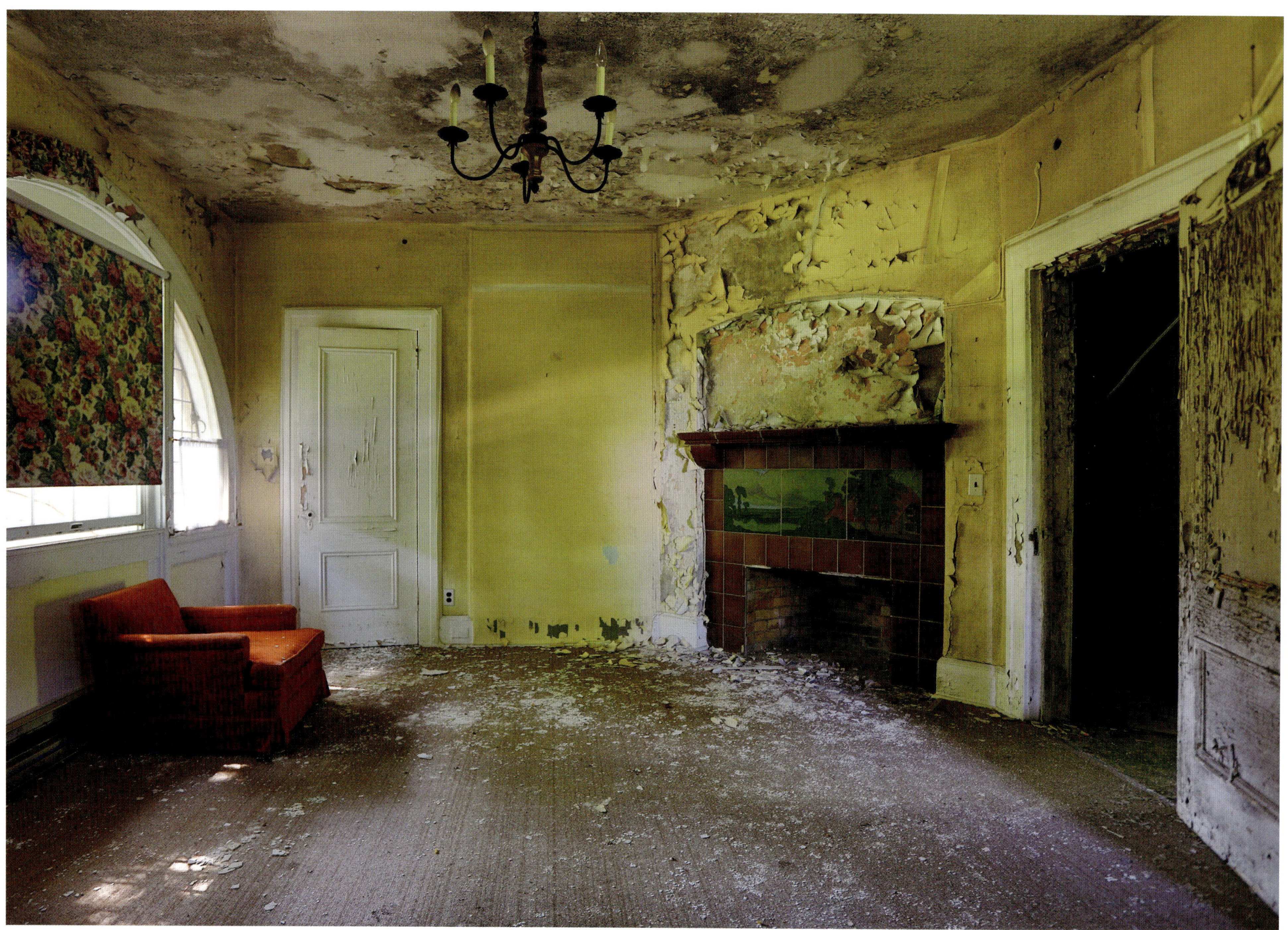

Typical resident room, Brandywine Estate

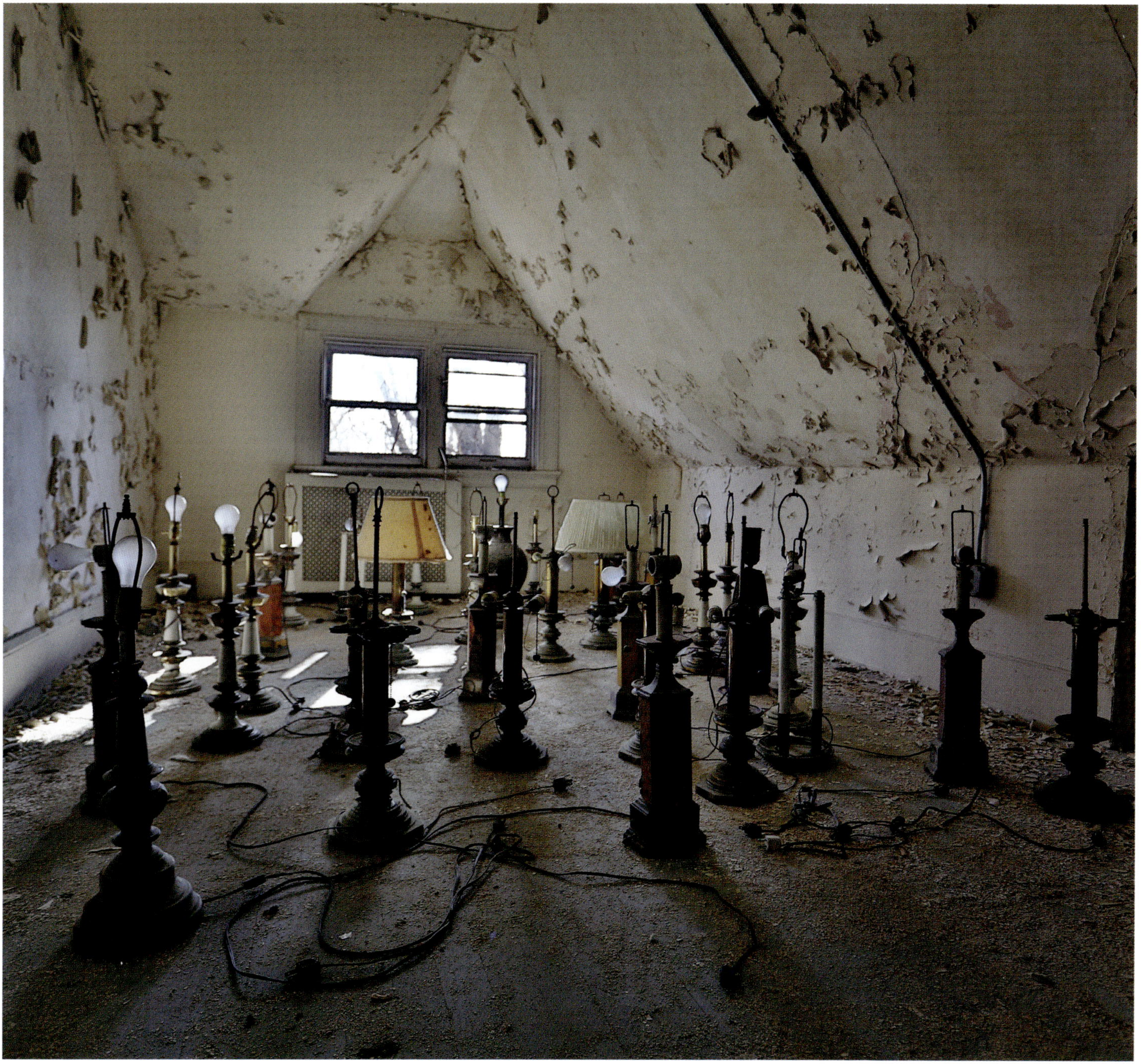

Attic storage, Brandywine Estate

CHAPTER 4.

CATSKILLS REGION

Catskill Game Farm

CATSKILL

About two and a half hours from New York City, up the Thruway to Exit 20 and off State Route 32, lie the remains of what was once the first privately owned zoo in the US—the Catskill Game Farm. Founded in 1933 by Roland Lindemann, the zoo grew from a single enclosure with a small variety of deer to a 1,000-acre farm with two thousand animals from all over the world. The game farm peaked in the 1960s, drawing half a million visitors each season. For decades, families would travel from near and far to visit this rural gem. Its primary attraction was the animal nursery and feeding ground, where visitors were able to pet, feed, and interact with a variety of quadrupeds, including deer, goats, and llamas.

Prior to the zoo's closing, Kathie Schultz, the owner of the game farm and daughter of Roland Lindemann, received several citations during the annual USDA inspections in 2004 and 2005. They included excess accumulation of manure, poor water drainage, and spoiled food. Finally, in 2006, Schultz was forced to close the doors to the Catskill Game Farm, citing years of declining attendance.

The controversy didn't end there. After the closure, there was considerable concern over the sale of the animals to unlicensed dealers for "canned hunts." A canned hunt is a trophy hunt where animals are kept in an expansive enclosure, making it easier for a hunter to attain a kill. Schultz refused to donate them to sanctuaries, leading protestors to picket the zoo. As a result of the press attention, animal advocates pooled their resources to form the Coalition for Catskill Game Farm Animals, the goal being to purchase as many animals as possible at the auction. They targeted the most "at risk" animals, including the nilgae, a type of antelope, the aoudad sheep, and two white rhinos. Although many of the animals were saved, several mammals, including bison, wisent, a red stag, and other rare antelope, were sold to traders tied to canned hunts.

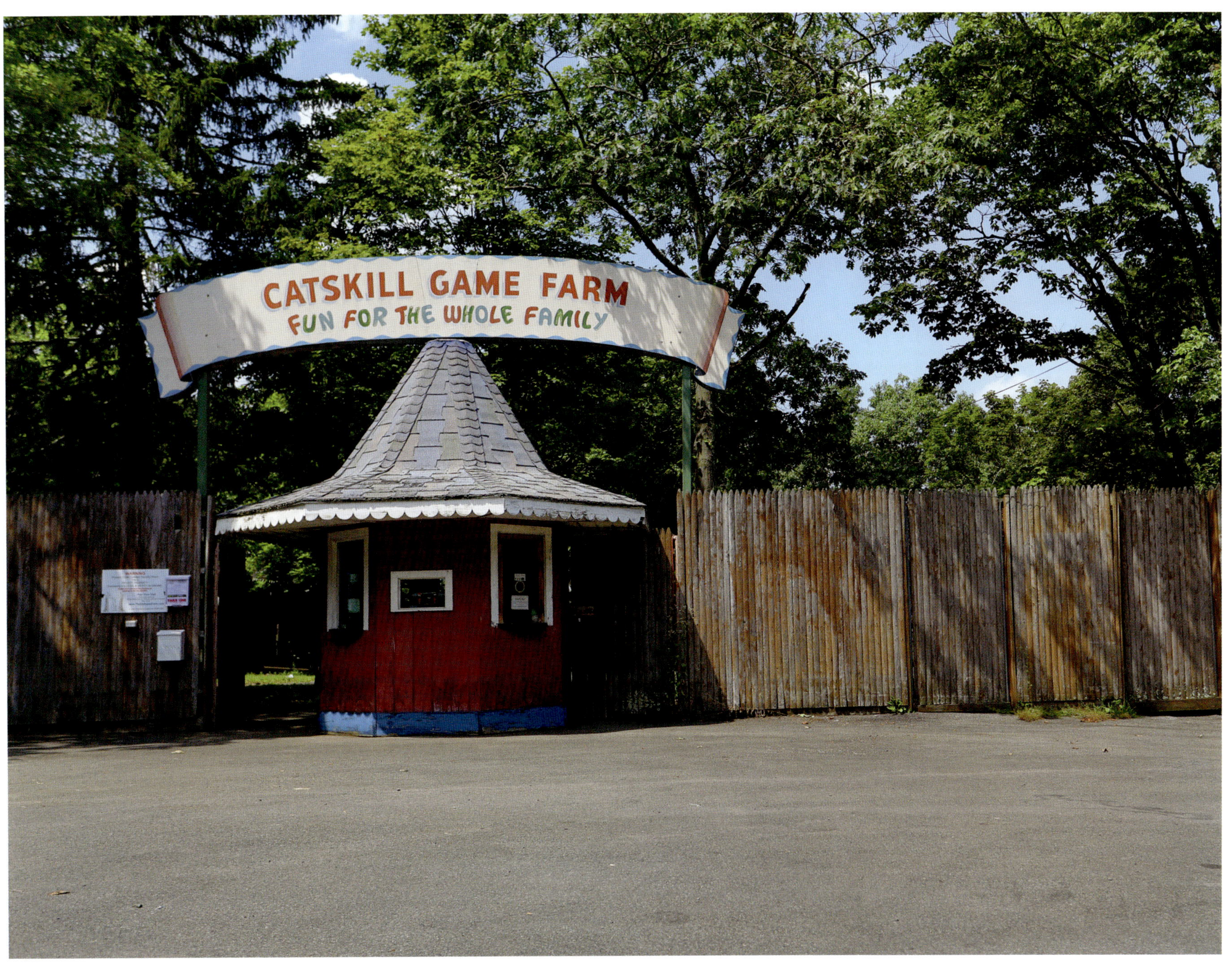

Main entrance, Catskill Game Farm

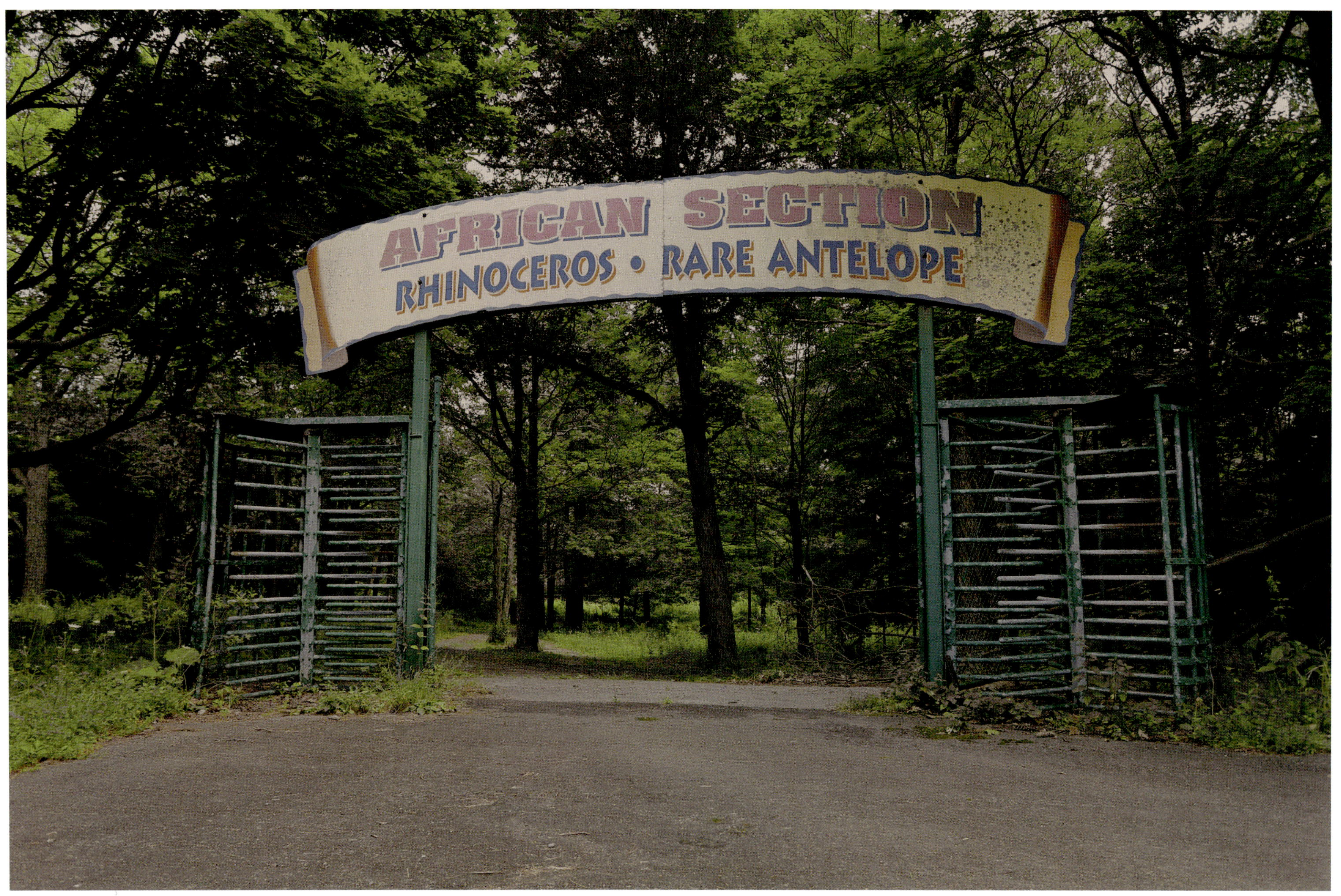

African Section entrance, Catskill Game Farm

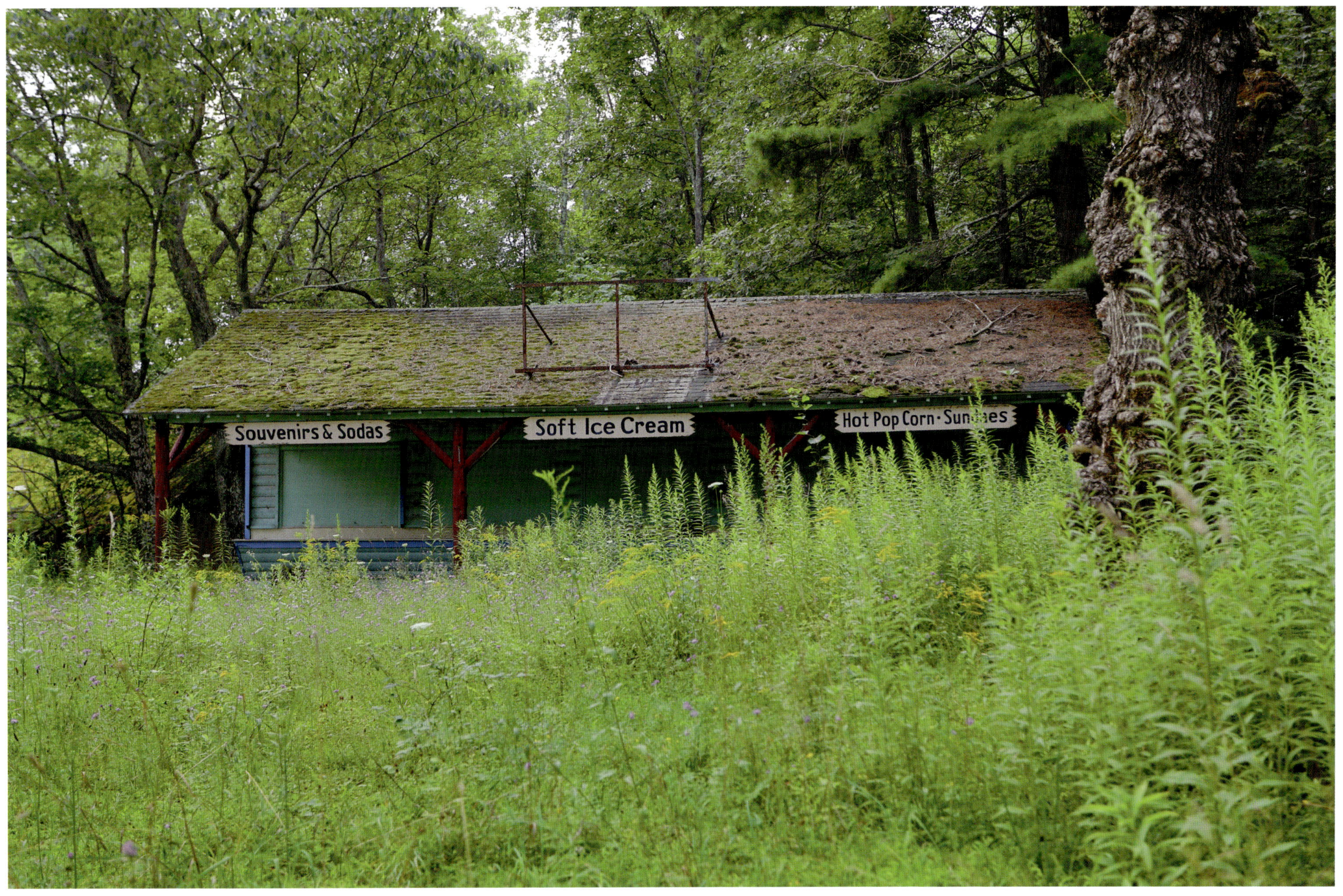

Souvenir shop, Catskill Game Farm

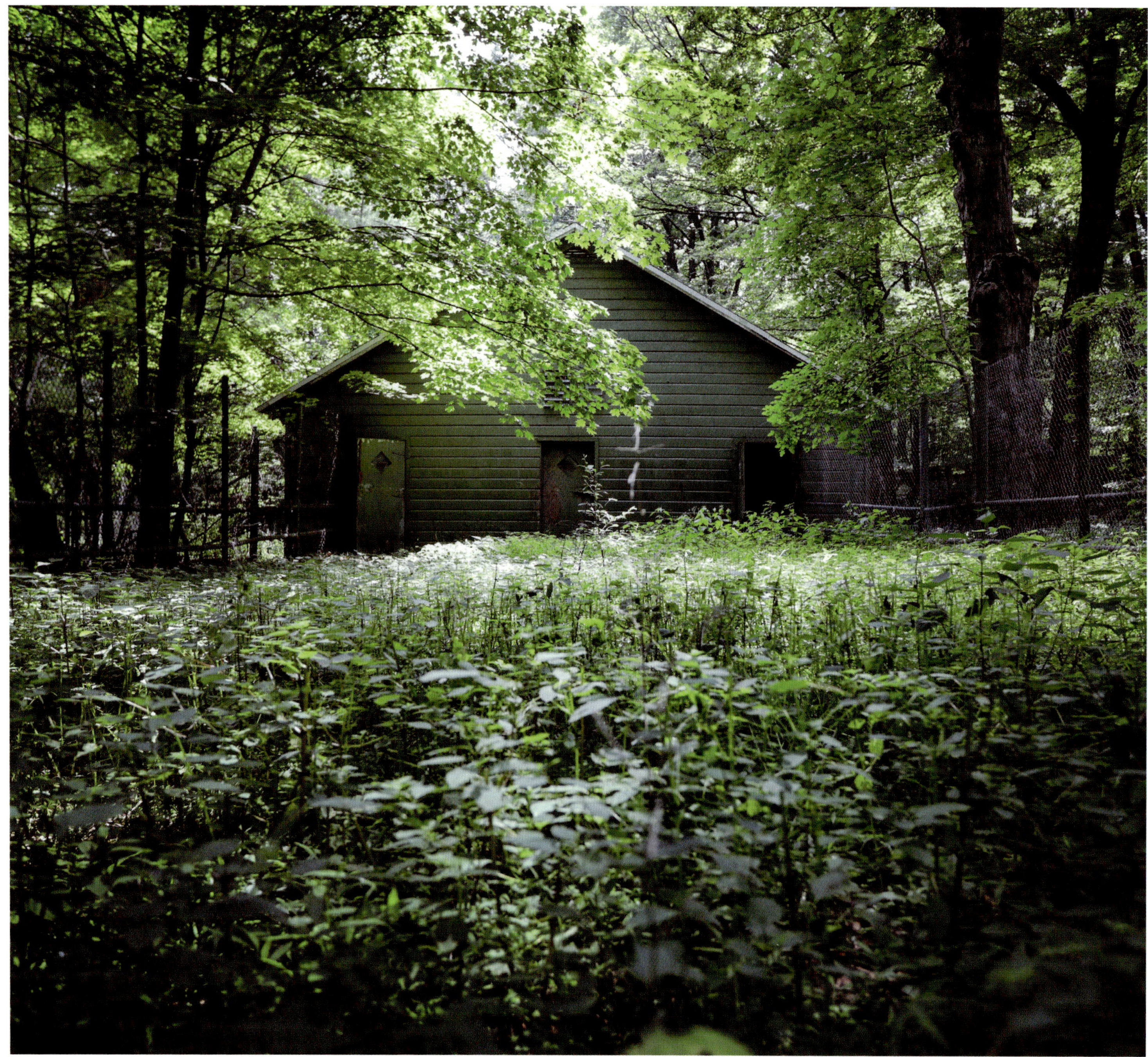

Animal enclosure, Catskill Game Farm

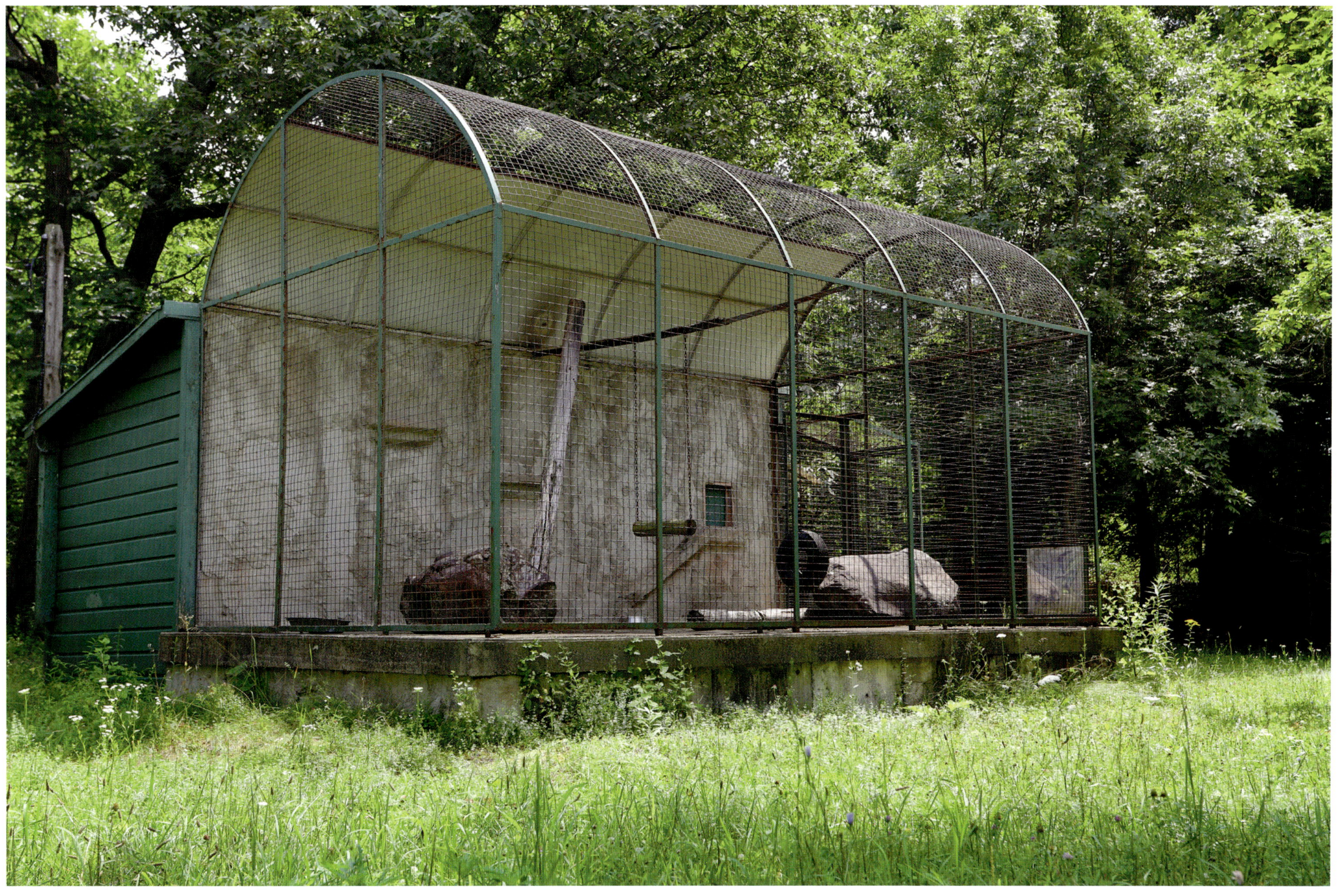

Animal enclosure, Catskill Game Farm

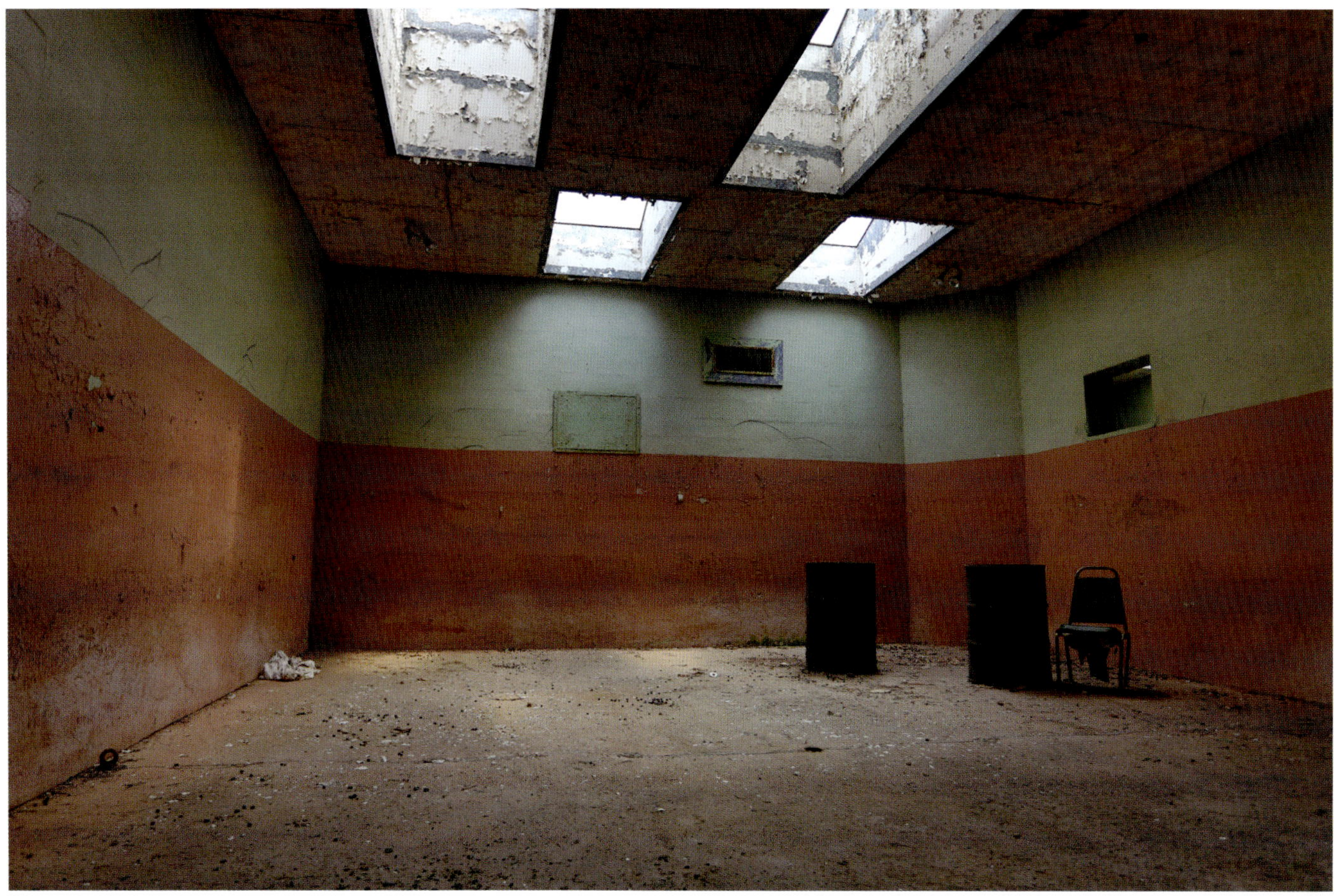

Rhinoceros house, Catskill Game Farm

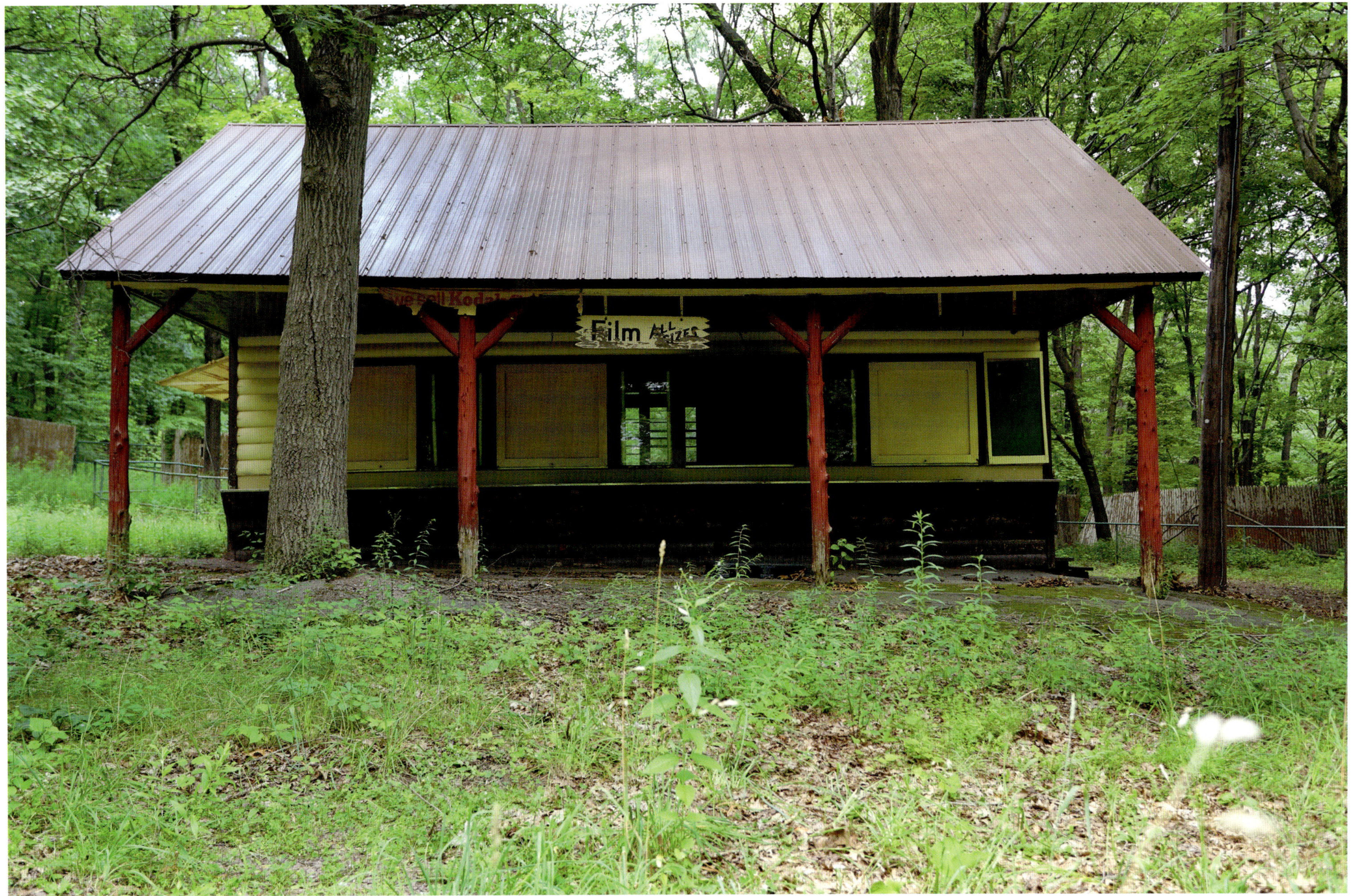

Camera film shop, Catskill Game Farm

Nevele Grande Resort & Country Club

WAWARSING

The remains of the Nevele Grande Resort—one of the largest destinations of the Borscht Belt, a colloquial term for the now-defunct summer resorts of the Catskills—are situated at the base of the Shawangunk Mountain Range outside Ellenville in Ulster County. In the early twentieth century, the Catskills served as a vacation area almost exclusively for Gentiles, since Jews were unwelcome in most resorts. As their peers prospered in the urban environment of New York City, many eastern European Jewish farmers who settled in the Catskill Region began taking on boarders seeking respite from the city.

At the turn of the century, one such farmer, named Charles Slutsky, purchased a tract of land in what is now Wawarsing, New York. By 1903 he constructed several cottages to house boarders, with the Nevele Falls Farm House being the first official accommodation. The word "Nevele" dates back to the late nineteenth century, when, according to local lore, eleven schoolteachers discovered Nevele Falls, a hidden waterfall on the property, thus inspiring the name "Nevele": simply "eleven" spelled backward.

Large resorts such as the Nevele were pioneers of the all-inclusive vacation. At its height, the Nevele employed eight hundred workers servicing 432 guest rooms, eight outdoor and four indoor tennis courts, five pools, a ski and tubing slope, the Stardust and Safari Lounges, a health club, an eighteen-hole golf course, and a nine-hundred-seat-capacity convention center. In 1964, Herbert D. Phillips of the New York Viola, Bernard, & Phillips architectural firm designed the Nevele tower, a ten-story dodecahedron structure intended to minimize the excessive corridor lengths seen in other hotels. One of the final additions was a brilliantly designed ski and skate chalet featuring glulam wood beams arching upward to a line of skylights.

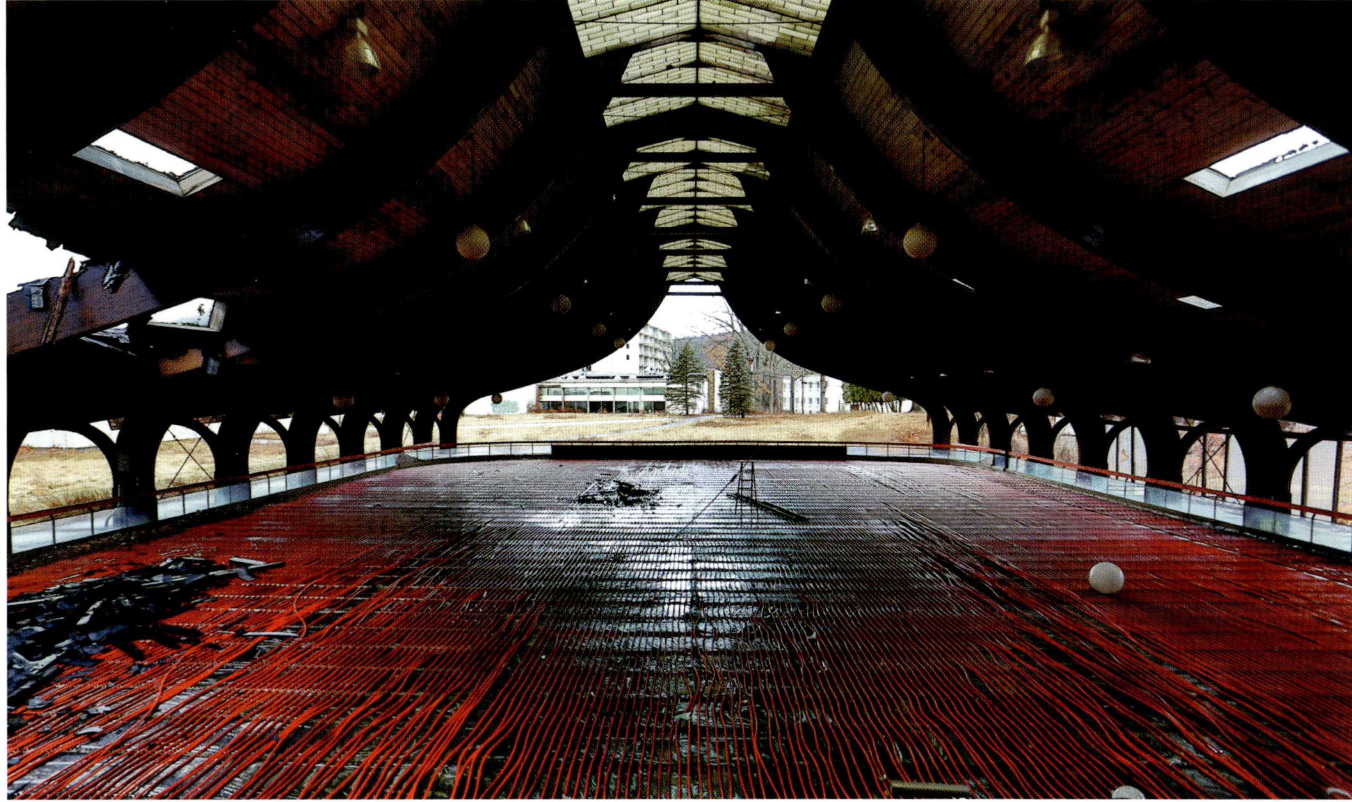

Ski & Skate Chalet, Nevele Grande Resort

By 1997, with Catskill tourism on a steep decline and the Nevele suffering from a decreasing number of visitors and continuous upkeep costs, the Slutsky family sold the resort to Fred Kassner, who combined Nevele with the nearby Fallsview Resort, renaming the former to the Nevele Grande Resort. Then, in 2000, the resort was purchased by Mitchell Wolff and Joel Hoffman, who oversaw massive renovations despite the continuous decline.

By early 2008, the Nevele had a 28 percent occupancy rate, barely generating a net profit of $2.5 million per year. Much of the resort had fallen into disrepair, with rooms having no heat or hot water. It was later revealed that Wolff and Hoffman owed $700,000 in back taxes to Ulster County. In early 2009, horrible conditions including the distinct presence of mold forced the Limmud NY learning convention to end early. On July 5, 2009, the Nevele Grande Resort closed without notice, displacing hundreds of workers.

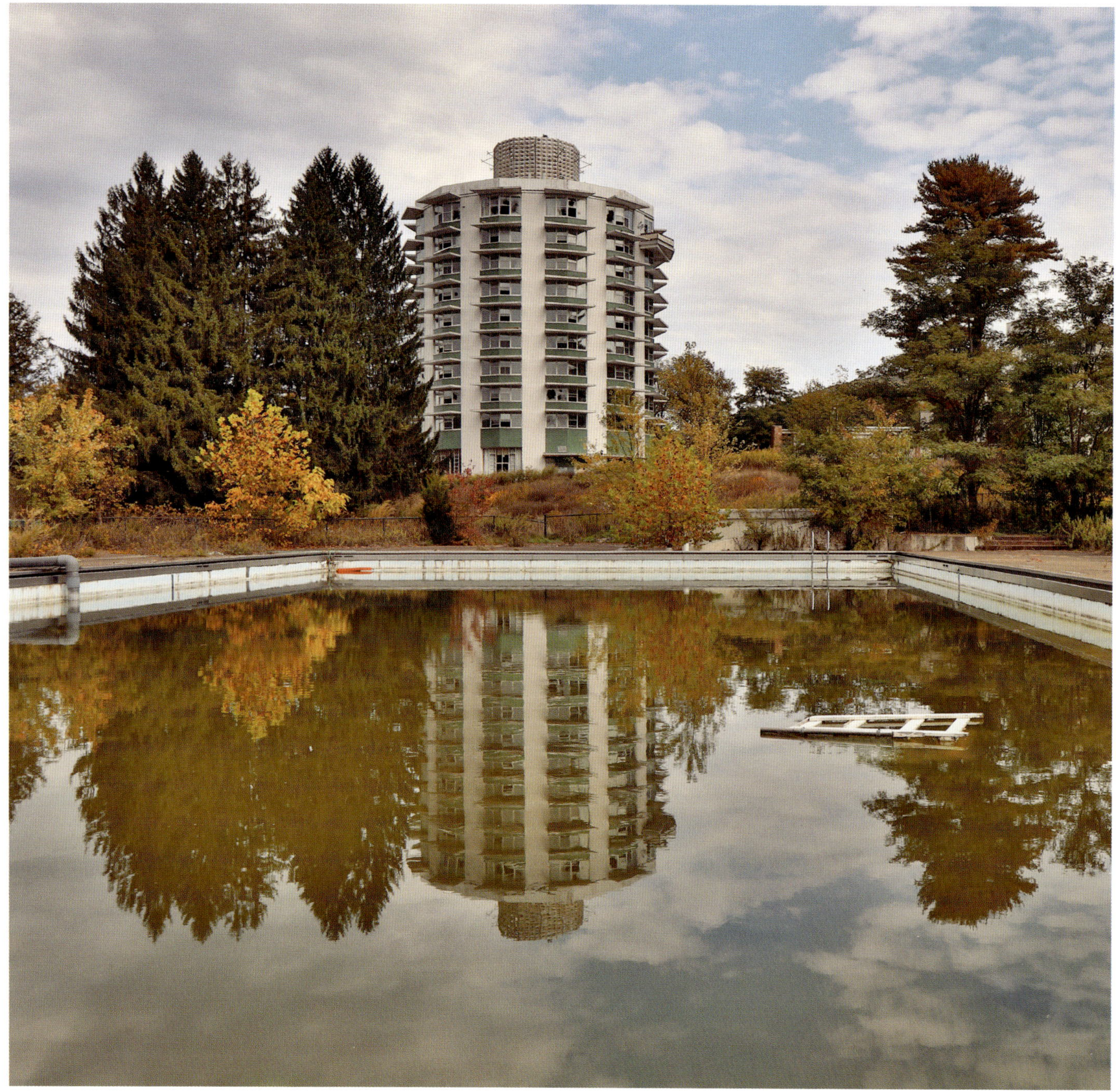

Nevele Tower, Nevele Grande Resort

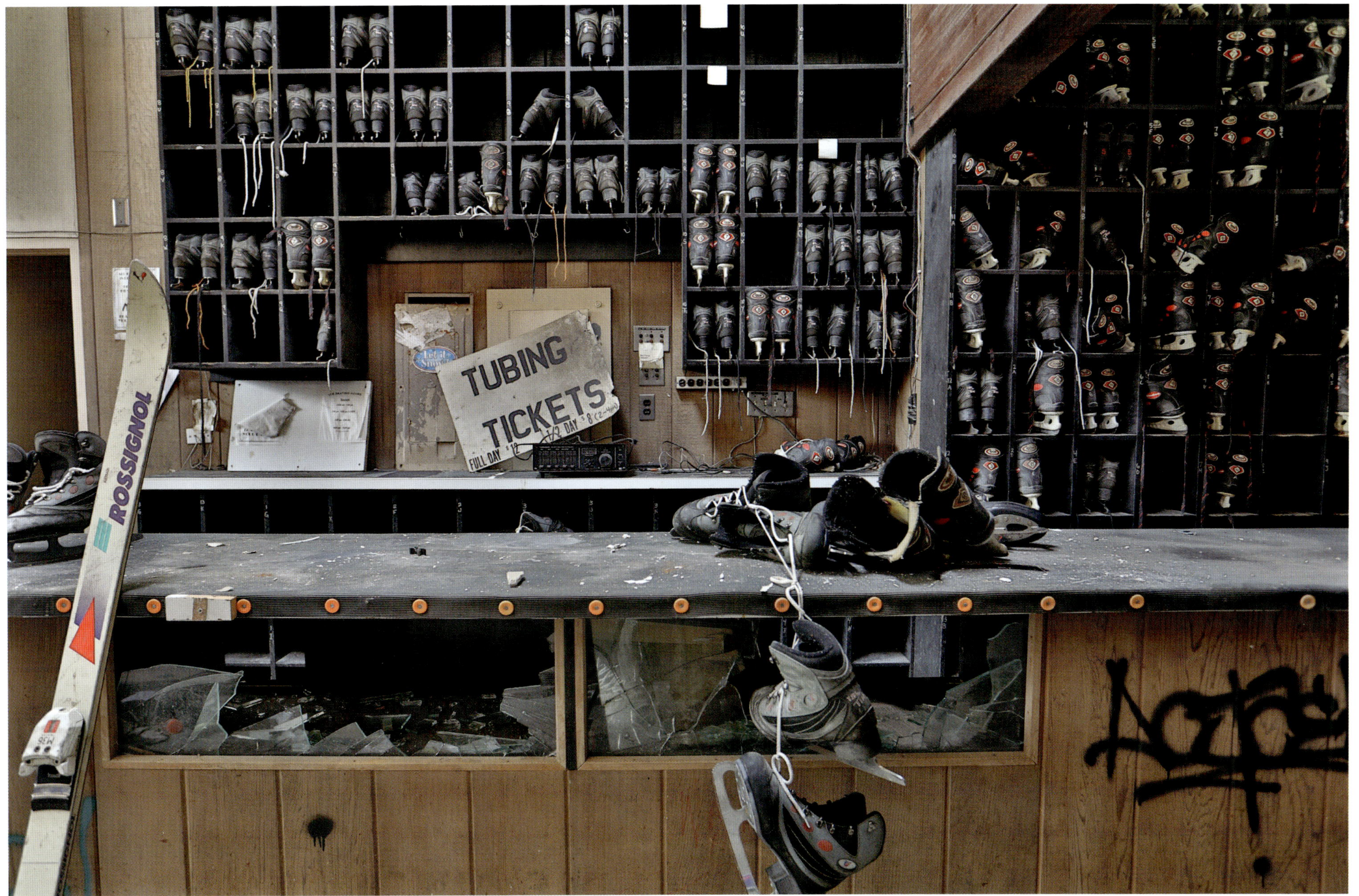

Ski/skate rentals at the Ski & Skate Chalet, Nevele Grande Resort

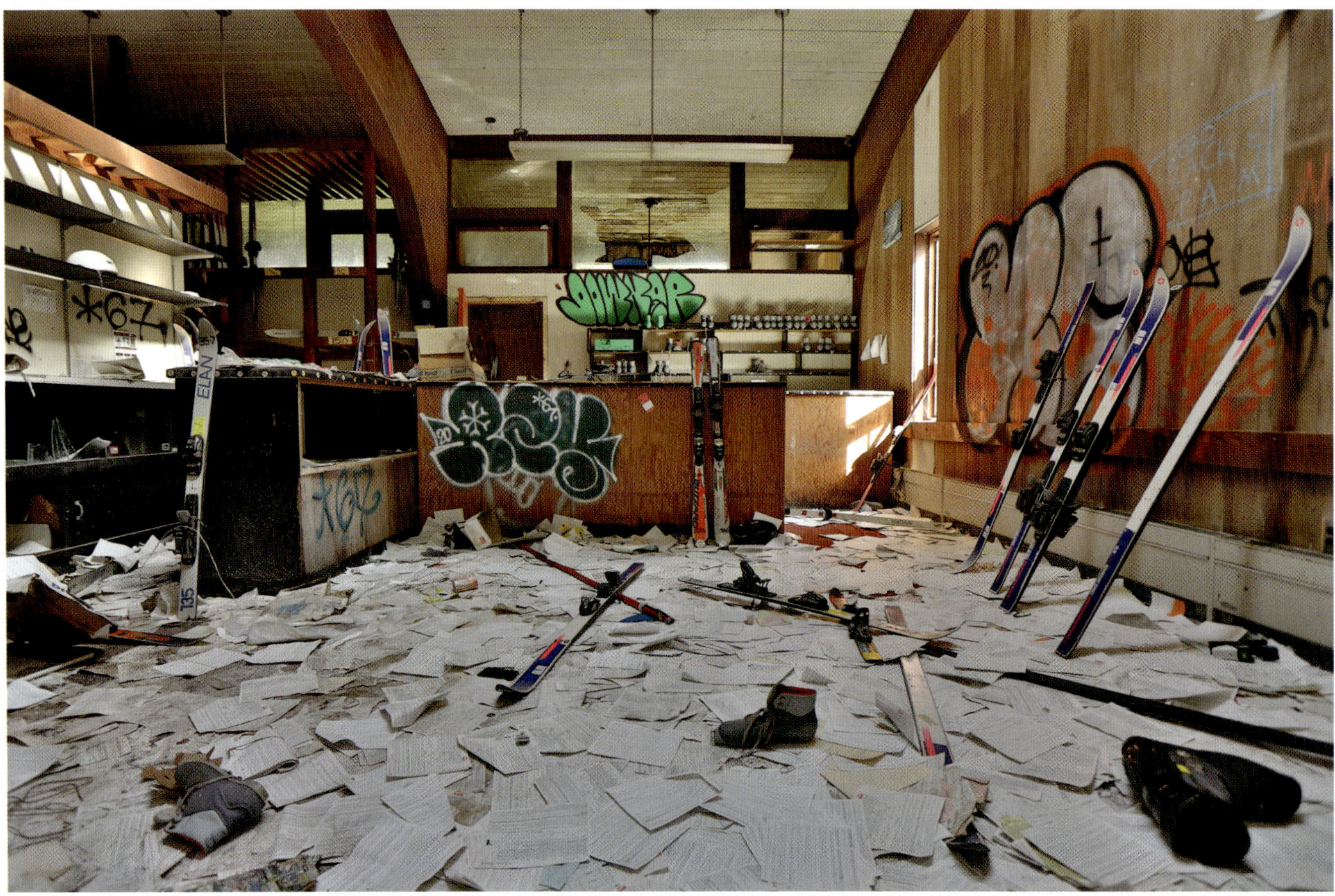

Ski/skate rentals at the Ski & Skate Chalet, Nevele Grande Resort

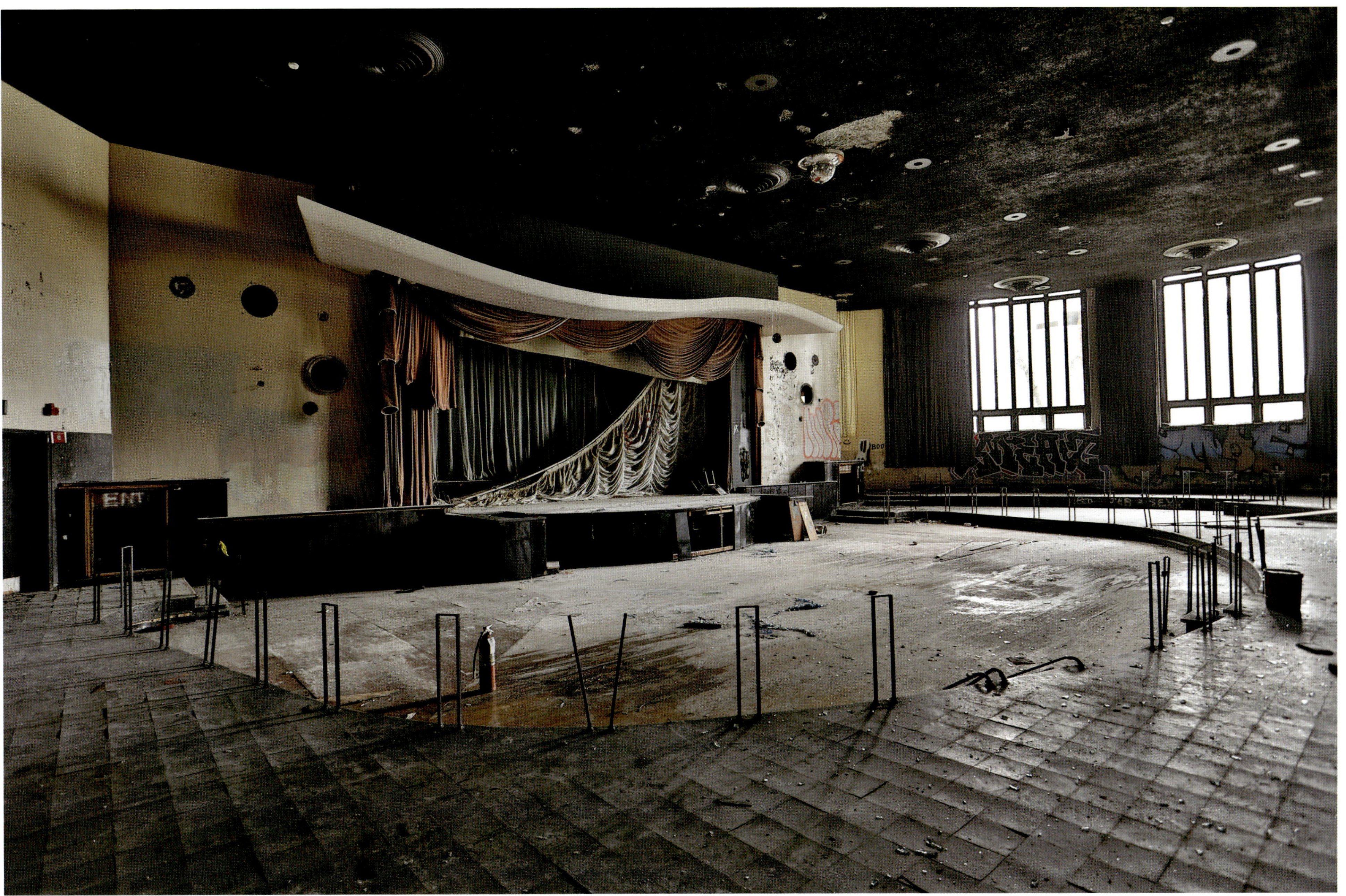

The Stardust Room, Nevele Grande Resort

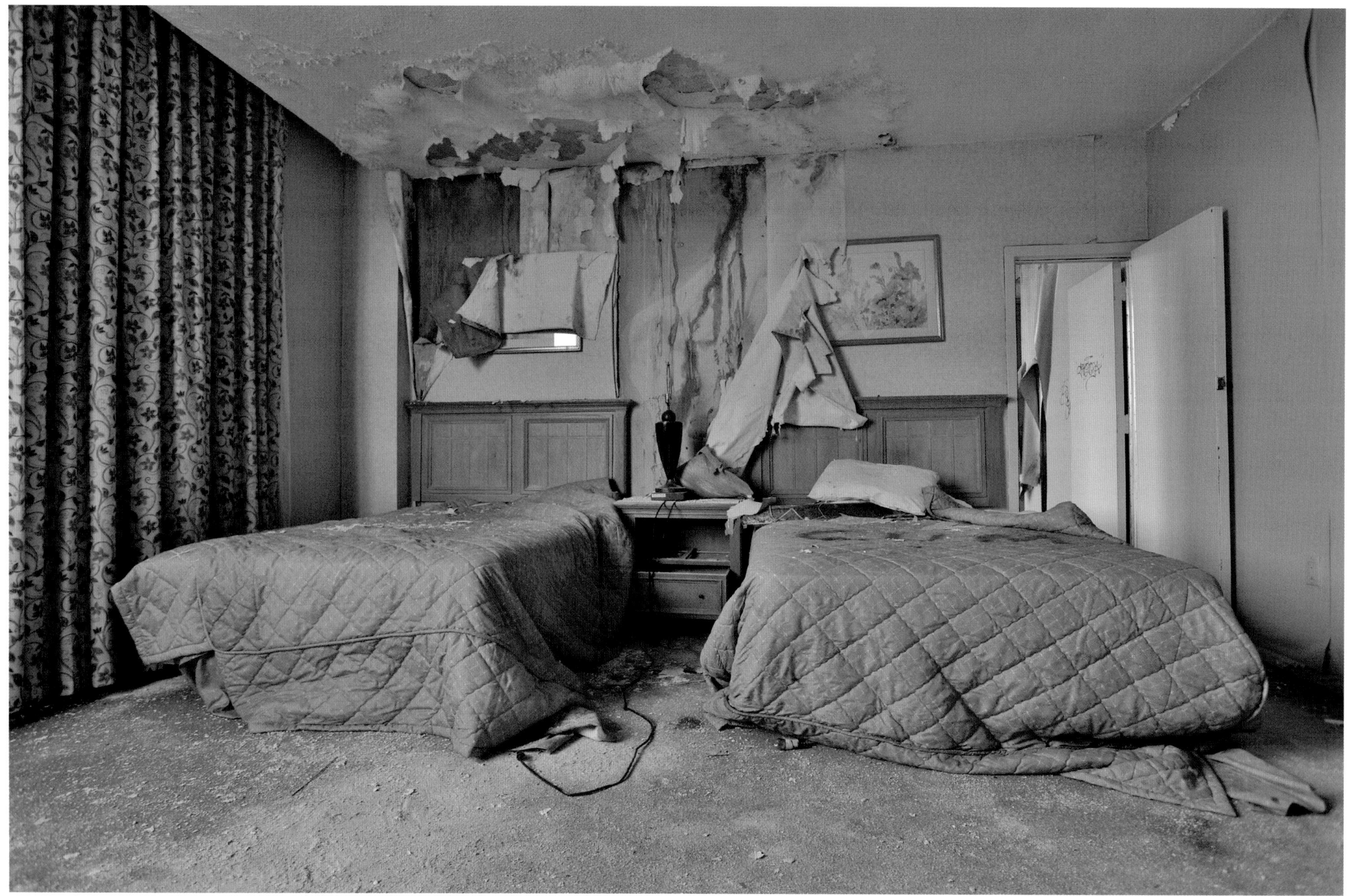

Nevele Tower guest room, Nevele Grande Resort

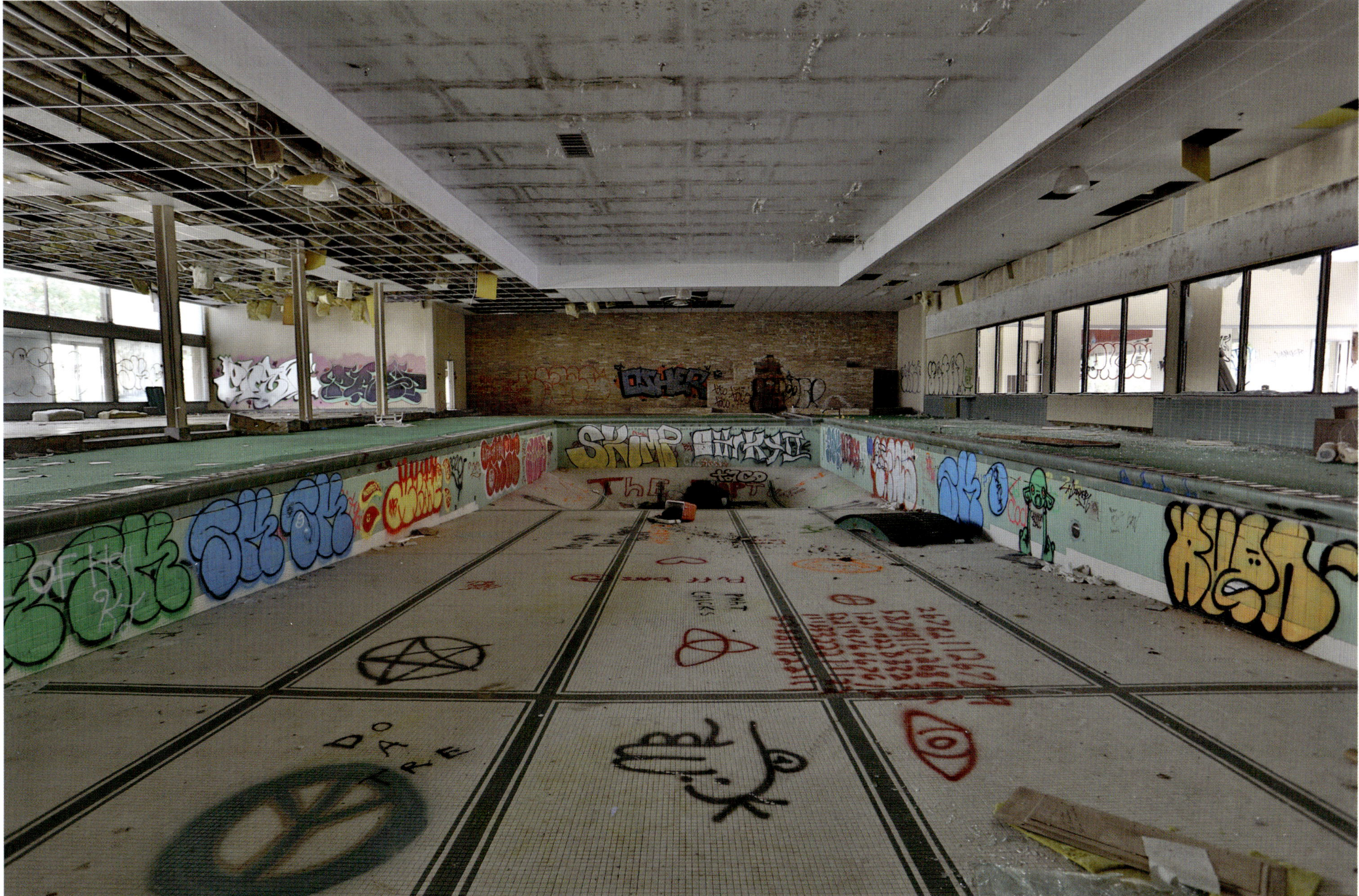

Indoor pool, Nevele Grande Resort

White Lake Mansion House

WHITE LAKE

Built in 1848 in Greek Revival style, the White Lake Mansion House is the oldest remaining summer hotel in Sullivan County. It was owned and operated by the Kinne family for over eighty years and offered 175 rooms, a restaurant, a casino, a ballroom, and tennis courts. During its heyday, the mansion was frequented by wealthy Manhattanites seeking a summer refuge. Due to the decline of tourism in the Catskills, the mansion closed in 2000.

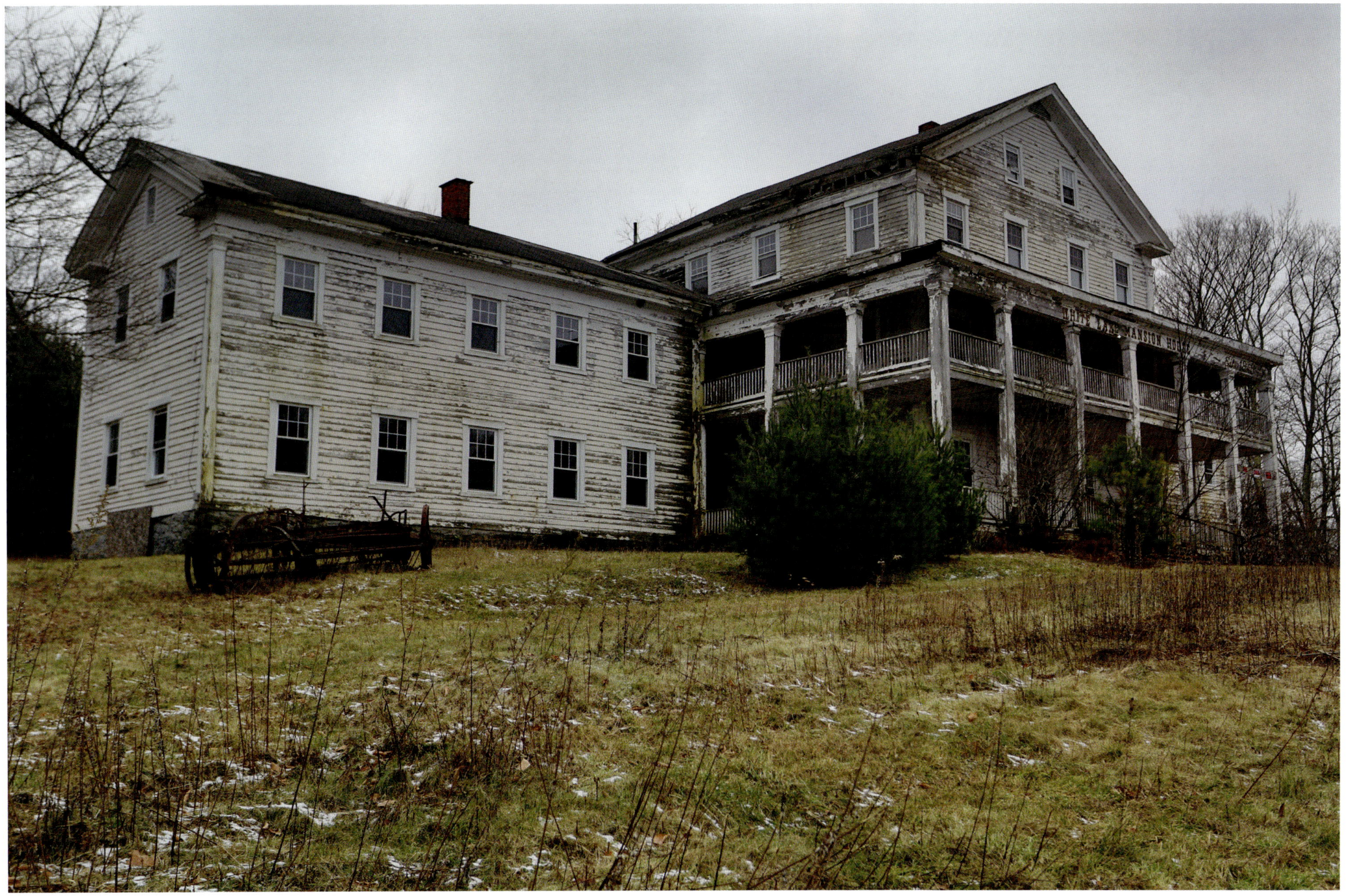

Today, the White Lake Mansion House sits on its original site in nearly all of its original condition.

Parksville Pharmacy

PARKSVILLE

The hamlet of Parksville shines a light into the economic hardships that plagued Sullivan County since the decline of tourism in the 1970s–1980s. Parksville was once a thriving hamlet boasting nearly fifty hotels and inns. Route 17 ran through the town center parallel to Main Street, making it a popular stopover for vacationers. When Route 17 was bypassed to Interstate 86, traffic was entirely rerouted from Parksville. Most businesses on Main Street, including the Parksville Pharmacy, were forced to close. As a result, many former storefronts sit abandoned.

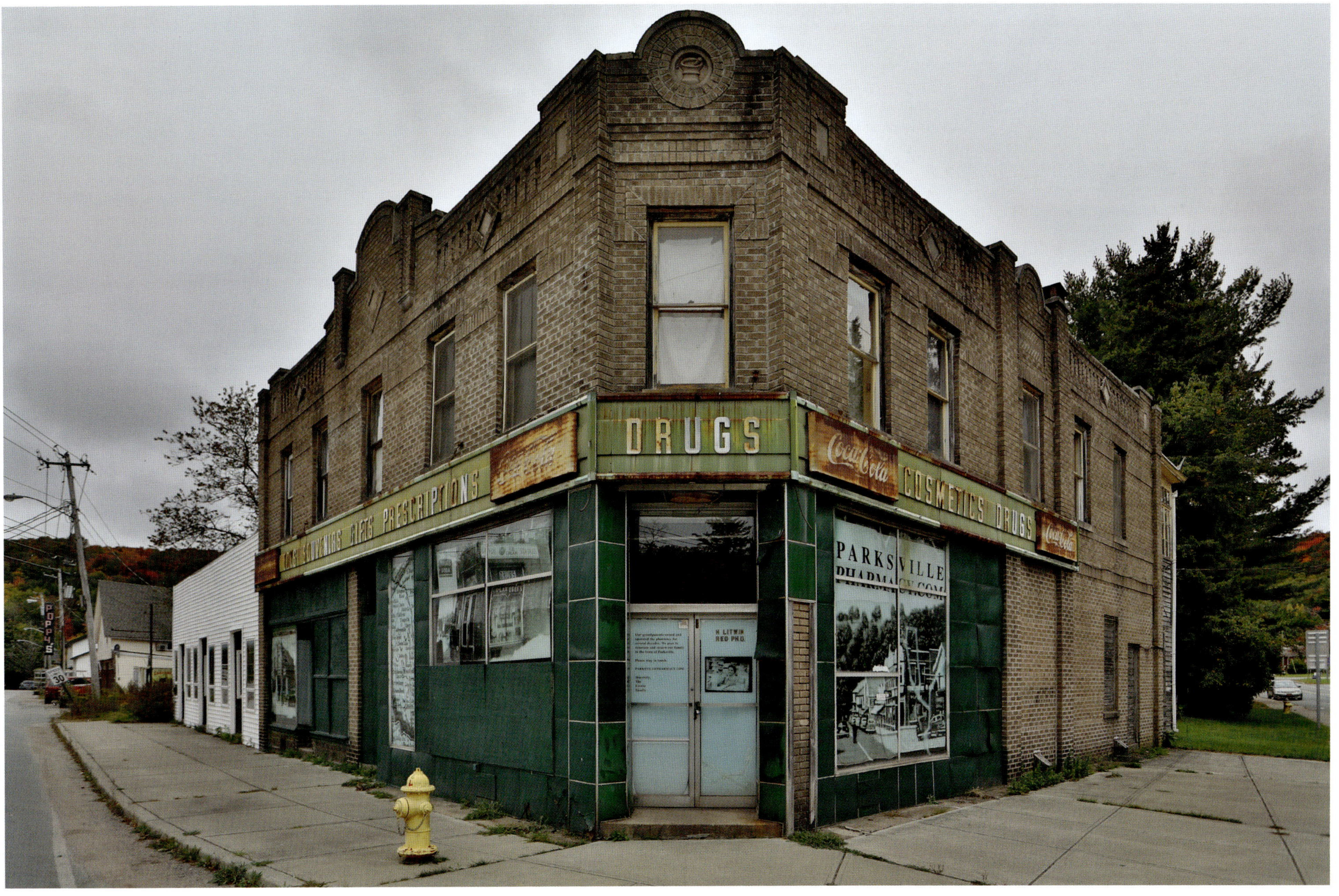

Parksville Pharmacy

Point Mountain Mausoleum

HANCOCK

The remains of this mausoleum rest at the summit of Point Mountain, overlooking the Delaware River into Pennsylvania. It was built sometime in the 1940s and was the brainchild of Delaware County coroner Dr. Lester E. Woolsey. After his death in 1962, Woolsey was buried here for several years until all human remains were moved due to frequent vandalism.

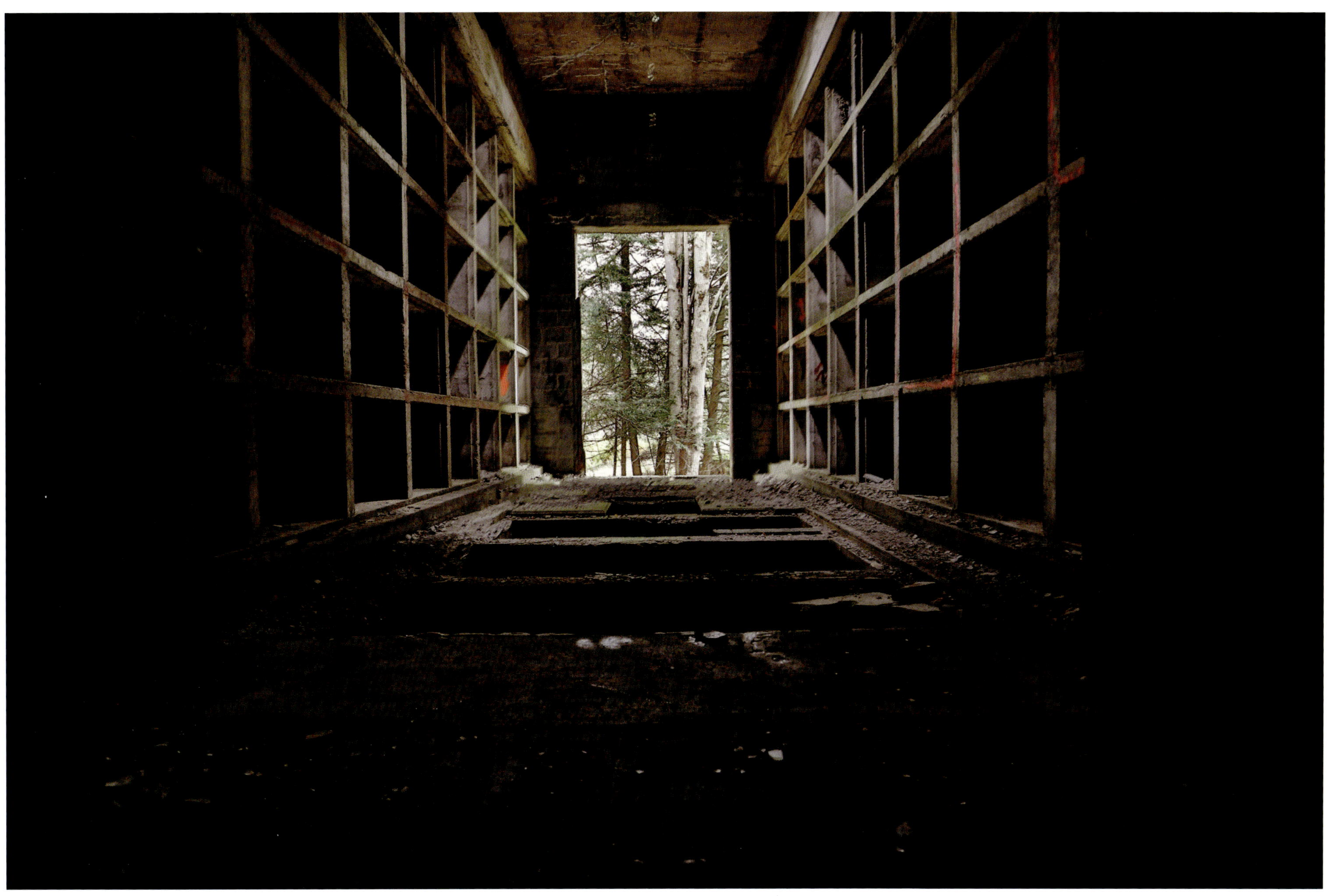

Point Mountain Mausoleum

CHAPTER 5.

CENTRAL NEW YORK REGION

Mohasco Power House

AMSTERDAM

The Chuctanunda Creek descends over 300 feet down to the shore of the Mohawk River, which in the early 1900s provided hydraulic potential, powering the surge in Amsterdam's industrial development. Water from the Chuctanunda Creek was filtered at the Mohasco Power House for use in steam conversion. The steam from the powerhouse's boilers powered its turbine generators, which in turn produced electricity for many of Amsterdam's mills. The remains of the Mohasco Power House are two different buildings, with one structure built in 1914 as a consolidation of several power plants, and the other, circa 1924 building being Mohawk Carpets. Like many industries served in Amsterdam, the steam efficiencies produced by Mohasco helped grow Mohawk Carpets to become a world leader in carpet making.

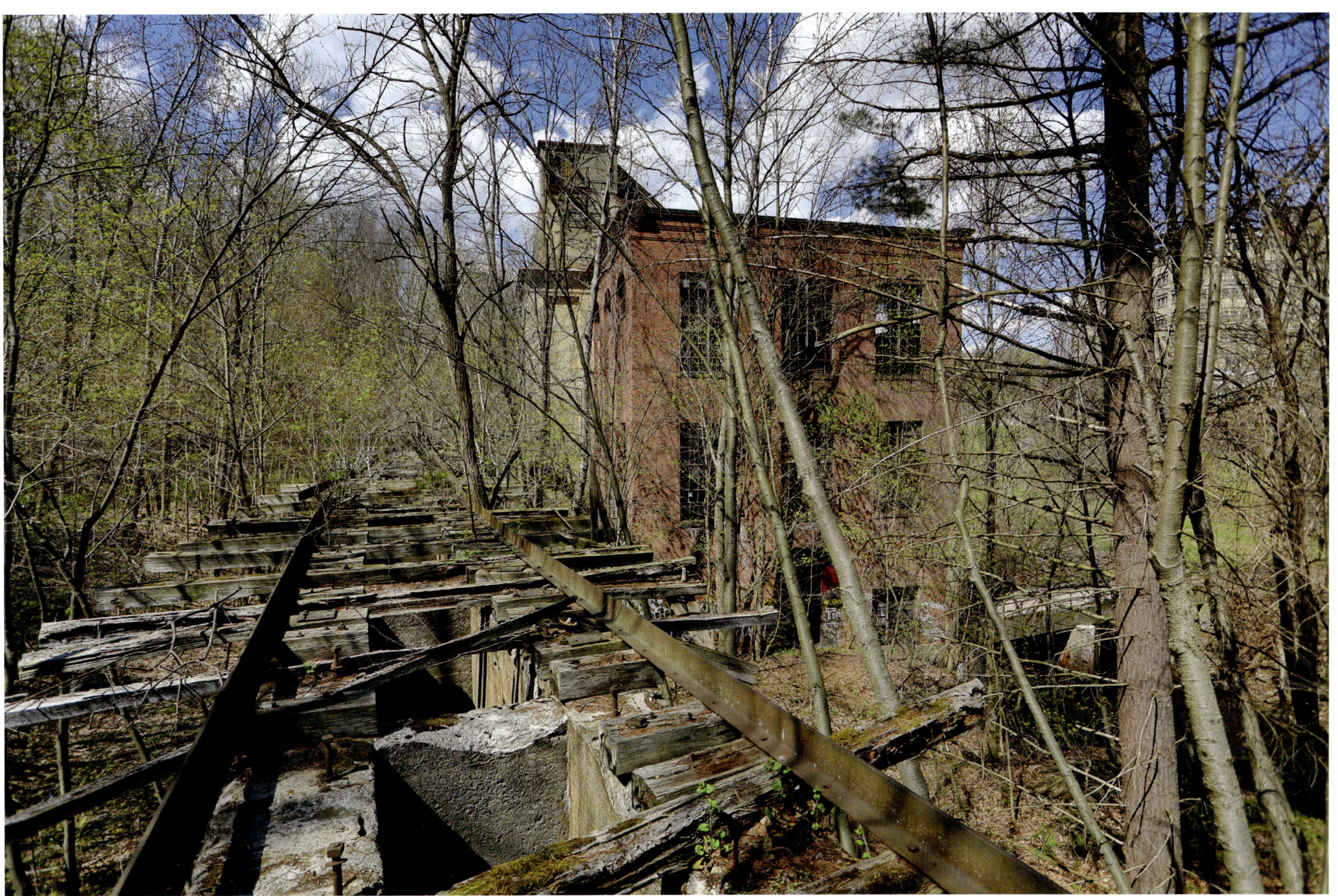

Train tracks leading to the Mohasco Power House, where freight cars would deliver coal

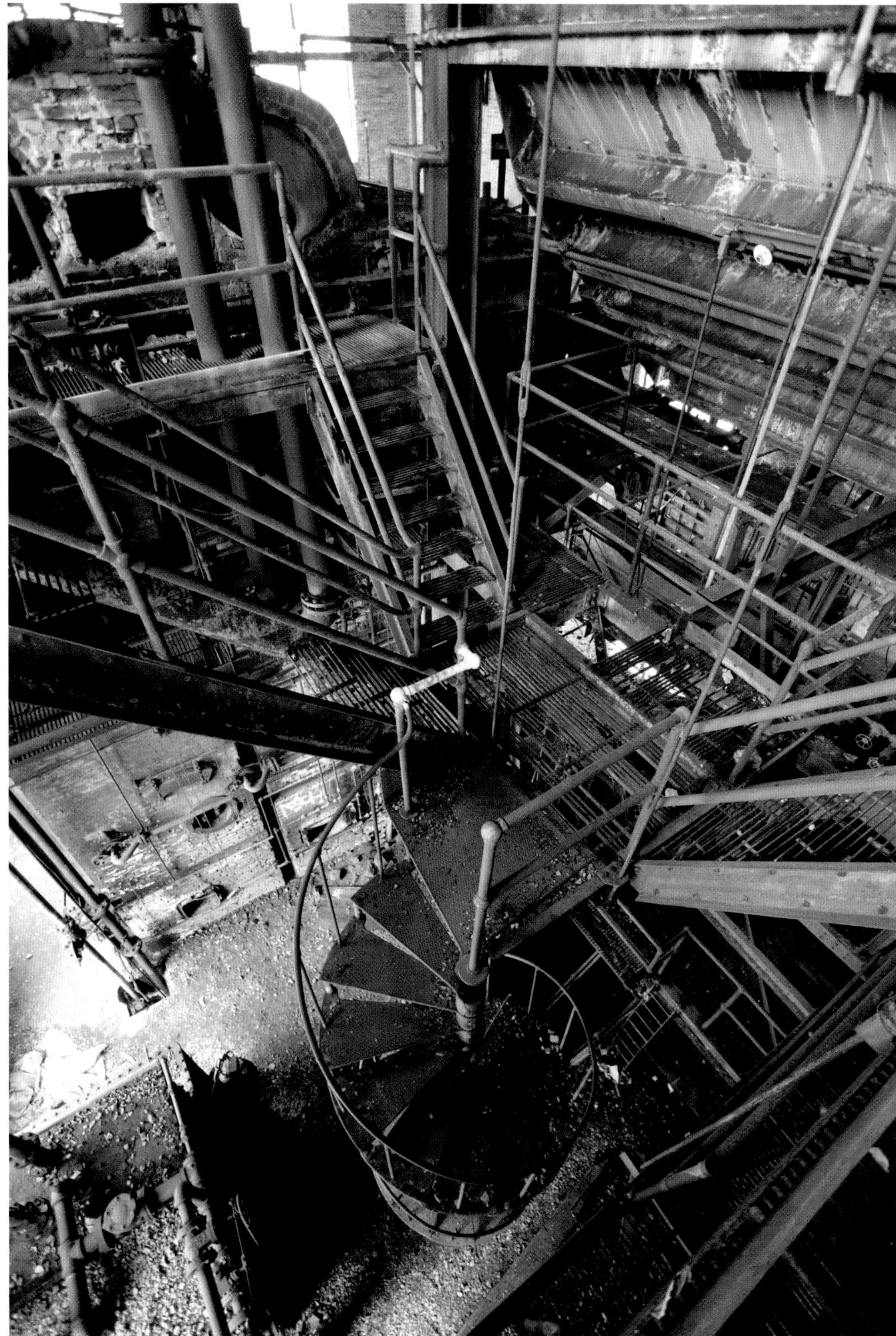

Boiler room, Mohasco
Power House

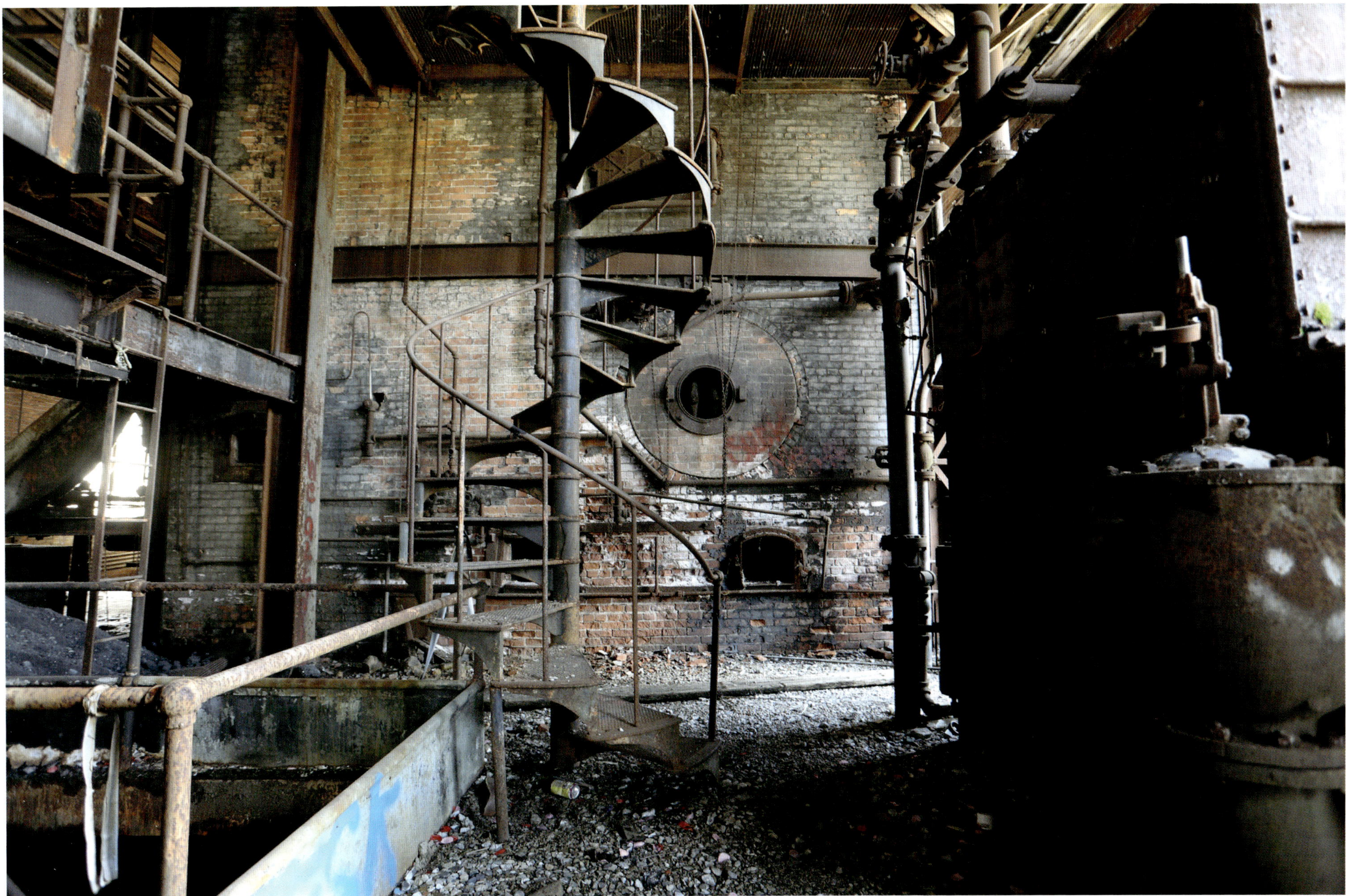

Boiler room, Mohasco Power House

Charlestown USA Outlet Mall

UTICA

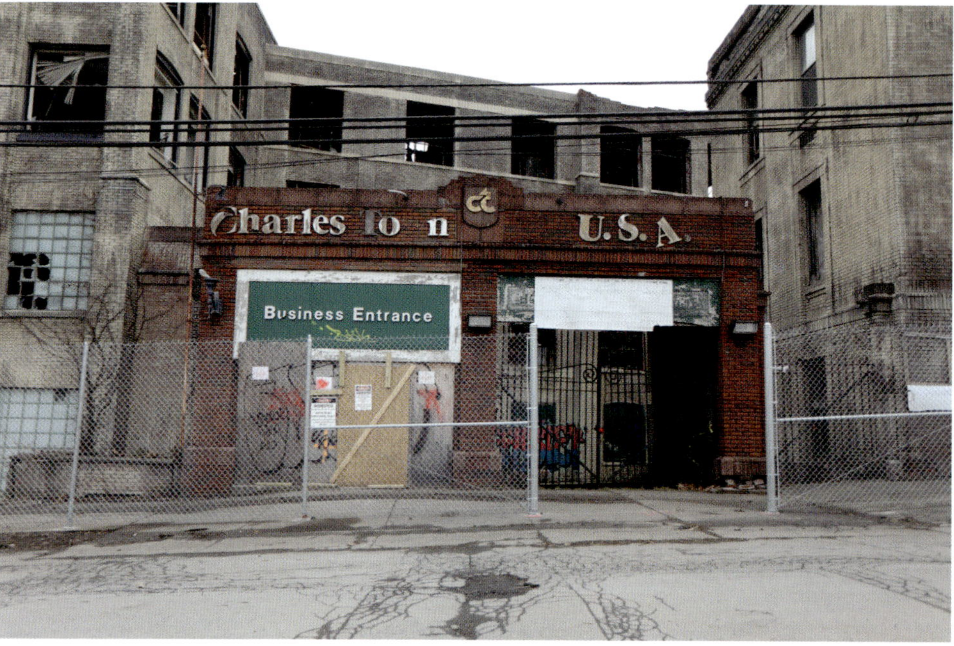

Charlestown USA business entrance

While most people remember this building as the Charlestown USA Mall, its use goes back to 1902, when it was occupied by Savage Arms, a weapons manufacturer for both world wars. In the 1950s, Sperry UNIVAC, a computer company, moved into the space and operated for two decades until the property was sold to Utica businessman Charles Gaetano.

Gaetano opened the Charlestown USA Outlet Mall in 1982. The complex stretched across 30 acres and contained over fifty stores, two restaurants, and an off-track betting parlor and operated until 1991.

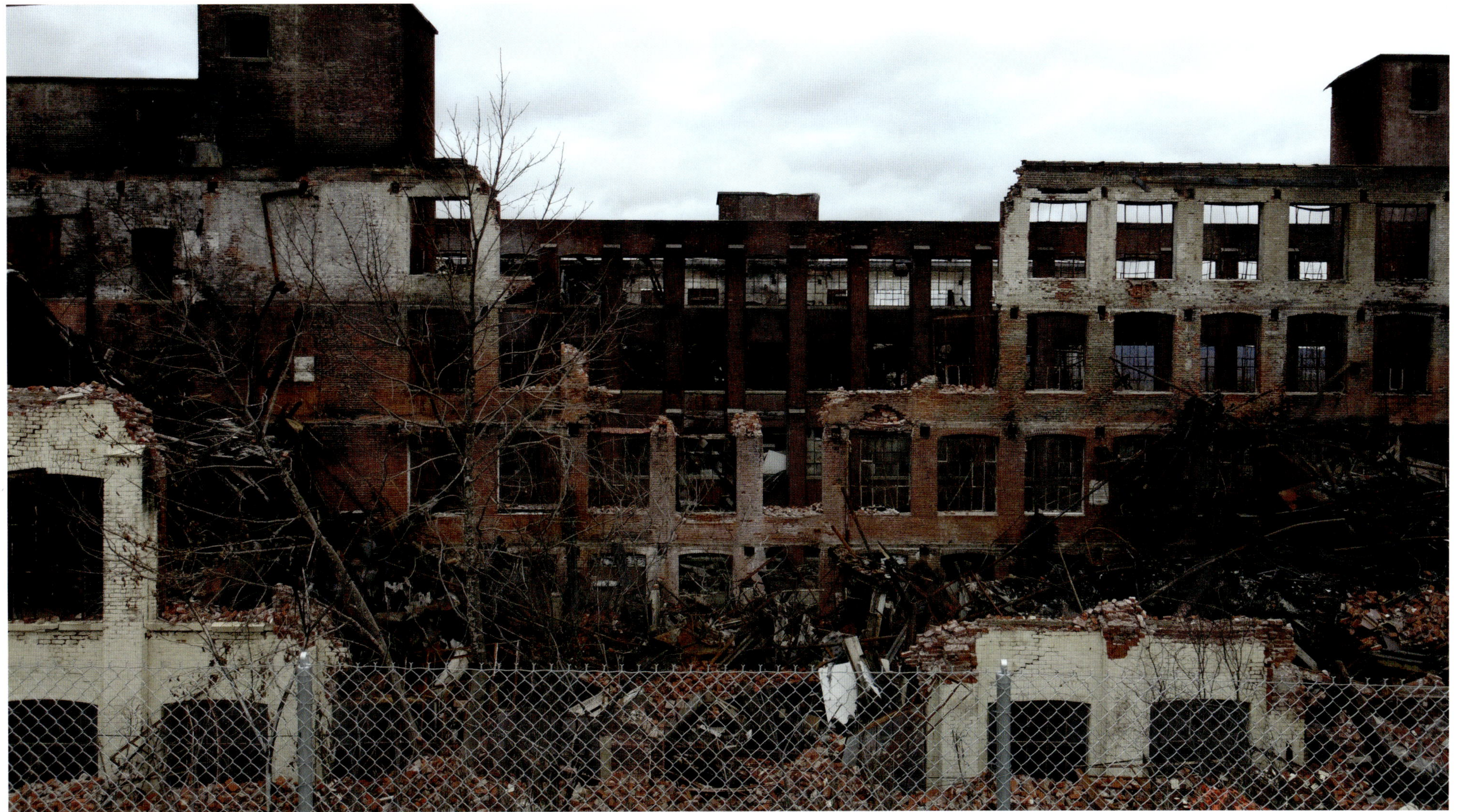

Following a massive fire that ripped through the abandoned mall on August 27, 2020, the City of Utica declared a state of emergency out of concern of the weather and wind patterns carrying ash and asbestos particles throughout the city.

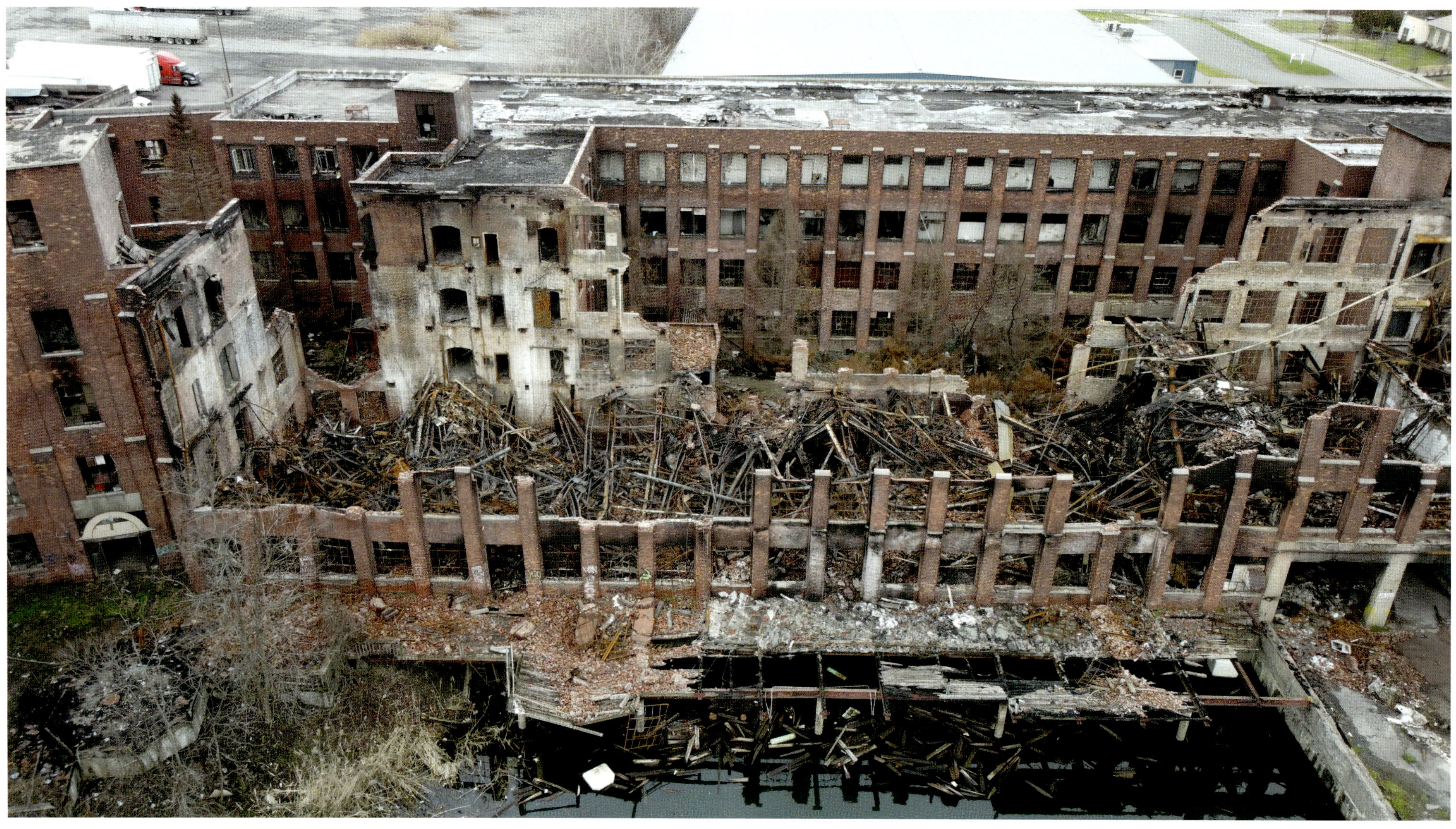

New York State Inebriate Asylum

BINGHAMTON

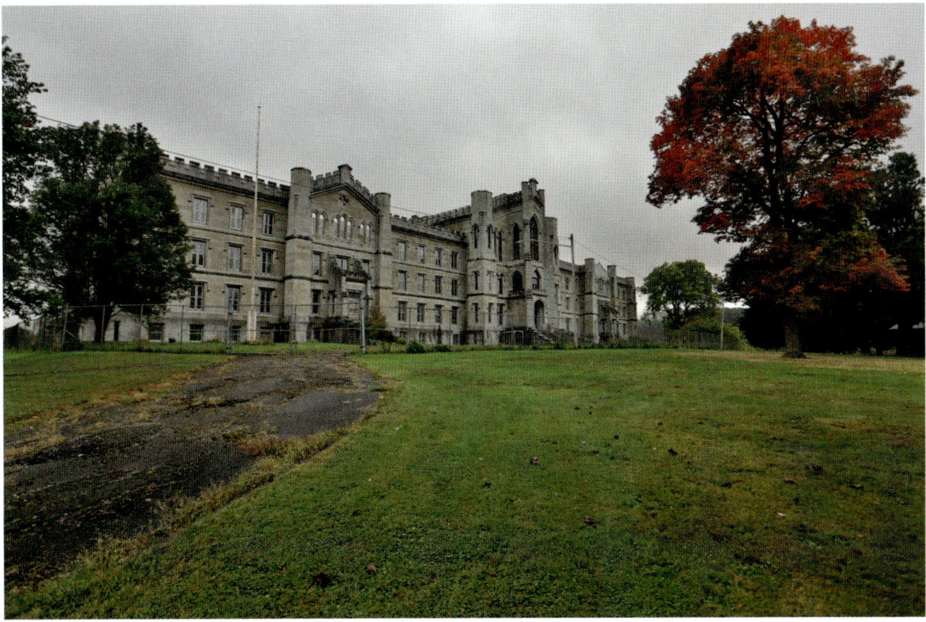

New York State Inebriate Asylum

Designed in the Gothic Revival style by New York architect Isaac Perry and built in 1858, the New York State Inebriate Asylum was the nation's first single-purpose hospital founded for the treatment of alcoholism, guided by the theory that alcoholism, like insanity, was a disease that required institutionalization. The asylum would serve this purpose for fifteen years until it was converted into Binghamton State Hospital, treating the chronically insane. As modern medicinal treatments for the insane were introduced, Binghamton State Hospital would fall into a steep decline before finally closing in 1993.

CHAPTER 6.

CAPITAL REGION

Saratoga County Homestead

BARKERSVILLE

The Saratoga County Homestead sits idly on a hill in the tranquil yet remote hamlet of Barkersville, New York, some 15 miles outside Saratoga Springs. Once a valiant hospital of its time, the homestead now resembles something out of an Edgar Allan Poe work of horror. Motorists on County Highway 16 slow down to admire its four regal-like columns of the road-facing facade. Decades of vandalism and decay give the building an ominous aura. Abandoned since 1973, the homestead served several purposes during its short period of operation, most notably being a tuberculosis hospital serving Saratoga County. While its history is short and seemingly less grandiose compared to New York City's Neponsit Beach and Sea View Hospitals of the time, the homestead served patients throughout the tuberculosis crisis that plagued much of New York during the first half of the century.

In 1909, New York State legislature mandated that every county open sanatoriums and hospitals to deal with the ongoing tuberculosis crisis, which had reached near-epidemic proportions by the end of the nineteenth century. Barkersville in 1914 saw the opening of the Homestead Sanatorium as a refuge from consumption for the people of Saratoga County. The property was described as a "secluded, well-wooded area with sweet and wholesome air." In the beginning, the sanatorium could accommodate and treat twenty-four patients. As the cases of tuberculosis in New York State increased, the homestead would undergo a massive expansion in 1936—its wooden structure being replaced by brick, embellished with decorative moldings, marble columns, and large windows and solariums to circulate the fresh Adirondack mountain air that was thought essential to the treatment process.

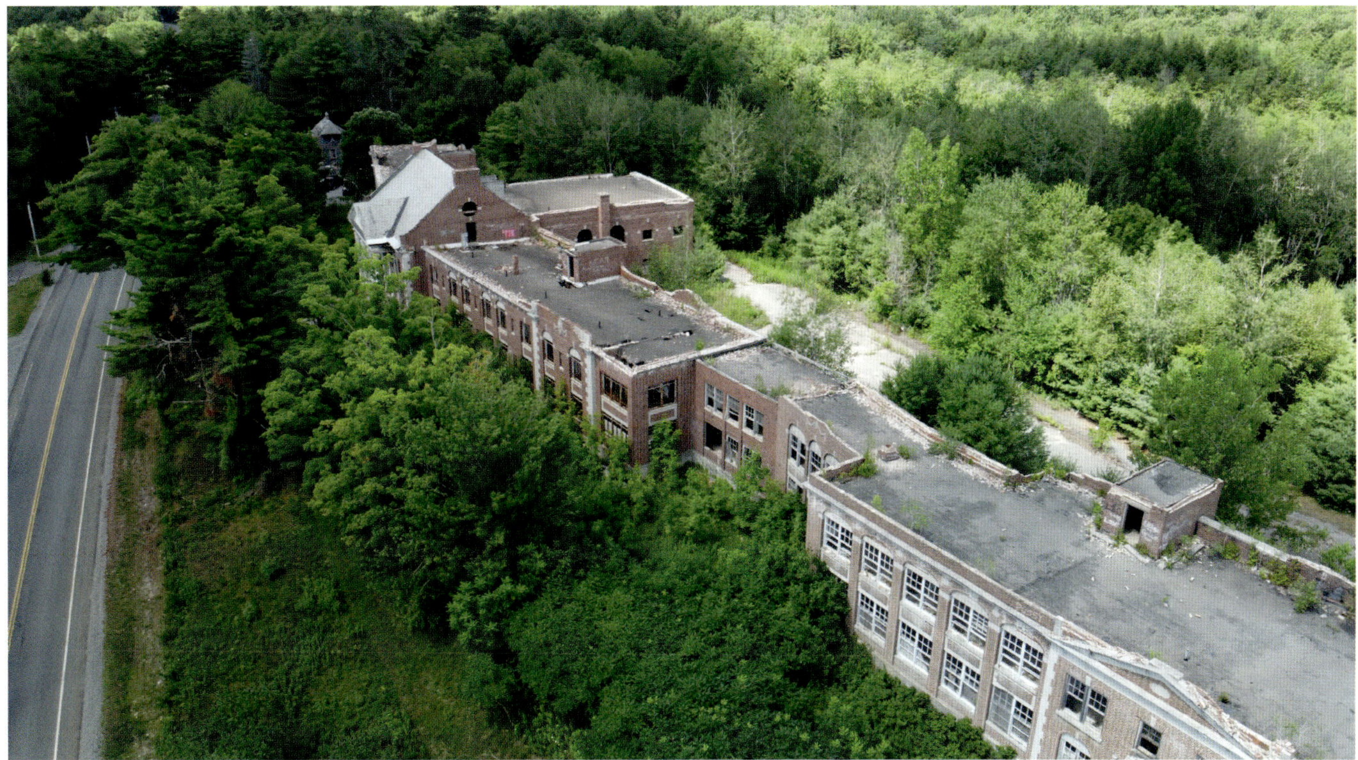

Aerial view of Saratoga County Homestead

Patients under the care of the homestead had a strict regimen of rest. Exercise was closely monitored. Dancing as well as alcohol, cigarettes, and foul language was prohibited according to the sanatorium's handbook. In order to reduce the risk of infection, patients were not allowed to carry handkerchiefs. Instead, patients carried a sputum box that collected phlegm, which in turn was collected by doctors to test for tuberculosis. Children patients attended school at the homestead and often attended class shirtless so that the fresh air could better penetrate their lungs.

By 1960, the development of antibiotics such as streptomycin led to the phaseout of sanatoriums across the country. Neponsit Beach Hospital in Queens had already closed as a tuberculosis sanatorium and was in the process of reopening as a nursing home. Staten Island's Sea View Hospital, which was instrumental in finding the cure for TB, closed in 1961. The last patients of Saratoga County Homestead left in August 1960, and it became the Saratoga County Infirmary the next year. It would treat geriatric patients until 1973, when it closed for good.

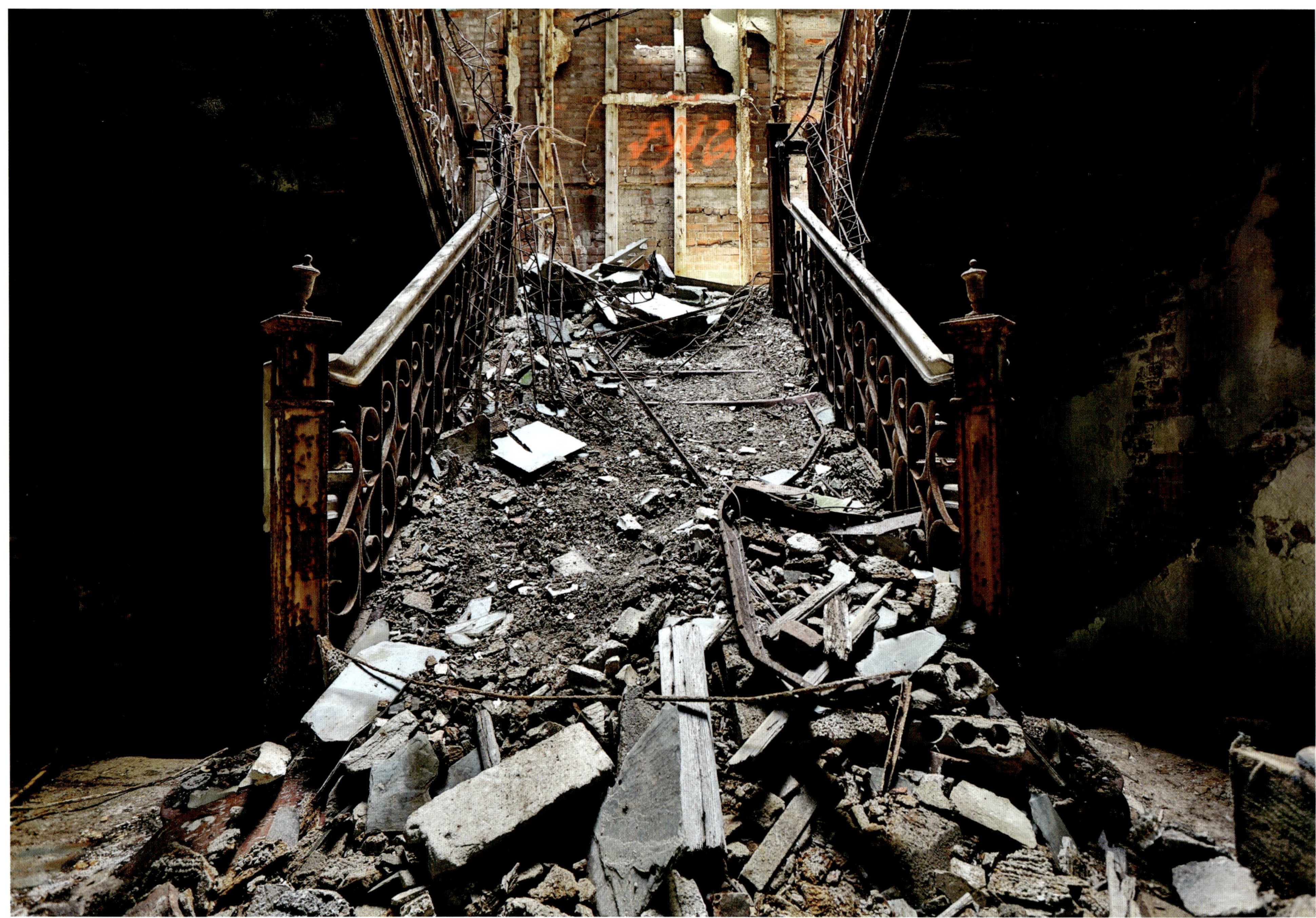

Main stairwell, Saratoga County Homestead

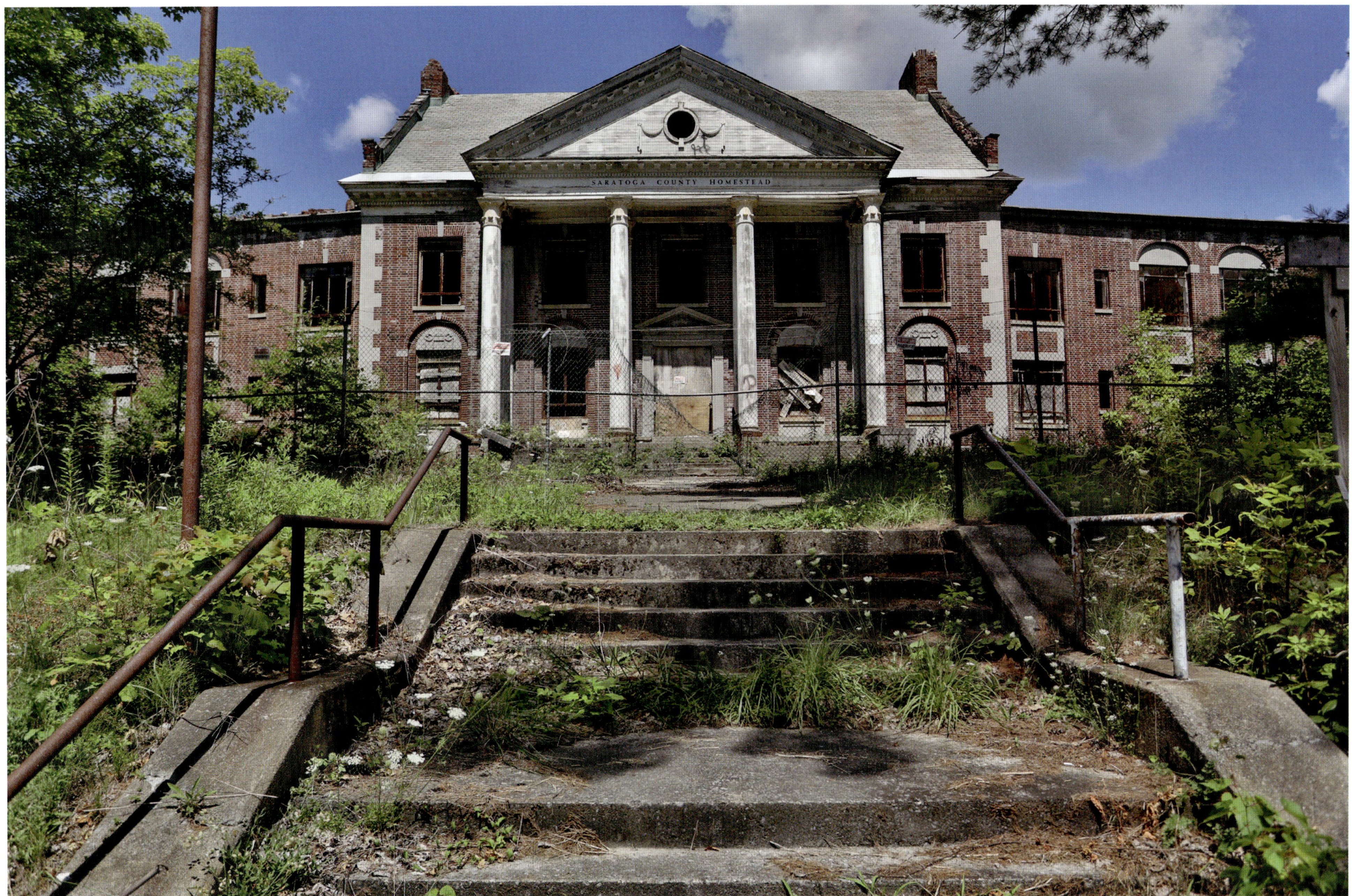

Front entrance, Saratoga County Homestead

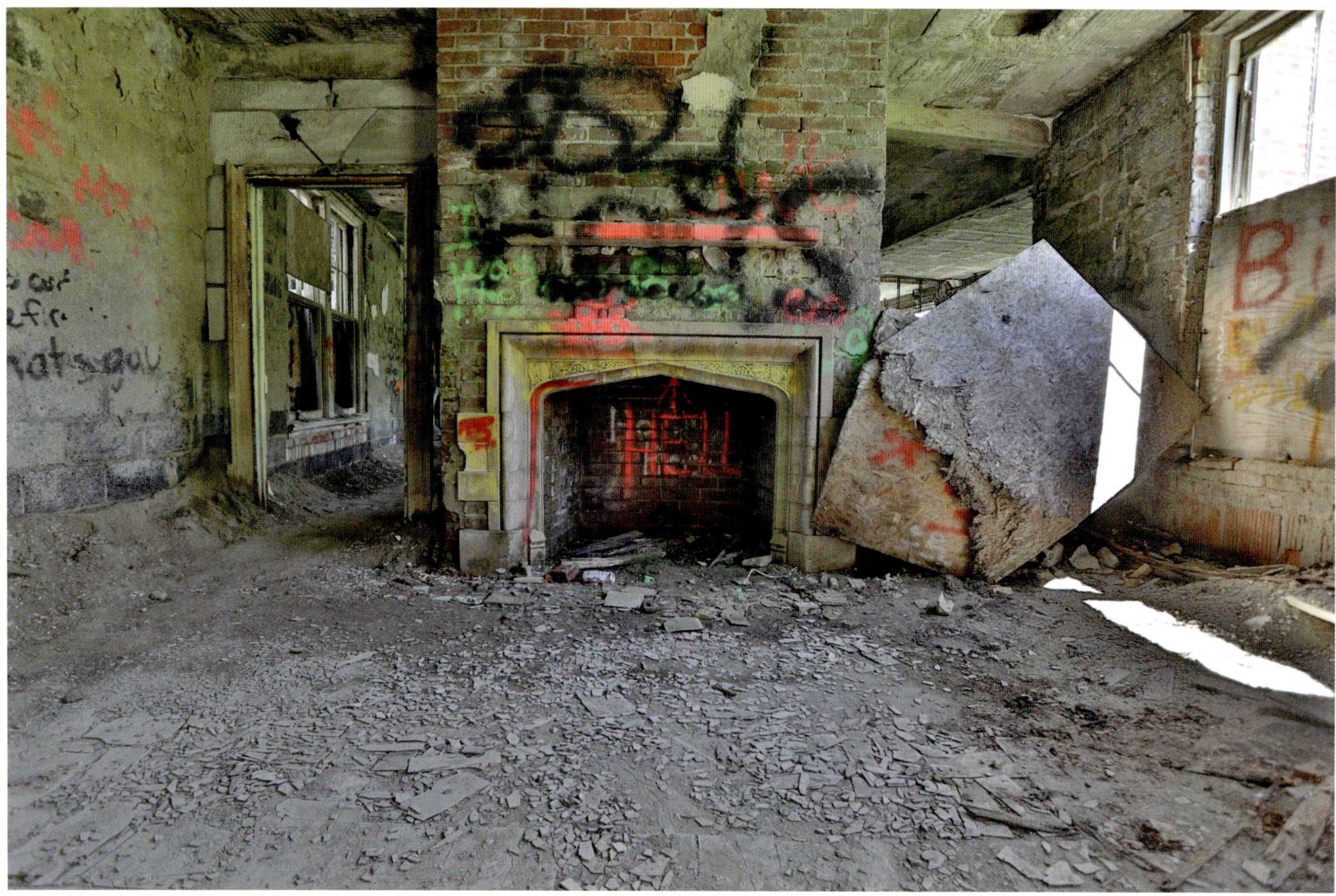

Drawing room, Saratoga County Homestead

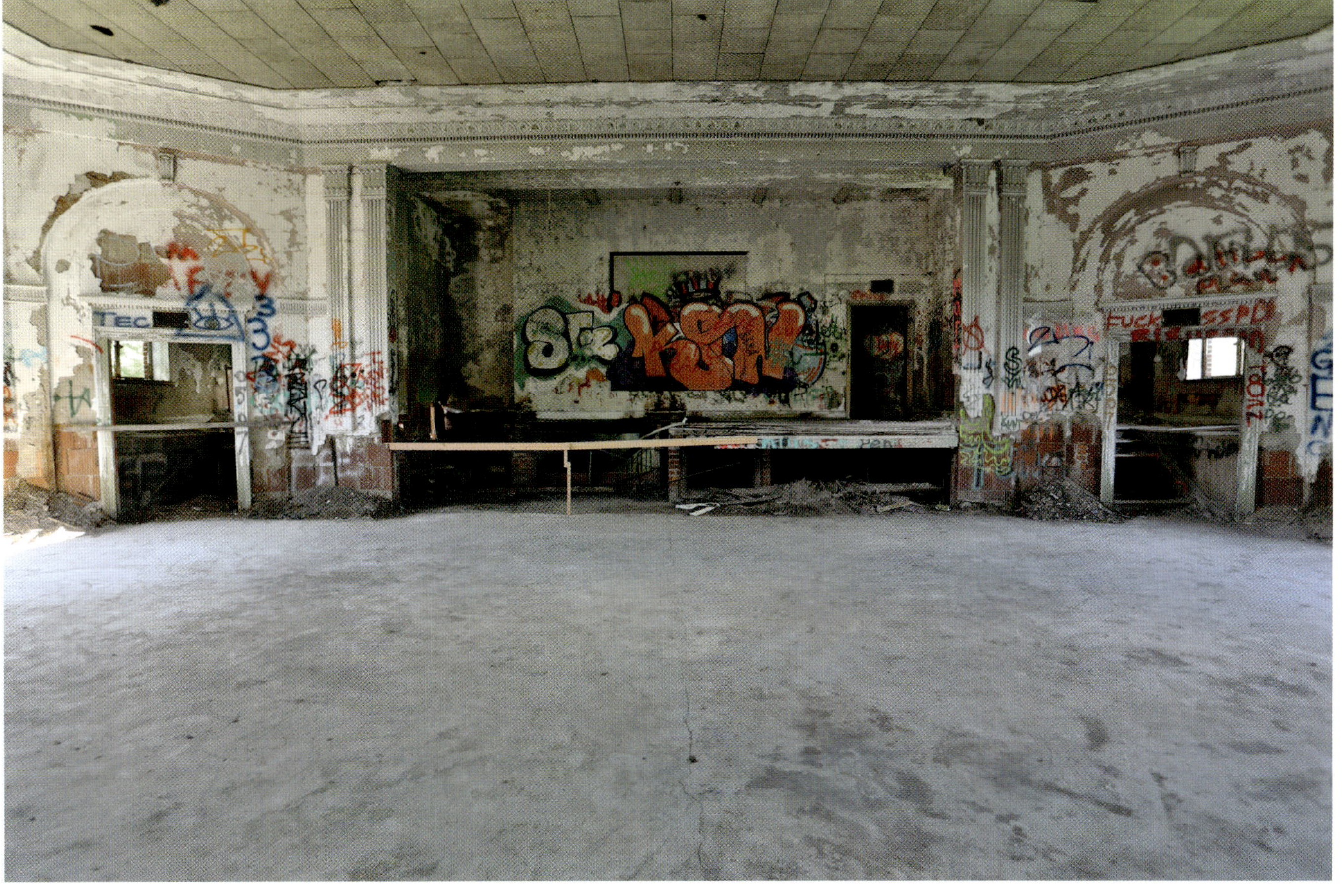

Theater, Saratoga County Homestead

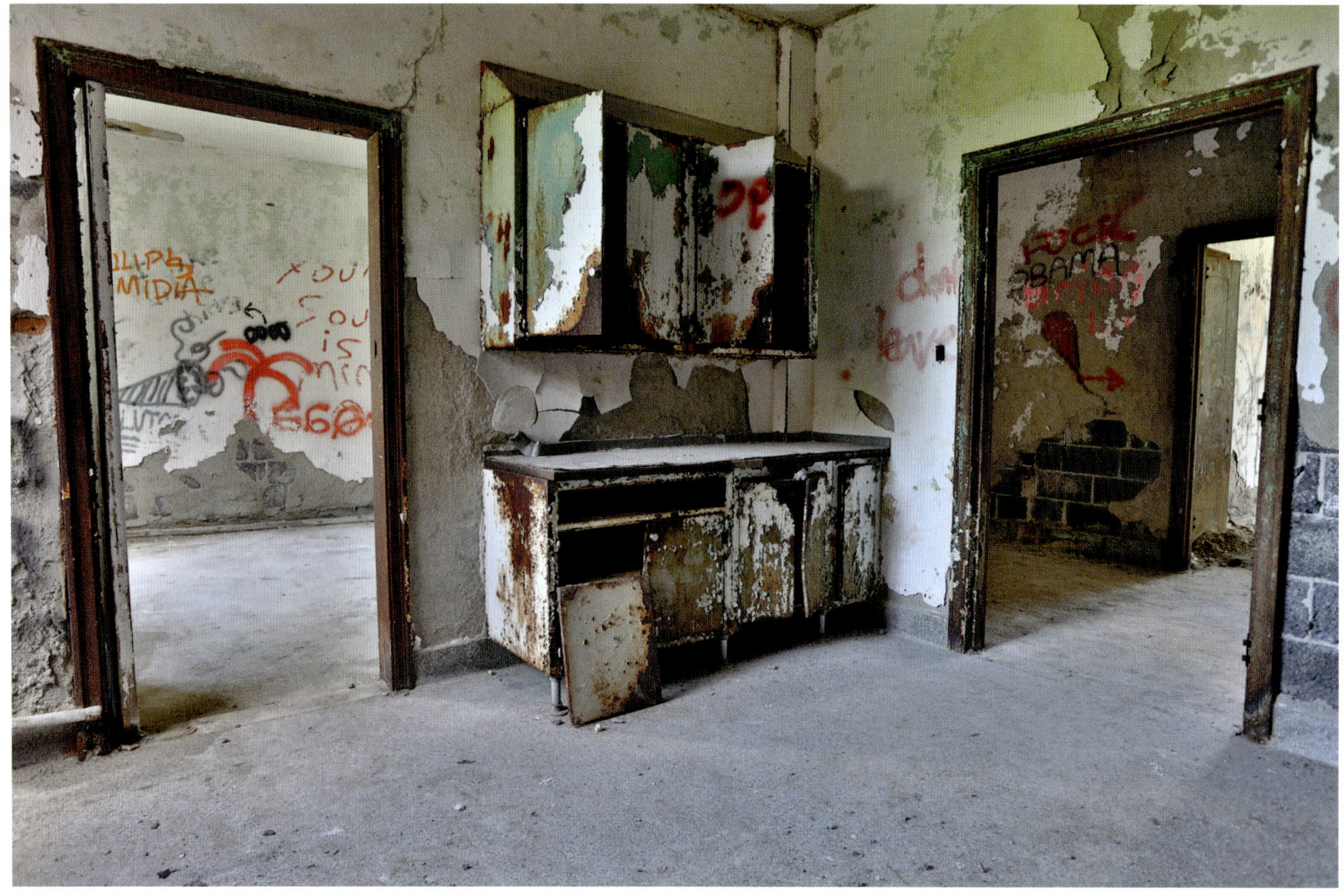

Medication room, Saratoga County Homestead

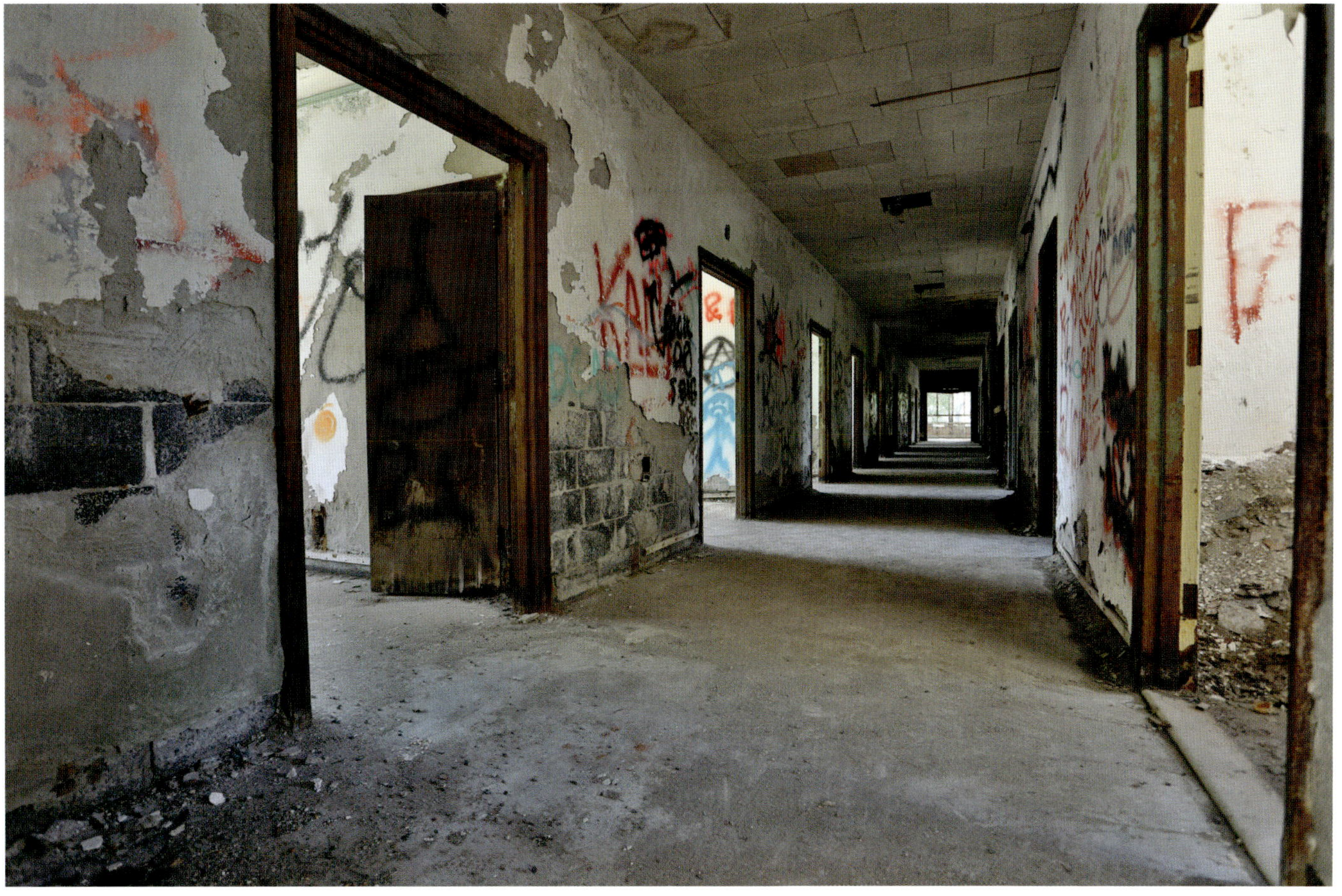

Male patient ward, Saratoga County Homestead

AL Tech Specialty Steel

WATERVLIET

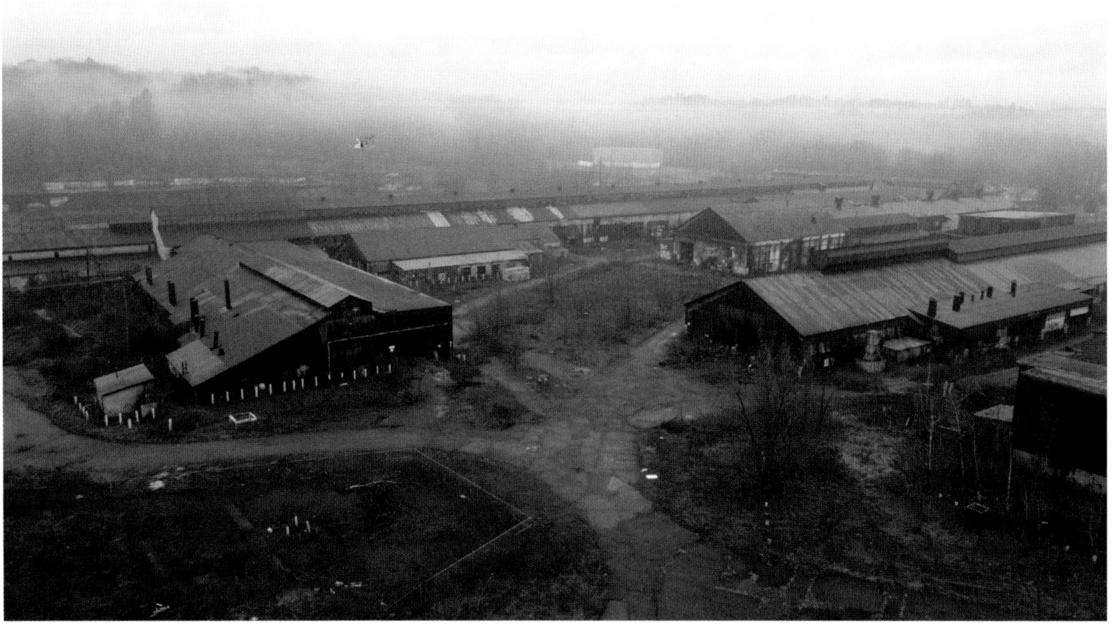

AL Tech Specialty Steel produced a myriad of steel parts for auto, medical, and aeronautical industries from 1908 until it went out of business in 1999. At the height of its operations during World War II, AL Tech employed five thousand workers.

The plant was started by the Corning family as the Ludlow Steel Company, which merged with Pittsburgh's Allegheny Steel Company in the 1930s and then became AL Tech Specialty Steel in 1976.

By 2019, AL Tech was listed as a Class 2 on the New York State Registry of Inactive Hazardous Waste Sites. The site is uninhabitable due to decades of pollution from the disposal of coal ash and the discard of acids for the pickling of steel transformers and capacitors, as well as the dispersal of electric arc furnace dust containing chromium. Proposed remediation included the removal of over 6,000 cubic yards of soil containing PCBs.

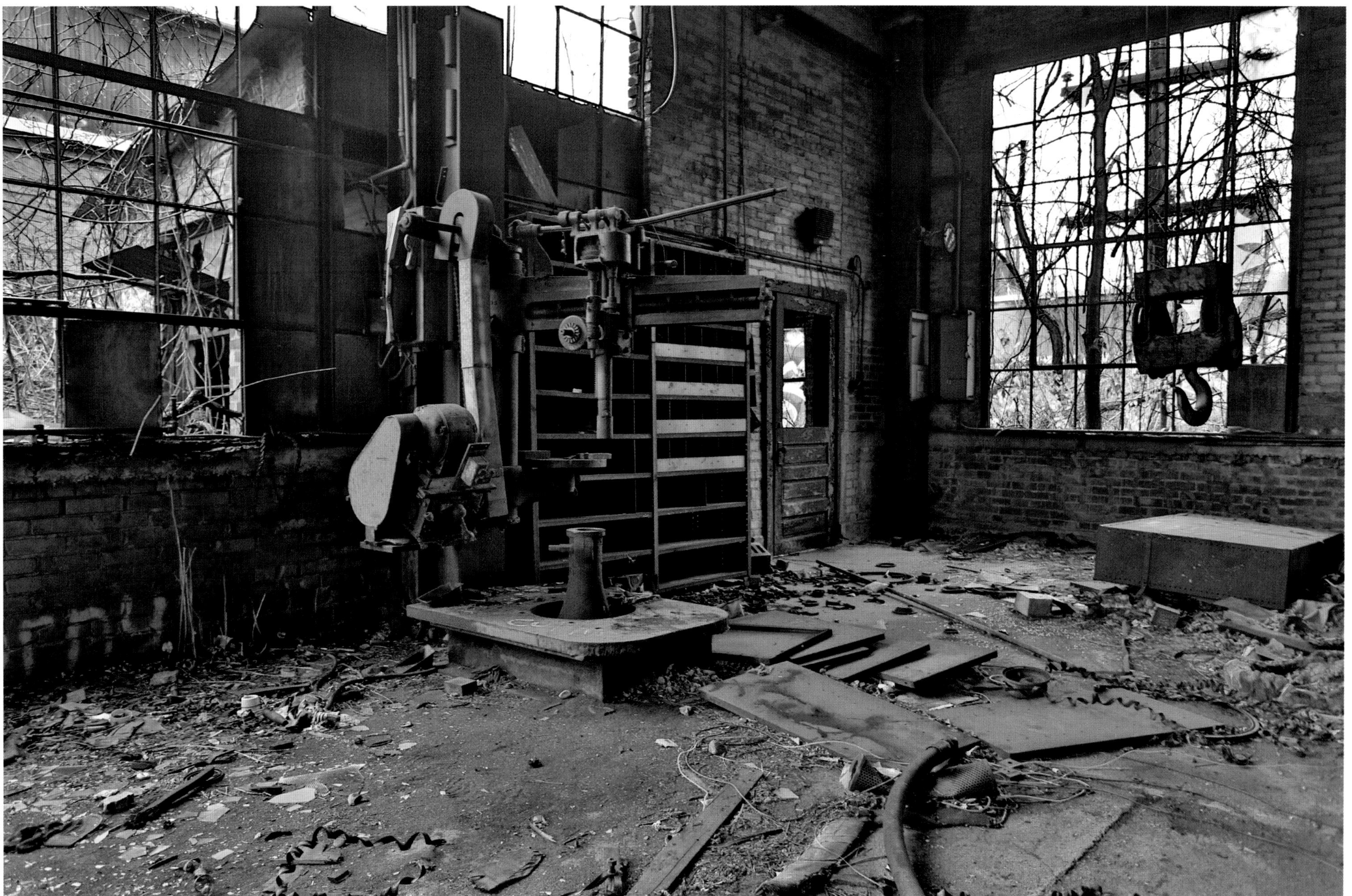

Workshop, AL Tech Specialty Steel

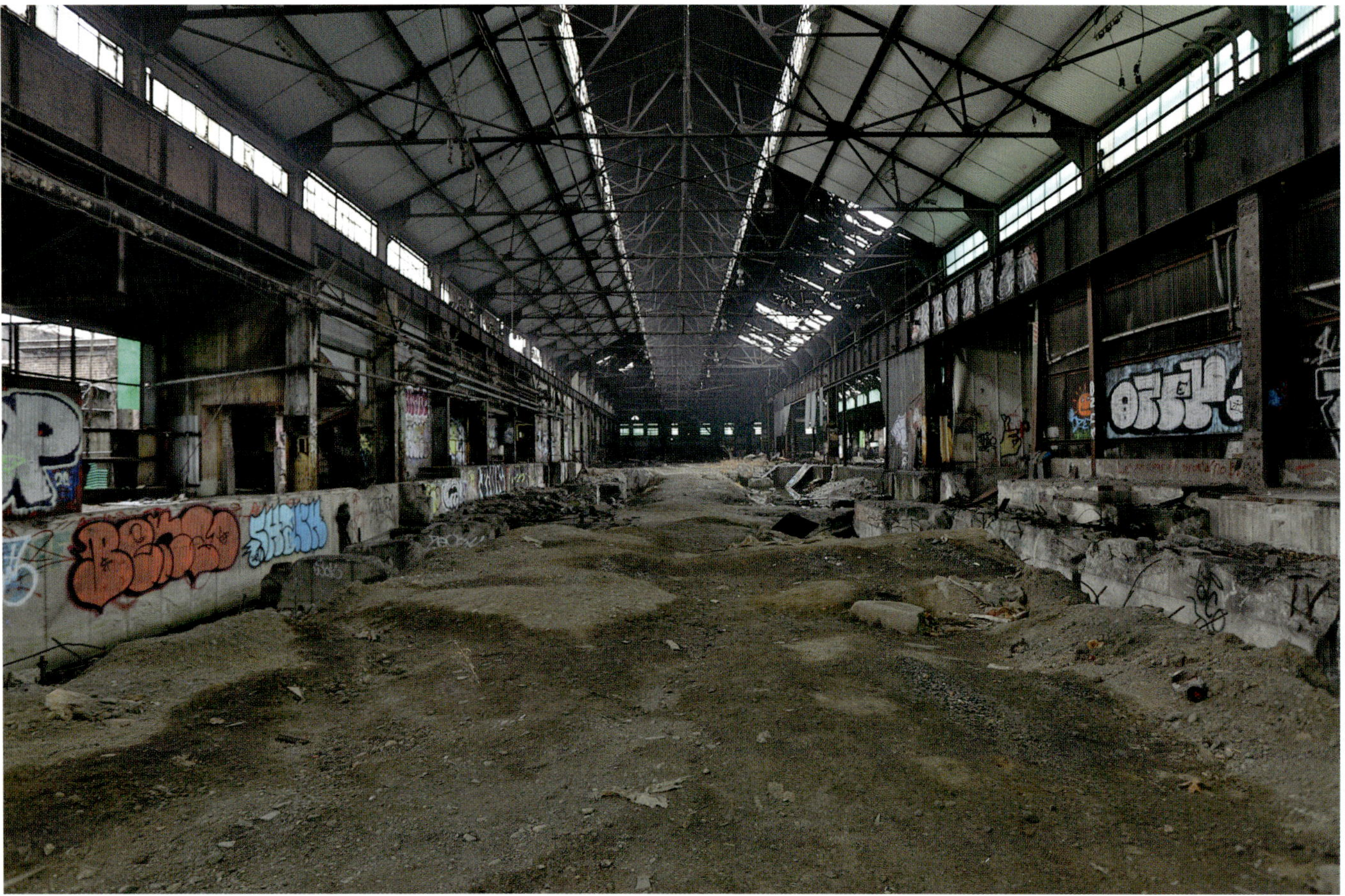

This cavernous space once served as the rolling mill, where steel was passed through rollers in order to reduce its thickness.

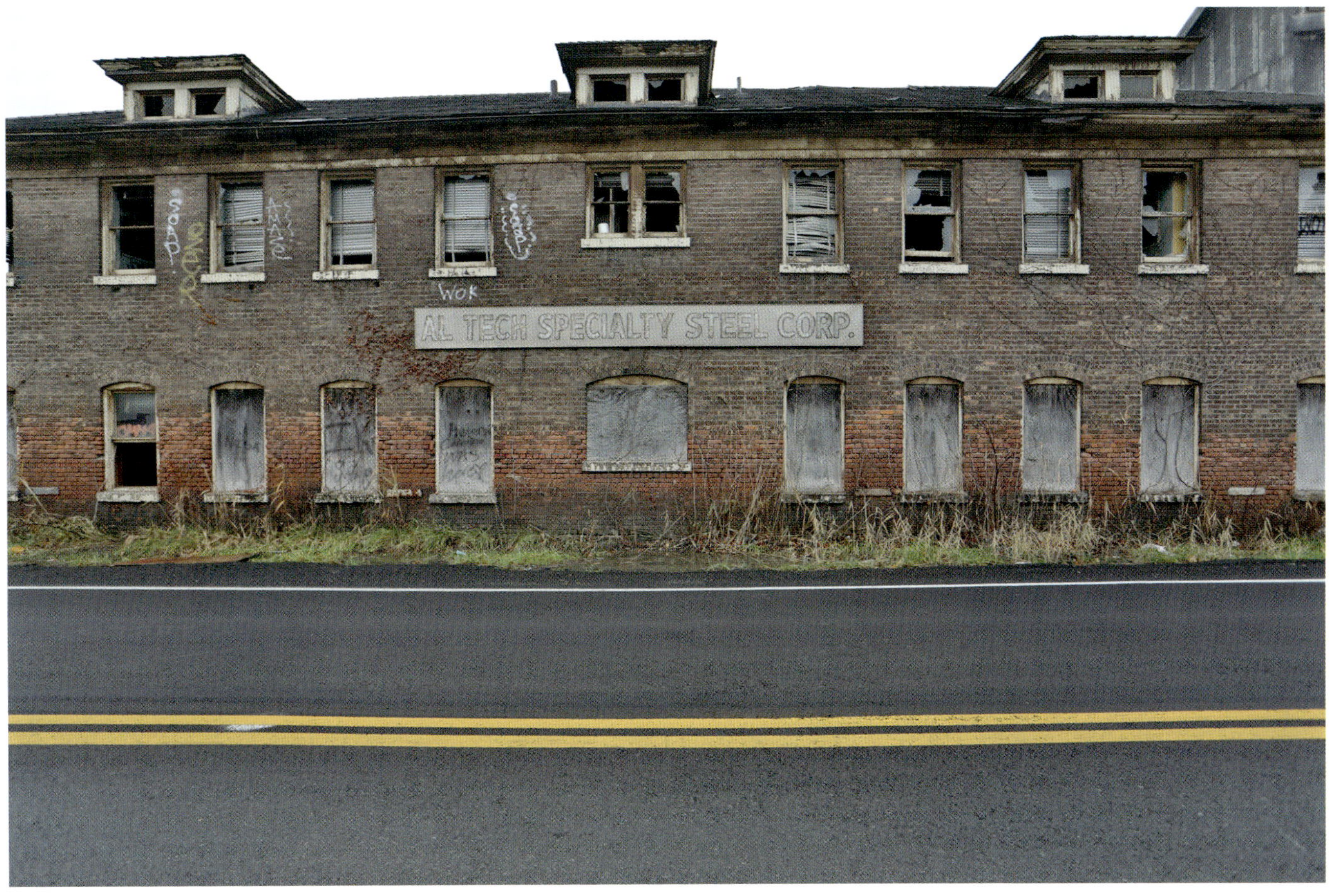

Office building, AL Tech Specialty Steel

St. Joseph's Roman Catholic Church

ALBANY

After 1850, almost every town and city in the Northeast had a Roman Catholic church designed by architect Patrick Keely dominating the skyline. Over his fifty-year architectural career, Keely designed nearly six hundred North American churches, including Albany's St. Joseph's Roman Catholic Church, which was finished in 1860.

St. Joseph's served Albany until 1994, when a steep decline in attendance and finances ultimately led to its closure.

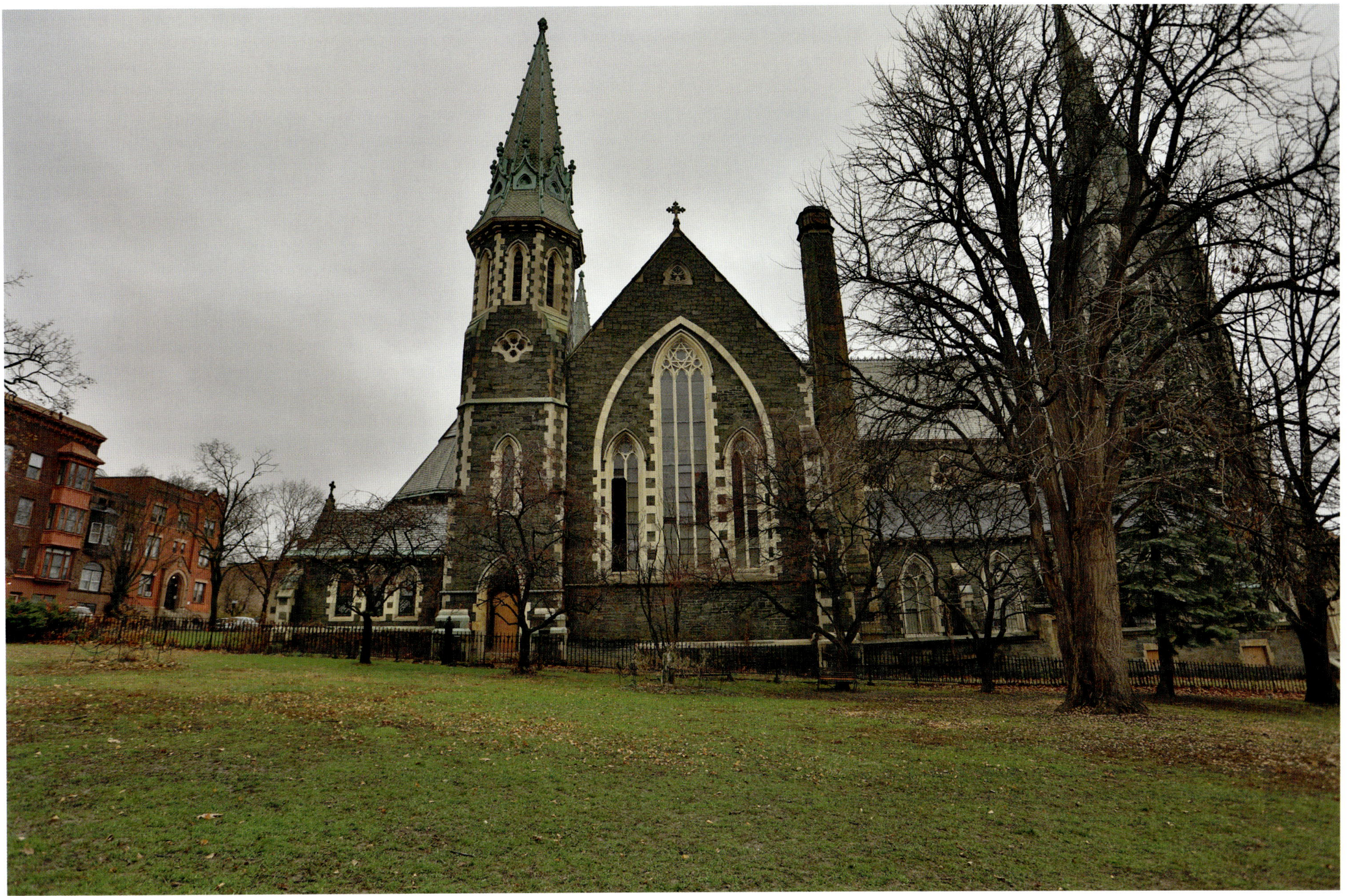

Side view of St. Joseph's

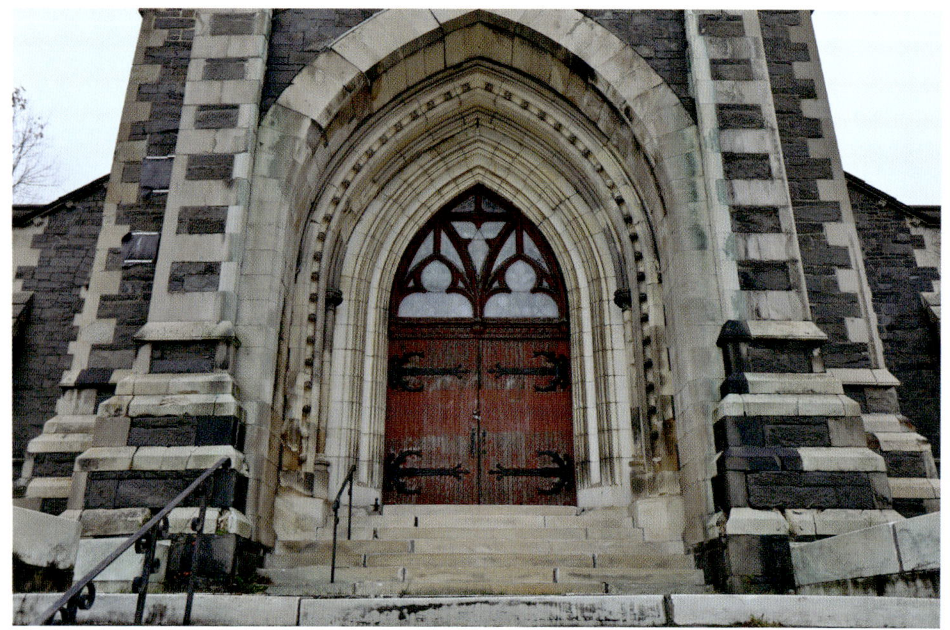

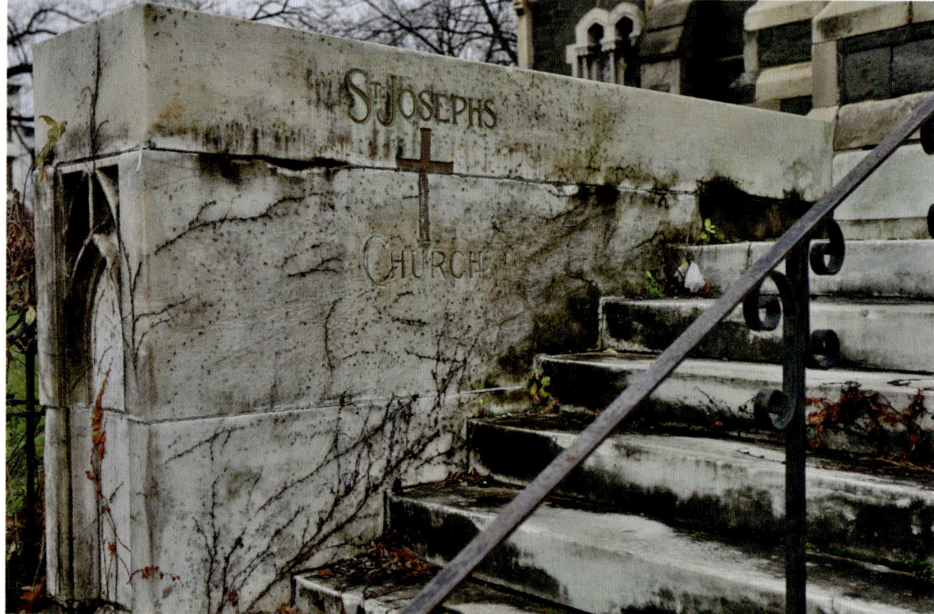

Front entrance, St. Joseph's

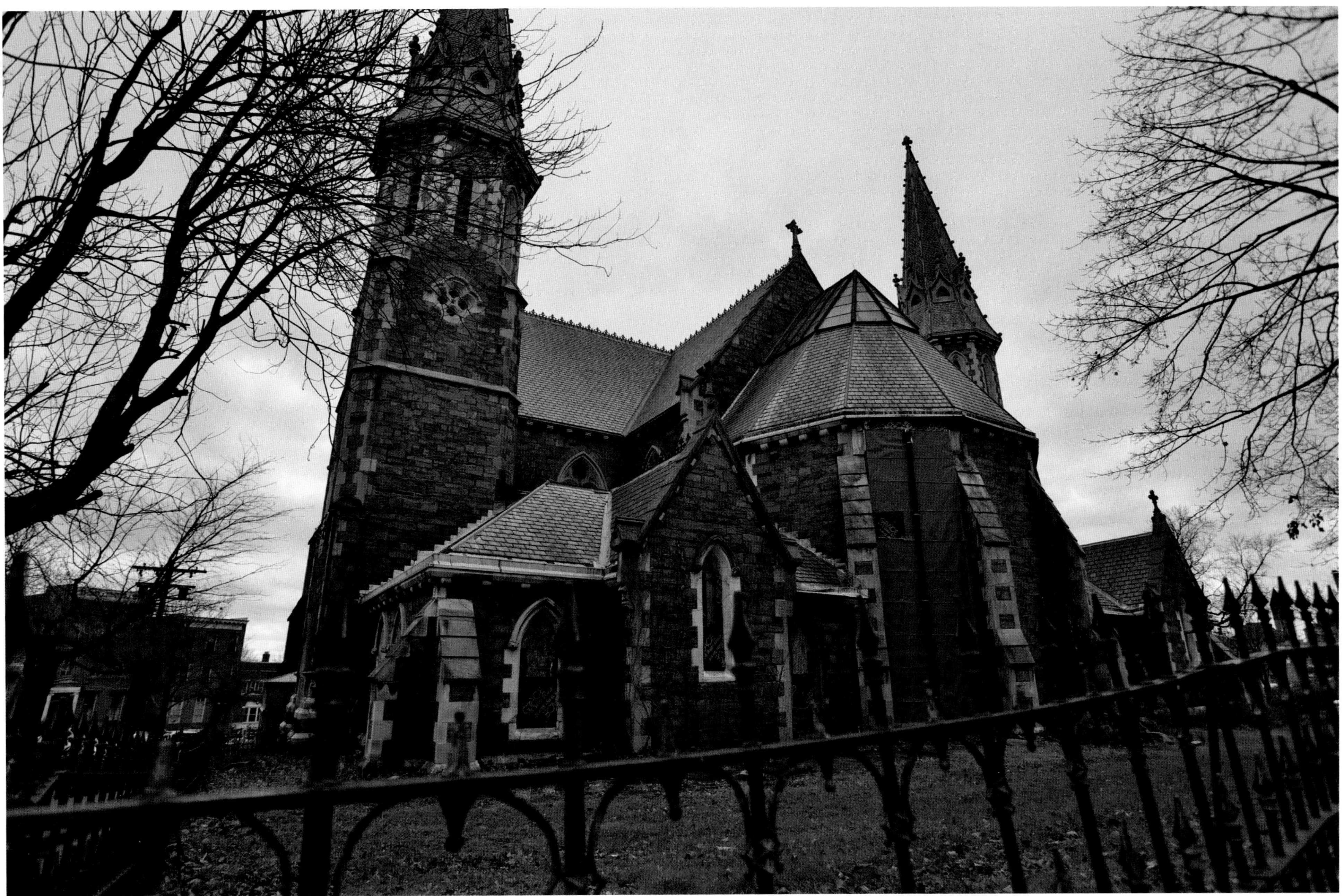

Rear view of St. Joseph's

Central Warehouse

ALBANY

Heading northbound or southbound on Interstate 787 outside Albany, one cannot miss the eyesore and regional landmark that is the Central Warehouse. This eleven-story, 508,000-square-foot cube-like structure was built in 1927 and served as a refrigerated food-storage facility. Its steel-and-concrete design insulated with cork and cooled with ammonia was capable of storing enough food to feed all of Albany for several months.

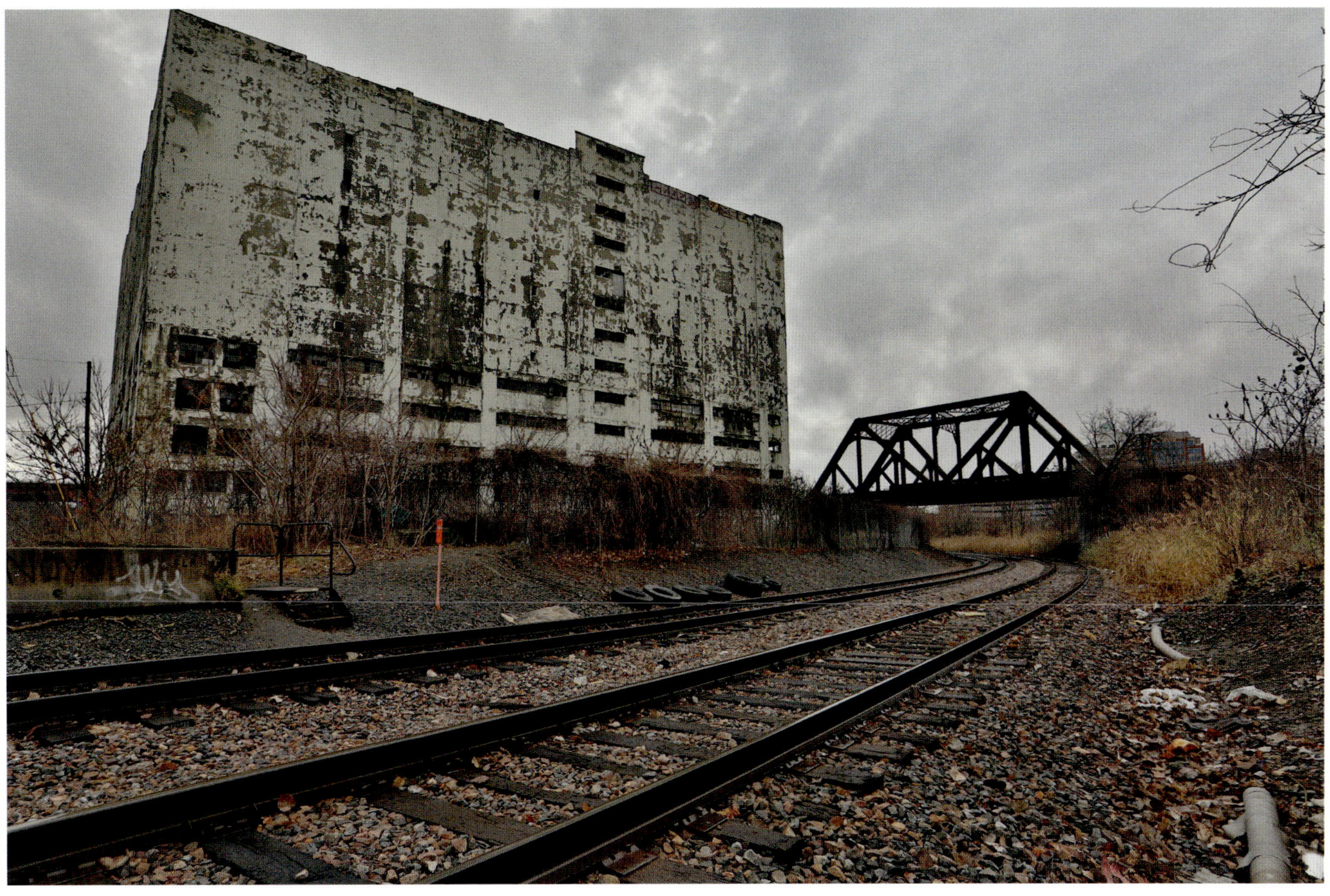

Central Warehouse

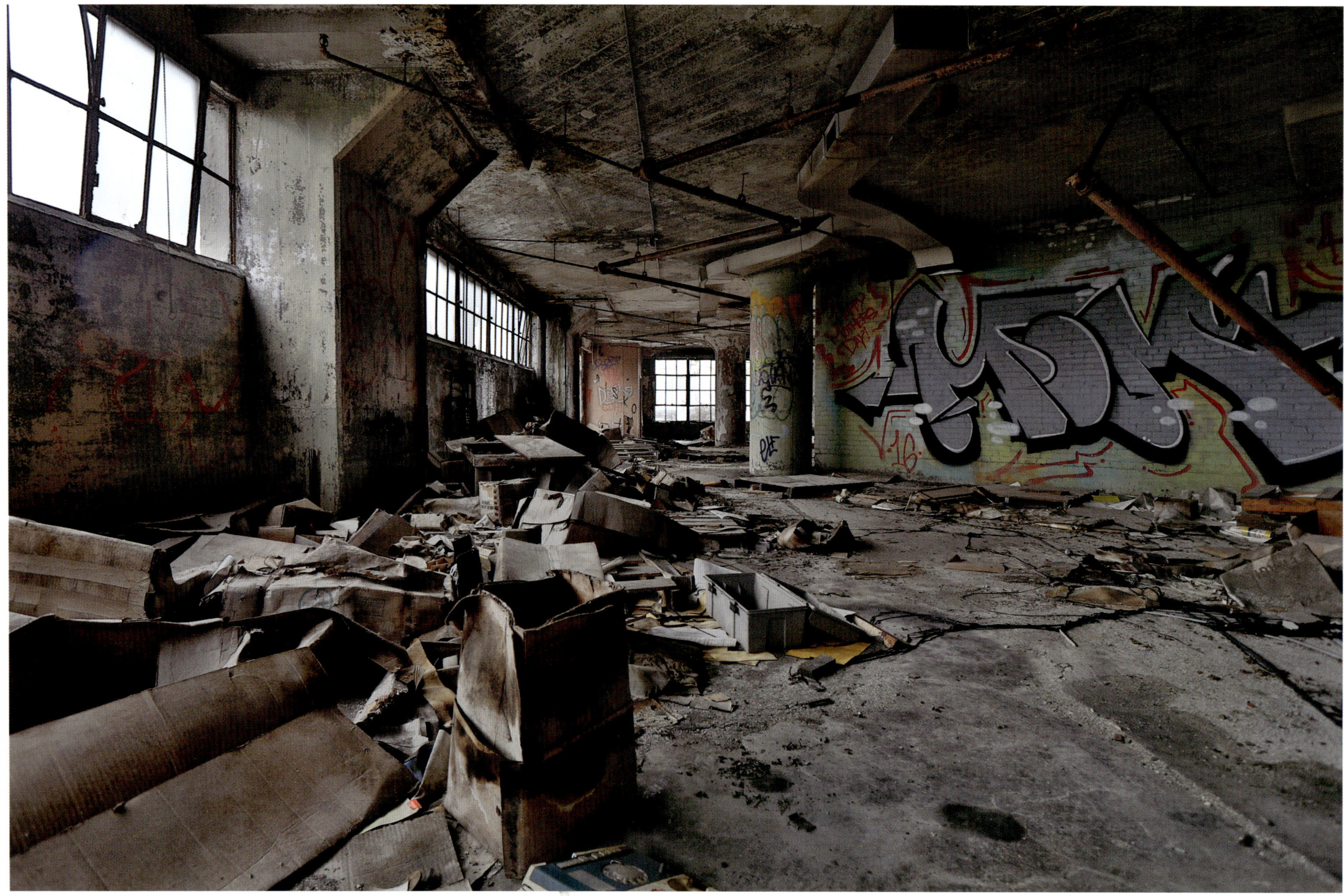

Storage floor, Central Warehouse

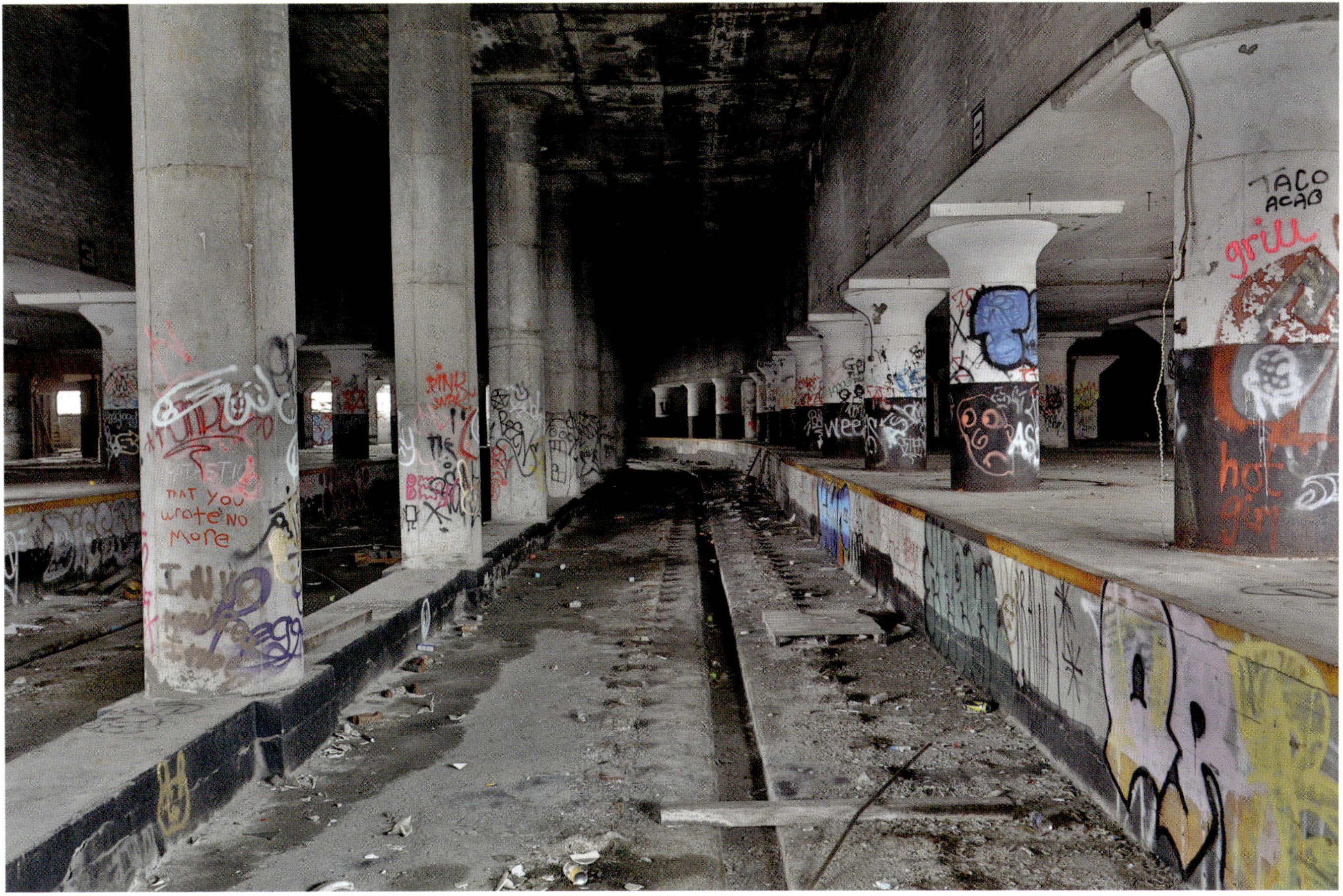

This railroad spur diverted into the warehouse, allowing goods to be unloaded and moved into storage via freight elevators.

CHAPTER 7.

ADIRONDACK REGION

Tahawus Upper Works

NEWCOMB

Throughout the nineteenth century, the Adirondack Mountains were explored by zealous prospectors looking to extract natural resources and secure new business opportunities in the region. In 1826, industrialist Archibald McIntyre and his partner David Henderson, along with the help of a Native American guide from the Saint Francis tribe, discovered iron ore deposits near the headwaters of the Hudson River, toward the base of Mt. Marcy. Together they started the Adirondack Iron & Steel Company, a mining operation that was extracting ore at the rate of 12–14 tons per day. A small village, later named Adirondac, was cut into the virgin forest around the operation, where some four hundred men labored during peak production.

By 1857, mining operations ceased when a series of circumstances led to the abandonment of the village. Of most impact was that impurities in the iron ore, later discovered to be titanium dioxide, hindered the production process. Despite the installation of a new $43,000 blast furnace, the equipment of the time was simply not advanced enough to process the impurities in the ore. Transportation issues also plagued Adirondac. Since the rural roads leading to the mines were so inadequate, supplies shipped from Albany had to be transported on sleds. In an attempt to modernize the ironworks operation, the Sackett's Harbor & Saratoga Railroad Company surveyed a line to within a few miles of Adirondac. Soon after construction began, it became clear that the tracks would never reach the ironworks.

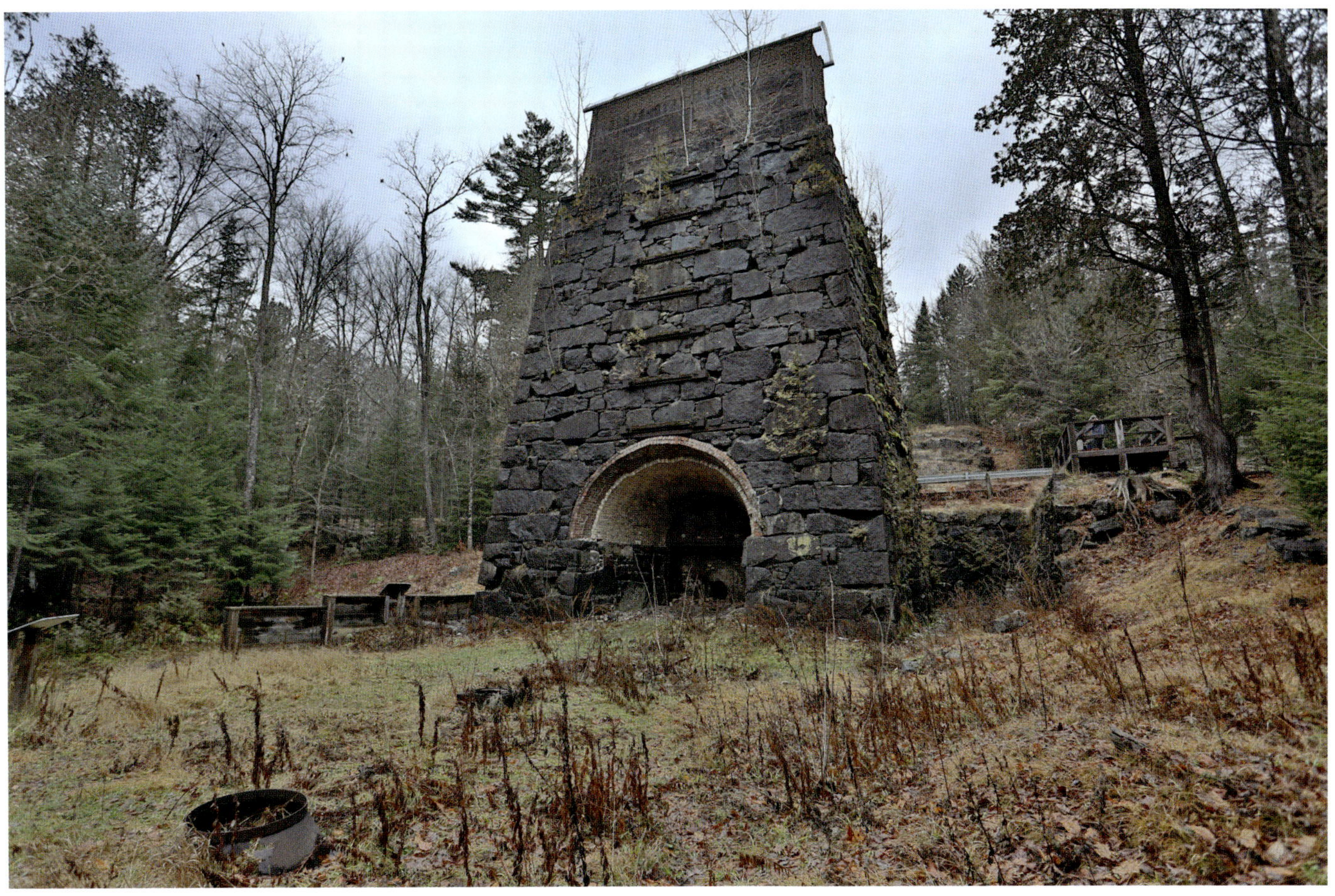

The McIntyre blast furnace was constructed in 1854 to help eliminate impurities in the iron ore.

Two decades after Adirondac became a ghost town, the Preston Ponds Club—a private fish and game club—moved into the village, renaming it Tahawus. At this time, most of the Iron Era buildings had deteriorated, so club owners rebuilt hunting lodges on the original foundations of the Adirondack Iron & Steel Company cottages. Ironically, the titanium dioxide that hindered mining operations in the 1800s served as the impetus for National Lead Industries reopening the mine prior to World War II. Hunting-club leases were terminated and the buildings were modernized for the mine workers. In 1962, after years of success, workers were transferred to Newcomb, New York, leaving Tahawus to become a ghost town once again.

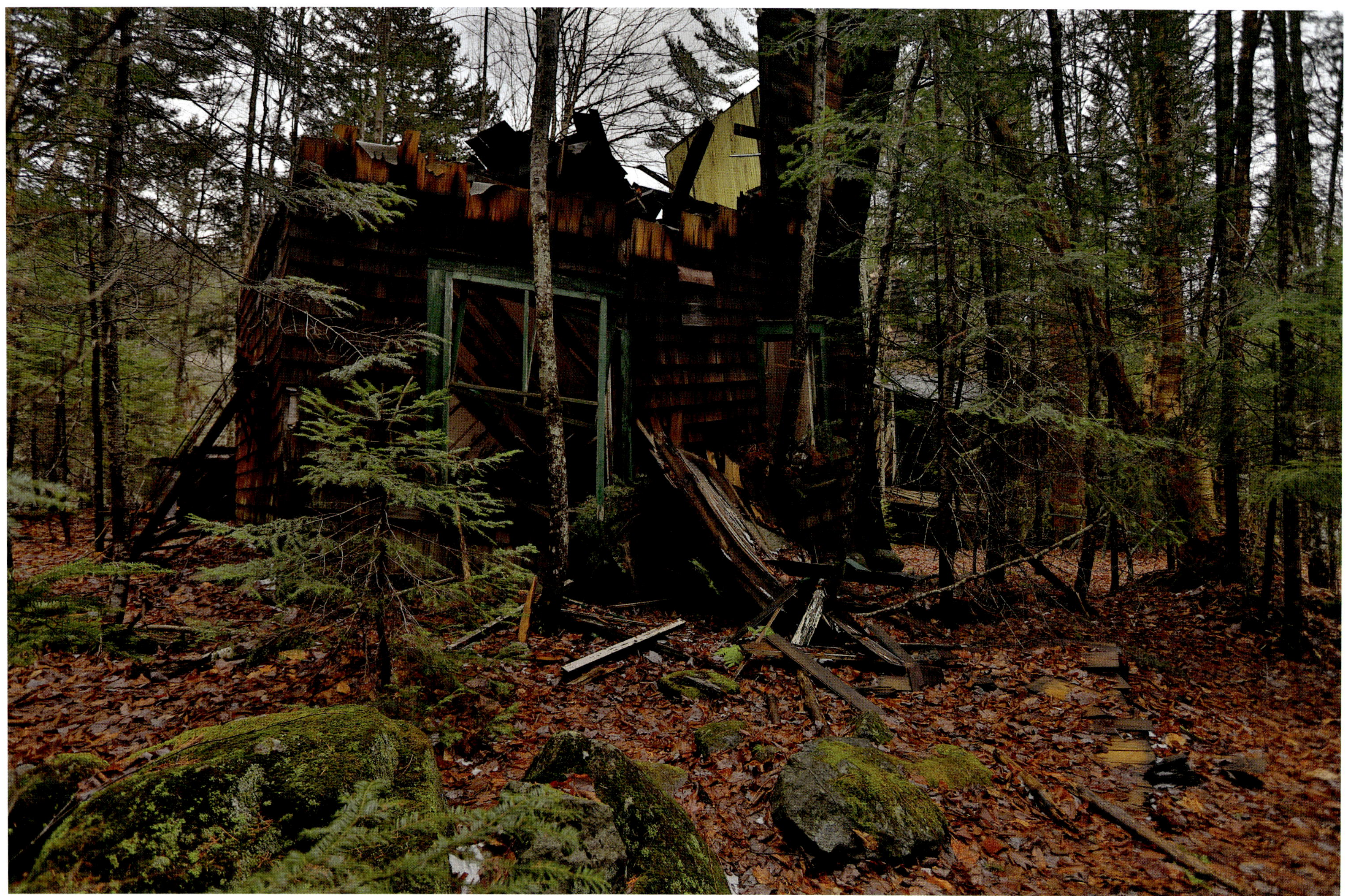

Worker's cottage, Tahawus Upper Works

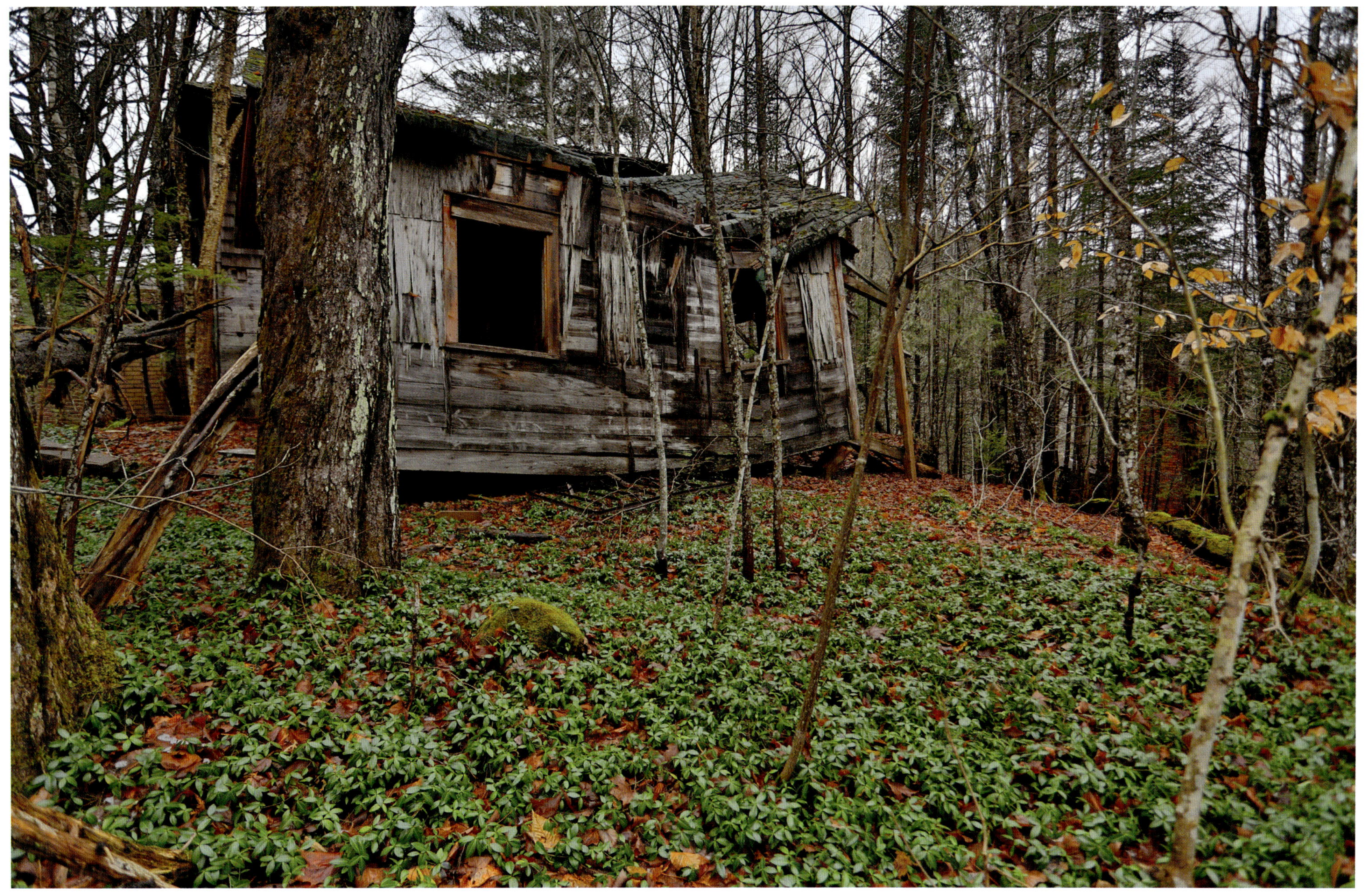

Workers' cottages, Tahawus Upper Works

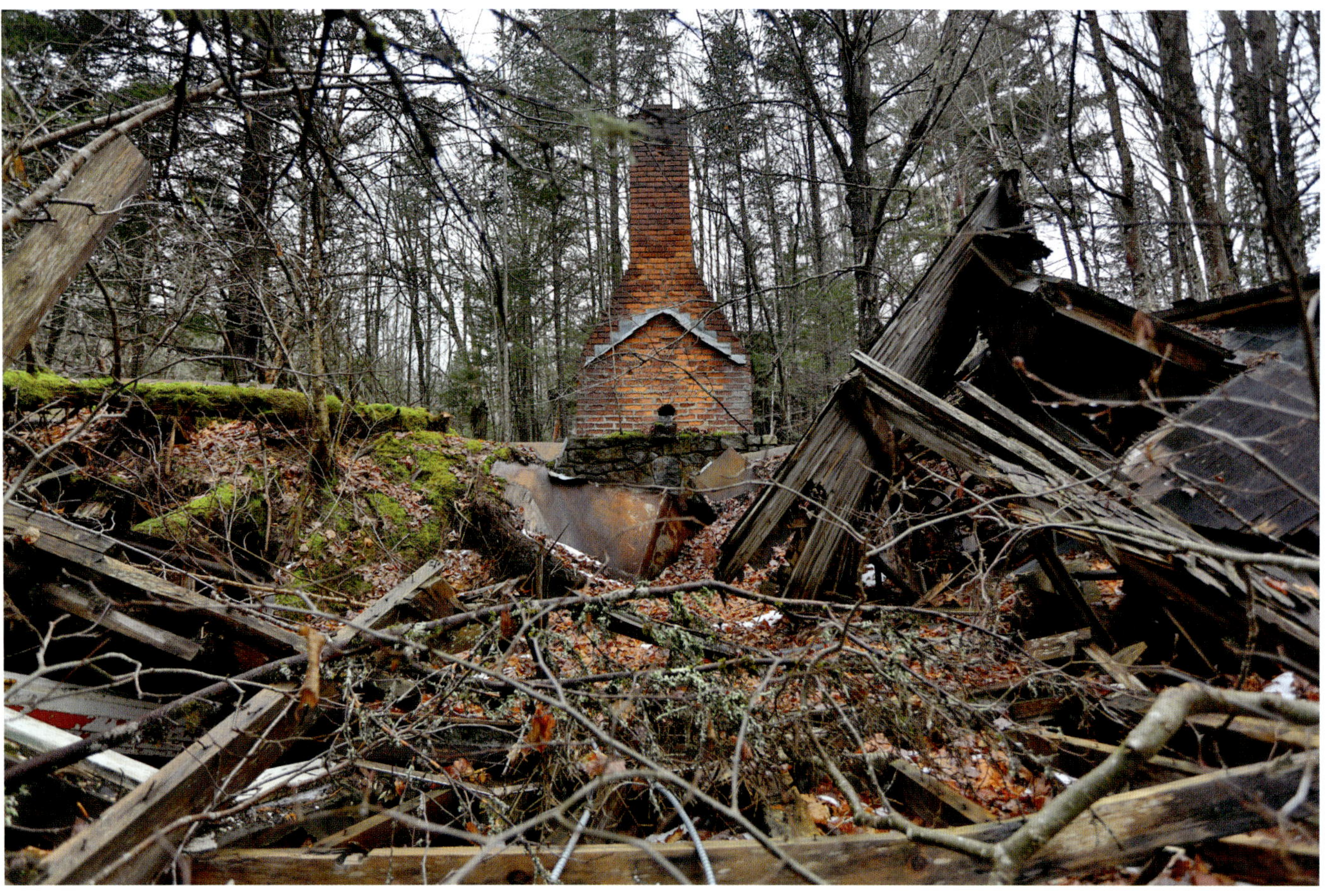

Worker's cottage, Tahawus Upper Works

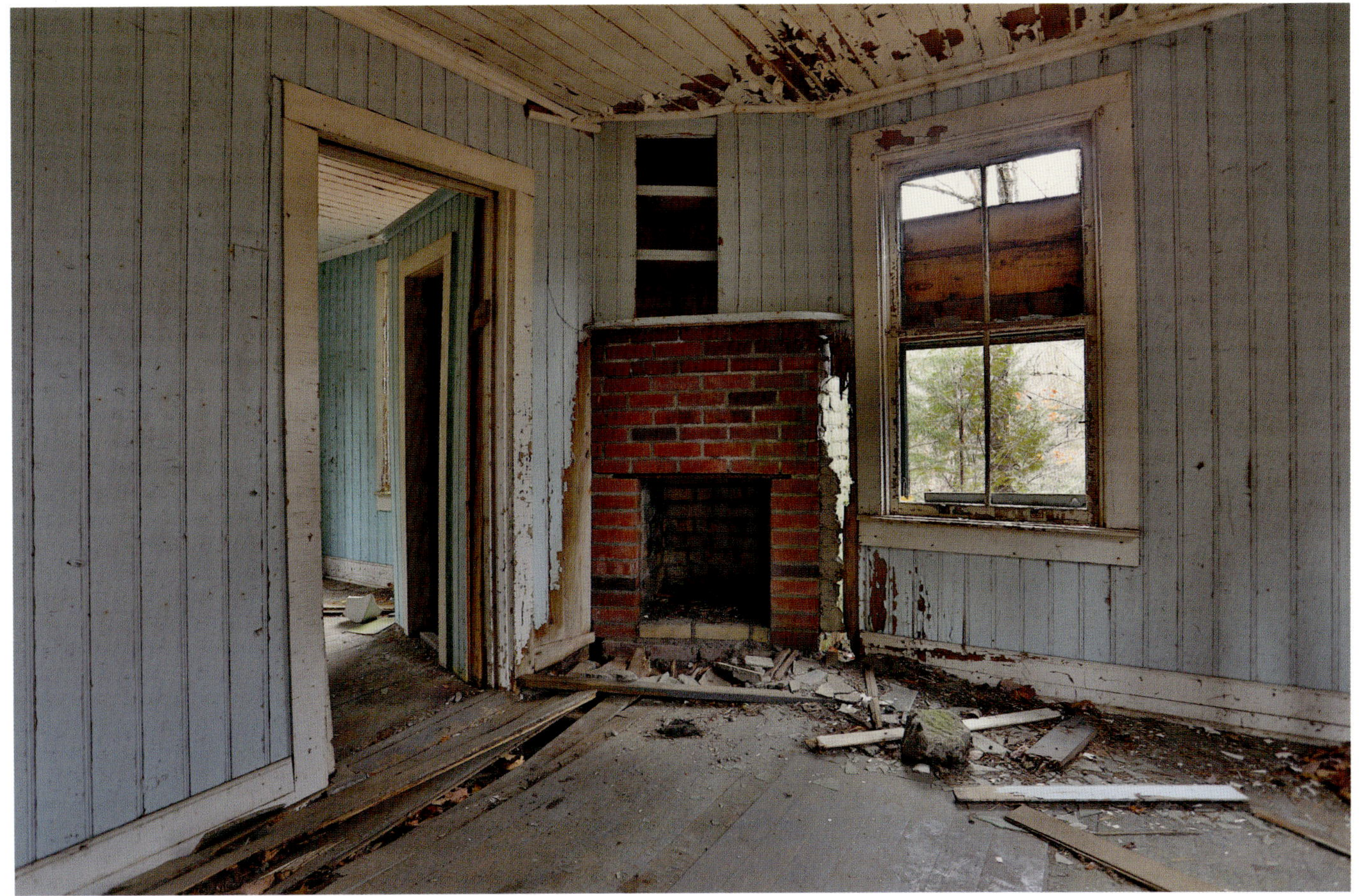

Interior of worker's cottage, Tahawus Upper Works

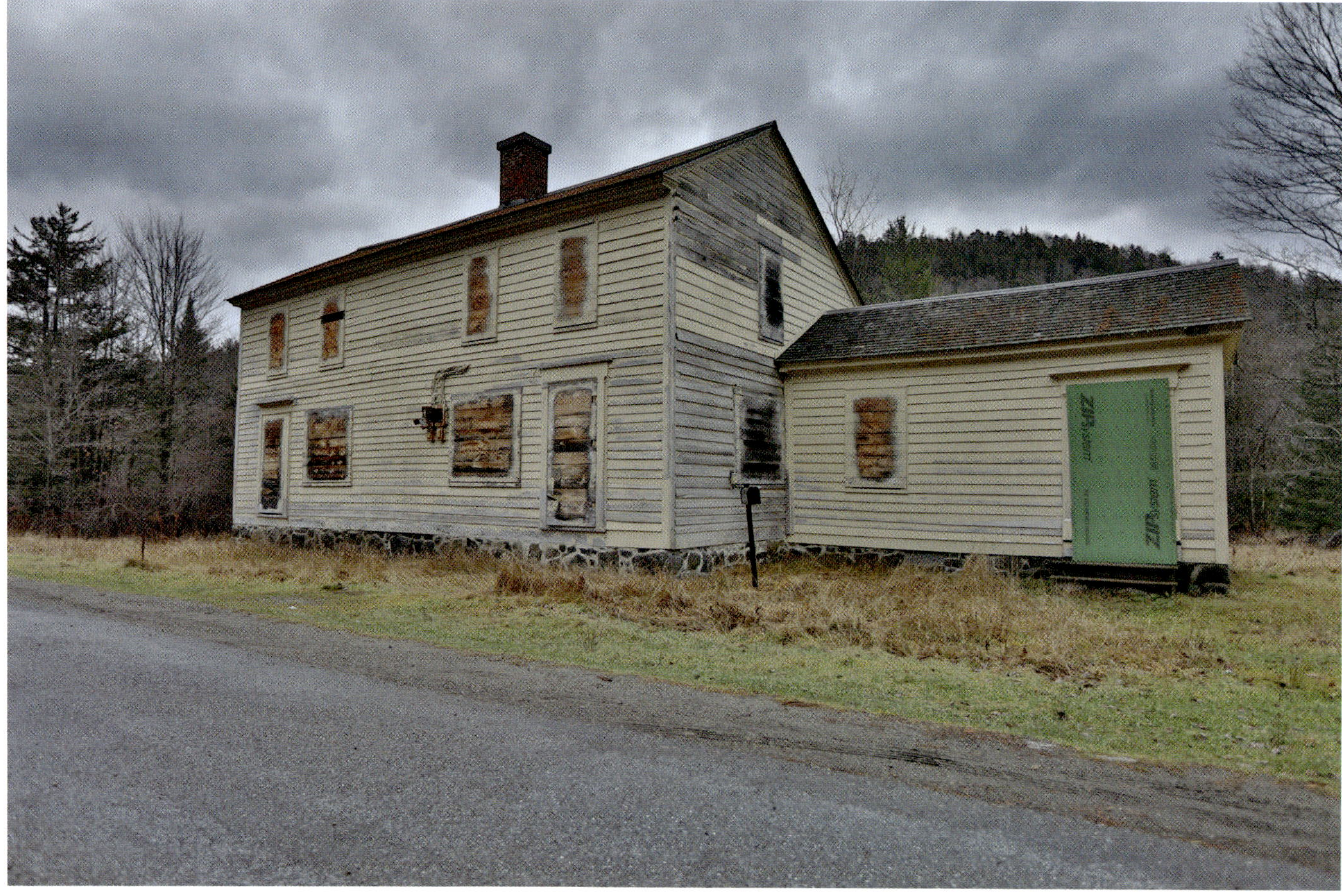

MacNaughton Cottage

The MacNaughton Cottage is the only remaining building of the Tahawus Upper Works still standing from the 1826 mining community.

In September 1901, Vice President Theodore Roosevelt and his family were staying at this cottage when they received word that President William McKinley was dying after being shot in Buffalo.

Mary McClellan Hospital

CAMBRIDGE

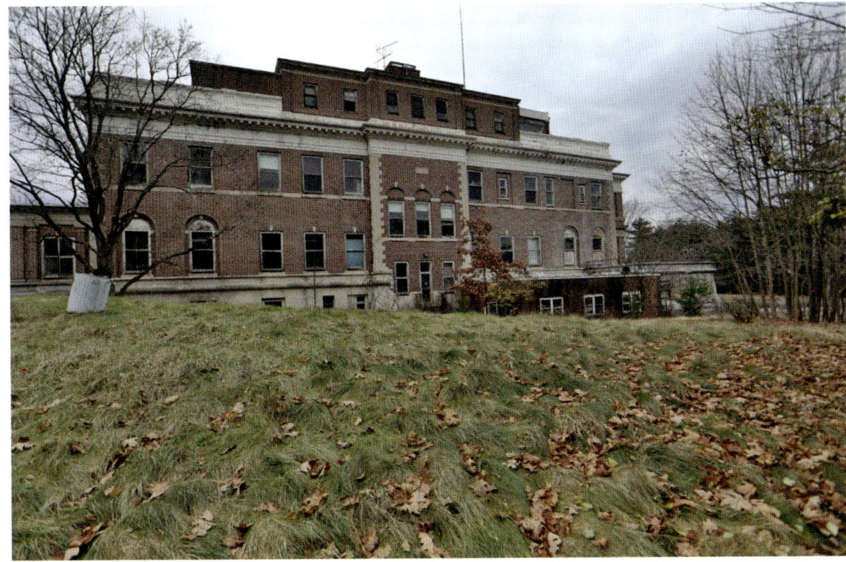

Mary McClellan Hospital

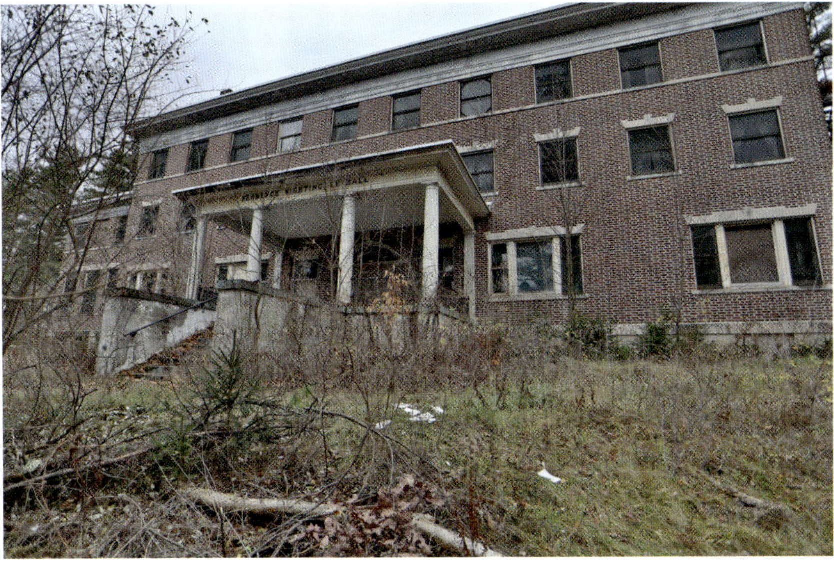

Tuition plus room and board for nurses at Florence Nightingale Hall was $625 per year.

Mary McClellan Hospital grew from the vision of Edwin McClellan, a native of Cambridge and branch manager of the Foster, Milburn & Company, a patent medicine manufacturer and distributor. In 1915, McClellan conferred with Cambridge's community members with plans to build a hospital, with the goal of improving the quality of medical care for local residents. With that, McClellan would oversee the construction of Mary McClellan Hospital, named after his mother. Shortly after opening in 1919, Mary McClellan Hospital would open a joint nursing school with Yale University and Skidmore College. Backed with a large endowment set up by Edwin McClellan, Mary McClellan Hospital became the most prominent medical facility in the region.

Ultimately, trends in the delivery of medical care made it difficult for small rural hospitals to prosper. Mary McClellan Hospital would transfer more and more patients to larger urban hospitals throughout the 1990s before closing in 2003.

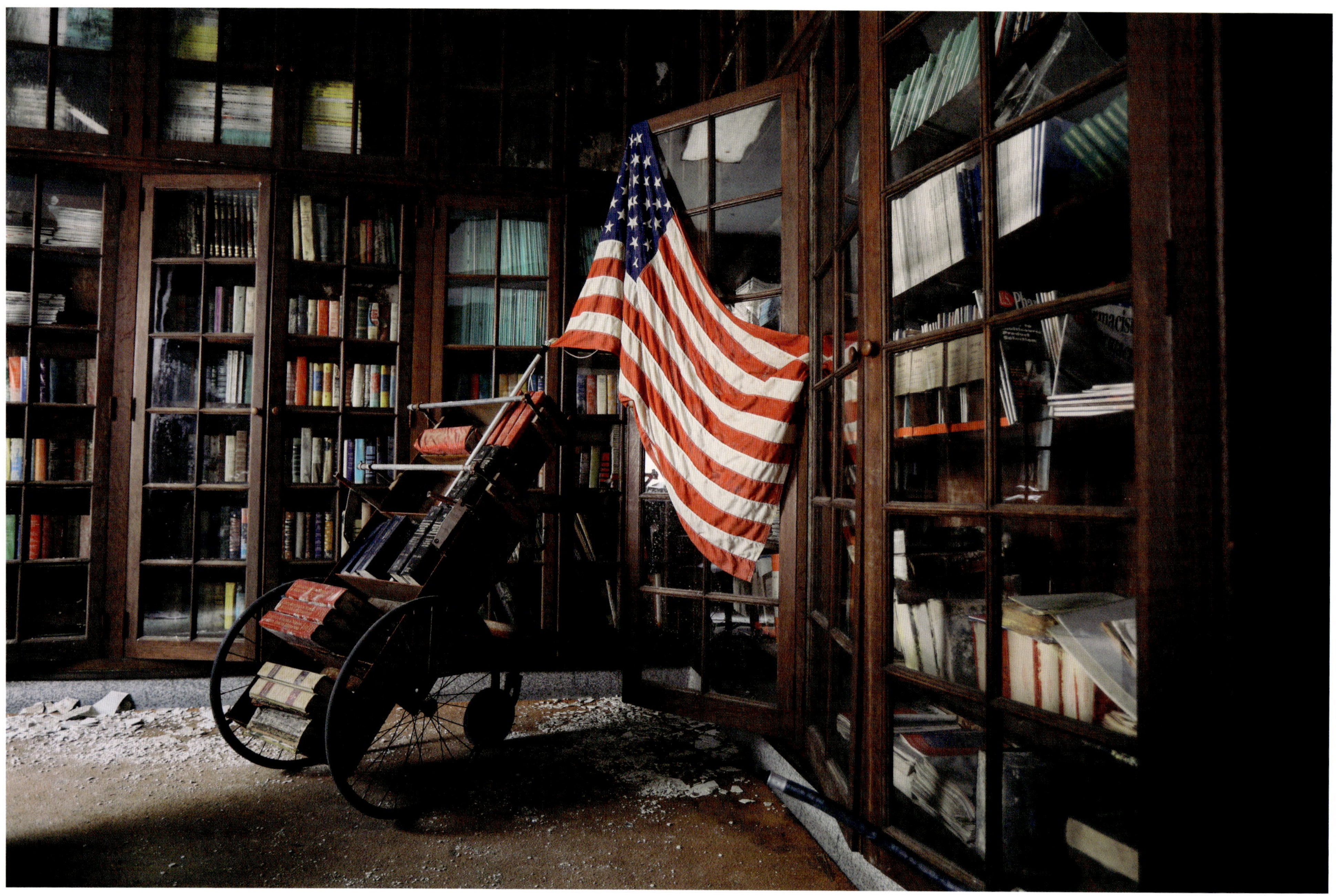

Medical library, Mary McClellan Hospital

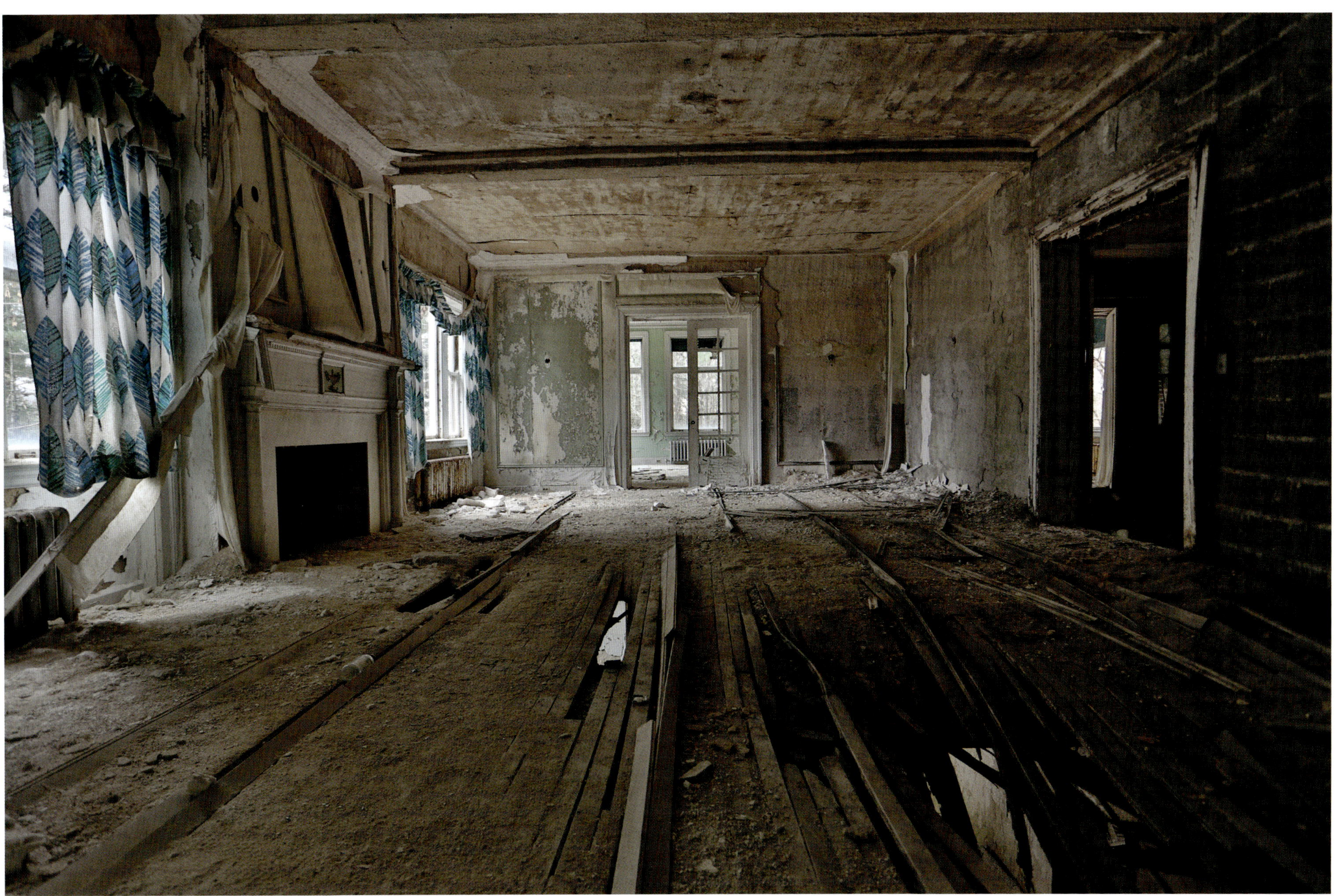

Living room in Florence Nightingale Hall, Mary McClellan Hospital

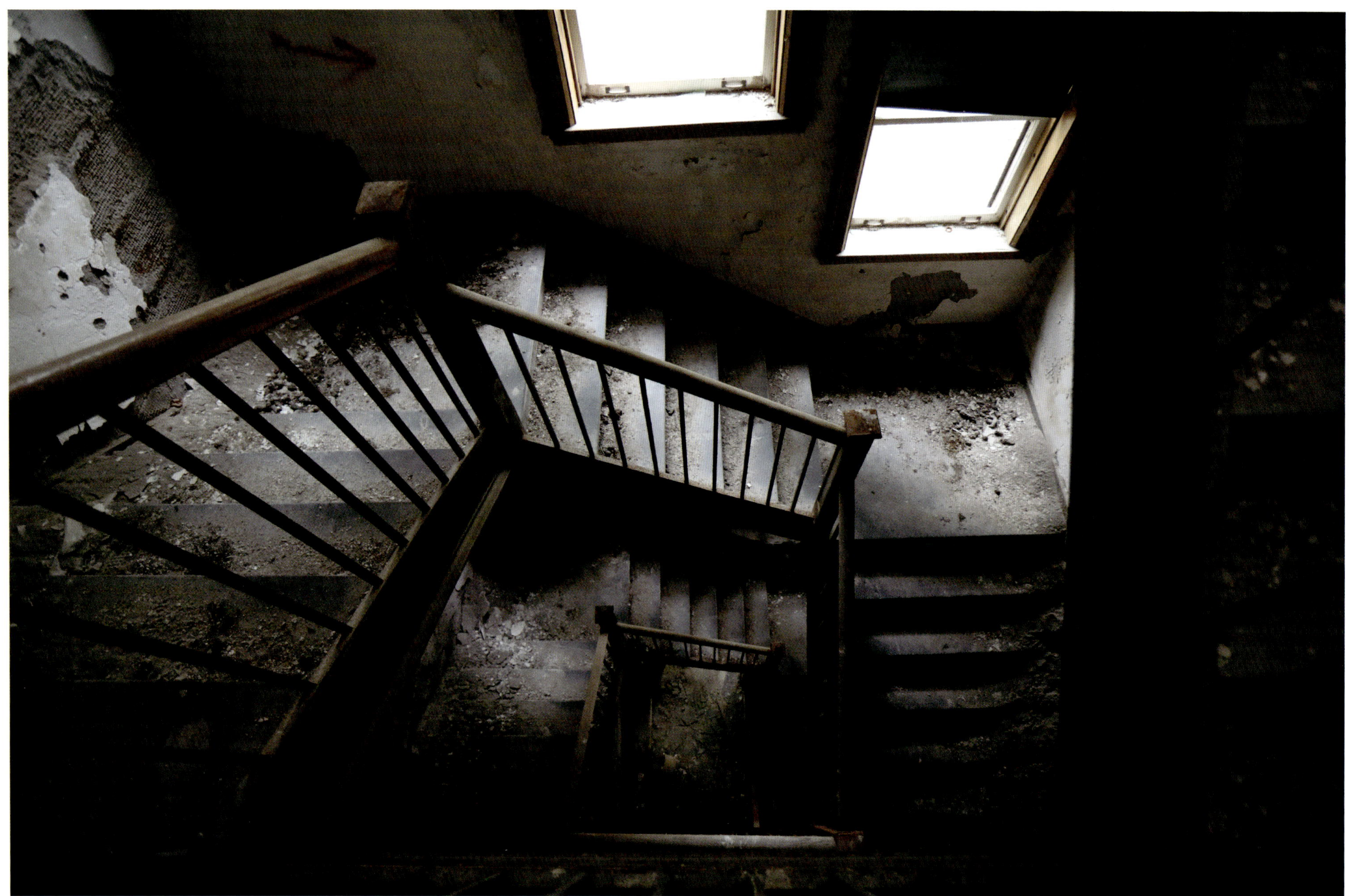

Stairwell in Florence Nightingale Hall, Mary McClellan Hospital

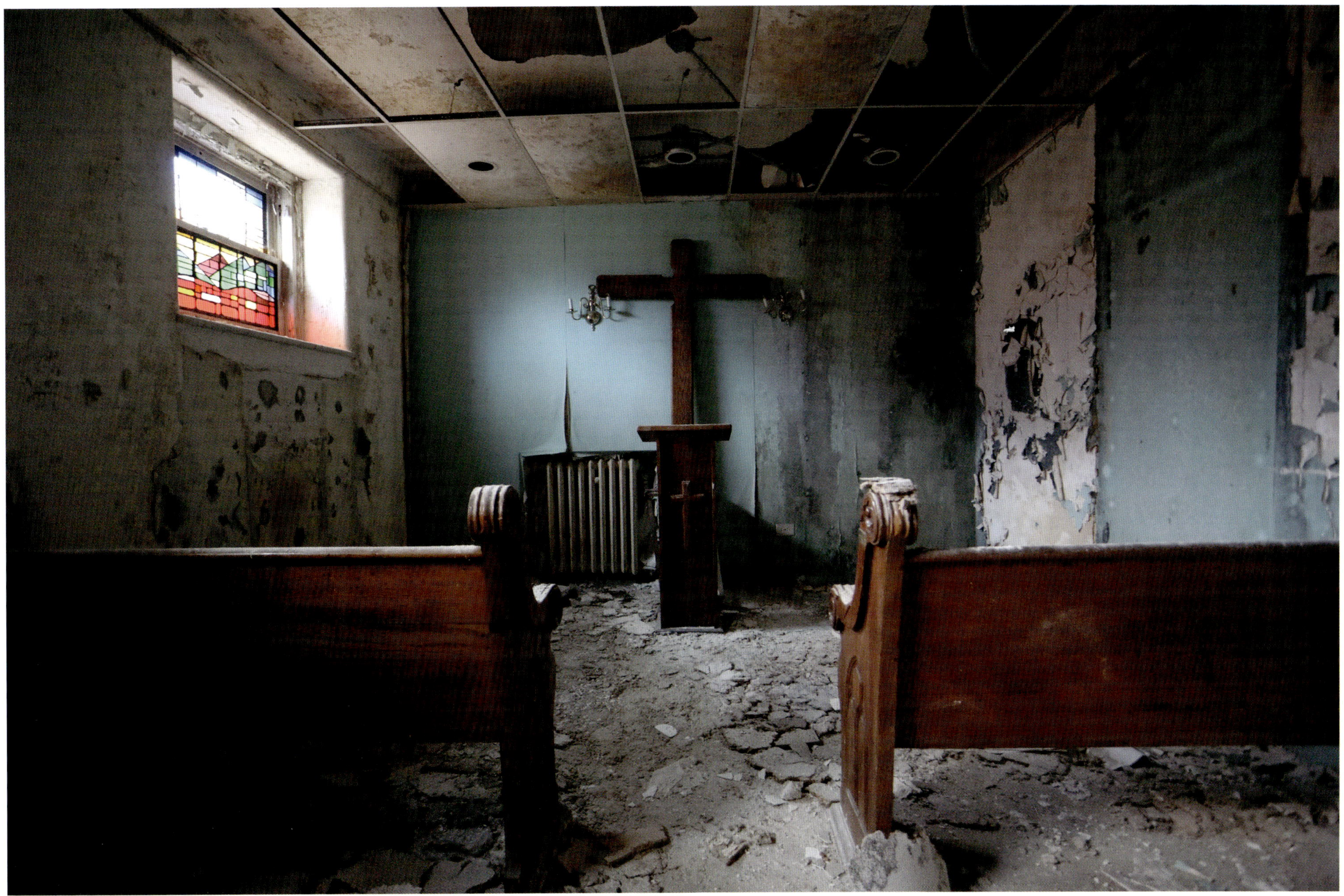

Chapel, Mary McClellan Hospital

Loraine W. Bills Elementary School

HERKIMER

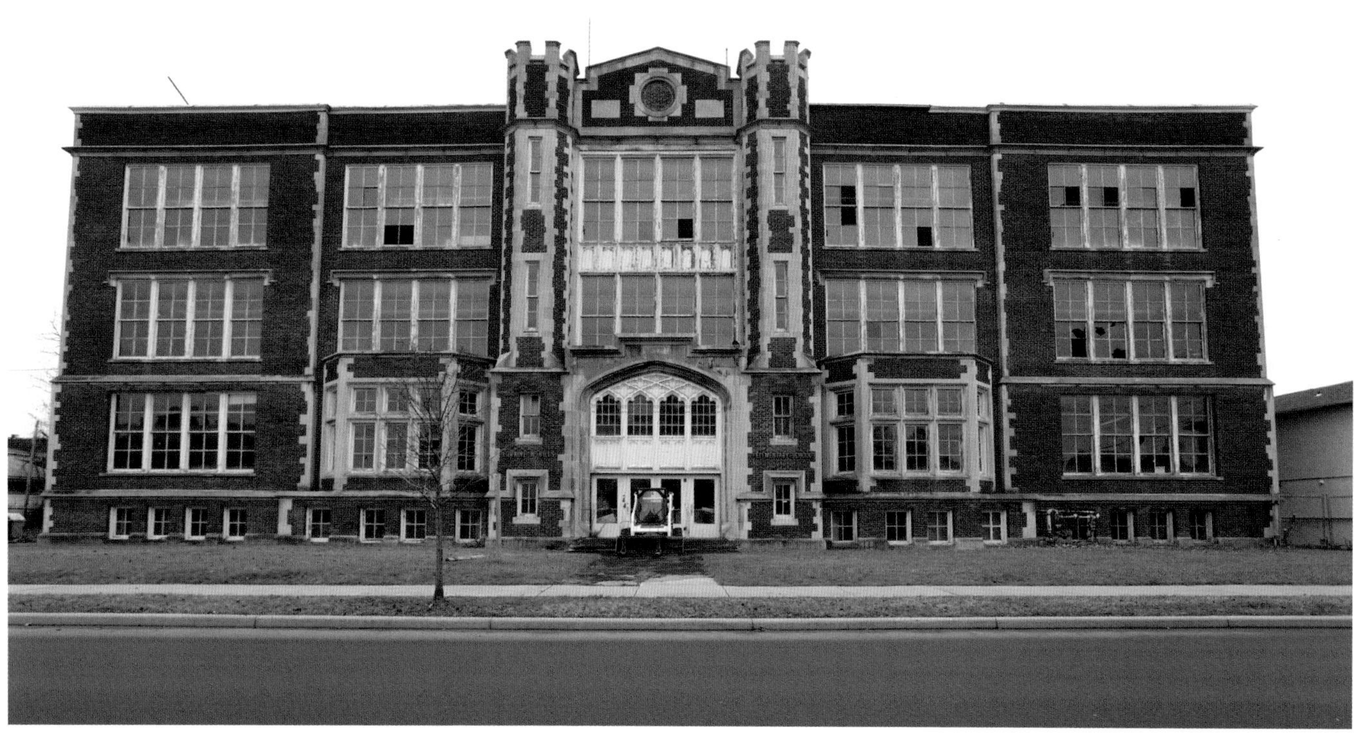

Front entrance, Loraine W. Bills Elementary School

The L. W. Bills School was one of two schools in the Herkimer Central School District that closed in 1991 after the opening of a newer facility. For years, L. W. Bills had been in need of repair, since its high ceilings and antiquated windows were not energy and cost efficient.

Built in 1921, L. W. Bills served approximately six hundred students in kindergarten through fourth grade. It is named after Loraine W. Bills, a former Herkimer superintendent of schools.

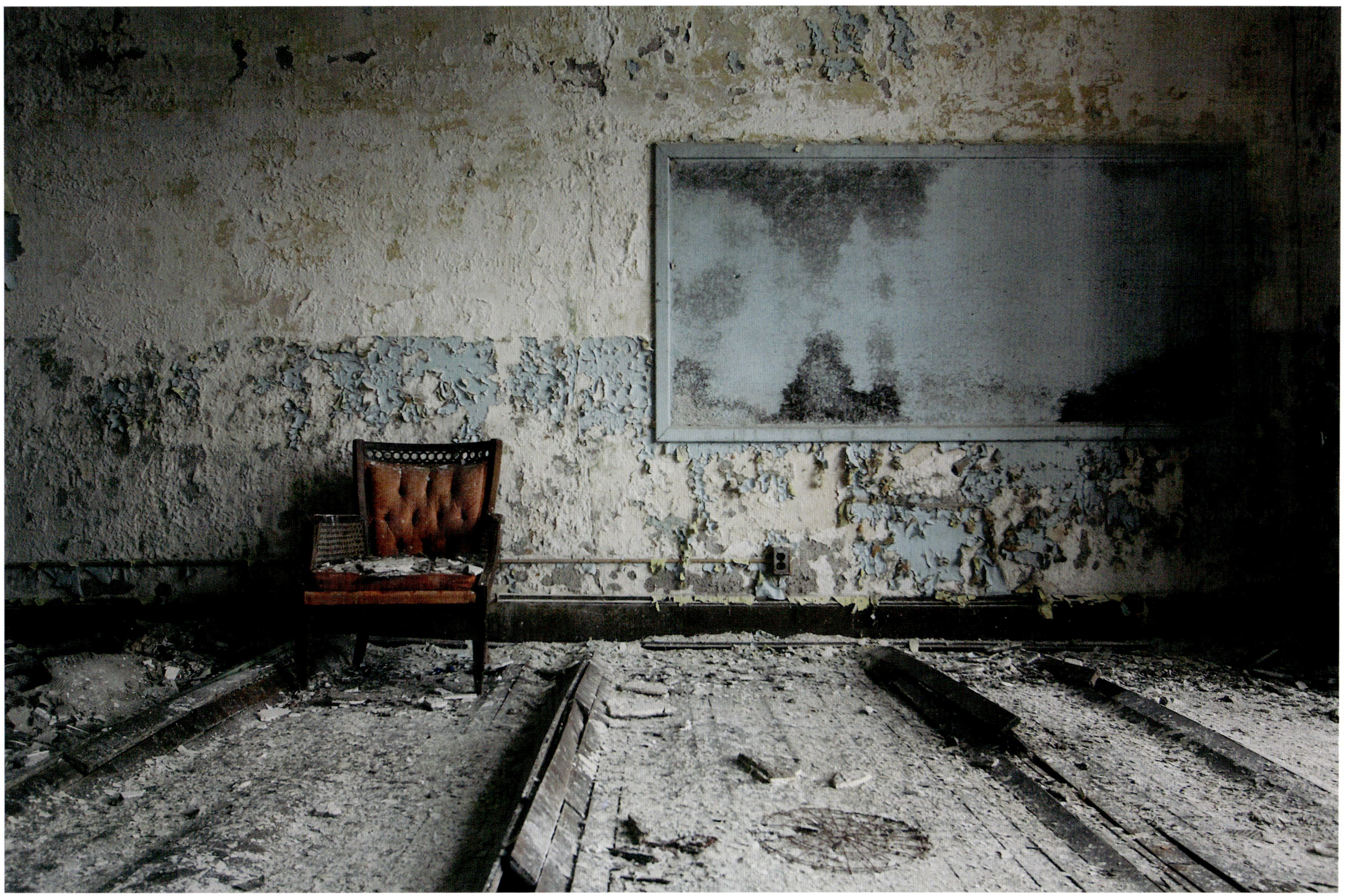

Classroom, Loraine W. Bills Elementary School

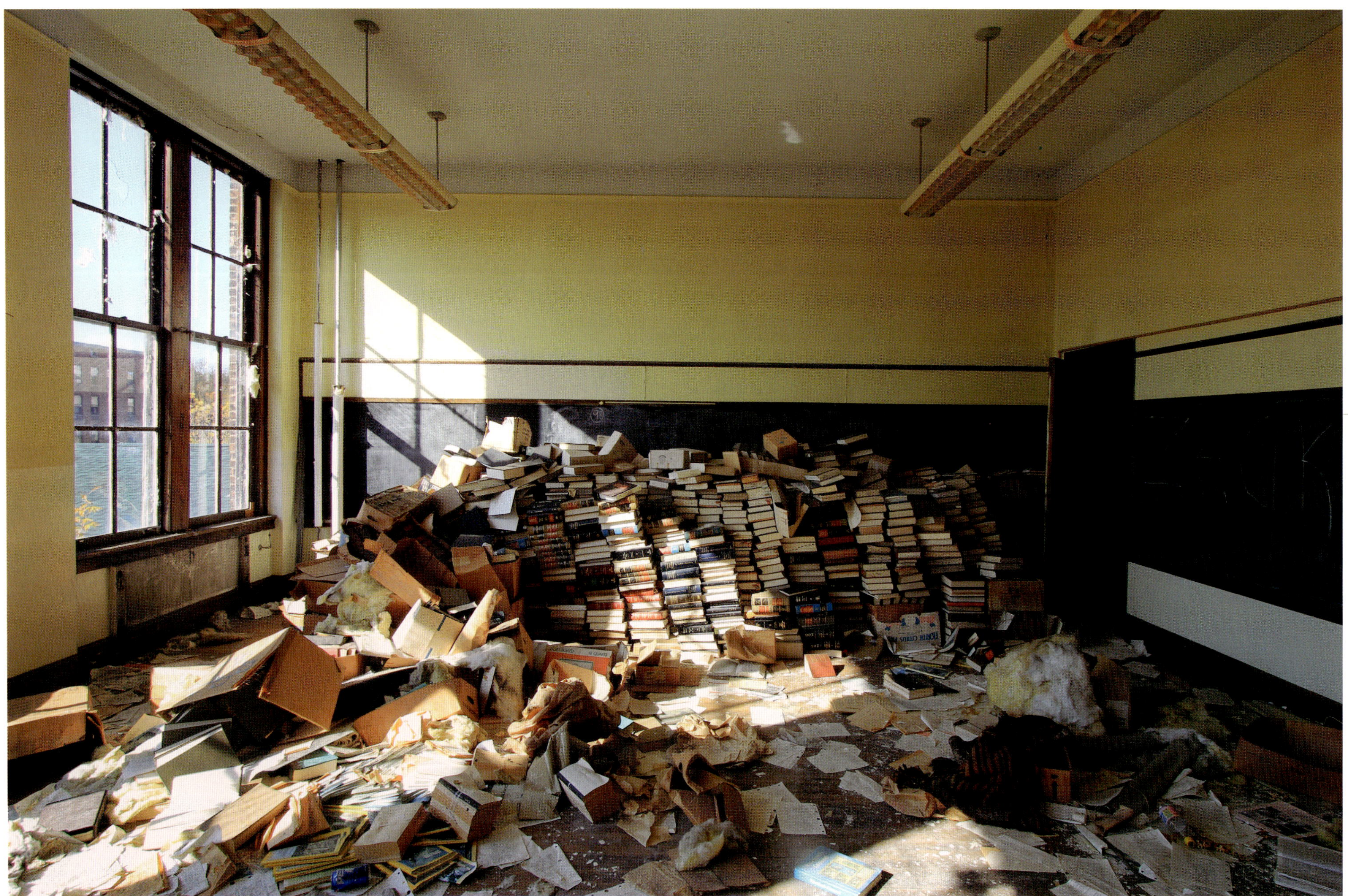

Classroom, Loraine W. Bills Elementary School

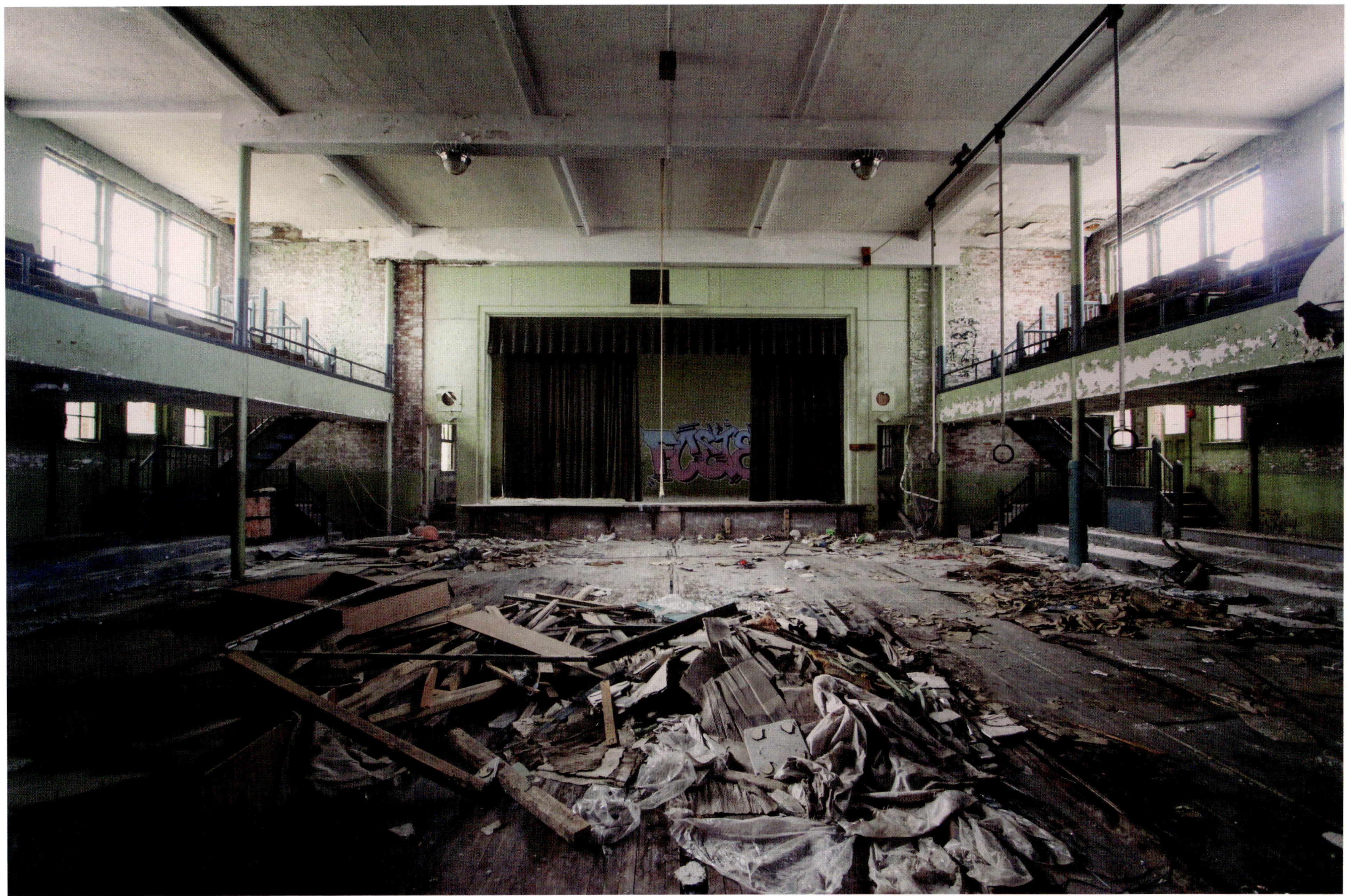

Auditorium/gymnasium, Loraine W. Bills Elementary School

Republic Steel's No. 7 Concentrating Plant

PORT HENRY

Demand for iron ore for the manufacturing of steel grew once the United States entered World War II in 1941. The Republic Steel Corporation reopened unused mines in the Port Henry area of New York and focused on the production of concentrated and sintered ore. At the No. 7 Concentrating Plant, ore was fed by a conveyor belt to magnetic separators at the rate of 300 tons per hour, where it was then separated by size. The waste tailings were disposed of nearby. The concentrated iron was then sent by rail to steel mills in Buffalo, Cleveland, and Youngstown.

High costs associated with the operations of the mines under Republic Steel led to the deterioration of No. 7 until the plant stopped processing ore in 1971.

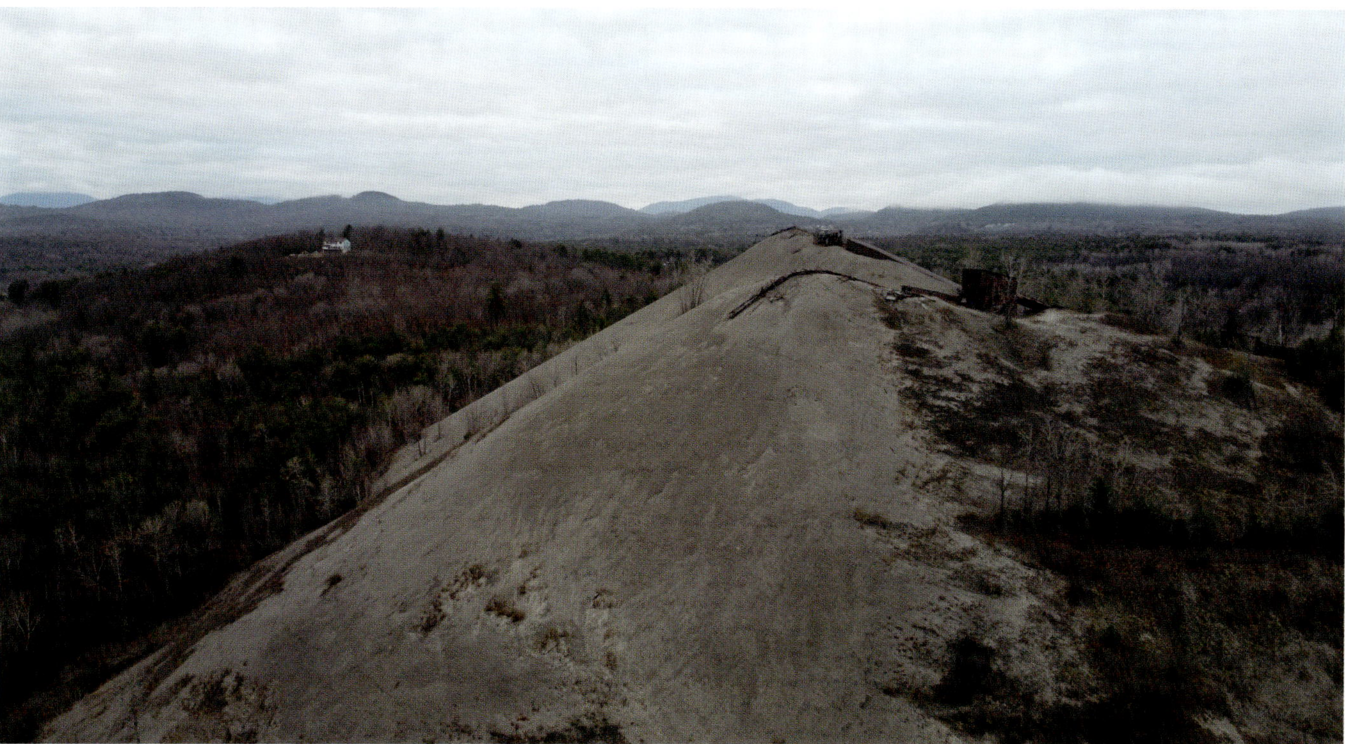

Ore tailing pile adjacent to the pant

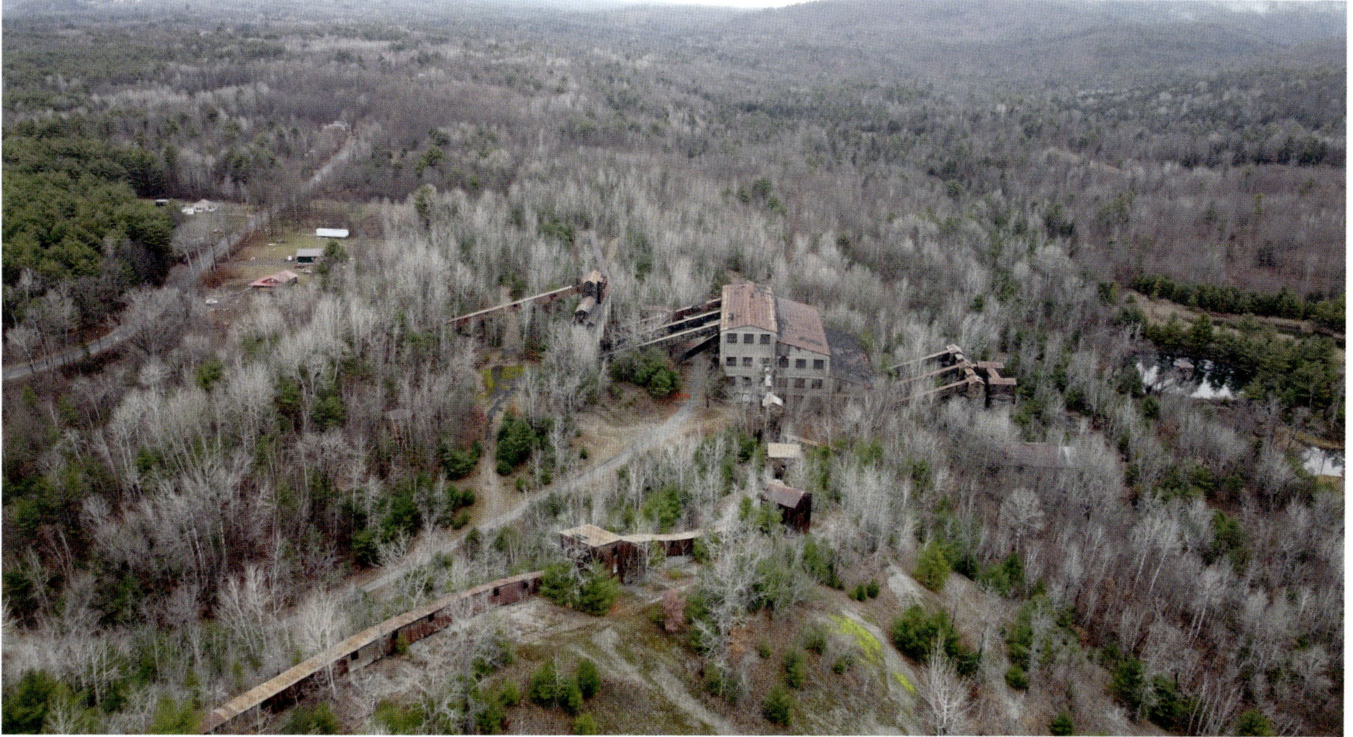

Republic Steel's No. 7 Concentrating Plant

CHAPTER 8.

THOUSAND ISLANDS–SEAWAY REGION

Newton Falls Fine Paper Company

NEWTON FALLS

In the western Adirondacks, pulp and paper mills were built along rivers, which provided mill power and transportation for floating lumber. While many suffered from the competition of larger, more efficient mills in Canada, Newton Falls prospered. The Newton Falls hamlet is named after James Newton, who built a sawmill in the area in 1894. By 1925, there were over eight hundred residents living in Newton Falls. Many immigrants traveled from Canada, Poland, Denmark, Finland, Latvia, Russia, and Norway and settled across the Adirondack Mountains looking for work. In turn, the paper mill built Sears Modern Homes for the workers, as well as a church, post office, school, and hotel for the greater community.

Over the following decades, with a variety of different ownership, Newton Falls Paper saw great renovations and equipment updates to keep up with industry giants in other states. Even though Newton Falls Paper was profitable, mill owner Appleton Coated of Kimberly, Wisconsin, announced in October 1999 that it was laying off half its workforce at Newton Falls. Mill workers were forced to learn new trades at schools in Canton and Saranac Lake. Others simply moved to find stable work.

Then, from 2007 to 2011, under new ownership, the mill briefly reopened as Newton Falls Fine Paper Company and became one of the largest private employers in St. Lawrence County before succumbing to the overall financial and pricing pressures in the paper industry.

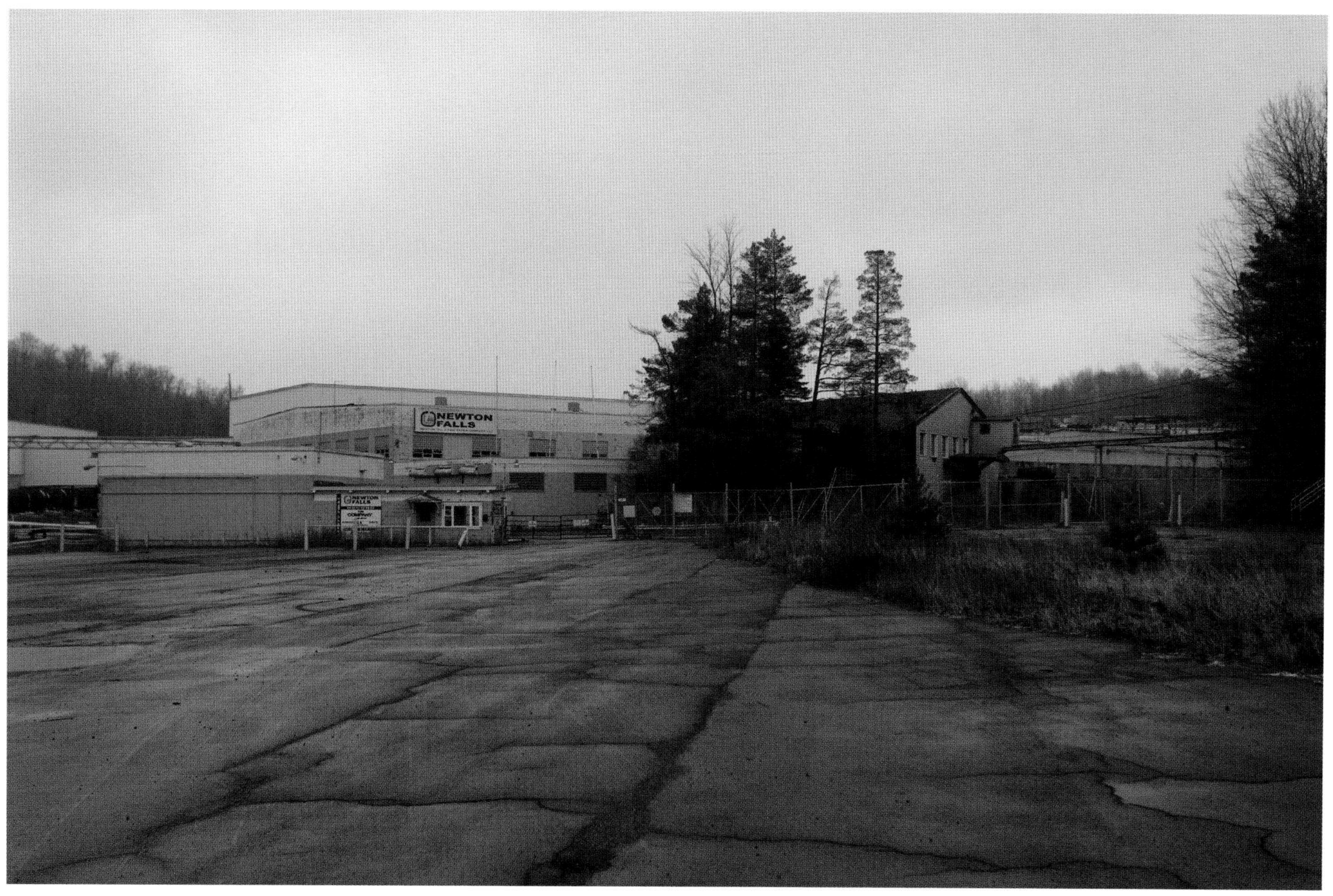

Newton Falls Fine Paper Co.

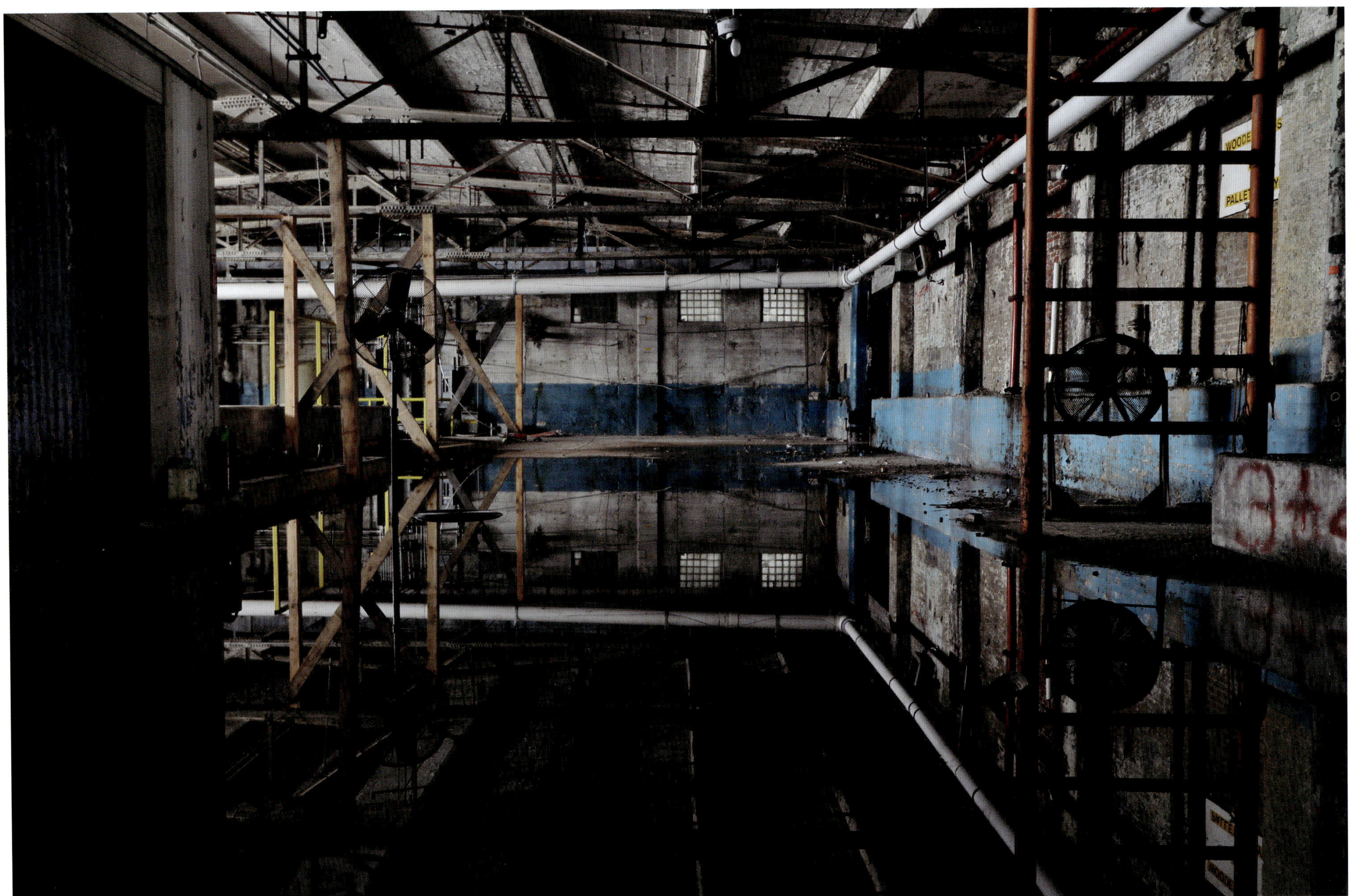

Work area, Newton Falls Fine Paper Co.

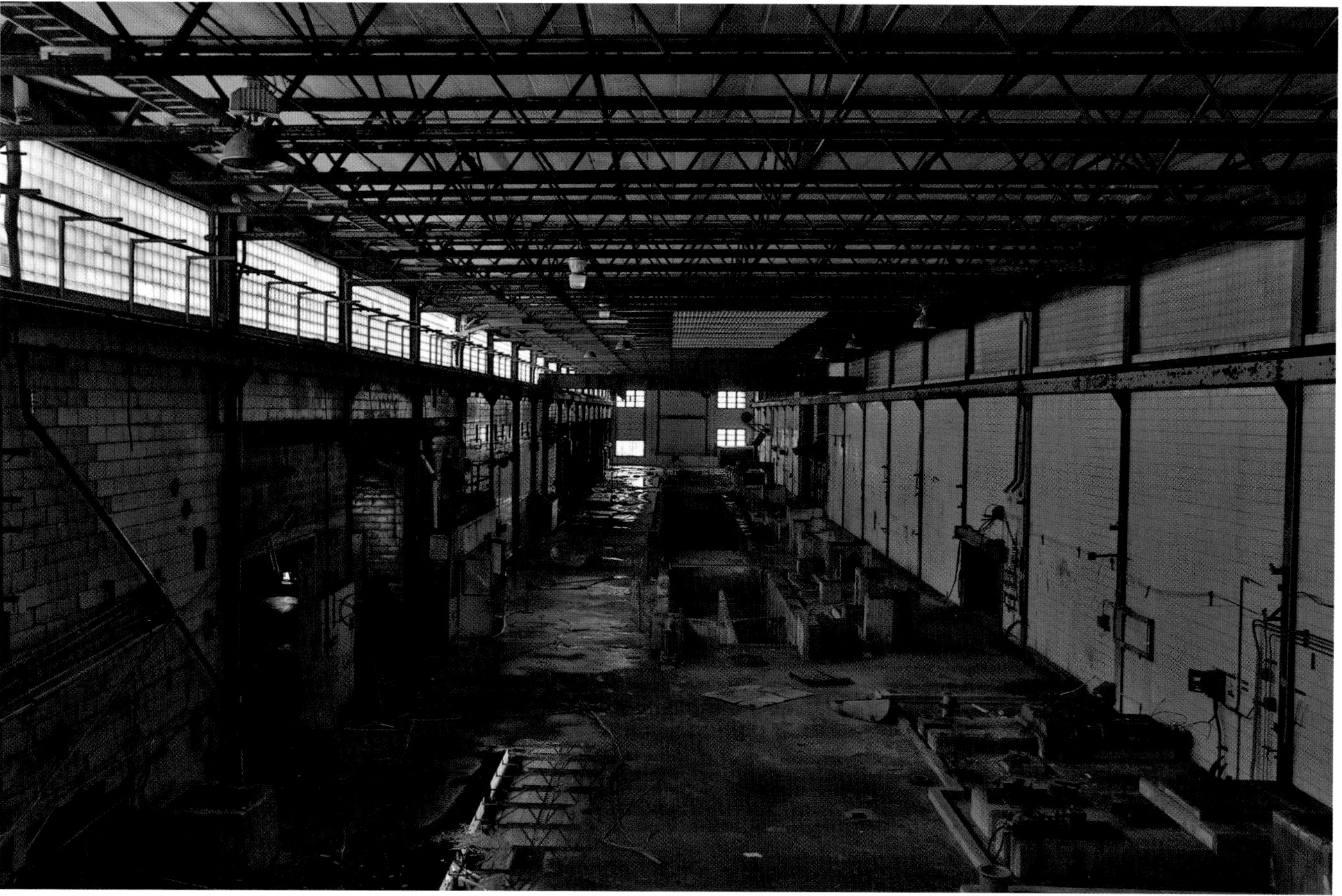

Main work floor, Newton Falls Fine Paper Co.

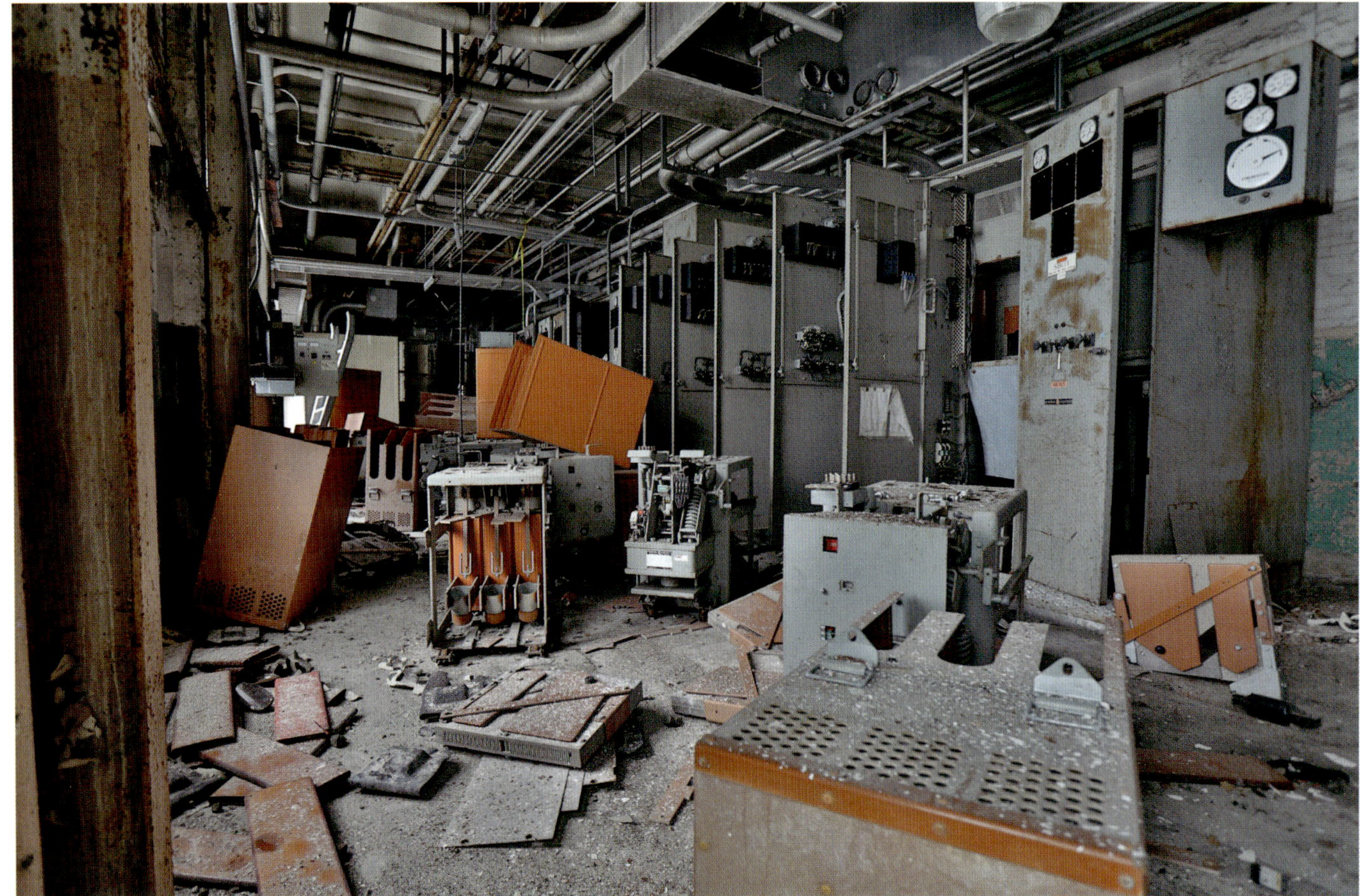

These synchroscopes measured the degree of synchronicity between Newton Falls' generators.

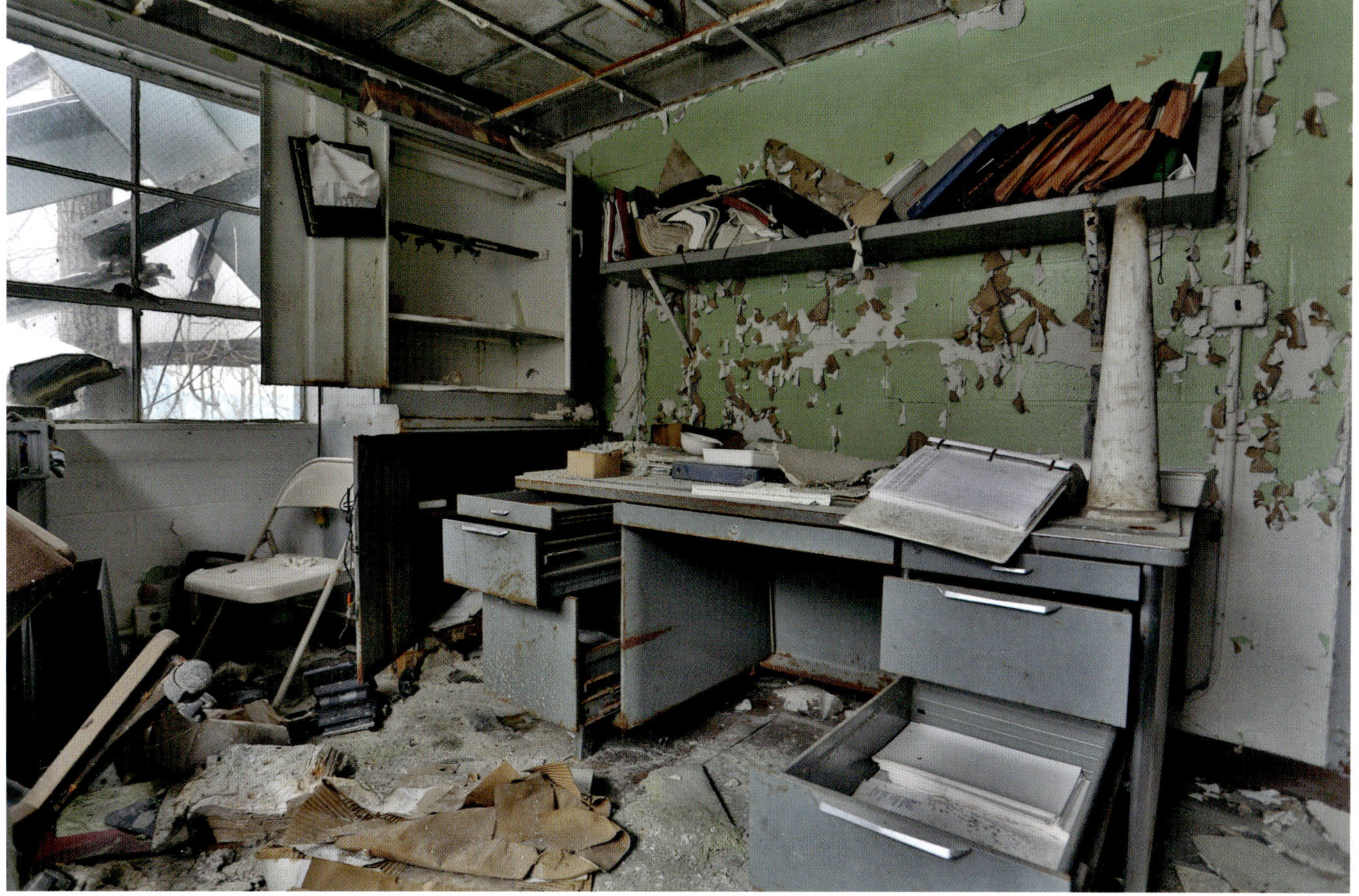

Office room, Newton Falls Fine Paper Co.

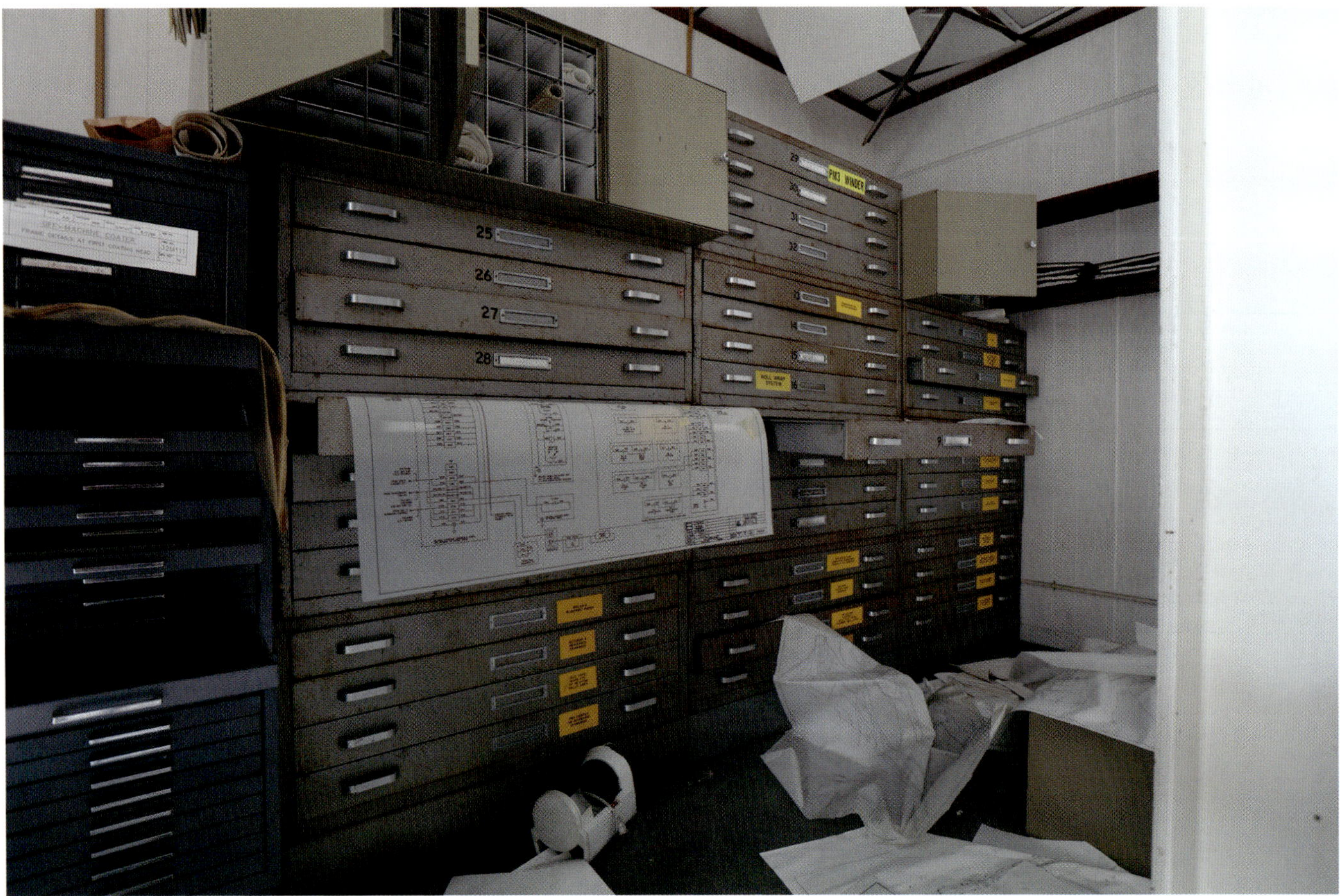

This room contained the blueprints for the entire mill.

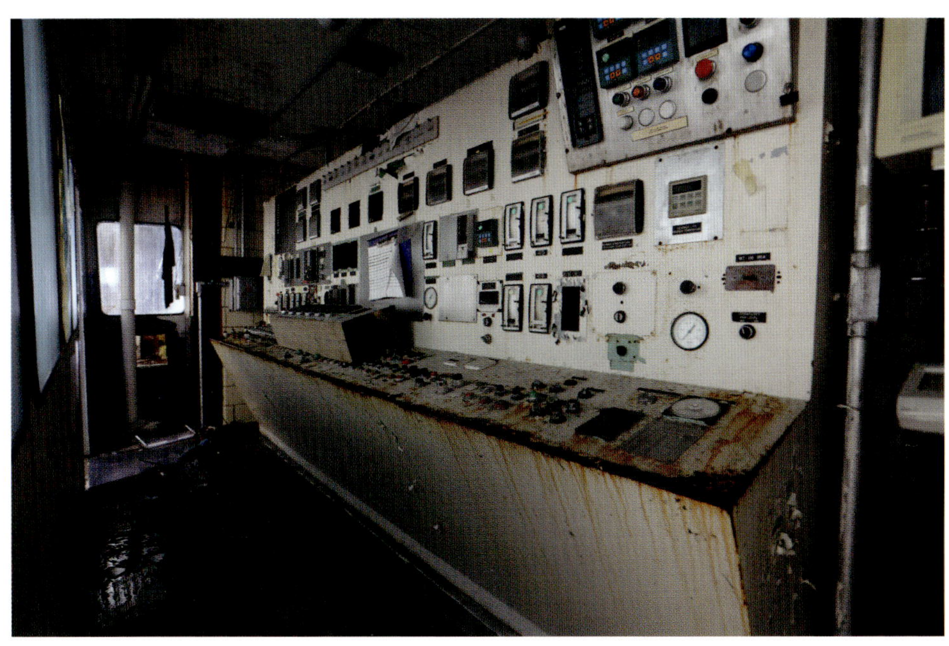

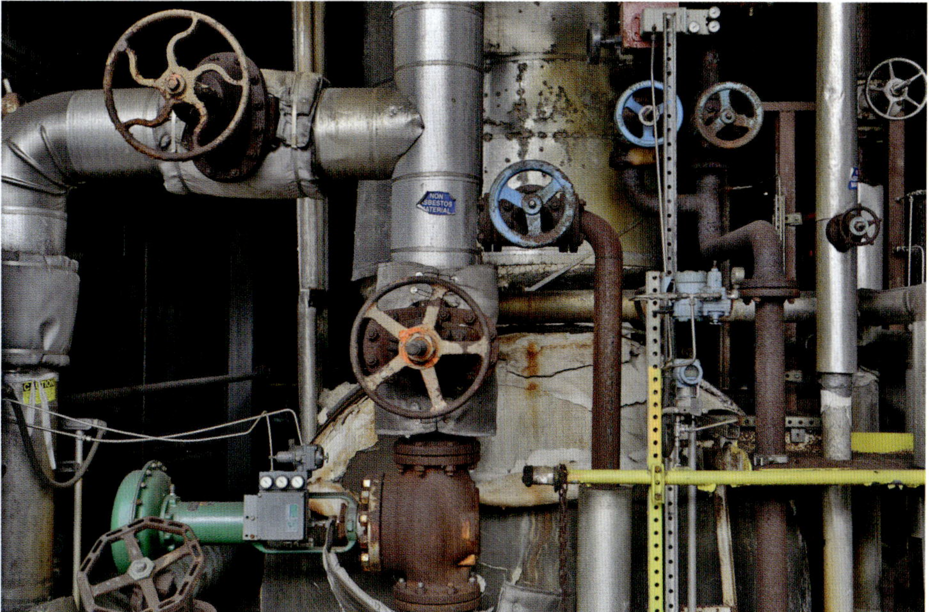

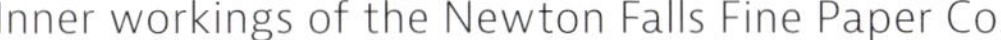
Inner workings of the Newton Falls Fine Paper Co.

Borden Milk Plant

EVANS MILLS

The Borden brand name traces back to 1856, when inventor and entrepreneur Gail Borden received a patent for his process of condensing milk, which allowed for the preservation of dairy products for long periods of time. He soon founded the New York Condensed Milk Company (which later became Borden Company) and opened many plants, with the first factory opening in Wassaic, New York, in 1861.

This particular factory in Evans Mill would cease operations in 1958. Abbass Food Corporation would then use the building for various warehousing operations until 2000.

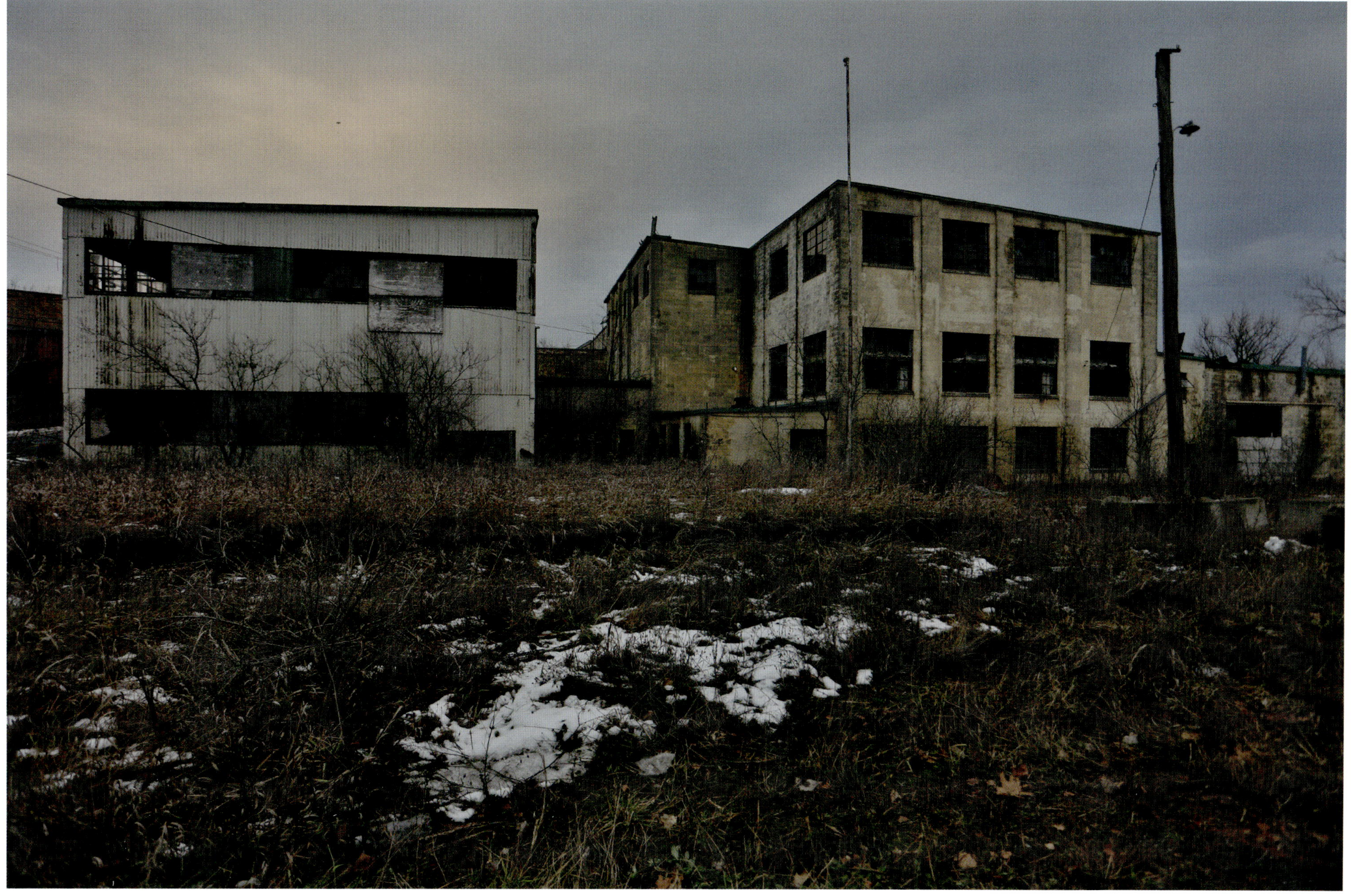

Borden Milk Plant at sunset

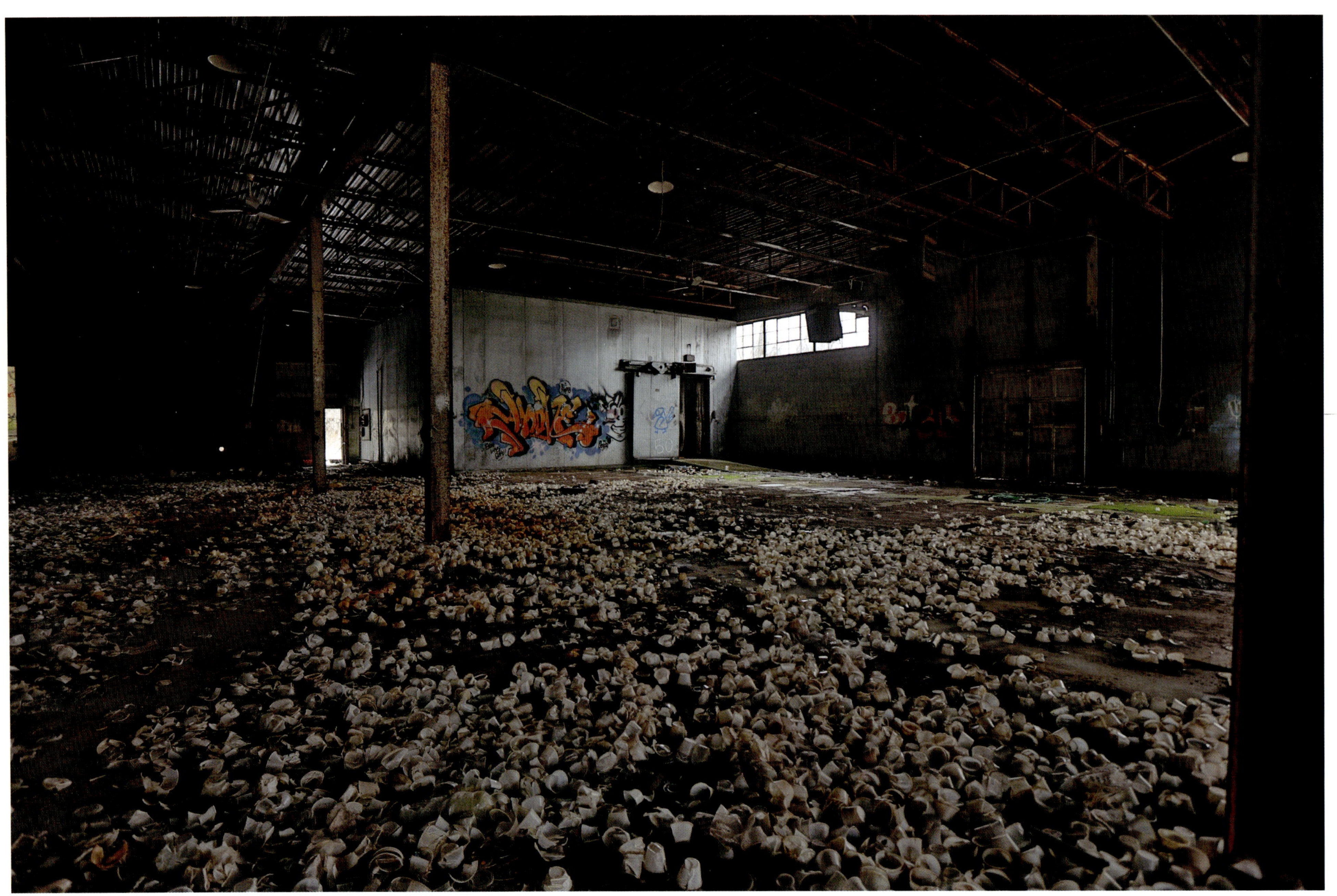

Main work floor, Borden Milk Plant

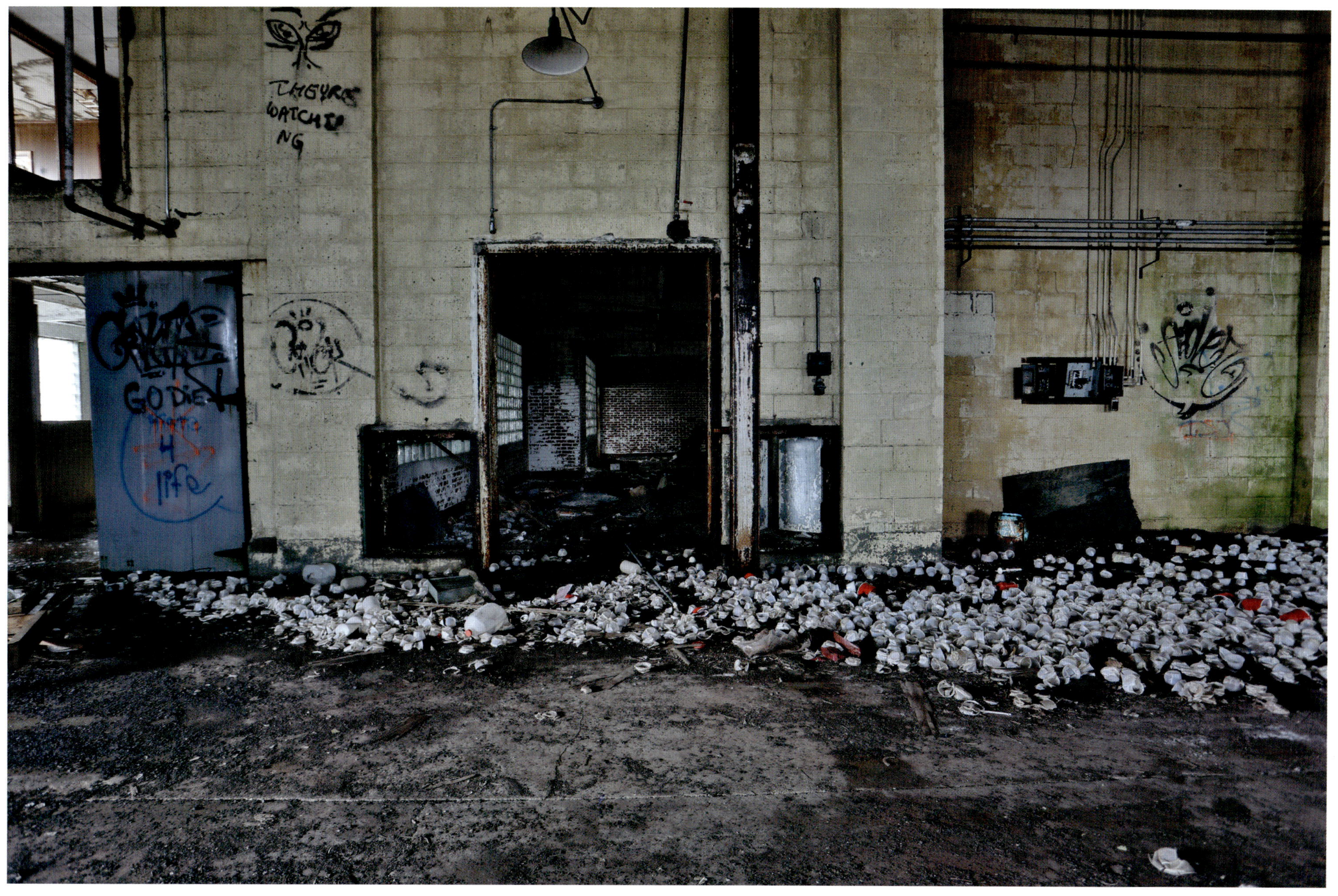
THEYRE
WATCHI
NG
GO DIE
4
life

CHAPTER 9.

FINGER LAKES REGION

Lehigh Valley Railroad Manchester Roundhouse

MANCHESTER

As diesel locomotives came into regular use, the Lehigh Valley Railroad constructed the Manchester Roundhouse in 1916, with the purpose of providing fuel and maintenance for freight cars and locomotives and coal/ash disposal for the antiquated steam engines. As part of the greater Manchester Yard, the 62,000-square-foot roundhouse had thirty bays, making it one of the largest rail support facilities in the country. The yard served as a division point where trains changed crews and were reconfigured for their next destination, similar to how airline hubs operate.

By the 1970s, industrial and commercial development was no longer concentrated in central locations but dispersed regionally. The interstate highway system allowed for the flexibility of trucking to bring cargo to more-dispersed locations. The Manchester Roundhouse would remain in service until 1975, when bankruptcy forced the Lehigh Valley Railroad to abandon the yards.

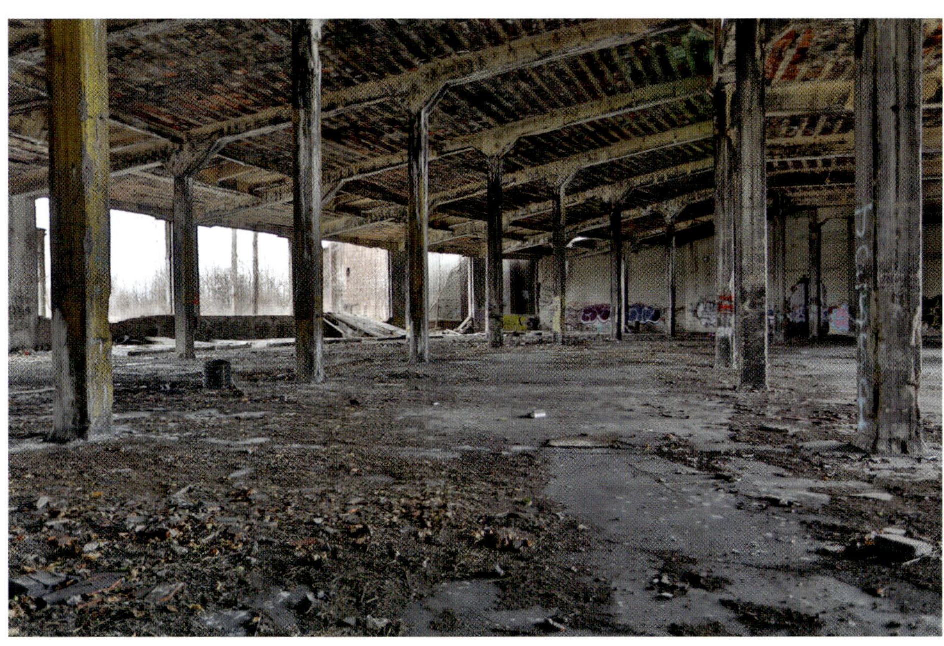

Lehigh Valley Railroad Manchester Roundhouse

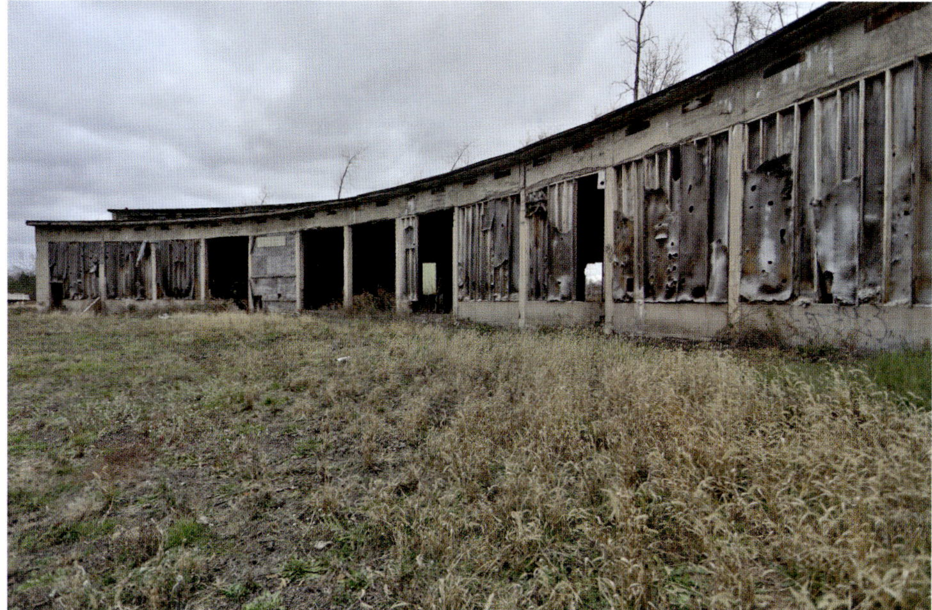

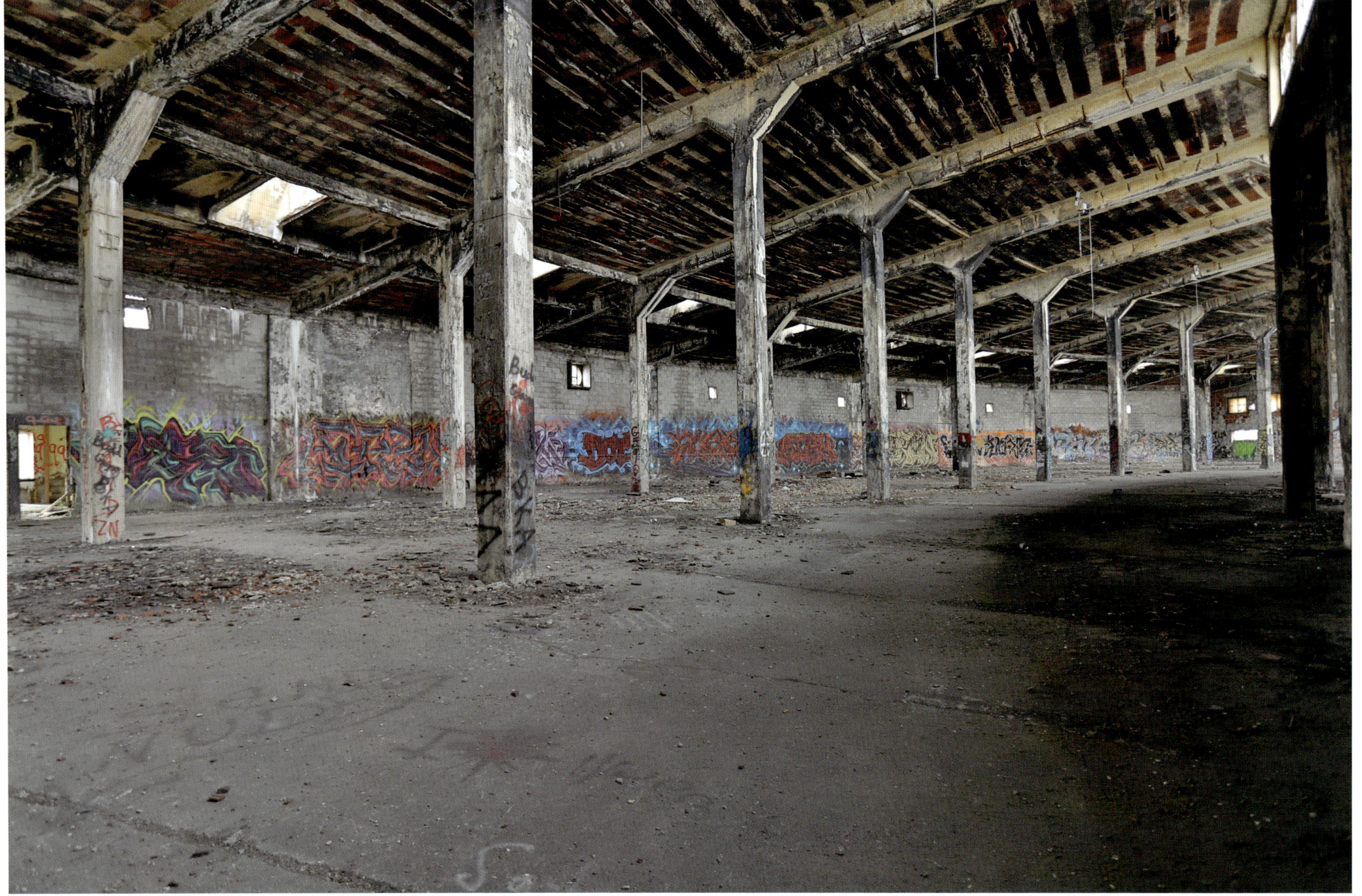

Freight car bays, Manchester Roundhouse

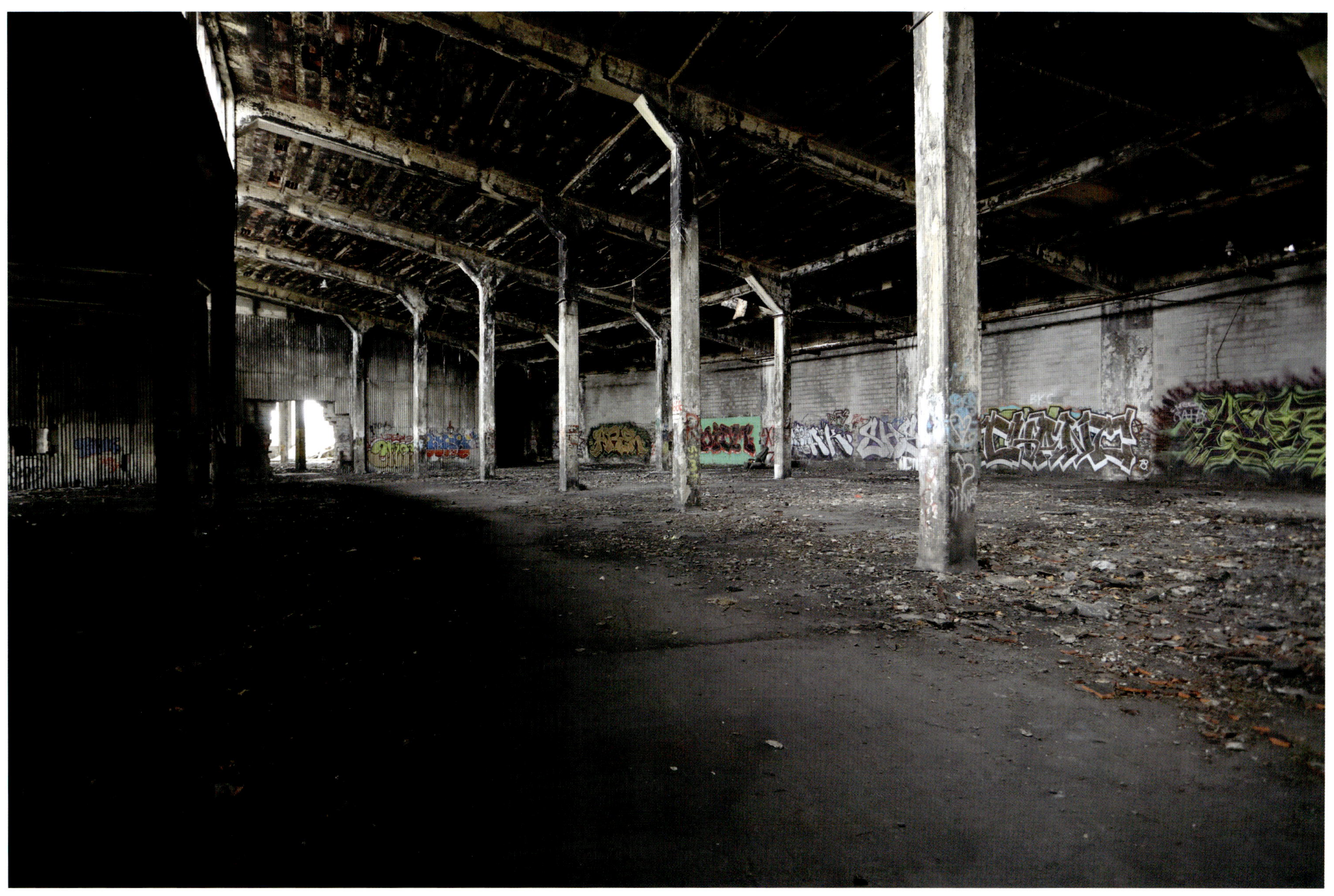

Rochester Incinerator

ROCHESTER

The Rochester Incinerator Plant was installed by the Decarie Incinerator Company in 1911 and could process 60 tons of the city's municipal trash daily. This newer structure (*pictured*) was added in the 1940s and served Delco, an automotive parts manufacturing company, before being decommissioned in the 1990s.

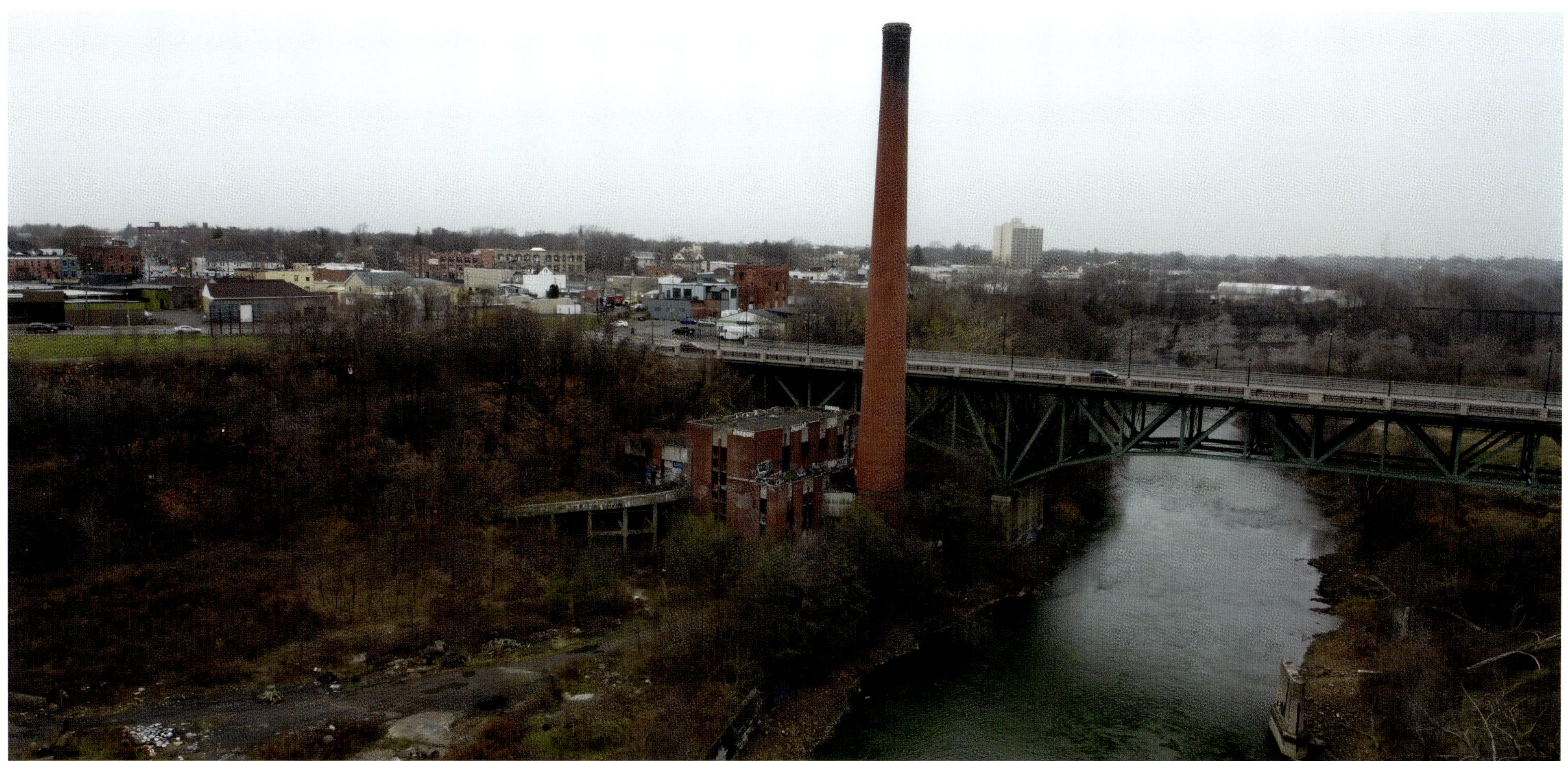

Aerial view of the Rochester Incinerator

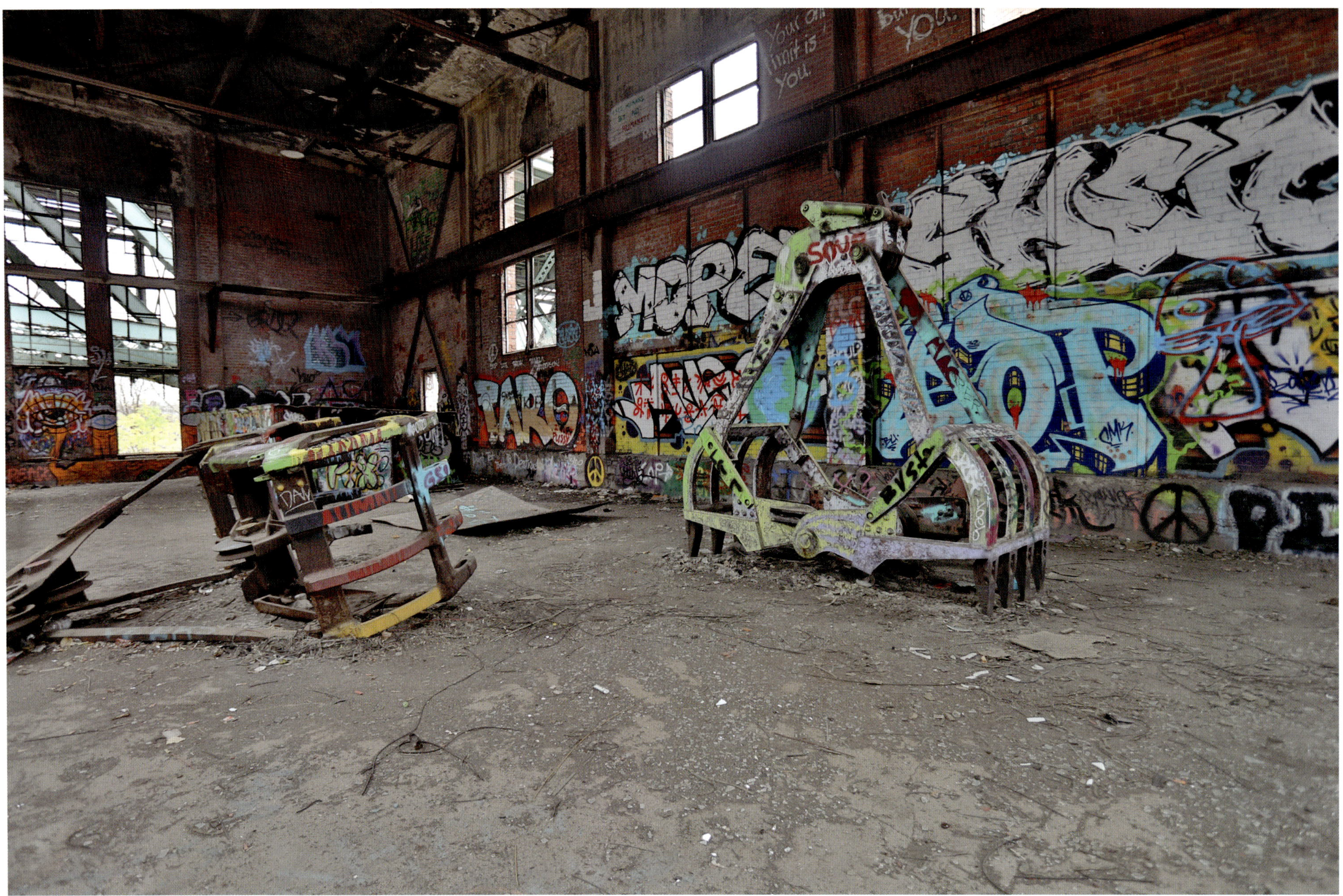

These steel claws were used to load municipal waste into the incinerator.

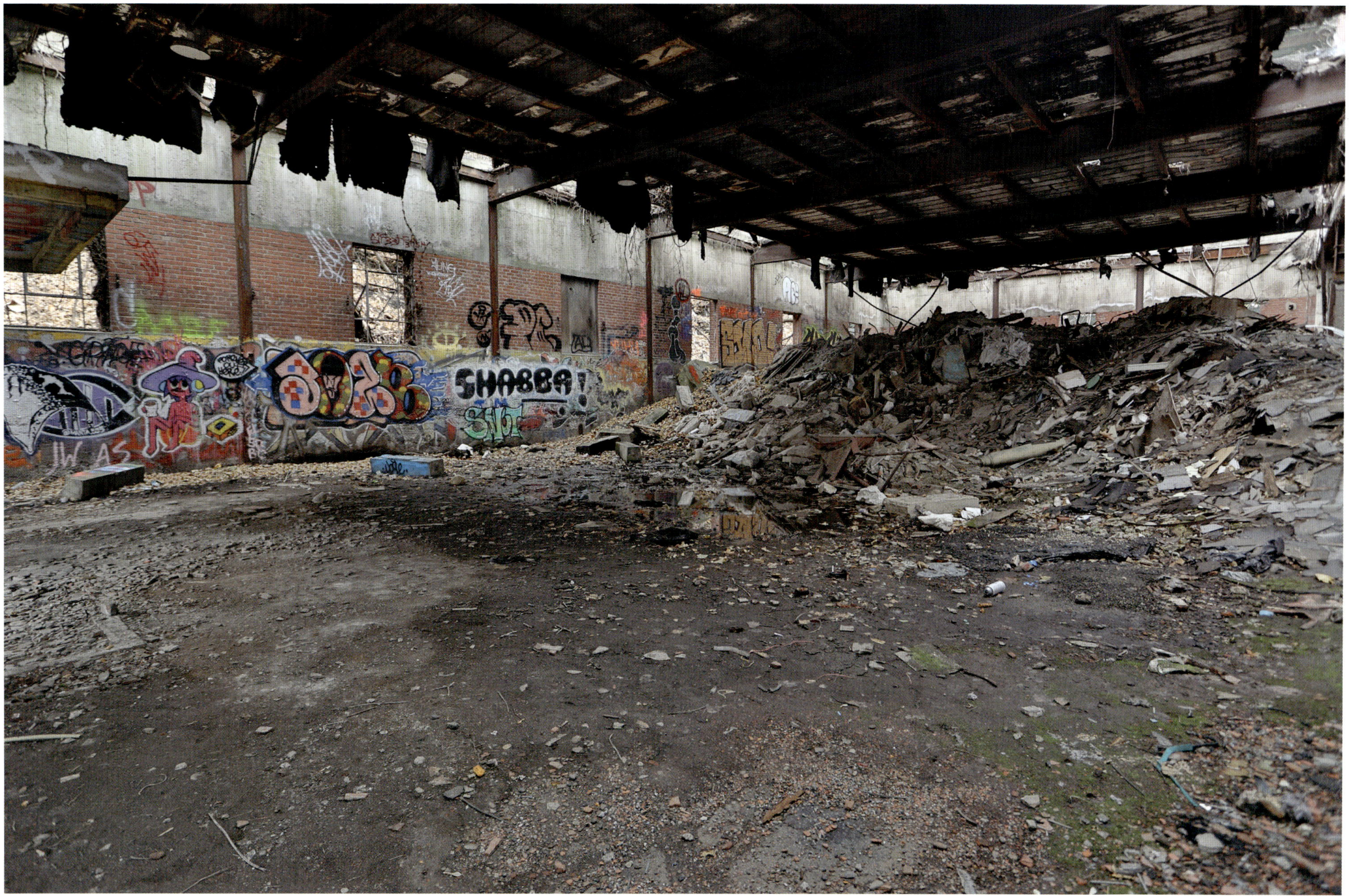

The incinerator plant also served as the location in the final scenes of ***The Alphabet Killer*** (2008), starring Eliza Dushku, Timothy Hutton, and Cary Elwes.

Walters Building & Terrence Tower, Rochester State Hospital

ROCHESTER

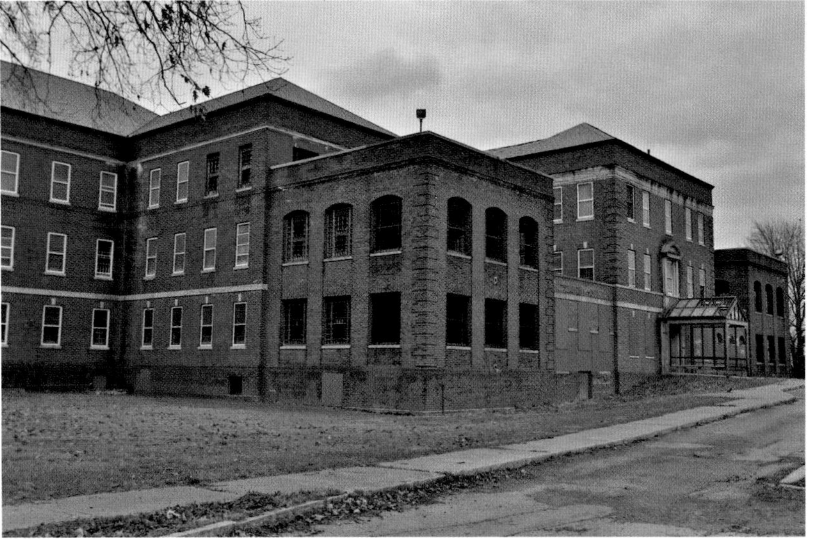

Walters Building, Rochester State Hospital

When the State Care Act passed in 1890, New York State assumed sole responsibility for the care of the mentally ill and established a statewide system of psychiatric hospitals. In counties where there was already an active hospital, New York State offered to purchase them and continue operation under state administration and funding. Monroe County accepted this offer, and the Monroe County Insane Asylum became Rochester State Hospital in 1891. By the Great Depression in the 1930s the hospital census had risen to 2,600, prompting the state to build additional patient wards, including the Walters Building, modeled in a Georgian Revival style.

At its peak, Rochester State Hospital sat on 200 acres of land and treated five thousand patients throughout eighty buildings. By the 1980s, however, the focus of treatment moved away from hospitals, ultimately leaving many of the campus buildings to be demolished or repurposed. The Walters Building and Terrence Tower are among the few remaining buildings from the hospital's peak operation.

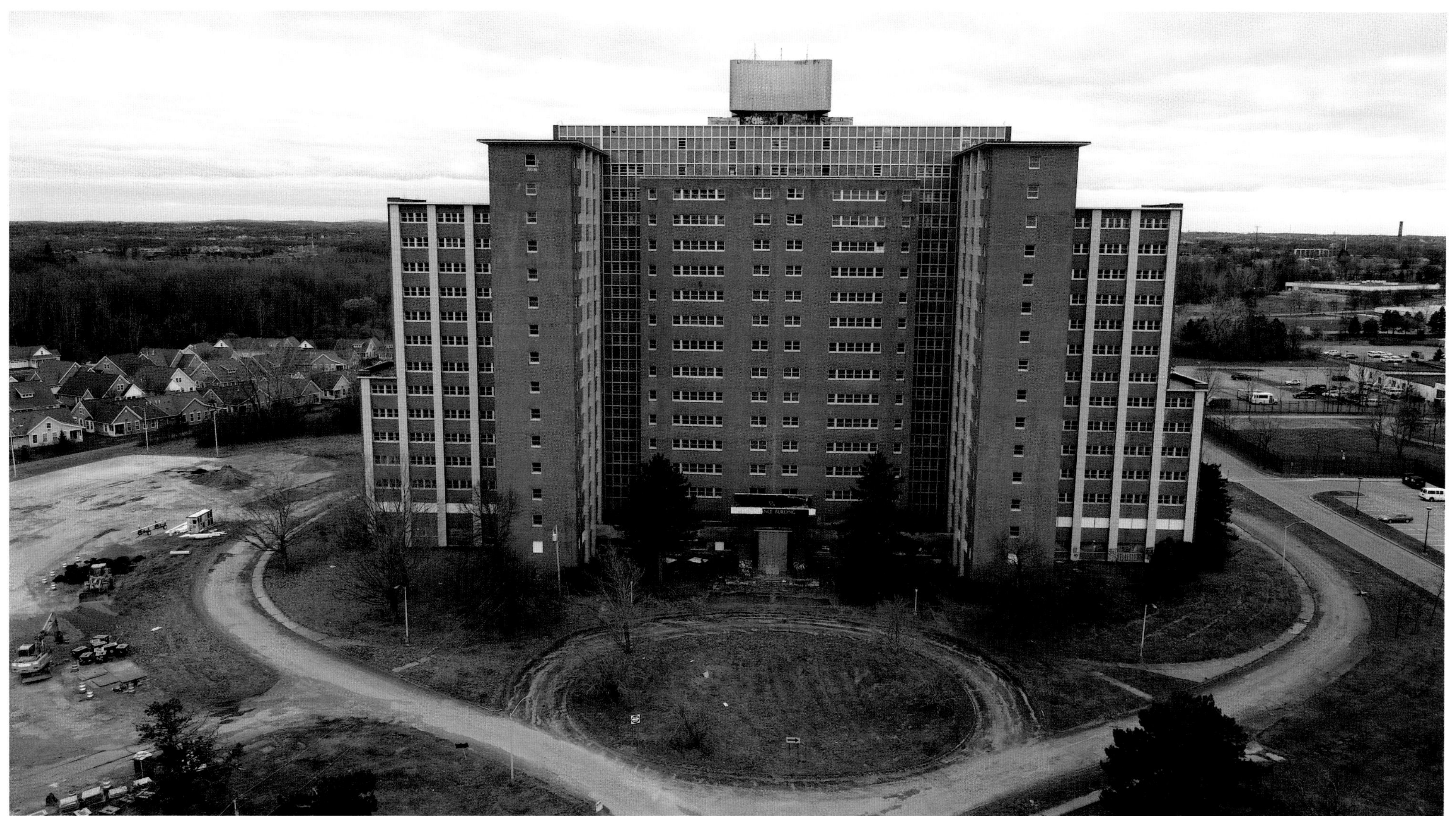

The sixteen-story Terrence Building, commonly referred to as "Terrence Tower," was built in 1959 and housed a thousand patients until 1995, when it was replaced by newer facilities.

Rochester Industrial & Rapid Transit Railway

ROCHESTER

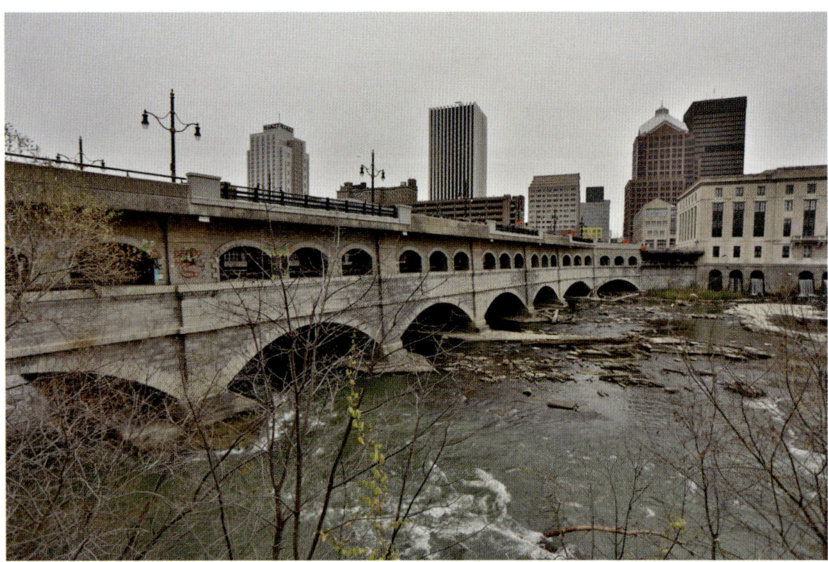

By the turn of the century, the Erie Canal was considered obsolete. After the New York State legislature allocated money for the relocation of the canal, bypassing downtown Rochester and with the last ships traveling through the locks in 1919, the city purchased the abandoned canal bed for construction of a subway to improve trolley passenger traffic and freight interchange.

The Rochester Industrial & Rapid Transit Railway opened to the public in December 1927. Ridership peaked during World War II due to gasoline rationing but declined by the 1950s as plans were developed for a system of expressways in and around Rochester. When construction on the Eastern Expressway (I-490) was completed, passenger service on the Rochester subway ended on June 30, 1956. The western end of the line continued to be used for freight service until 1976.

The last of the subway cars of the Rapid Transit Railway reside at the Rochester & Genesee Valley Railroad Museum.

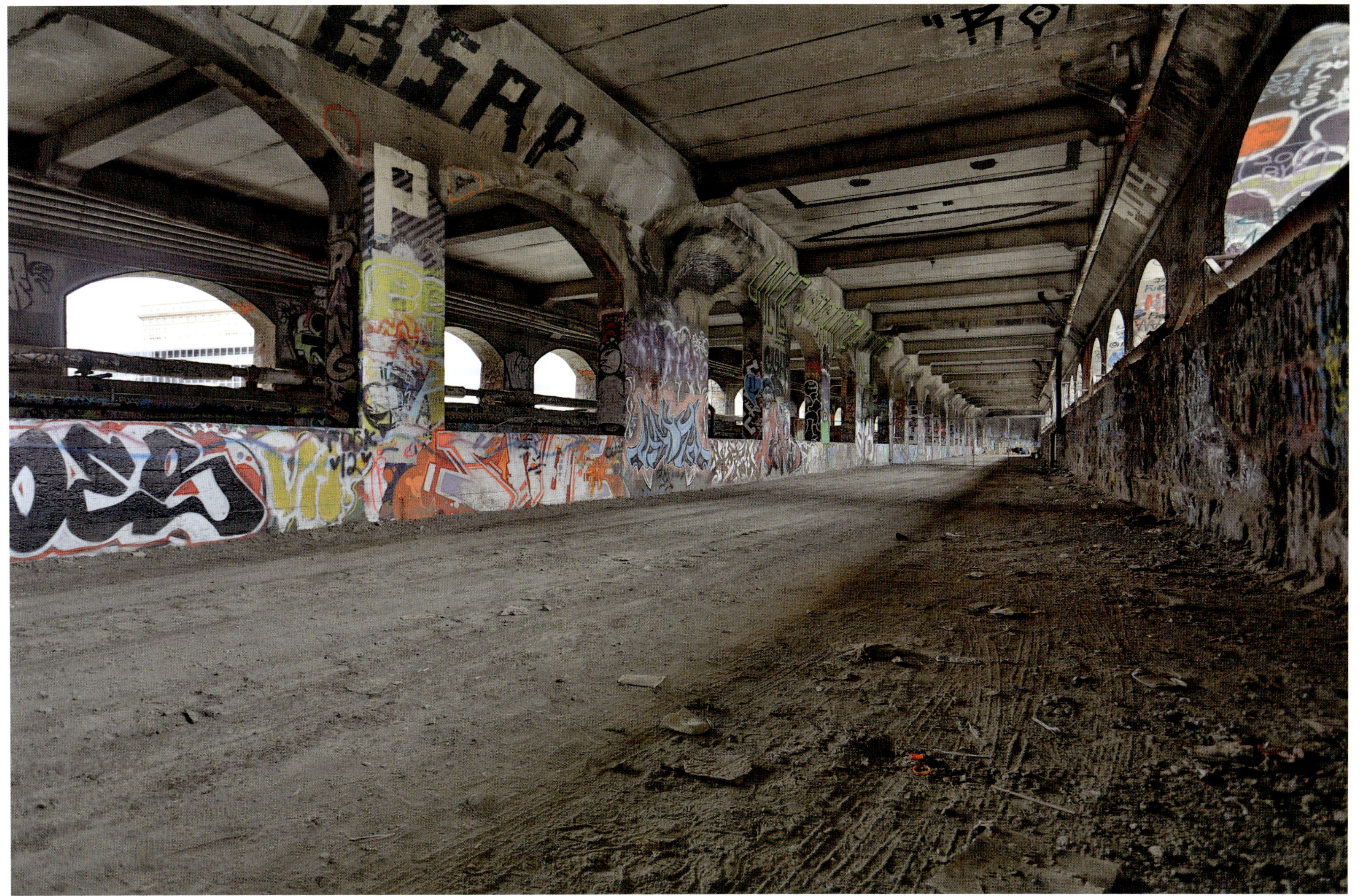

Rochester Industrial & Rapid Transit Railway

Jackson Sanatorium

DANSVILLE

This sprawling, castle-like structure peering through the treeline overlooking the city of Dansville, New York, is Jackson Sanatorium. Its story begins in 1854, when Dr. Caleb Jackson opened the institute as "Our Home on the Hillside" during a time when hydrotherapy—a practice using various water treatments to cure such ailments as anxiety, depression, and stress—was a popular alternative medicine. Dr. Jackson also encouraged his patients to follow a strict diet emphasizing fruits, vegetables, and unprocessed grains. His concoction of twice-baked graham flour had to be soaked in water overnight, later becoming granola, America's first breakfast cereal.

The Jackson Sanatorium remained successful throughout the 1800s, drawing such visitors as Frederick Douglass, Elizabeth Cady Stanton, and Clara Barton, who would eventually establish the first chapter of the American Red Cross in Dansville. It would go through many names and uses, with the most recent being Bernarr Macfadden's Castle on the Hill, a hotel that operated until Labor Day 1971.

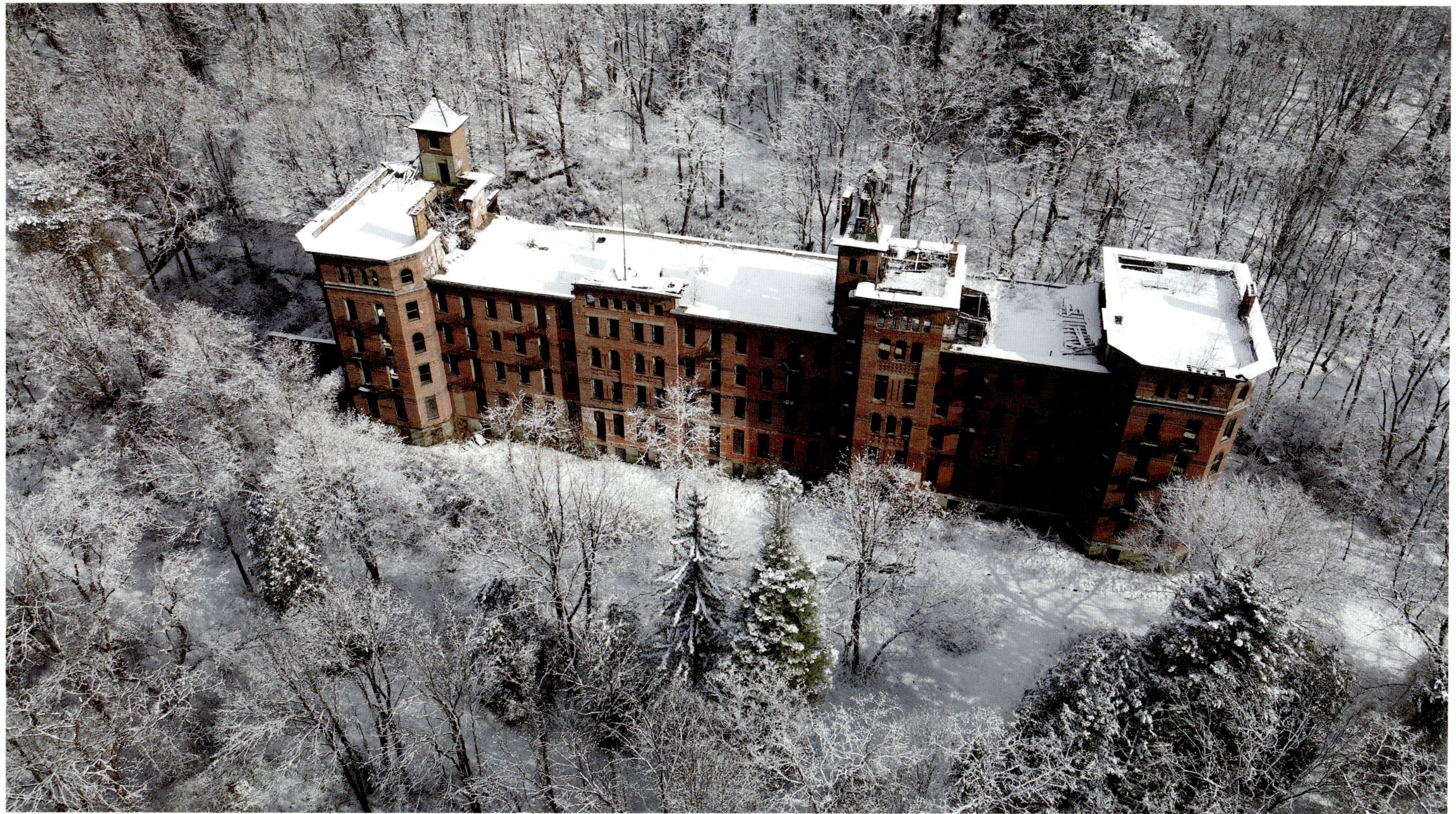

Jackson Sanatorium

CHAPTER 10.

CHAUTAUQUA-ALLEGHENY REGION

J. N. Adam Memorial Hospital

PERRYSBURG

Following the rise of tuberculosis cases in Erie County, Buffalo mayor James Nobel Adam, following the recommendation of Dr. John H. Pryor, purchased a 293-acre hillside in Perrysburg, New York, to build a tuberculosis hospital in 1909. Named after Mayor Adam, J. N. Adam Memorial Hospital officially opened on November 12, 1912, under the ownership of the City of Buffalo.

Sitting at an elevation of 1,322 feet with a 140-patient capacity, J. N. Adam Hospital afforded spectacular views of Buffalo and Canada to the north, Lake Erie to the west, and vast farmland and forests to the east and south. The hospital would treat tuberculosis patients until 1960, when it was reformatted to treat the developmentally disabled until 1993.

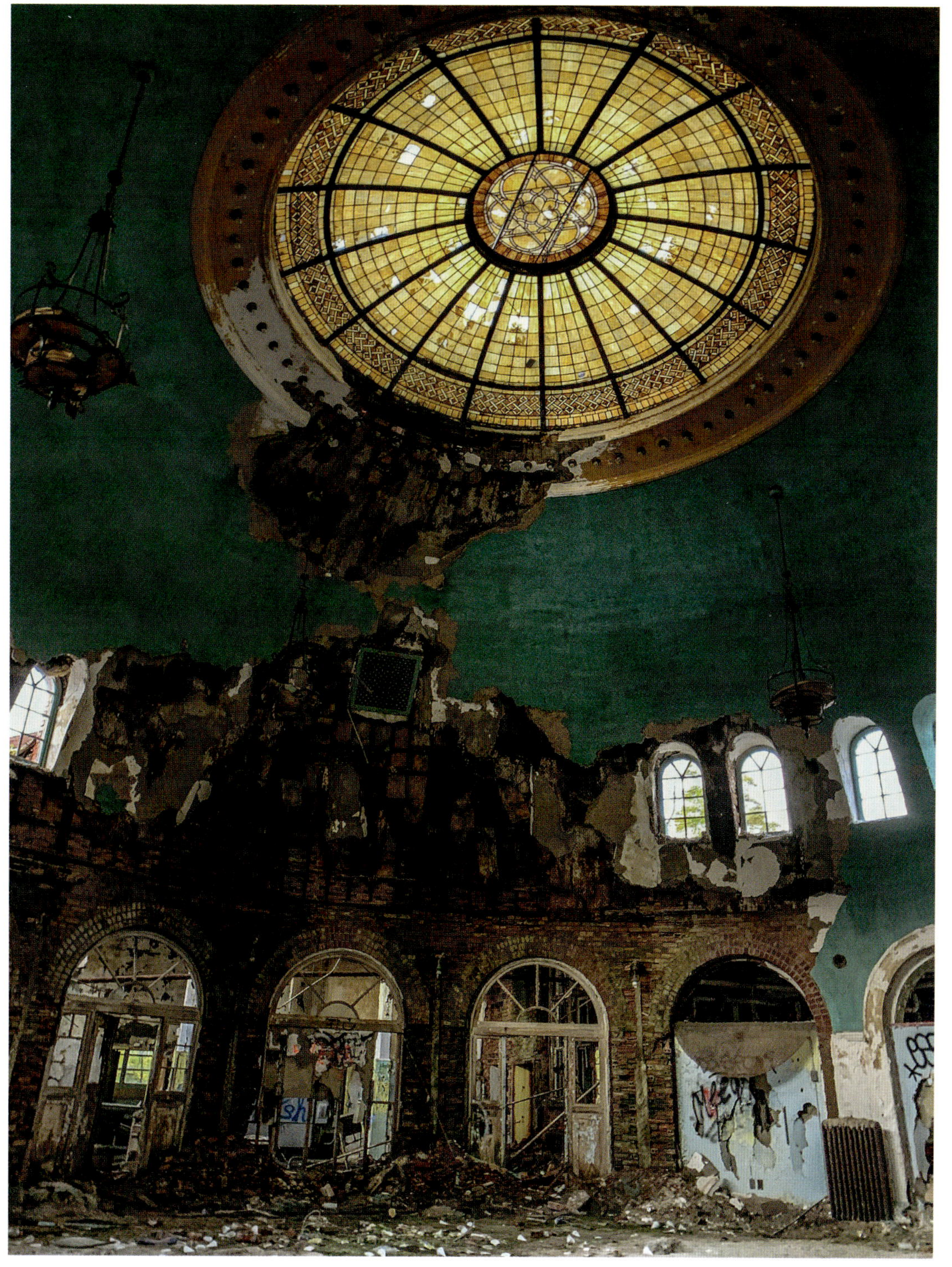

Dining Hall, J. N. Adam Memorial Hospital

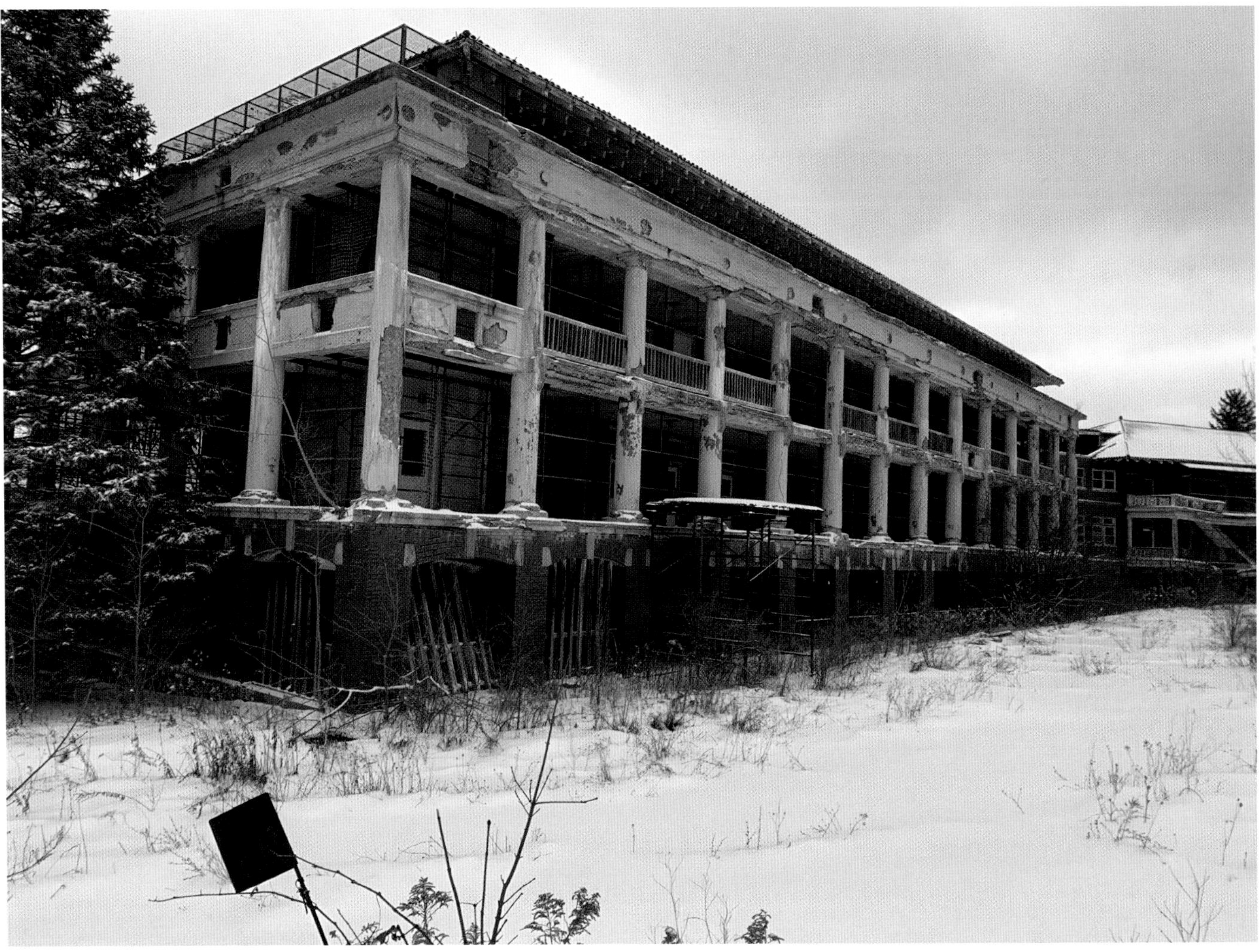

J. N. Adam Memorial Hospital

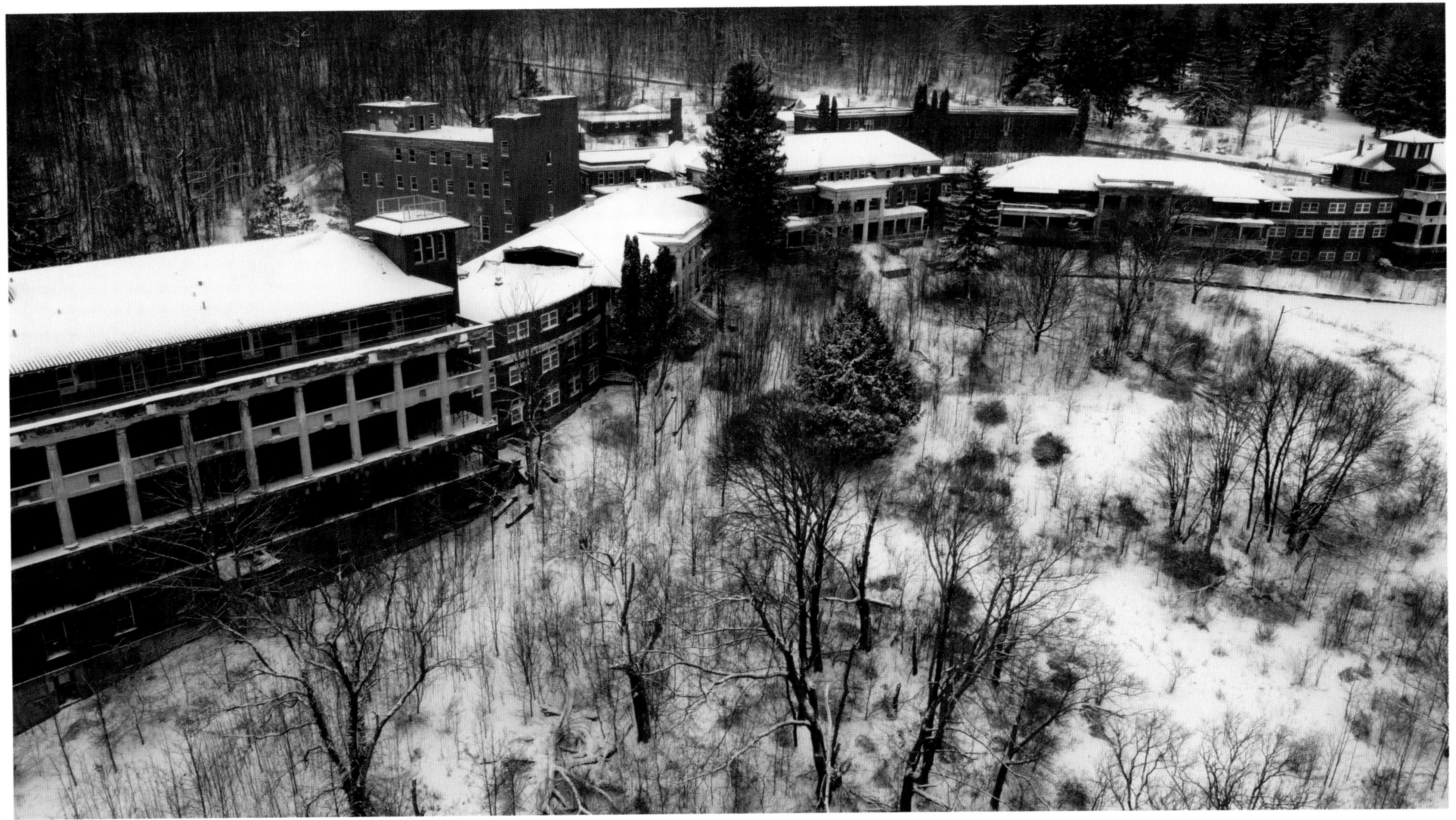

Silver Creek High School

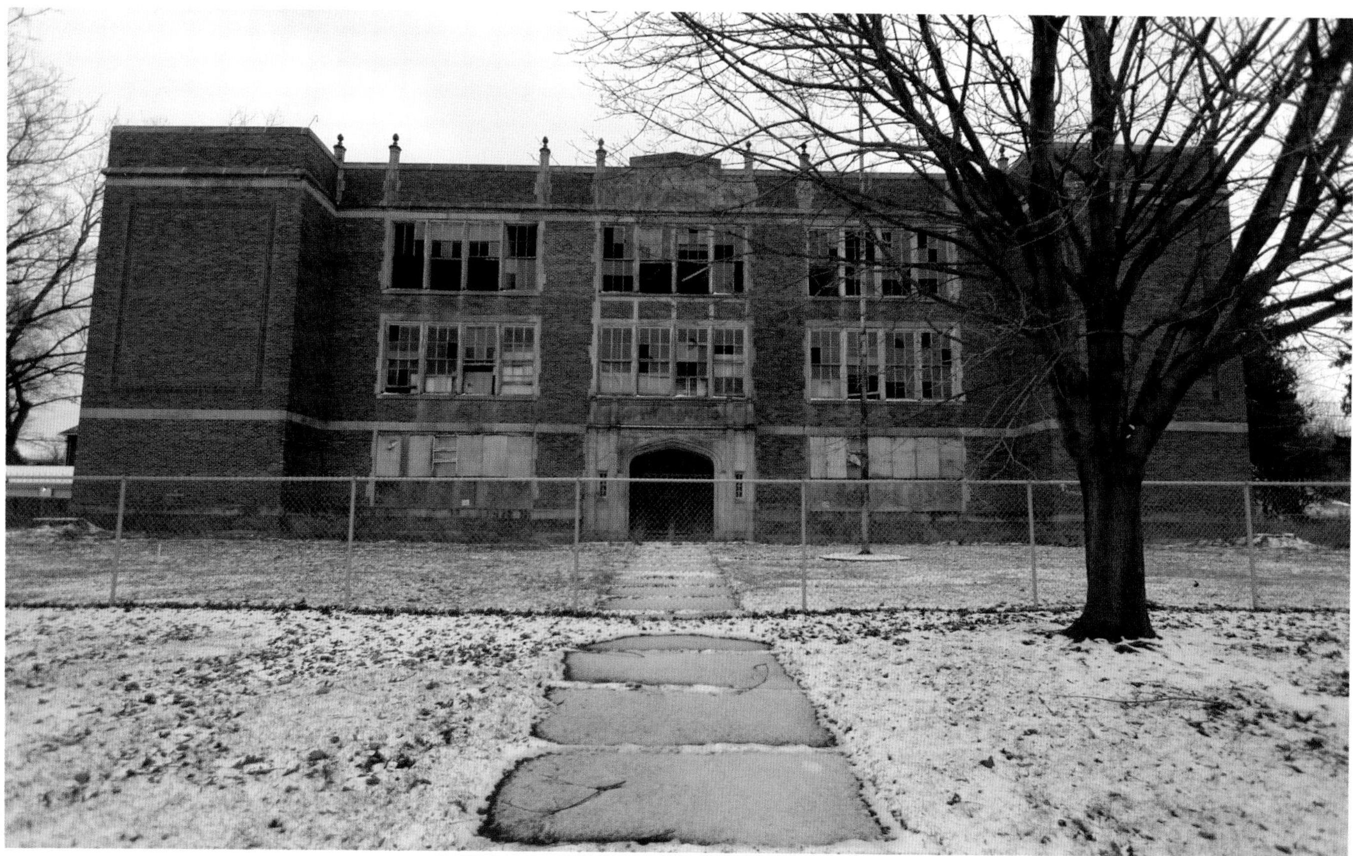

SILVER CREEK

The first settlers of what is now Silver Creek, New York, hailed from Massachusetts at the turn of the nineteenth century, many of them veterans of the Revolutionary War. In 1823 the first class in Silver Creek took place in a one-room schoolhouse on Main Street. As Silver Creek's population expanded, the local school board purchased a plot of land in 1916 for the Silver Creek Junior-Senior High School. It operated for fifty years and was replaced by a newer facility on Dickinson Street that still operates today.

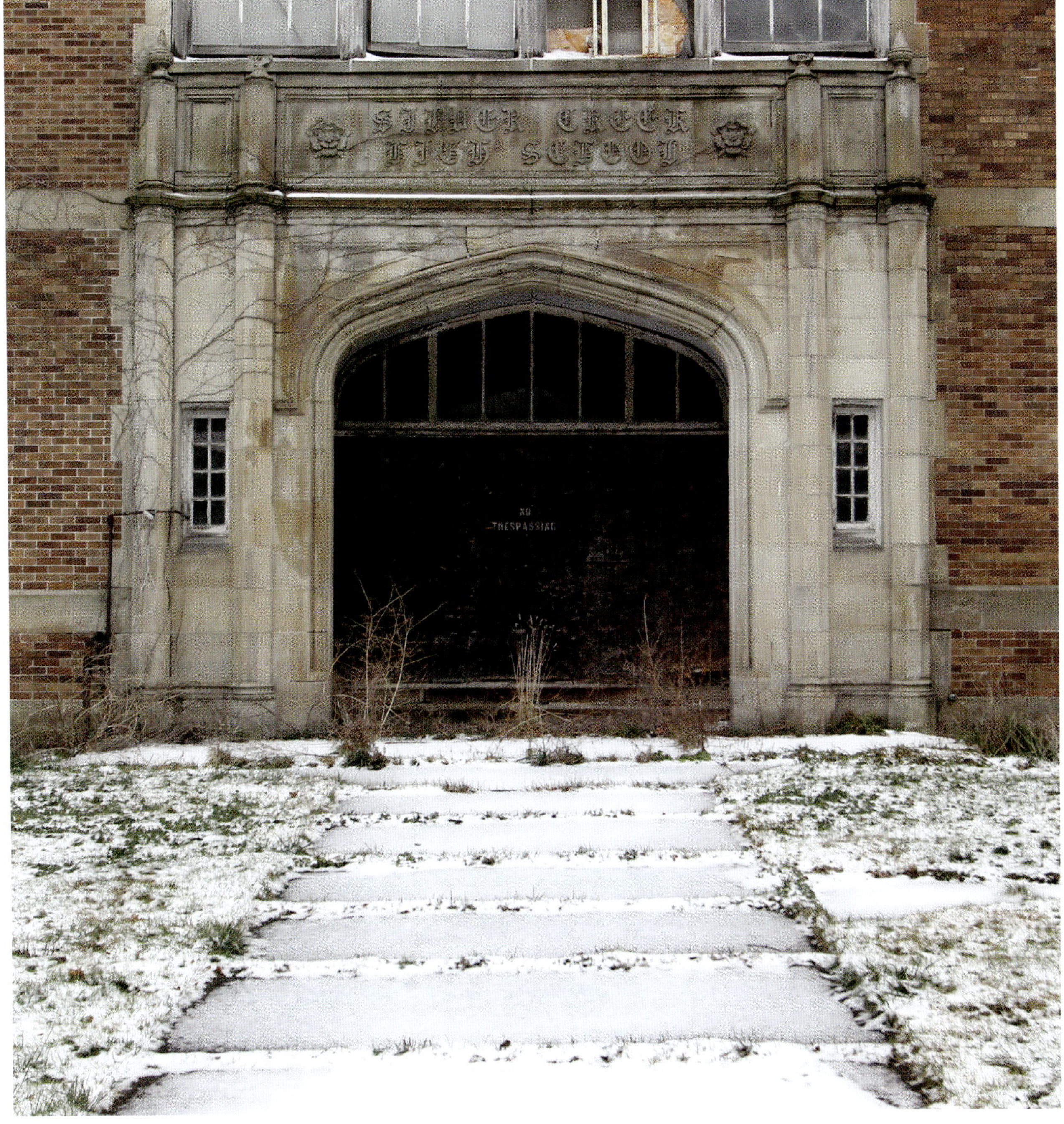

Silver Creek High School

CHAPTER 11.

NIAGARA FRONTIER REGION

Buffalo Central Terminal

BUFFALO

The New York Central Railroad opened the Buffalo Central Terminal on June 22, 1929, months before the Great Depression. The seventeen-story art deco terminal could handle two hundred trains and ten thousand passengers daily, serving as the midpoint for the New York Central Railroad, one of the largest mainline railroads in the country, extending from New York City's Grand Central Terminal to LaSalle Street Station in Chicago.

After years of declining passenger rail travel following the stock market crash, and again after World War II with the rising popularity of auto and air travel, Buffalo Central Terminal merged with Penn Central Railroad until the 1970s, when Amtrak assumed operation of nearly every major intercity rail system in the US. The last passenger train departed Buffalo Central Terminal in October 1979, just fifty years after it opened.

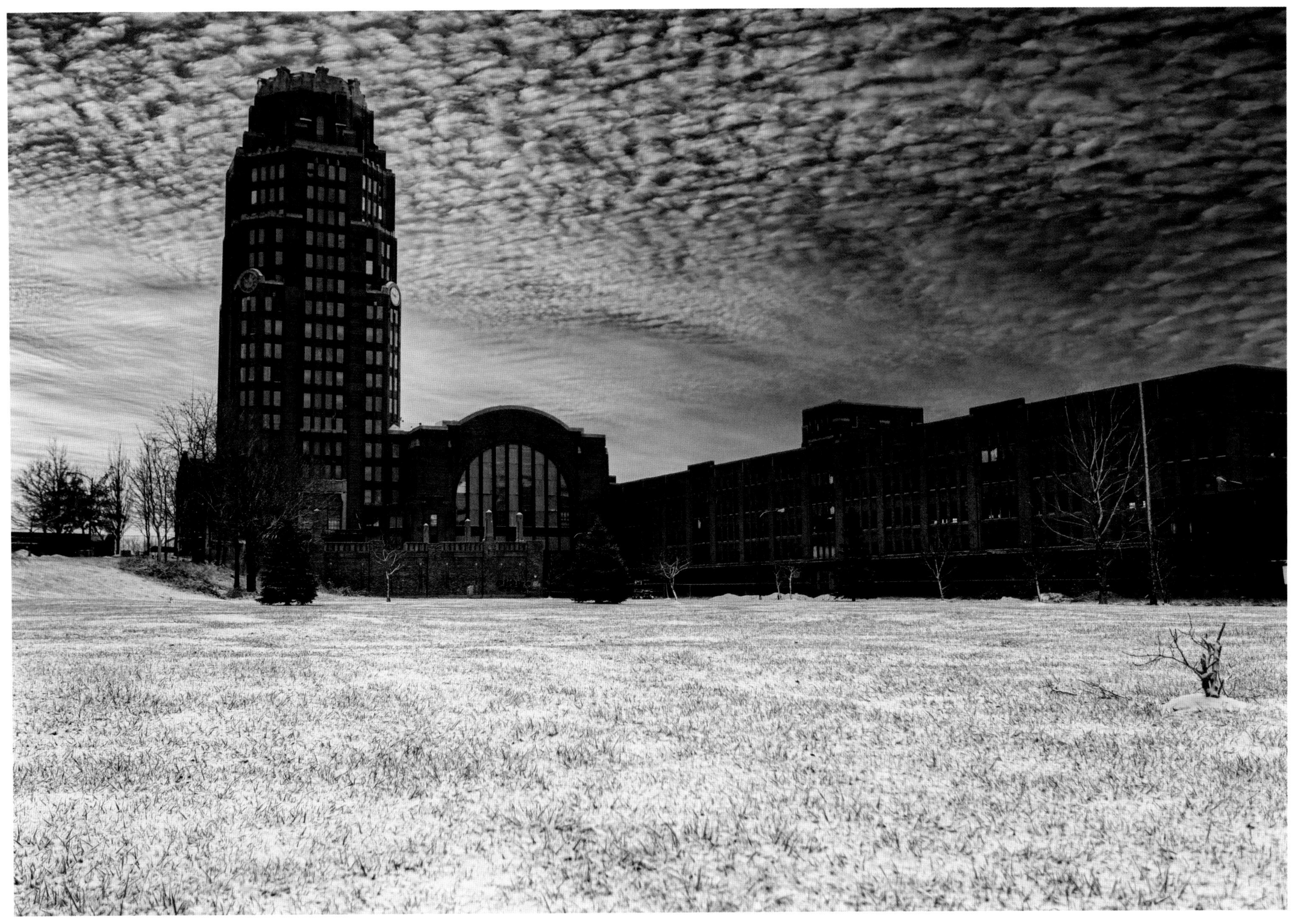

Buffalo Central Terminal

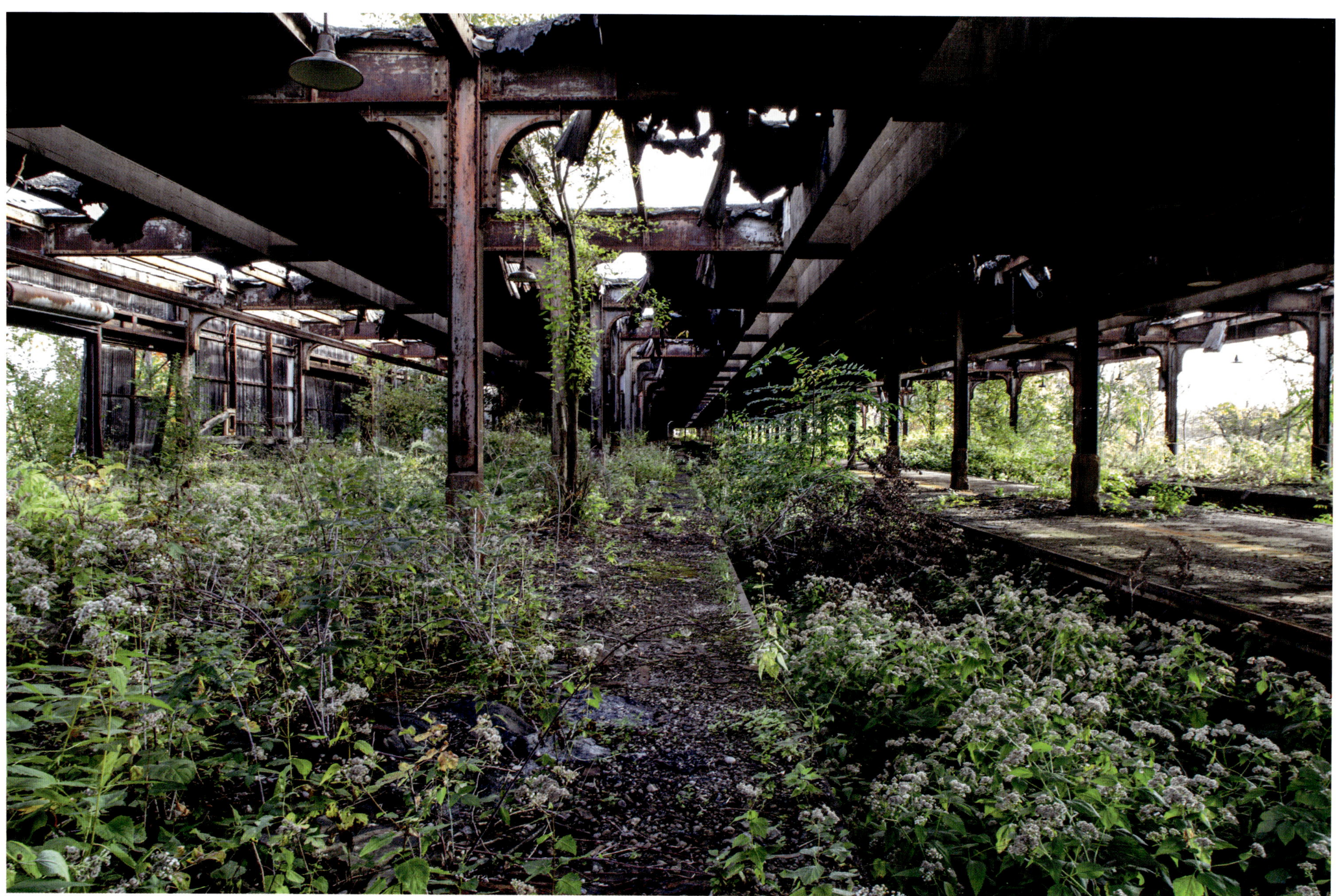

Remains of a train platform, Buffalo Central Terminal

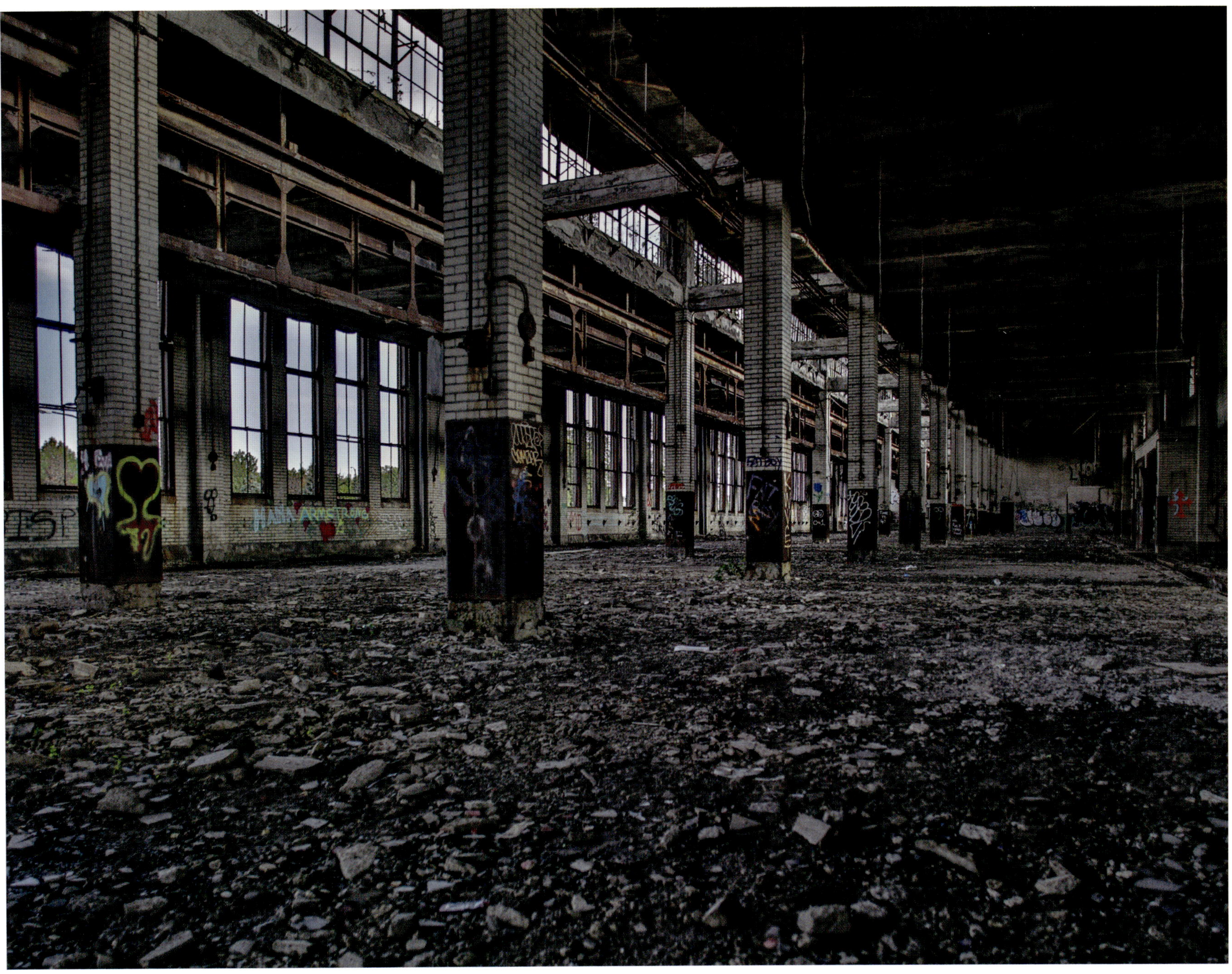

Baggage building, Buffalo Central Terminal

Wonder Bread Factory

BUFFALO

Sitting on a 2.88-acre site on Fougeron Street on Buffalo's East Side is the shell of the five-story Wonder Bread Factory. The circa 1915 factory was modeled after Brooklyn's Ward Baking Company bakery, with blond brick representing the standard of cleanliness maintained inside. Ward & Ward had a daily production rate of 100,000 loaves, 50,000 cakes, and 20,000 rolls and emphasized its "free from human touch" production process. In 1925, Continental Baking Company acquired Taggart Baking, makers of Wonder Bread, and went on to open ninety-eight plants in forty-one different cities, including Buffalo.

The Continental Baking Company declared bankruptcy in 2004, with the Wonder Bread Factory slated for redevelopment into an apartment complex as of 2019. The smokestack to the rear of the building still reads "Ward's Bread."

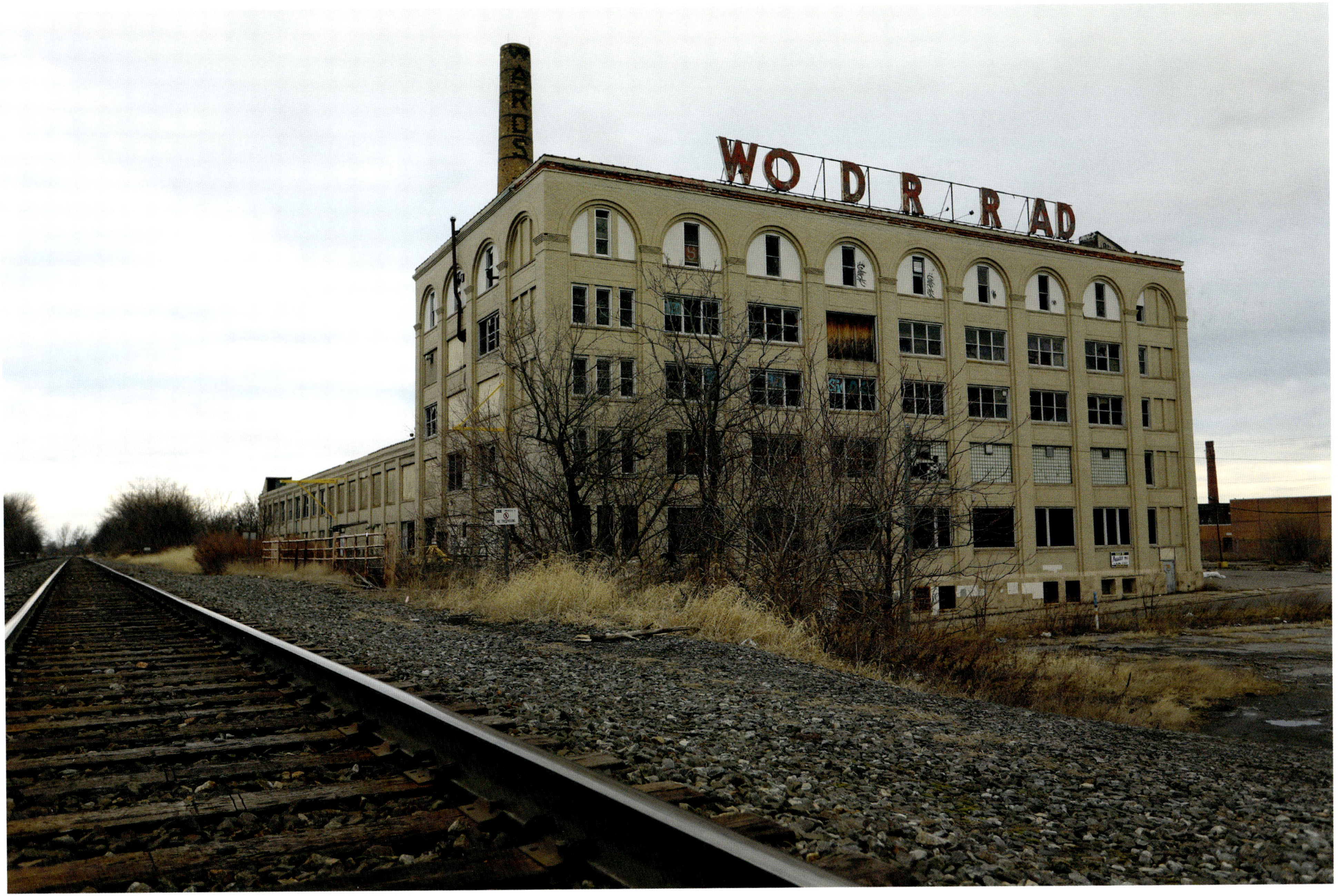

Wonder Bread Factory

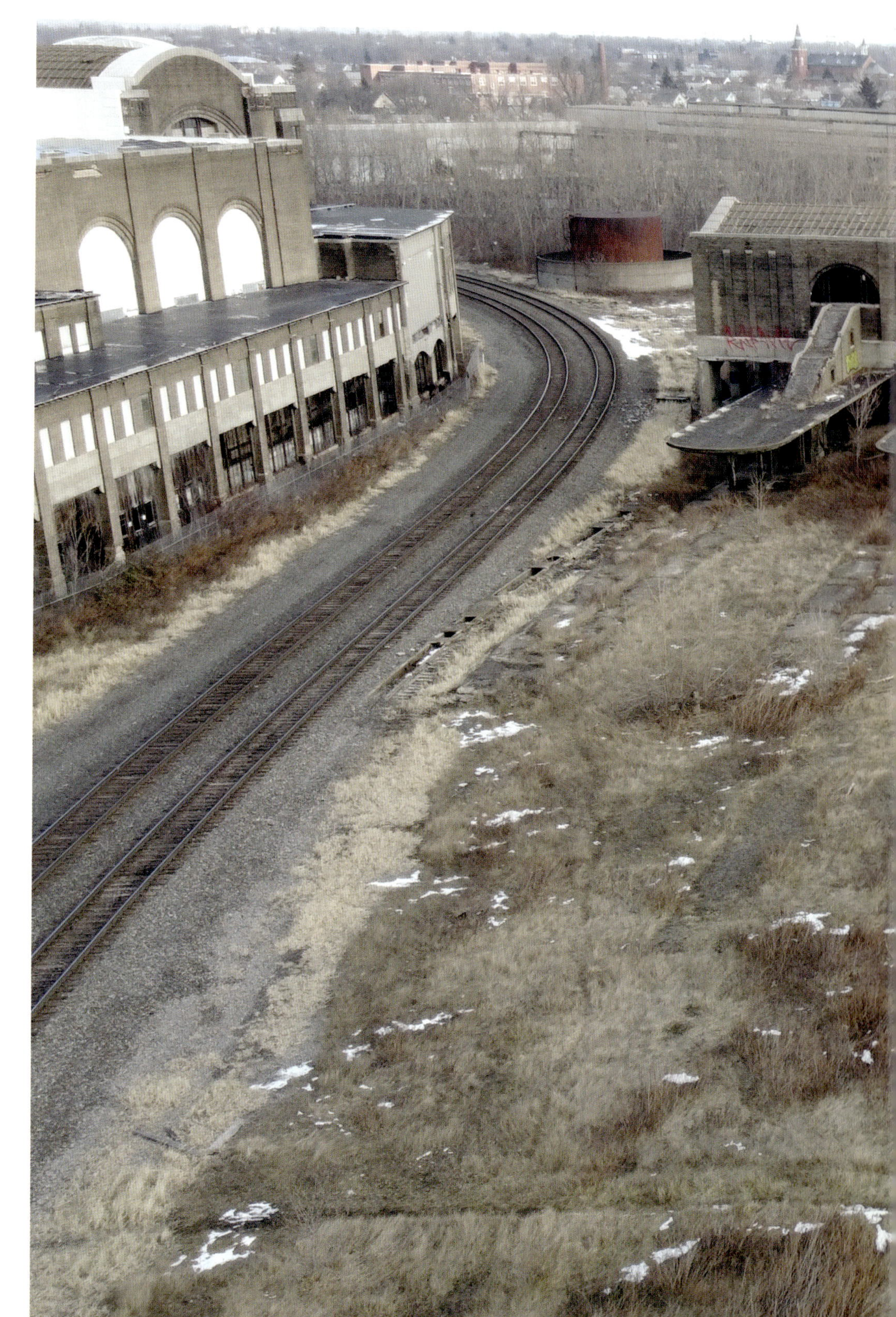

The 450-foot-long Buffalo Central Terminal train concourse had fourteen passenger trains served by seven platforms.

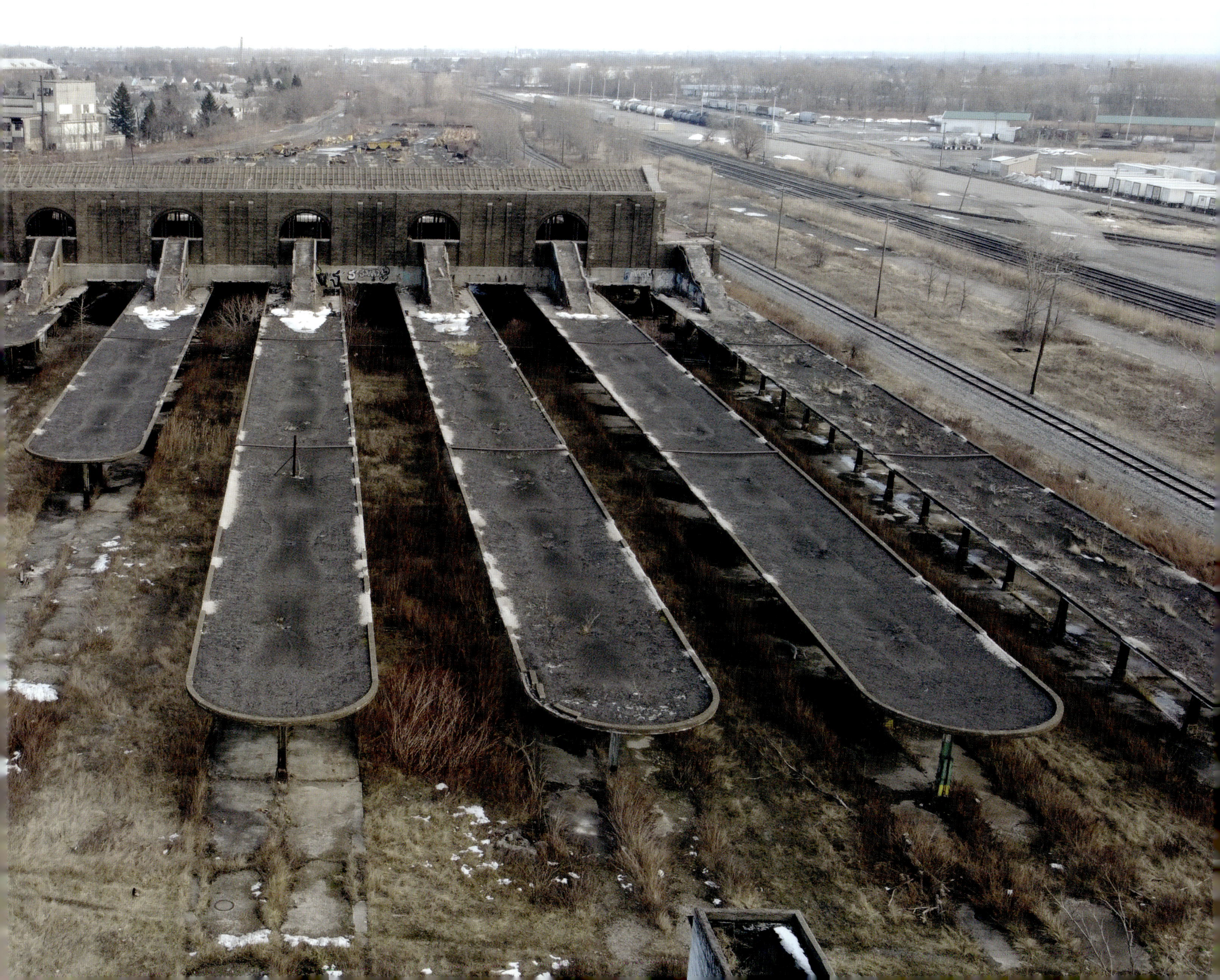

BIBLIOGRAPHY

Abramovich, Chad. "The Ruins of Tahawus." Obscure Vermont. August 8, 2012. https://obscurevermont.com/the-ruins-of-tahawus.

Adirondack Park Agency. "Historic Tahawus Tract." Town of Newcomb, Essex County. https://apa.ny.gov/Press/OSI_Tahawus.htm.

Albert Wisner Public Library. *A Legacy of Justice & Social Reform: The History of the Mid-Orange Correctional Facility, the New York State Training School for Boys, & the N.Y. City Farm*. Warwick Valley History. http://www.albertwisnerlibrary.org/Factsandhistory/History/MOCF.

Barry. Dan. "A Mill Closes, and a Hamlet Fades to Black." *New York Times*, February 16, 2001. https://www.nytimes.com/2001/02/16/nyregion/a-mill-closes-and-a-hamlet-fades-to-black.html.

Borden Dairy. "The Story behind the Name: Borden, an American Heritage Brand." Borden Dairy History. https://www.bordendairy.com/press-room/history.

Buffalo Central Terminal. "History & Restoration." Buffalo Central Terminal. https://buffalocentralterminal.org/about/history-restoration.

Buffalo Rising. "Landmarking: Wonder Bread Factory." Buffalo Rising. September 7, 2018. https://www.buffalorising.com/2018/09/landmarking-wonder-bread-factory.

Cahal, Sherman. "Minnewaska Resort & Country Club." Abandoned Online. https://abandonedonline.net/location/minnewaska-resort-and-country-club.

Cahal, Sherman. "No. 7 Concentrating Mill." Abandoned Online. https://abandonedonline.net/location/no-7-concentrating-mill/#google_vignette.

Chung, Jen. "Massive Greenpoint Fire 'Suspicious' and Still Being Fought." Gothamist. May 3, 2006. https://gothamist.com/news/massive-greenpoint-fire-suspicious-and-still-being-fought.

City of Amsterdam, New York. "Chuctanunda Creek Trail: Power House." https://www.amsterdamny.gov/our-city/things-to-do/chucktrail.

Conway, John. "White Lake Mansion House—My View." *Catskill Chronicle*. https://thecatskillchronicle.com/letters-to-the-editor/letters-to-the-editor-archives/white-lake-mansion-house-my-view.

Devivo, Elijah. "Forgotten History: The Saratoga Homestead." HubPages. December 26, 2019. https://discover.hubpages.com/travel/Forgotten-History-The-Saratoga-Homestead.

Fanelli, Gino. "The Castle on the Hill: A Story of American Decay." *Reporter*, October 5, 2015. https://reporter.rit.edu/leisure/castle-hill-story-american-decay.

Farmingdale Observer Staff. "Minute of History." *Farmingdale Observer*, August 29, 2013. https://farmingdale-observer.com/2013/08/29/minute-of-history-2.

Fego, Sami. "The Bennett College." April 17, 2017.

Fischer, Molly. "Faded Catskills Classic Has Mystery Buyer; Currently Seeking Backup." *The Observer*, September 1, 2009. https://observer.com/2009/09/faded-catskills-classic-has-mystery-buyer-currently-seeking-backup.

Flock, Elizabeth. "Remembering the 'Forgotten City,' Greenpoint Terminal Market." *Bedford + Bowery* (blog), December 31, 2013. https://bedfordandbowery.com/2013/12/remembering-the-forgotten-city-greenpoint-terminal-market.

Franco, Jim. "A $16.6 Million Plan to Clean Up the AL Tech Site." SpotlightNews.com. January 3, 2019. https://spotlightnews.com/towns/colonie/2019/01/03/a-16-6-million-plan-to-clean-up-the-al-tech-site.

Gray, Christopher. "Streetscapes: The Farm Colony; 'Historic or Not, It's a Jungle in There." *New York Times*, September 22, 1991. https://www.nytimes.com/1991/09/22/realestate/streetscapes-the-farm-colony-historic-or-not-it-s-a-jungle-in-there.html.

Guerrasio, Jason. "The Crazy Government Conspiracy Theory That Inspired 'Stranger Things.'" *Business Insider*, September 17, 2016. https://www.businessinsider.com/what-inspired-stranger-things-montauk-project-2016-9.

Hernandez, Miguel. "An Ossining Castle: David Abercrombie's 'Elda.'" *New York Almanack* (blog), February 2013. https://www.newyorkalmanack.com/2013/02/an-ossining-castle-david-abercrombies-elda.

Historical Marker Database. "Rochester State Hospital." Rochester in Monroe County, New York. Last modified on February 26, 2020. https://www.hmdb.org/m.asp?m=145716.

Historic Path of Cattaraugus County. "JN Adam Facility." https://historicpath.com/article/j-n-adam-facility-192.

Jordan, John. "Orange County Takes Back Camp LaGuardia Property." *Real Estate In-Depth*, April 18, 2016. http://www.realestateindepth.com/news/orange-county-takes-back-camp-laguardia-property.

Kachejian, Brian. "Pilgrim Psychiatric Center History: Days of Past and Present." Classic NY History. https://classicnewyorkhistory.com/pilgrim-psychiatric-center-history-days-of-past-and-present.

Kelly, Brian. "Soured Situation." NNY360. March 14, 2019. https://www.nny360.com/news/soured-situation/article_a35c0e9f-5738-5270-a826-d20a63775ff2.html.

Lakes to Locks Passage. "21. Driving Switchback and Cheney Roads: Republic Steel and the #7 Sintering Plant." The Story of Iron in Crown Point & Moriah. https://passageport.org/journey/the-story-of-iron-in-crown-point-moriah/21-driving-switchback-and-cheney-roads.

Lemire, Paula. "Central Warehouse Fire." Albany History. October 25, 2010. http://albanynyhistory.blogspot.com/2010/10/central-warehouse-fire.html.

Levine, David. "The Real History of Letchworth Village." *Hudson Valley Magazine*. https://hvmag.com/life-style/history/letchworth-village-thiells.

Liberatore, Wendy. "Once a Refuge for TB Patients, Saratoga Sanatorium Is in Terminal Condition." *Times Union*, last modified June 8, 2019. https://www.timesunion.com/news/article/Once-lively-Saratoga-County-sanatorium-a-grim-13937126.php.

Luther, Roger. "History." Castle on the Hill. 2015. http://nysasylum.com/biahist.htm.

Mary McClellan Foundation. "About Us." https://marymcclellanfoundation.org.

McConnell, Stephen. "The Old Pier 1—Brooklyn, New York." Behance. https://www.behance.net/gallery/86099221/The-Old-Pier-1Brooklyn-New-York.

Meier, Eric. "The Legend of the Point Mountain Mausoleum in Hancock." Lite 98.7. September, 18, 2015. https://lite987.com/the-legend-of-the-point-mountain-mausoleum-in-hancock.

Municipal Journal & Engineer. "American Refuse Disposal Plants." *Municipal Journal*, September 5, 1912, 321.

O'Connor, Anahad. "Farm's Fate Is Certain, but the Future of Its Animals Is Not." *New York Times*, October 6, 2006. https://www.nytimes.com/2006/10/06/nyregion/06catskill.html.

Ontario County, New York. "Manchester Yard Site Redevelopment Project." https://www.co.ontario.ny.us/1205/Manchester-Yard-Site-Redevelopment-Project.

Ossining History on the Run. "Brandywine Estate, Briarcliff Manor." February 16, 2019. https://ossininghistoryontherun.com/2019/02/16/brandywine-estate-briarcliff-manor.

Perkins, Susan R., and Caryl A. Hopson. *Herkimer Village*. Images of America. Charleston, SC: Arcadia, 2008.

Phelan, Kevin. "Tappan's Masonic Home Prepares for Second Life." *Lohud*, May 25, 2003. https://www.lohud.com/story/life/2016/05/25/tappan-masonic-home-renovation/84605656.

Polaski, Leo. *The Farm Colonies: Caring for New York City's Mentally Ill in Long Island's State Hospitals*. Kings Park, NY: Kings Park Heritage Museum, 2003.

Rochester Subway. "Into the Incinerator." March 3, 2014. https://www.rochestersubway.com/topics/2014/03/rochester-garbage-incinerator.

Ross, Kenneth R. "Newton Falls in 1925." *St. Lawrence County Historical Association Quarterly* 46, no. 2 (Spring 2001): 16–19.

Sblano, Nicolette, Sabrina Sucato, and Raphael Beretta. "A Massive, Abandoned Zoo Is Reborn in Catskill." *Hudson Valley Magazine*, February 11, 2021. https://hvmag.com/life-style/history/old-catskill-game-farm-zoo-hudson-valley.

Siener, Christian D. *From Prison to Homeless Shelter: Camp LaGuardia and the Political Economy of an Urban Infrastructure*. New York: Graduate Center, City University of New York, 2018.

Sommer, Jesse S. "Mr. Blum, Tear Down This Eyesore!" *Altamont Enterprise*, January 29, 2020. https://altamontenterprise.com/opinion/columns/so-swears-new-scot/01292020/mr-blum-tear-down-eyesore.

Sorrell-White, Stephanie. "Former L. W. Bills School Sells for $4,000." *Times Telegram*, August 5, 2011. https://webcache.googleusercontent.com/search?q=cache:aRFAwqKCb-MJ:https://www.timestelegram.com/article/20110805/NEWS/308059961+&cd=1&hl=en&ct=clnk&gl=us.

Southampton Press. "Amagansett House on Stilts, Surrounded by Water, Is Still Loved." Residence. *Southampton Press*, January 12, 2017. https://www.27east.com/home-garden/amagansett-house-on-stilts-surrounded-by-water-is-still-loved-1378206.

Sparks, Leonard. "Bypass on Route 17 Reshapes Parksville." *Times Herald-Record*, June 17, 2012. https://www.recordonline.com/article/20120617/News/206170324.

Thomas, Cara. "Your Hometown: Charlestown USA Factory Outlet." Spectrum News 1. January 3, 2016. https://spectrumlocalnews.com/tx/austin/news/2015/12/31/your-hometown-charlestown-usa.

University of Rochester Medical Center. "Rochester State Hospital." Edward G. Miner Library. https://www.urmc.rochester.edu/libraries/miner/rare-books-and-manuscripts/archives-and-manuscripts/record-groups/rochester-state-hospital.aspx.

Village of Silver Creek, New York. "Our Village's History." June 11, 2002. http://silvercreekny.com/old/Silver%20Creek%20History.htm.

Vondrak, Otto M. "About the Once Vital, Now Abandoned Rochester Subway." Rochester Subway. https://www.rochestersubway.com/topics.

Wheeler, Walter Richard. *Architects in Albany*. Albany, NY: Mount Ida, 2009.

Wolf, Craig. "Dilapidated Hall in Millbrook to Make Way for Park and More." *Poughkeepsie Journal*, May 13, 2014.

Zavin, Shirley. "New York City Farm Colony—Sea View Hospital Historic District Designation Report." Landmarks Preservation Commission. 1985. http://s-media.nyc.gov/agencies/lpc/lp/1408.pdf.

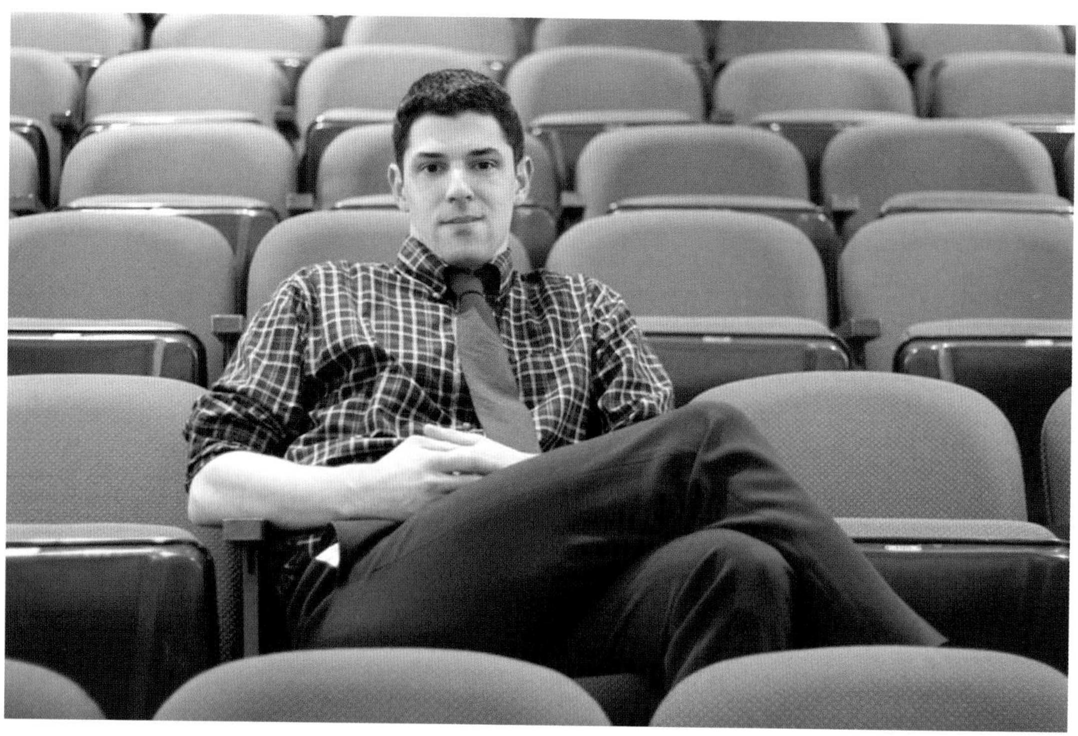

John Lazzaro is a documentary filmmaker and documentary photographer based on Long Island, New York. In his approach to photography, Lazzaro draws upon his experiences from documentary filmmaking in order to create a realistic, visual, and thought-provoking dialogue of the macabre. His main focus is capturing abandoned buildings and vanishing architecture throughout New England.

He is fascinated by history, storytelling, and visual design, and his documentaries address topics of social awareness. *Hindsight* (2010) offered a painful look at Long Island's heroin epidemic. His most recent documentary, *Masters of Cruelty* (2018), takes an eye-opening look at New York's animal abuse laws as told through those fighting against cruelty cases on Long Island. His photo book *The Walls Still Talk* documents the decades of neglect and decay of the Kings Park Psychiatric Center in Kings Park, New York, as a result of deinstitutionalization.

Lazzaro is a member of the Firefly Gallery in Northport, New York, and fotofoto gallery in Huntington, New York.